Legitimacy and Politics

In recent years, national and internationa. ___
public awareness about cases of political corruption and the impact of
globalization on domestic institutions and policies, have put the role of
the State at the centre of contemporary political debates. In one way or
another, these issues and the debates they generate raise the question
of the legitimacy of established powers. The result is that legitimacy, a
key notion of political thought in general, has today become a burning
issue.

Bringing together approaches drawn from philosophy, political science, law, history, and sociology, as well as the epistemology of the
social sciences, Coicaud takes up the issue of legitimacy and explores its
significance and relevance for modern politics. In the process, he offers
insightful views on questions such as the connection between morality
and politics, the role of values, political responsibility, and political justice, while at the same time challenging crude positivism and scientism
in the theory and practice of the social sciences.

Coicaud argues that, far from bidding one to abandon the principle
of the 'right to govern' (as illustrated, for example, by the Weberian
reduction of legitimacy to a mere belief) and, more generally, any idea
of practical truth, modernity invites a search for normative criteria of
justice that are compatible with plurality within and among societies and
with the historical dimension of social reality. As such, the book provides
a useful framework of analysis for addressing the issue of legitimacy in
contemporary democratic culture.

JEAN-MARC COICAUD is Senior Academic Officer in the Peace and
Governance Program of the United Nations University (Tokyo). He
also teaches social and political philosophy at the New School University (New York). From 1992 to 1996, he served as a speech writer in the
Executive Office of the United Nations Secretary-General, and, from
1986 to 1992, he was a Fellow at Harvard University (Center for International Affairs, Department of Philosophy, and Harvard Law School).
He holds Ph.D.'s in philosophy and political science (University of the
Sorbonne and the Institut d'Études Politiques, Paris). He is the author
of *L'Introuvable Démocratie autoritaire* (1996), co-author of *Power in
Transition: The Peaceful Change of International Order* (2001), and co-
editor of *The Legitimacy of International Organizations* (2001) and *Ethics
and International Affairs: Extent and Limits* (2001).

Legitimacy and Politics

A Contribution to the Study of Political Right and Political Responsibility

Jean-Marc Coicaud

United Nations University, Tokyo
New School University, New York

translated and edited by David Ames Curtis

CAMBRIDGE
UNIVERSITY PRESS

PUBLISHED BY THE PRESS SYNDICATE OF THE UNIVERSITY OF CAMBRIDGE
The Pitt Building, Trumpington Street, Cambridge CB2 1RP, United Kingdom

CAMBRIDGE UNIVERSITY PRESS
The Edinburgh Building, Cambridge CB2 2RU, UK
40 West 20th Street, New York, NY 10011-4211, USA
477 Williams town Road, Port Melbourne, VIC 3207, Australia
Ruiz de Alarcón 13, 28014 Madrid, Spain
Dock House, The Waterfront, Cape Town 8001, South Africa

http://www.cambridge.org

The translation presents Jean-Marc Coicaud's *Légitimité et politique.*
Contribution à l'étude du droit et de la responsabilité politiques
by Presses Universitaires de France 1997
and © Presses Universitaires de France 1997
First published in English by Cambridge University Press 2002 as
English translation © Cambridge University Press 2002

Printed in the United Kingdom at the University Press, Cambridge

Typeface Plantin 10/12 pt   *System* LaTeX 2$_\varepsilon$ [TB]

A catalogue record for this book is available from the British Library

ISBN 0 521 78261 9 hardback
ISBN 0 521 78782 3 paperback

To my parents,
and to Catherine and Françoise

In the last analysis . . . our decisions about right and wrong will depend upon our choice of company, through thinking in examples, with whom we wish to spend our lives. And this company again is chosen through thinking in examples, in examples of persons dead or alive, and in examples of incidents, past or present . . . But the likelihood that someone would come and tell us that . . . any company will be good enough for him is, I fear, by far greater. Morally and even politically speaking, this indifference . . . is the greatest danger. And in the same direction, only a bit less dangerous, does this other very common modern phenomenon lie, the wide-spread tendency to refuse to judge at all. Out of the unwillingness or inability to choose one's examples and one's company, and out of the unwillingness or inability to relate to others through judgment arise the real skandala, the real stumbling-blocks . . . There lies the horror and, at the same time, the banality of evil.

HANNAH ARENDT
Hannah Arendt Papers (1949–75)

Contents

Translator's foreword

It is one of the startling surprises in a translator's life to discover that the labour of translation – his creative transformation of a work, so that it may be read and received in another language – does not necessarily become easier as his experience increases and his so-called expertise grows. On the contrary, words and phrases may become more of a problem for him, more difficult to render satisfactorily, as he learns more about the intricacies and nuances of a foreign tongue and encounters more vividly and viscerally the complexities involved in 'interpreting' these expressions for a new audience in the transnational republic of letters. Experience and reflection are certainly not the natural enemies of accuracy and clarity, but they create a new level of exigency that is unsettling, even as they offer new opportunities for extension, elaboration, and refinement that are welcomed as an invitation and a challenge.

The title of Jean-Marc Coicaud's book, *Légitimité et politique. Contribution à l'étude du droit et de la responsabilité politiques*, is rather straightforward in French; I have translated it as *Legitimacy and Politics: A Contribution to the Study of Political Right and Political Responsibility*. And its basic themes and insights, if they may be summarised quickly and in unsystematic fashion – namely, that legitimacy must be related to politics, that legitimacy is not mere conformity to law, and that all these terms (legitimacy, politics, law) as well as the notions they imply and implement (consent, norms, the identity of a society, etc.) are not wholly separable from their historical instantiations – are presented by the author with considerable rigour and precision. Yet as a translator, questions were raised in my mind as soon as I was confronted with the task of translating this title and of coming to terms with its key words and concepts. An account of these questions and my responses to them may be of value to the reader as she embarks upon, or seeks to reflect back upon, the present translated work.

A brief incident from my own life may serve here as an introduction. A little more than two decades ago at Harvard University, the same institution Coicaud attended while writing his book, I took a course in political philosophy from Professor John Rawls, author of the celebrated volume *A Theory of Justice*. To my disappointment 'political philosophy' turned out to mean not much more than 'moral theory', so that any political manifestations and issues could be viewed only upon a very distant, almost invisible or unrelated horizon. Curiously, Marxism was discussed and dismissed in one lecture, Rawls treating it as minor variation in the way one writes utility functions. Neither it, nor the constant challenge anarchism poses to the predominant tendency of 'political philosophy' to seek theoretical justifications for present or alternative political arrangements, were given serious consideration. Nor were the similarities between Marxism and anarchism, on the one hand, and liberalism, on the other, ever highlighted or investigated, even though it was beginning to dawn on me that the former two doctrines evince as much of a reticence to deal forthrightly with political questions and power considerations as the latter one does.

As was already my habit by then, I engaged in a self-invented 'education through opposition': after having discerned the biases and preferences of the instructor, I proceeded to write a paper (in this case, one later reworked for publication)[1] that sought systematically and savagely to contest his views.[2] Specifically, here I attempted 'a class and state analysis' of the utilitarianism of Rawls's favourite moral theorist, Henry Sidgwick, author of *The Methods of Ethics*; and I endeavoured to show that utilitarianism must be understood in historical perspective, starting from the interpretation thereof offered in *The German Ideology*. Instead of viewing the growing formalisation present in this late nineteenth-century Englishman's writings as a triumph of theoretical distillation and purification – the view of Rawls, who regarded the reduction of moral precepts to a discreet and decreasing number of axiom-like propositions to be a mark of progress (and not, for instance, a process of desiccation or degeneration leading to ultimate historical irrelevancy and demise) – or as merely a reflection of changing class interests – a mechanical extrapolation of Marx and Engels's not wholly unenlightening historical overview of the utilitarianism of the elder Mill, Jeremy Bentham, and their predecessors

[1] David Ames Curtis, 'A Class and State Analysis of Henry Sidgwick's Utilitarianism', *Philosophy and Social Criticism* 11:3 (Summer 1986), 259–96. Errata in 12:4, 387–88.
[2] That same school year I wrote a paper for Robert Nozick's course on 'metaphilosophy', challenging its major premises, too. To my great disappointment, Nozick rushed up to me after I had completed my year-end blue-book exam to tell me that he had given me an 'A' of some sort on my paper – something, he pointedly told me, that he rarely grants. Not glimpsing in him the slightest sense that he was being challenged and ridiculed by my essay, I was overcome with a sense of failure.

in English political economy[3] – I argued that such formalisation must be analysed in a *non-reductionistic* way; it would be seen, rather, as a creative, independent articulation of the growing rationalisation and impersonal-isation characteristic of the bureaucratic mind-set in capitalist society during a period in which, after the political triumph of the bourgeoisie (1832 Reform Bill) and in the context of working-class demands for an extension of the suffrage in England as well as for other rights that create a strain upon hierarchical governance, an impersonal state apparatus comes into existence, silently seizes power, and undertakes to impose social har-mony and tranquillity from the outside upon all classes and segments of the population – enfranchised, unenfranchised, or about to be enfran-chised – by employing the difficult-to-contest language of an 'impersonal decider'. Needless to say, such an interpretation challenged both liberal and Marxist modes of explanation and interpretation as well as their efforts at justification or counterjustification.

Now, liberal thought prides itself, certainly, upon its willingness to entertain a plurality of viewpoints. In the response of Rawls, perhaps the pre-eminent liberal theorist at the time, I discovered with a certain perverse inward satisfaction the limits to such professions of openness and pluralism. He refused to grade the paper and instead scrawled a page of comments . . . to explain why he would not comment upon it. Initially mystified and yet also intrigued, I requested a meeting at his office. We spoke, cordially, for about a half an hour, at the end of which time he asked me, point-blank, 'What *are* you: a sociologist, a historian, or what?', each term, perfectly articulated, falling from his lips with a distinct expression of disdain – as if the very idea of introducing social considerations or just historical context into philosophical thinking about the political world had only now occurred to him for the first time and was immediately experienced with utter revulsion. My explanation that I was a student in his very own philosophy department and not some alien discipline's import only increased our mutual sense of bafflement, and the interview quickly ended. When I pointed out to his teaching

[3] I had already, in the Sidgwick paper, added a corollary to Marx/Engels's interpretation of utilitarianism by contrasting the radical egalitarian implications of Bentham's hedonistic calculus, articulated at the time of a rising bourgeoisie, with the 'poetry versus pushpin' moral hierarchy of pleasures espoused by J. S. Mill in the aftermath of the bourgeoisie's successful passage of the 1832 Reform Bill (elimination of 'rotten boroughs' held by the aristocracy and large landowning gentry, partial extension of the suffrage to middle-class citizens, prospect of a wider suffrage and of broader political changes starting to threaten in the rising workers' movement). See John Stuart Mill, 'Bentham', in *Utilitarianism, On Liberty, Essay on Bentham together with selected writings of Jeremy Bentham and John Austin* (London: Collins, 1979), p. 125, and 'Utilitarianism', p. 259.

assistant a few days later, with mock innocence and shock, that I had still not received a grade for the paper, she told me that it was 'too different' (so much for liberal tolerance . . .) and that she and Rawls had decided that it 'would not receive any grade at all: A, B, C, D, or F', adding that I would receive a B of some sort for the course, as if that was what should be of paramount concern and might somehow placate me. She quickly fled, running off to watch a Red Sox–Yankees game – a response that greatly upset me at the time, but which I, now older, less serious about myself, and more serious about baseball, can fully appreciate in retrospect.

What a difference a few decades can make! Thanking Rawls in his Acknowledgements but also, in the body of his book, engaging in criticism of Rawls's views, Coicaud asserts in the very title of his work that legitimacy must be understood in its political context. Moreover, in developing his key assertion that legitimacy is a matter of political judgement of a practical truth that must be understood in its historical rootedness, Coicaud points out that

> Rawls has been led, in his later writings, to attune his rhetoric to what constitutes, in *A Theory of Justice*, his practice, but without him then wanting to admit it. His revisions are not lacking in breadth. He gives up on the universal import of his categories of analysis. He recognises that the ends of political philosophy depend upon the society to which this philosophy addresses itself. And he comes to affirm that his objective is to construct a theory of justice that is the most reasonable for us. Fittingly, he acknowledges that his understanding of justice corresponds to the conception of the individual belonging to liberal-democratic culture, and that it concerns that culture alone. Rawls almost goes so far as to set the United States and its basic values as the limit for his reflections.

It is more than doubtful that my minor, intemperate undergraduate challenge to Rawls's abstract moral liberalism might have had any effect upon his subsequent decision to adjust his language in a more historically informed political direction, and I certainly would not want to claim any credit for the resulting changes in his point of view. Still, it is refreshing to see now in Coicaud's work an explicit will to relate questions of justice to political and historical considerations that are deemed inseparable from those questions while also refusing to accept liberal precepts unquestioningly in their actual historical incarnations (as Rawls, Coicaud reports, now seems to be doing).

And yet, questions arise as soon as we consider the translation of the term *politique*. First, we note its pronounced importance: the word appears as a noun in the title and is repeated, as a plural adjective, in the subtitle. This double assertion is perhaps inelegant but certainly is to be welcomed for its forcefulness. As a substantive noun associated, via a conjunction, with 'legitimacy', but lacking a definite or indefinite article, the appearance of *politique* in the title can, however, be rendered in several distinct ways.[4] In French, the well-known feminine noun *la politique*, derived from the Greek via the Latin, translates as 'politics' (or 'policy'). *Le politique*, as a masculine noun of relatively recent origin (the older meaning, 'statesman', also appears in Coicaud's writing), is usually rendered in English by the less familiar phrase 'the political', which derives from the conservative Nazi-era jurist Carl Schmitt's usage (coinage?) of *das politische* in German. This unusual noun, *the political*, has been employed and reflected upon in various ways by a number of German-born twentieth-century authors, including Schmitt's former student Leo Strauss, and it has been associated with Martin Heidegger's anti-totalitarian student Hannah Arendt. Some anti-totalitarian French-language political thinkers, Cornelius Castoriadis and Claude Lefort,[5] explicitly distinguish *politics* from *the political*, treating the former as historical in character and the latter as a basic attribute of any society –

---

[4] I had previously discussed these terms in my Translator's Foreword to Claude Lefort's *Writing: The Political Test* (Durham, N.C.: Duke University Press, 2000), p. xii, referring more expansively there to: 'the curious masculine noun of recent vintage, *le politique* – 'the political' or "the political sphere", as is sometimes said now in English – which contrasts in French with the more straightforward, concrete, and familiar feminine noun *la politique* – "politics" or "policy", depending upon the context – and which derives from *das politische*, a neuter German word popularized by the Nazi-era German constitutional scholar and political thinker Carl Schmitt and then by his American emigrant former student Leo Strauss . . . "The political" has been associated, too, with the writings of Hannah Arendt (wrongly, according to one young political scientist, who claims that "this term, developed by the right-wing jurist Carl Schmitt, has been ascribed to her by Marxist thinkers more influenced by Schmitt than she is") . . . and *le politique* is employed today by a wide variety of other French-speaking writers besides Lefort, including the late emigrant Greek political and social thinker Cornelius Castoriadis, whose usage of the *le/la politique* distinction differs markedly from his, and leading French classicist Jean-Pierre Vernant, who, in insisting that "the political", like "politics", has a datable birth and origin in the *poleis* of Ancient Greece, differs from both Castoriadis and Lefort on this score. Yet, "the political", as substantive noun, still reads rather inelegantly on the cover of an English-language book – even if we note the existence of *Reinterpreting the Political*, a recently published American anthology of "Continental" political theory that borrows its title directly from a passage in Lefort's influential 1985 essay, "The Question of Democracy".'

[5] Ibid., p. xxxiv, note 7: 'Lefort calls "the political" the "form" of a society. In "Power, Politics, Autonomy" (1988), Castoriadis defines "the political" as "a dimension of the institution of society pertaining to *explicit power*, that is, to the existence of *instances capable of formulating explicitly sanctionable injunctions*" (*Philosophy, Politics, Autonomy*, ed. David Ames Curtis (New York: Oxford University Press, 1991), p. 156). As such, it does and must pertain to *any* society. By way of contrast, "Greek politics, and politics properly conceived, can be defined as the explicit collective activity which aims at being lucid (reflective and deliberate) and whose object is the institution of society as such" (ibid., p. 160). "Politics" thus appertains, for Castoriadis, only to those societies in which the "project of autonomy" has already emerged and become operative.'

though the two do not agree upon the precise definitions to give the two terms – while a classical historian, the distinguished former French Resistance figure Jean-Pierre Vernant,[6] views even *the political* as historically datable and localisable, it having its origin, like politics, in ancient Greece – the birthplace, of course, of the *polis*.[7]

In consultation with Coicaud, I have not eliminated this polysemy but resolved it in a provisional way by generally favouring *politics*. Despite the fact that he discusses Schmitt's *The Concept of the Political*, Coicaud himself does not make any hard-and-fast distinctions between *le politique* and *la politique*, nor does he offer a definition of either term or even take a position on the historicality or the essential (that is, here, non-historical) character of the one or the other in relation to society and its institution. Coicaud freely acknowledged to me that he has not yet reflected upon these terms sufficiently to take a stand of his own. An honest admission – and a prudent stand, as well, considering the distinguished writers who still disagree among themselves on this topic. Given that these two similar nouns (the term 'homonym' is not quite applicable here, since it is their respective genders that create the difference) are not employed in any systematic or technical way, I have upon occasion, with the author's approval, even changed (what would be) 'the political' to 'politics', as it renders the result more familiar to an English-speaking audience without in any way violating the author's deep-seated intentions.

The definitional deficit of this decisive but polysemous term *politique* rebounds, however, upon his primary expository term, *legitimacy*, as regards its historical status. Coicaud wishes to place the study of legitimacy in a historical (but not historicist) perspective, so as to salvage it as a key element of social and political analysis and to defend it from attacks on several fronts. The *historical* element comes into play when he argues that legitimacy must always be studied on the basis of concrete historical

[6] Ibid., pp. xxxiv–xxxv, note 8: 'See my . . . Jean-Pierre Vernant translation, "The Birth of the Political", in the Australia-based social theory journal *Thesis Eleven* (60 (February 2000), 87–91). Like Lefort, and despite their differing definitions of *le* and *la politique* (see preceding note), Castoriadis too considers "the political" to be an essential and inescapable element of any human society. Vernant's argument could be summarized by saying that it makes no sense to speak of either "the political" or "politics" before the advent of the *polis* as an effective social-historical institution. That raises the question whether both of these terms might be datable (and thereby *historical* in character), instead of one or another or both being a "form" or "dimension" of *all* societies. But what would one then call this element, in pre-*polis* times, whereby a society gives itself its "form" through social division (Lefort) or organizes its "explicit power" (Castoriadis)?'

[7] One could also phrase the question in terms of whether the *polis* and politics/the political are *translatable* into prior languages, societies, and cultures – or whether, instead, such a translation effort is futile because anachronistic, it being an unjustified reverse extrapolation of a social-historical form that had not yet been created as a distinctive realm.

situations; when he questions orientations that challenge the relevancy or applicability of legitimacy, for he places these orientations (positivism, Marxism, Weberian social theory) themselves in revealing historical perspective; and when he tellingly exposes their inability to come to terms with the historicity of Modern Times without indulging in a 'nostalgia' for premodernity.[8]

Yet, it is in quite *general* terms that Coicaud defines the elements that go to make up legitimacy. Legitimacy, he asserts, assumes an 'unequal distribution of power', an 'asymmetric relationship constituted by the command relations between the governors and the governed', as well as 'political differentiation', for a 'division that separates those individuals who command from those who obey is that upon which the logic of legitimacy rests'. Moreover, 'in order to understand how a theory of legitimacy is based upon the separation of the governors and the governed, one must', he states, 'first distinguish it from those political concepts that find it impossible to justify the power of the State' – which seems to imply that legitimacy, by way of contrast, necessarily involves a justification of *the State*'s power (this creates an additional potential for anachronism, even though he emphasises that the State is not to be taken as equivalent to the 'bourgeois State'). The general theory of legitimacy also introduces the notions of consent and laws, as well as that of the norms – or 'values', to employ the neo-Kantian and post-Nietzschean axiological language Coicaud usually prefers – by which the identity of a given society serves to posit and then to judge the effectiveness and appropriateness of its actual laws. Thus, as stated previously, legitimacy is not understood by him as mere conformity to the existing law. Nor is Coicaud adopting a conservative or reactionary authoritarian viewpoint regarding either political arrangements or their legitimation via discourse. Here, Coicaud quotes Michael Walzer, who states that, 'in the context of consent theory, we do not say that the government is just, therefore the citizens are obligated, but rather that citizens have committed themselves, therefore the government is just' – a crucial point, but one which would pack a bunch of historical elements into a general theory of legitimacy. For, Coicaud decidedly wants to apply legitimacy theory's study of consent not only to regimes that include 'citizens' but to *all* societies whose governments do not rely solely upon force (and no governmental apparatus can perpetually rely solely upon force). He goes so far in one place as to derive 'the question of justice in human life' from a sweeping analysis of the demands and dynamic development of the newborn child.

[8] On 'the nostalgia for the origin', see my Fabio Ciaramelli translation, 'The Self-Presupposition of the Origin', *Thesis Eleven* 49 (May 1997), 45–67.

There is still considerable force as well as some substantial benefit to Coicaud's approach, even though the general and historical expositions of legitimacy sometimes seem at odds or enjoy an uneasy coexistence. Viewed in relation to politics/the political, the 'problematic of legitimacy' (to use his terminology) prevents him from turning his historically informed approach into a hermeneutic – i.e. merely interpretational – undertaking: a political judgement of legitimacy is such that it cannot simply retrace what the laws have decreed in order to come up with an answer to the question of where justice lies. Moreover, his insistence upon always examining a potential for legitimate command–obedience relationships in their historical context strongly militates against the tendency to 'adopt an anachronistic point of view, wishing to evaluate the past on the basis of criteria for judgement borrowed entirely from the present' – the sort of confused retrospective moralism characteristic, for example, of much 'left-wing' political correctness in academia today, which is a flip side of the tendency of traditionalists to judge the present solely on the basis of what they (presently) consider to be values consecrated by the past.

Nonetheless, the question of historical connection between legitimacy and politics is still posed: if legitimacy is related to politics, does the historical character of the former have anything to do with the birth of the *polis* in the ancient world? Coicaud broaches the subject of legitimacy theory by citing Jose Guilherme Merquior's historical reconstitution of the term *legitimacy*, noting that Merquior cites Cicero's 'use [of] the expressions *legitimum imperium* and *potestas legitima* when he refers to legally established power and magistrates or when he distinguishes the legitimate enemy (*legitimus hostis*) from the thief or pirate because of the treaties signed with the former and because such treaties were valid as legal documents'. He also relies upon Merquior when he establishes that 'the signification of the word *legitimacy*, whose employment is observed for the first time in medieval texts, preserves the idea of conformity to the law. The political character of legitimacy is accentuated by a reflection upon the justification of the delegation of power.' While Merquior is not a major authority for Coicaud, it is worth noting that the former had introduced his remarks on legitimacy, however, by stating that 'the cradle of legitimacy theory' – i.e. its historical birthplace, or at least the site in which it was first nurtured – 'was legal philosophy'. That assertion might bring us back to the Greeks, since philosophical reflection upon the law certainly predates Roman and medieval times, and it makes us wonder about the applicability of the study of legitimacy to pre-Hellenic societies (a Coicaud thesis, we noted), since one places oneself upon dangerous, perhaps anachronistic ground when one claims that the existence of philosophy, legal or otherwise, might somehow predate these same Greeks. Interestingly, the relevancy of the Greeks to legitimacy theory is questioned by Merquior himself in another passage on the same page – one that Coicaud, however, does not cite: 'Apparently, ancient Greek did not possess a special word for legitimate (as distinct from lawful).' Indeed, as Merquior goes on to say,

the rise of the concept of legitimacy as a political problem [and it is as a 'political problem' that we are discussing it here – D. A. C.] was prompted by *the collapse of direct rule in the ancient world* [my emphasis – D. A. C.]. It owes much to the substitution of imperial authority for the direct democracy of the *agora* [a particularly nonsensical, counterhistorical expression – D. A. C.] or the personal rule of local tyrants. Thus the medieval application of 'legitimate' to persons in office reflects the long acquaintance with the power of deputies of the emperors or popes.

The author whom Coicaud cites, and to whom he refers us in order to consider 'the history of the term *legitimacy*', seems to be telling us that it is the *death* of the *polis* as a self-governing, collectively autonomous political entity that serves as the historical context for the rise of political legitimacy theory, articulated as the possibility of a critical evaluation of separate authority that also involves or implies a (grudging or enthusiastic) acceptance thereof. This would tend to confirm Coicaud's general definition of legitimacy in terms of political differentiation, an unequal and asymmetrical distribution of power, as well as consent, by the governed, of the actions of a separate state apparatus run by governors – notions contested in the Greek political imaginary – just as it would be consonant with the historical struggle of early Renaissance cities to carve out a realm of political rule for themselves at the expense of, but also in the context of nearly inevitable compromises with, aristocratic, monarchical, imperial, and papal authorities. Yet this set of political-linguistic circumstances might now serve to circumscribe legitimacy historically, excising therefrom the very period in which the *polis*, and thus politics and perhaps also 'the political', came into existence as distinct social-historical forms.

While we may find merit in Merquior's historical vantage point on the origins of legitimacy theory in the demise of direct democracy and in the rise of the sort of unbalanced and detached forms of command–obedience power relationships characteristic of the post-*polis* politics of imperial, feudal, and early modern times (and, let us add, in the emergence of a *conditional resistance* thereto), we might also be tempted to challenge his linguistic assertion regarding the lack of any distinction in ancient Greek between mere lawfulness and something that goes beyond simple unlawfulness (i.e. beyond plain non-observance of the existing law) – a lack that was also characteristic, he had asserted, of ancient

xviii   Translator's foreword

Rome's single-edged usage of *legitimus*. In *Democracy Ancient and Modern*,[9] the blacklisted American classicist M. I. Finley highlighted what Castoriadis was later to describe as the 'apparently strange but fascinating procedure called *graphē paranomon* (accusation of unlawfulness)'.[10] *Graphē paranomon* – you have written (proposed and won acceptance for) a 'para'-law, a faulty or abnormal law – had introduced the possibility of a subsequent review and, eventually, an abrogation of a specific law into the procedures by which laws were, after deliberative consideration by the council (*boulē*), democratically adopted by the assembly (the *ekklēsia* – and *not* the 'agora', whose political functions were more diffuse). This legal procedure, explains Castoriadis, involved an 'accusation by a citizen against another citizen that the latter had induced the Assembly to adopt an "illegitimate law"', and it led to an adjudication by a jury of the assembly's peers, selected by lot from the entire citizenry (or at least among those who had registered for this remunerated civic responsibility). 'We need to reflect on the abysses opened by this phrase', *illegitimate law*, Castoriadis says after having placed it in quotation marks – indicating thereby that, with regard to the question of justice, ancient

---

9   M. I. Finley, *Democracy Ancient and Modern* (New Brunswick, N.J.: Rutgers University Press, 1973), pp. 26–7, 118. Finley's translation of *graphē paranomon* is 'illegal proposal'. Clearly, a translation problem of colossal proportions arises here, and whatever solution one offers will depend upon one's view of the relevancy and applicability of legitimacy theory to the ancient *poleis*. In 'Max Weber and the Greek City-State' (in *Ancient History: Evidence and Models* (New York: Viking, 1986), pp. 88–103; see p. 99), Finley explains that 'Greek law has been notoriously a stepchild in modern study. Weber was no exception to the universal neglect of the subject.'

10 Cornelius Castoriadis, 'The Greek *Polis* and the Creation of Democracy', *Philosophy, Politics, Autonomy*, p. 116, n. 25, where Castoriadis also mentions Victor Ehrenberg's discussion of two similar provisions: *apate tou demou* (deceit of the *demos*) and the exception *ton nomon me peideion einai* (inappropriateness of a law). Castoriadis describes *graphē paranomon* in depth in the following terms: 'You have made a proposal to the *ecclesia*, and this proposal has been voted for. Then another citizen can bring you before a court, accusing you of inducing the people to vote for an unlawful law. You can be acquitted or convicted – and in the latter case, the law is annulled. Thus, you have the right to propose anything you please, but you have to think carefully before proposing something on the basis of a momentary fit of popular mood and having it approved by a bare majority. For the action would be judged by a popular court of considerable dimensions (501, sometimes 1,001 or even 1,501 citizens sitting as judges), drawn by lot. Thus the *demos* was appealing against itself in front of itself: the appeal was from the whole body of citizens (or whichever part of it was present when the proposal in question was adopted) to a huge random sample of the same body sitting after passions had calmed, listening again to contradictory arguments, and assessing the matter from a relative distance. Since the source of the law is the people, "control of constitutionality" could not be entrusted to "professionals" – in any case, the idea would have sounded ridiculous to a Greek – but only to the people themselves acting in a different guise. The people say what the law is; the people can err; the people can correct themselves. This is a magnificent example of an effective institution of self-limitation' (p. 117).

Greek democracy and politics create a decisive break in relation to traditional and religious (heteronomous) ways of relating to and evaluating
a society's own norms and laws, and perhaps also expressing concern
whether 'legitimacy' and 'illegitimacy', as usually understood, can be applied meaningfully and accurately (i.e. not anachronistically) to Greek
political arrangements, which did indeed allow existing laws to be called
into question.[11]

Furthermore, when Merquior turns to medieval and early modern
times, he adds that

the first definition of governmental legitimacy as derived from consent grounded
on natural law is due to William of Occam (first half of fourteenth century), the
thinker whose nominalism so revolutionized medieval philosophy. The basis of
Occam's reasoning was the older medieval argument *quod omnes tanget* – what
touches all must be approved by all.

An apparently similar, but in fact more far-reaching political view had
already been staged, however, during the first third of the fifth century
BCE at democratic Athens in Aeschylus's *The Suppliant Maidens* (with
the political anachronism characteristic of tragedy).[12] King Pelasgus of
Argos tells the daughters of Danaus, who are seeking asylum after having
fled the prospect of forced marriage with their Egyptian cousins:

> You are not suppliants at my own hearth.
> If the city stains the commonweal,
> In common let the people work a cure. (365–67)

To this assertion, that what touches all must be not only approved by all
but also resolved in a participatory way by all, is added an all-inclusive
idea of sharing:

[11] Cornelius Castoriadis, 'The Greek and the Modern Political Imaginary', in *World in Fragments*, trans. and ed. David Ames Curtis (Stanford: Stanford University Press, 1997), p. 93.
[12] Aeschylus, *The Suppliant Women*, in *The Complete Greek Tragedies*, ed. David Greene and Richmond Lattimore, 2nd edn (University of Chicago Press, 1991), *Aeschylus*, vol. II, p. 19. It is in this play (lines 603–4) that for the first time a juxtaposition of the two words that go to make up *democracy* – *dēmos* (people) and *kratos* (power) – can be documented (see Pierre Vidal-Naquet, 'The Tradition of Greek Democracy', *Thesis Eleven* 60 (February 2000), 78, and Pierre Lévêque and Pierre Vidal-Naquet, *Cleisthenes, the Athenian: An Essay on the Representation of Space and of Time in Greek Political Thought from the End of the Sixth Century to the Death of Plato*, with a new discussion *On the Invention of Democracy* by Pierre Lévêque, Pierre Vidal-Naquet, and Cornelius Castoriadis (Atlantic Highlands, N.J.: Humanities Press, 1996), p. 19; on p. 150, n. 11, Lévêque and Vidal-Naquet cite Ehrenberg as the source for this observation). In light of Coicaud's concern with the theme of 'exclusion', it is worthwhile mentioning, as well, that this play concerns the acceptance and integration of aliens (the daughters of Danaus) who have only the slenderest of claims to a common heritage with the city of Argos and the Argive king.

> But I would make no promises until
> I share with all the citizens. (368–69)

Moreover, when these ideas are reiterated, they are articulated in terms of an explicit rejection, by he who is in a position of command, of any *separation* from the people:

> I said before that never would I act
> Alone, apart from the people, though I am ruler; (398–99)

Indeed, the fact that the decision is tougher and more complex than usual militates *in favour of more* participation and sharing, *not less*, for the king had just said:

> The choice is not easy: choose me not as judge. (387)

It is thus doubtful, at least according to some observers and for varied reasons, whether legitimacy as an analytical concept can apply to the political imaginary of ancient Greece – but also doubtful, in light of the foregoing, whether one can think legitimacy theory historically without reference to the contributions made by the ancient Greek *poleis*, without reference to the *poleis*'s demise as well, and, finally, without reference to the rise of early modern cities within a nearly overwhelming set of hostile circumstances.

The historical relationship between legitimacy and politics, then, is evidently highly complex, one continually fraught with the dangers of anachronism. Thanks to the reading of an author Coicaud himself cites, further historical reflection reveals that Coicaud's general theory of legitimacy could conflict at times with legitimacy theory's own historical development. It has even been asked whether the very term *legitimacy* is Eurocentric – and Sinocentric, too (the 'Mandate of Heaven') – instead of being an overall term of political analysis that is then potentially applicable to the study of every particular political situation within history where governance does not rely solely upon force.[13] Coicaud believes that legitimacy and the consent it presupposes may be at work in primitive societies, since he asserts, on the authority of the Structuralist anthropologist Claude Lévi-Strauss, that such societies include 'deliberative procedures'. But another French author whose name is to be found among Coicaud's footnotes – the political anthropologist Pierre Clastres, who challenged anthropological tenets of Structuralism and Marxism, just as Coicaud wishes to do – wrote of a 'society against the State' in

---

[13] Cornelius Castoriadis, 'The Greek and the Modern Political Imaginary', *World in Fragments*, p. 86.

primitive Amerindian cultures.[14] That phrase ill accords with a theory of legitimacy involving possible justification of a State, let alone with what Coicaud believes is entailed by the existence of legitimacy: 'the right to govern'. In those cultures, Clastres argues, the chief is instituted and installed not as a governor with separate powers but as a 'servant' lacking them, hemmed in as he is on all sides precisely because, according to the political norms of Amerindian tribes, any permanent division in governance that would lead to the creation of a separate state apparatus must be conjured away *at all costs* – including the 'torture', applicable to all on an equal basis, involved in rituals of initiation as well as incessant tribal wars, which ensure that population will not increase too rapidly and resources will remain at near-subsistence levels.[15]

Certain salutary effects still flow from Coicaud's determination to relate legitimacy theory to a historically informed politics (and not just to *de facto* law, on the one side, and an ahistorical morality, on the other). In particular, his exposition of legitimacy theory in his book, written near the dawn of the twenty-first century, challenges a number of nineteenth-century political theories (liberalism, Marxism, and anarchism) that, prolonged into the twentieth century, still encounter considerable difficulties when it comes to thinking about legitimacy. They encounter such difficulties precisely because these theories display ambiguous, if not downright hostile, attitudes towards politics. This is obvious for the *laissez-faire* tendencies of classical liberalism that have been developed into that 'solemn complement of justification' (what Marx also called *ideology*) by such exponents of a loony 'libertarian' liberalism as Friedrich August von Hayek and Milton Friedman, as well as for contemporary liberals who tend to view politics itself as a potential danger to 'the individual', to 'pluralism', and to 'tolerance'. It is perhaps less apparent, for some, in the cases of Marxism and anarchism, because of their overt political engagements. Yet one need only reflect upon Marx's critique of 'political' rights as merely 'formal' (instead of historically *partial*, in both senses of the term) or classical anarchism's nearly self-definitional rejection of all power relationships. Coicaud is constantly endeavouring to show, through his demonstrations of liberalism's, Marxism's, and anarchism's inability to come to terms

---

[14] Pierre Clastres, *Society Against the State: The Leader as Servant and the Humane Uses of Power Among the Indians of the Americas*, trans. Robert Hurley (New York: Urizen Books, 1977).

[15] See my recent translation of Claude Lefort's 'Dialogue with Pierre Clastres', in *Writing: The Political Test*, pp. 207–35. Those who saw Richard Harris in *A Man Called Horse* have a vivid picture of what 'the "torture" . . . involved in rituals of initiation' may entail in Indian societies. Clastres treats such 'torture' as an integral and necessary part of what he considers their anti-statist social institution.

with the concept of legitimacy, how each of those doctrines rejects politics in one way or another. An added benefit: even though, generally speaking, Coicaud opts for a variation[16] on a Weberian 'norm-legitimacy' theory over the 'power-legitimacy' theory of a Rousseau (the terminology here is Merquior's),[17] he emphasises over and over again that all attempts to consider and to comprehend a society without explicitly including therein its power relationships are as incoherent as they are vain. This is a decided advantage over these various nineteenth-century doctrines (not that political power considerations, of course, have been entirely absent therefrom

[16] Coicaud's distinctive response, in relation to a Weberian 'norm-legitimacy', is to refuse to reduce legitimacy to a *belief* in legitimacy; he does so by challenging the so-called separation of facts and values championed by Max Weber.

[17] Rousseau, Merquior noted, is the archetypical exponent of 'power-legitimacy'. Coicaud's integration of power considerations into his 'norm-legitimacy' approach, which takes values seriously and does not reduce legitimacy to mere belief, moves him from Weberian 'norm-legitimacy' to a position that does not wholly repudiate the outlook of 'power-legitimacy', so long as 'values' are recognised and given their due. For Coicaud, Weberian 'norm-legitimacy' does not really secure legitimacy at all, given Weber's inadequate notion of objectivity, his neutralist stance on neutrality, his consequent debilitating refusal to take a stand in relation to values, and his faulty view of the benefits and scope of legal positivism.

Coicaud avails himself of a keen observation from Raymond Aron to illustrate a further indication of Weber's inability to come to terms with legitimacy as a political judgement, based upon values, that is not reducible to *de facto* belief. There is a discrepancy between the four Weberian types of action (goal-related rational action, value-rational action, affective behaviour, and traditional action) and the three Weberian types of political legitimacy (rational, traditional, and charismatic). 'It is easy to notice', Coicaud comments, 'that the failure of these two typologies to coincide with each other is due to the absence of a power relationship that would be the equivalent of value-rational action.' A practical consequence of this discordance may be seen on the level of civilisational analysis, and it relates directly to the question of the status of the *polis* in relation to the study of legitimacy. In 'Max Weber and the Greek City-State' (in *Ancient History: Evidence and Models*, pp. 93–9, 103), M. I. Finley criticises Weber's contortions and the lengths Weber had to go in order to force the Athenian democratic *polis* into the 'charismatic' model. In these matters, historical falsification is not the province of Marxism alone; it extends to Weber's neo-Kantianism, where the 'separation of facts from values' prolongs into social theory the incoherent instituted split between Kantian pandeterminism (in the first *Critique*, Kant states that 'everything which exists is completely determined') and Kantian moral theory (its unattainable polar star).

As we noted above, Coicaud also points out the connection between Weber's inadequate notion of objectivity and his neutralist view of neutrality, on the one hand, and his debilitating refusal to take a stand in relation to values, on the other. Building upon this insight, we might go further and, challenging Weber's neo-Kantianism, say that there is a revealing homology between his notion of ideal types, which he treats as a 'utopia', both useful and unrealisable, and his assertion, in a 1908 letter to Robert Michels, that 'any thought . . . of removing the rule of men over men through even the most sophisticated forms of "democracy", is "utopian"'. Coicaud quotes, but does not challenge, this last statement – which is, indeed, consonant with his own view that legitimacy entails an 'asymmetry' in the 'political differentiation' of governors and governed, instead of a possible *reversibility* of the roles of governor and governed (Aristotle's definition of a citizen as someone capable, by turns, of ruling and being ruled).

on the practical and even theoretical levels). Nor is power viewed by
Coicaud as inherently evil or corrupting, as an acosmic moral theorist
might do. 'The mechanism of political legitimacy', Coicaud explains,
'aims at establishing recognition for the right to govern. It is therefore
not a matter of doing away with the existence of power.'

It is unfortunate, in this respect, that Coicaud does not take into account political and associational practices that date at least from the
1871 Paris Commune and have their roots further back in a variety of
modern efforts at individual and collective autonomy – e.g., the English,
American, and French Revolutions, as well as the workers' movement
(and, more recently, the student, women's, and ecology movements) –
and that have been extended on the practical plane as well as theorised
throughout the twentieth century (Council Communists, Spanish anarchists and POUM-ists, Hungarian workers' council revolutionaries, or
the students of the May 1968 movement in Coicaud's native France, to
take a few striking examples). Along with his assessments of what I consider the dogmatic buffooneries of authors like Louis Althusser and Pierre
Bourdieu – who, in a highly conservative move, attempt to *salvage* classical Marxism by adding thereto a few 'scientific' updates – as well as of the
invariably immobile views of doctrinaire anarchists, it would have been
interesting for Coicaud to have examined thinkers and movements that,
over the course of the century just ending, have challenged anti-political
tendencies and biases in classical liberalism, Marxism, and anarchism.
How would a former Marxist committed to a direct economic and political democracy and inspired by classical Greece, like Castoriadis (whom
Coicaud cites in his bibliography but not in his text or in his notes), or
an ecologist quite critical of many strains of anarchism and favourable
to a municipal libertarianism also inspired by ancient Greek democratic
practices, like Murray Bookchin, fare when the question of legitimacy is
raised? How might an engagement with their thought have led to a more
complex and nuanced appreciation of legitimacy in its historical context,
a finer understanding of the origin, applicability, advantages, and perhaps also limits of legitimacy theory? We can nevertheless benefit from
Coicaud's reflections – which are intended as a defence and advancement
of the concept of legitimacy – as a basis for our pursuing such questions
further, a process the author would certainly not consider unwelcome,
and which he would be sure to explore with the same penetrating inci-
siveness that, in his book, he has shown himself capable of illustrating
and exemplifying.

Let us now return to the title – or, more precisely, the subtitle – of
Legitimacy and Politics in order to allow a reflection upon the translation

process to shed further light upon this book. The volume is intended as 'a contribution to the study of political right and political responsibility'. Like Rawls's *A Theory of Justice*, with its indefinite article most prominent in its title, this subtitled 'contribution' is modest and intentionally undogmatic in its ambitions. Indeed, Coicaud champions the values of tolerance and pluralism, as do Rawls as well as Weber, though he believes that one can no longer do so in the same ways as they have done, given their inadequate conceptions of legitimacy and the contradictions into which their respective brands of tolerance and pluralism have led them. The word that captures the translator's attention, however, the one that proved to be the most difficult term in the entire translation, is the word *droit*, which means 'right' but also 'law'.

We can begin to get an idea of the difficulties this word poses when we focus on its usage in the subtitle. What is *droit politique* – which, when framed in terms of legitimacy, Coicaud calls *the right to govern*? The translation 'political law' would sound strange to many an English speaker and might conjure up, for some, disturbing images of a politicised law wherein it is men and not laws that govern. 'Political right' is not a phrase with which English speakers are very familiar, either. But, as Coicaud himself pointed out to me, *droit politique* is found in the subtitle of Jean-Jacques Rousseau's famous treatise, the standard translation of which is *On the Social Contract, or Principles of Political Right*. 'Political right' for Coicaud would involve not just the specific laws enacted to regulate the political process, nor simply the extant political rights recognised in a community, but would concern, too, the norms that stand behind and govern (in the broad sense of define, guide, and control) the concrete rules a society adopts in order to conceive, implement, oversee, monitor, and guarantee the political life of a community.

The Marxist response to political right – and to the laws and rights that embody it – is, of course, thoroughly negative. Coicaud quotes Marx and Engels that, 'as far as law is concerned, we with many others have stressed the opposition of communism to law, both political and private, as also in its most general form as the rights of man'. Herein we see the translation overlap of these two English terms – which in German, as in French, are both expressed by a single word: *Recht*. (Hegel's treatise on legal philosophy, for example, is sometimes translated as *The Philosophy of Right* and sometimes as *The Philosophy of Law*.) Choice thus becomes necessary, and it is not always easy. I have had to decide between 'right' and 'law' on nearly every page of Coicaud's book, a situation sometimes further complicated by the presence of a second French word meaning 'law': *loi*, which has both general and specific connotations, just as *droit* does. Short of indicating the French original each and every time within brackets or of employing some other such artificial and encumbering device that would again detract from the flow of the printed translation,[18] I have, after careful consideration and, I hope, judiciously, opted for one or the other, often doing so in consultation with the author – who, fully appreciative of the difficulties the translation of *droit* poses in English, patiently communicated to me his hesitations, his decisions, and sometimes his reconsiderations.

The rendering into English of another phrase involving right/law, *l'État de droit*, is also worth mentioning, for it too involves this vexing interface of the French, German, and English legal and linguistic traditions. Challenges of this sort make of translation an imperfect, and often maddening, but always passionately interesting transnational art – an encounter, indeed, with social imaginary significations that go well beyond the horizon of any individual author's (or translator's) intention or understanding – instead of a ready-made and easily applicable science, ripe for computerisation. In English, one tends to speak of 'the rule of law'. This has become a particularly empty and useless phrase, as its usage *ad nauseam* by all sides has driven home to me once again as I write these very lines (the Elian Gonzalez custody case in America). Taken by itself, the 'rule of law' decidedly does *not* fit the 'problematic of legitimacy' laid out by Coicaud, for it is hardly distinguishable from the 'conformity to the law' rhetoric that, in his correct view, falls short of the standard for legitimacy.

One can avoid this now nearly barren expression by using *l'État de droit*'s somewhat more familiar German equivalent: *Rechtstaat*. This solution sidesteps the issue, however, by simply displacing the problem into a third language. Yet it also has one minor advantage: it is better as a translation than 'rule of law', for it is consonant with Coicaud's association of legitimacy with the establishment of recognition for the justification of a *State*. But an ambiguity also intervenes between the French and German. At times, Coicaud himself takes a break from state justification to speak of positive contributions to 'the life of the city' – *cité*, in French. Unlike *État*, *Staat* is used – in the phrase *autonomer Stadtstaat* – to talk about the *polis*. And yet, just like the English-language expression *city-state*, its German counterpart *autonomer Stadtstaat* actually is nothing more than an abusive mistranslation of *polis*, for it is of doubtful value to consider the latter to be a state formation, a separate governmental apparatus. These

---

[18] One can imagine a not-too-distant future where, with the advent of the 'e-book' or another such electronic device that presents text and other information in a hyperlinked format, it will be possible to place the original language for key words and phrases 'underneath' the translated text and thereby enable the reader to call up the original at will for examination, consideration, and reflection. Of course, such an artifice, while perhaps highly informative to the reader, by itself does nothing to resolve any concrete problems of translation.

English and German phrases are particularly egregious anachronisms, their usages as erroneous as they are widespread.

I have therefore settled upon 'rights-based State' as the most appropriate translation for Coicaud's understanding of *l'État de droit* ('constitutional State', the standard translation of *Rechtstaat*, packs too much historical specificity to be appropriate here). But at times I have called upon 'the rule of law' and *Rechtstaat* to supplement (double or triple) this term or to indicate specific technical or historical features of its meaning. The reader is thus forewarned by this specific discussion of *droit* – as she will also be alerted by Coicaud's general theme of legitimacy as being something more than and different from mere conformity to the law – that it must always be kept in mind that my imperfect but forced choices of either *right* or *law* may very well result in ambiguities and misperceptions at any particular location in the text. It will be in reading *through* and *beyond* these difficulties in translation that the reader will perhaps gain a greater understanding of the political and philosophical stakes involved and thus be able to reflect further upon this transnational linguistic conundrum for herself.

One last feature of my labour as a translator should be highlighted in order for the reader to comprehend this volume in the most well-informed manner possible. In contrast to most of the texts I have worked on during my fifteen years as a professional translator, I did not myself propose this one to a publisher. Instead, Cambridge University Press offered me a translator's contract after my name was recommended to Coicaud by the French Publishers' Agency in New York. Both my editor at the Press, John Haslam, and the Agency are to be thanked for their interest and support.

It has been my general policy, in writing translator's forewords, not to take advantage of my position as the first reader of the work in translation, prejudicing subsequent readers' experiences by telling them in advance what to think about what they are about to read. I have sought, rather, to offer background information they might not otherwise have had available about the author and his work, now rendered into English. If I have dwelt here at length, and not for the first time, upon difficulties in my translation efforts, it is to offer the reader a glimpse of the struggle the translator undergoes each time he undertakes the strange and daunting task of writing in another person's voice – that of a foreigner, to myself and to other readers of the translated text – endeavouring thereby to make him speak in a language that is not his native tongue. As with all the other authors I have translated, my goal has been to render that foreign voice familiar enough to be read by an English-speaking public while preserving a sufficient degree of its foreignness to allow for a new and distinct contribution to the transnational republic of letters. In this effort, I have been assisted by the unparalleled openness and accessibility of Jean-Marc, who, entering into the spirit of the struggle himself, patiently answered my many translation questions and generously assisted me in the preparation of the notes and bibliographical apparatus for the English-language edition. The privilege of becoming acquainted with him aided me considerably in the imaginary creation of a native English-speaking Coicaud, a persona I gladly adopted as my own for several months, and has transformed him from foreigner into friend. Any defects or deficiencies in the establishment of that character are nevertheless mine.[19]

Winchester, Massachusetts, April 2000   DAVID AMES CURTIS
– Peloponnesus, Greece, October 2000

---

[19] In addition to reviewing the translation, Coicaud has also made a number of alterations in the text, nuancing some points, suppressing others outright, and clarifying eventual ambiguities. The present text therefore is, in this respect, more than and different from a faithful translation.

Acknowledgements

This work could not have been written without the faith and support bestowed upon me by a number of institutions and persons. Allow me to take this opportunity to thank them.

The main part of this work was completed while I was doing research and teaching at Harvard University. Whether at the Center for European Studies, at the Center for International Affairs, in the Department of Philosophy, or at the Law School, I have always benefited from a warm and stimulating environment. Among the professors whose support I have particularly prized, I wish to thank Patrice Higonnet, Stanley Hoffmann, Samuel P. Huntington, Harvey C. Mansfield, Hilary Putnam, John Rawls, and Roberto Mangabeira Unger.

The Sachs Foundation of Harvard University and the French Ministry of Foreign Affairs gave me crucial financial support. Without this support, it would have been difficult for me to free up the time necessary to write the present text.

Through our discussions and with their encouragement, a number of my friends have aided me in my research. In Cambridge, Massachusetts, I am thinking of Vincent Cortes, Michael Daumer, Jacques Delisle, Aleksa Djilas, Jeffrey Gross, and Jean-Michel Roy. In France, I thank Maïlys de Bernède, Olivier Broche, Gabriel Girard, Didier Louvel, Christophe Naulleau, Jean-Marie Pellerin, Henry Rousso, Sophie Sebirot-Nossof, Jean-Bernard Sire, and Patrick Weil. I also thank Jean-Christophe Brochier for having helped me make the present text more readable.

Assistance for the translation was provided by the French Ministry of Culture.

Introduction

What is political legitimacy? Under what conditions can one speak of a politically legitimate situation? Though simple in their formulation, these questions are nevertheless complicated. Providing satisfactory responses to them presupposes that one is able to surmount a certain number of problems, one of the foremost being the notion of political judgement.

Facing up to such a notion boils down, in effect, to appealing to a 'faculty of judgement' in the political domain. That faculty consists in evaluating the decisions and actions of rulers and institutions who are charged with ensuring that society runs well. It presupposes that the question of the criteria for political judgement has been elucidated – that is to say, that the conditions for the validity of those elements that allow for an evaluation of the just character of political relations have been established. Now, in what, precisely, do those conditions consist? Where are they to be found? How is one to assure oneself of their reliability?

Because of its complexity, the theme of legitimacy occupies a para-doxical position in contemporary political thought. On the one hand, it is granted that legitimacy is essential to the operation of political life. Legitimacy is therefore taken into account in analyses whose objective is to describe and to explain its mechanisms. And if one were to rank the terms to which political observers have recourse in their work, the word *legitimacy* would arrive in the top grouping. Only rarely do writings on this topic and observers of the political scene ignore this notion.

On the other hand, the treatment of the concept of legitimacy often brings out a certain reticence. Although legitimacy is indissociable from the faculty of judgement, most works and reflections that make use of it are loath to take into account the dimension of judgement it implies. They refuse to conduct research into the conditions for the right to govern by inquiring about the criteria used to evaluate political life. Max Weber's analyses of legitimacy, as we shall see, have a great deal to do with this phenomenon.

The situation surrounding this question is therefore quite troubling. The importance of the notion of legitimacy is recognised, as is attested to by the fact that the observers of political life cannot prevent themselves from referring to it. But this recognition goes hand in hand with a reluctance to broach the question of political judgement.

Thus, to the question 'What is political legitimacy?' is quickly added another one: How is one to explain the fact that, in contemporary political thought, the study of the idea of legitimacy does not seem to integrate any reflection upon the faculty of judgement in politics? This 'oversight', or 'denial', compels us to try to understand the signification of the notion of legitimacy from a relatively general point of view and to explain its paradoxical status in the field of contemporary political studies.

We shall begin by analysing a certain number of key themes regarding legitimacy. The examination of the question of legitimacy and of the faculty of judgement will then lead us into the heart of a history of ideas – but also a history of modern societies. On that basis, it will become possible to formulate some hypotheses, ones likely to allow us to surmount the aporias characteristic of the conventional approach to the topic of legitimacy.

Thus, in the first chapter we provide a definition of legitimacy and try to sort out its meaning on the political level. The idea of legitimacy is first of all defined in connection with the notions of consent, a network of norms – around which is made the pact [*accord*] among individuals in society – and law, which is conceived as a factor in the protection and promulgation of agreement [*accord*] about legitimacy. In the effort to understand the political from the angle of legitimacy, we seek from this perspective to set out the relationships of command and obedience in terms of right [*droit*] and to bring into play a dynamic of responsibility on the part of the governors and the governed – a dynamic that itself requires an idea of political judgement. This orientation, which places the accent on the search for the conditions political relationships are to fulfil in order to be seen to assume a right and just character, therefore breaks away from Marxist and positivist conceptions of political analysis.

The second chapter offers an account of the objections that have been formulated against analysing politics in terms of legitimacy, and shows their limitations. These objections lie at the heart of the paradoxical situation this notion finds itself in within contemporary political thought and can be entered under the following two headings: the theoretical and the methodological. A complementary relationship obviously exists between these two levels.

The theoretical objections consist essentially in rejecting the possibility of studying politics in terms of the right to govern. These objections are lodged either because the idea that legal action has any privileged connection with the theme of justice is contested or because the consent of individuals is thought not to play any role therein, or because the problematic of legitimacy is likened to a moral perception of the political, whereas the latter is said to have strictly nothing to do with ethical principles.

The objections of a methodological order lie primarily in a challenge to the validity of approaching political reality from the standpoint of values. They are based on a sort of empiricism that is defined above all by a separation of facts and values. Such a separation rules out the possibility of implementing the faculty of judgement and of taking practical reason into account in any way.

Such criticisms, which basically stem from Marxist and positivist currents of thought, take us back to such classical authors as Machiavelli, Marx, and Weber as well as to some contemporary authors, in particular Pierre Bourdieu and Theda Skocpol. Criticisms of this sort have some serious drawbacks and contain some grave contradictions: while the field of law is not the paradise of fairness some people depict it as, it is not to be reduced for all that to a more or less disguised use of violence. It is appropriate to give things their due and to examine in what way the field of law does indeed authoritatively express, for those living in society, the idea of social and political justice and contributes towards its realisation. Moreover, the role played by individual consent cannot systematically be denied. It is one of the essential factors in political relationships. And furthermore, morality is not alien to politics. Without our being able to identify it strictly with ethical principles and actions, politics could not disregard morality completely without the risk of seeing relationships among the members of one and the same community turning into open warfare. Finally, as much on the theoretical as on the methodological level, the separation of facts from values seems neither possible nor desirable. The analysis of legitimacy must therefore be distinguished from a narrow empiricism or positivism.

Chapter 3 shows that these theoretical and methodological objections, which take up a considerable, though often diffuse, space in contemporary political thought, are set within a history of social theories and of modern societies. They are in line with the scientistic conception of how to analyse social and political reality, as that conception was developed beginning in the seventeenth century under the influence of natural scientific study. Here, the reflections of Thomas Hobbes and Montesquieu serve as a point of departure. After the Age of Enlightenment, during which there was a convergence between theoretical reason and practical reason, a divorce ensued. Max Weber's reflections on the separation of facts and values is illustrative of this situation. But this division between theoretical reason and practical reason would not have been possible unless societies themselves had gone through a crisis as to the groundedness of their own values and, by way of extension, of values in general. Now, while this crisis is in part the product of that characteristic movement by which the world we know breaks with the premodern one, it is also the result of the developmental process of the ideals of modernity. In developing and in seeking to fulfil their ambition of universality, these ideals are turned against themselves and come to pose the question of legitimacy as one of the central stakes in both political reflection and political practice: they constitute legitimacy at once as a point of origin and as a line on the horizon. In their reality, our societies cannot fully align themselves upon them both. Legitimacy becomes therefore a key problem of modern political life.

How is it possible to surmount the aporias to which modernity is condemned as regards legitimacy? The last three chapters of the book attempt to answer that question. They offer three complementary paths of reflection, which deal with the relations between the idea of legitimacy, on the one hand, and the experience of history and of the community, on the other. By combining them, we can rehabilitate the roles of practical reasoning and the faculty of judgement in the analysis of social and political phenomena.

In Chapter 4, we establish that an authentic reflection upon practical truths has to break away from a scientistic interpretation of history. From this point of view, the Marxist and Weberian conceptions of history are equally unreliable. Each one in its own way presents the risk of pegging the idea of legitimacy on that of legality. As for Carl Schmitt's theories, which are analysed as a prolongation of the path laid out by Max Weber, they offer a good illustration of the dangers to which one is exposed when one subjects law to the imperatives of politics. In any case, we shall see that the scientistic, Marxist, and Weberian orientations all share a nostalgia for the absolute. That nostalgia forbids them to pose the question of truth within history in a way that would allow them to think legitimacy in satisfactory terms.

In opposition to these theories, it is emphasised in Chapter 5 that the exercise of the faculty of judgement in modernity – wherein the plural and shifting character of human reality and of the referential systems used to evaluate this reality occupy a place of key importance – necessitates a revision of our conception of history and of history's relations with social and political theory. This is indicated by two points of view, which are complementary. In the first place, while it is useful to take empirical data into account when reflecting upon legitimacy, it can be so only when such a practice is articulated in tandem with what are called *values*.

That is what bids us to remain attentive to the impact of values on the constitution of human phenomena and not to describe the axiological domain as irrational, the consequence of which would be to prevent us from being able to establish a hierarchy among its component parts. But it also implies the implementation of a neutral and objective point of view that integrates an engaged approach to human reality. In the second place, in order to deploy one's faculty of judgement, one has to shed light on the kind of relation that exists between the analysis of social and political phenomena and history. To render the criteria for judgement explicit, one must determine the domain within which the faculty of judgement is applicable. Here, in fact, it is a matter of being careful that the analysis of social and political phenomena and the evaluations of the right to govern that may result therefrom will not be established in terms of criteria that are alien to the situations under examination.

The sixth and final chapter shows that, in working out a theory of political deliberation, it is important to do so in connection with the meaning of the possible and of the necessary. This is a meaning with which individuals identify, and it is starting from this meaning that they evaluate their situation, asking whether or not it corresponds to their criteria for what is just and unjust. It is from this standpoint that the aforementioned reflections on history take on their full strength. Indeed, it is in questioning oneself about the way in which individuals recognise themselves in the values that define the identity of the society in which they live – indeed, it is in examining whether they consider the place reserved for them acceptable or unacceptable – that it is possible to go further in one's reflections on legitimacy. In other words, it is a matter of seeing how individuals position themselves within the community to which they belong. From this point of view, it is possible to explicate the legitimate or illegitimate character of a political situation by taking into account both the idea of right promoted by the identity of a given society and the attitudes of adherence or rejection individuals exhibit as regards this idea of right. The ruled may reject the way in which they are governed, and this opens up forms of contestation and, in some cases, more or less strategic forms of political change. Whether or not they do so depends upon the configuration of the relations of forces, and notably upon the chances opponents have to succeed in their efforts at contestation, as well as upon the (material and symbolic) cost such an undertaking represents. In any case, without necessarily witnessing radical upheavals, it is possible to spot indications of political legitimacy or illegitimacy through the ways in which, and the degrees to which, individuals invest themselves in the life of their society. This aspect of the question of legitimacy can be examined by analysing the process by which one passes from demands that are discredited, even criminalised, by the existing authorities, to points of view that begin to be listened to and are ultimately legalised.

Of course, one has to assume some methodological and intellectual positions when following this line of research. In the first place, although the present work belongs to the field of political science, it does not limit itself thereto, and it also calls upon the disciplines of philosophy, sociology, and law. Indeed, by virtue of its configuration and its position, at the place where the social bond is brought together, the question of legitimacy has to be grasped from the outset in a pluridisciplinary perspective. Let us add that to a great extent the present book calls upon the history of social and political ideas. And yet, it is not for all that a matter of offering an exhaustive account here of these intellectual and historical phenomena for their own sake. Such phenomena are treated, rather, as revelatory indices of the movement that is constitutive of the problematic of legitimacy. In the end, it is also a matter, when studying the question of legitimacy, of taking seriously the normative dimension of human reality and of examining how one might rehabilitate that dimension.

These methodological and intellectual positions go to explain the dual nature of the present work. On the one hand, our investigation takes the form of a historical reconstitution or reconstruction. On the other, this reconstitution is placed in the service of an analysis of the conditions of possibility for a reflection upon practical truths. It is obviously not a question of proposing solutions and answers *in abstracto*. The objective, on the contrary, is to show that, far from forbidding one to question the faculty of judgement in politics or from rendering that questioning superfluous, historical rootedness urgently requires such questioning. To put it briefly: it is a matter of implementing a normative approach to the question of legitimacy, while endeavouring to set things in historical perspective.

From this point of view, the analysis proposed here offers an alternative to political reflection as it has been developed in a certain number of conventional ways.

- First of all, it distinguishes itself from a positivist approach to political reality. Without denying, obviously, the usefulness of the latter approach, it contests that approach's pretensions to hegemony, which are the combined product of the ambient scientism, force of habit, and a certain intellectual laziness. These three factors have led researchers to turn away from basic questions, whose complexity and nature entail provisional, ever-revisable answers and which, in another connection, go against received ideas within the French scientific community;

• Secondly, history is used here, but it is not studied for its own sake. Without contesting the role historical works play in reappropriating the past and in constituting our memory, it is just too easy a solution to ask oneself what so-and-so said, what he meant to say, what he thought, rather than to ask oneself what is to be thought in and for the present time. Certainly, we always reflect while aided by others, and with others. But when one reduces political reflection to dwelling upon the past, to commentary upon previous works, political thought itself atrophies. And yet, the present work also breaks away from the anti-historical temptation that frequently characterises philosophical works in the Anglo-Saxon world. A result of the legacy of English empirical philosophy (which, traditionally speaking, is not very history oriented), of the specific cultural background of the New World, and of the importance granted to analytical philosophy, that temptation ends up creating repetitious situations. One is reduced to various forms of historical ignorance and amnesia, which must be avoided as much as possible.

• Finally, to broach the question of legitimacy is to take the theme of right seriously and to interrogate oneself about the conditions that make for the just exercise of political command. To tackle this question is therefore to go against an orientation that has been cultivated to excess in certain French intellectual and academic circles: that is, a refusal to recognise the connection legal authority has with justice. This situation can be explained by the combined action of positivism, which does not connect law to the substantive dimension of values, and of Marxism, whose critique of legal authority is well known. But it can also be explained by the relationships that exist in France between law and the State, as well as by the resulting status legal training enjoys there. The fact that, inside the French Hexagon, law turns out to be intimately tied up with the State – a situation quite different from what obtains in the United States, for example, where the birth of the State does not proceed the unfurling of democratic ideals and where the State does not dominate civil society as much as it does in France – as well as the conservative tendencies of law schools, has not facilitated the flowering of a balanced form of legal reflection. It is, moreover, in part for this reason that the philosophy of law remains a discipline that has hardly developed at all in France. To put it briefly: law has for a long time been either discredited or revered there, on account of its alliance with the State.

Reflecting upon legitimacy consequently amounts to taking an interest in law from a perspective that is not traditionally adopted in France. Of course, with the ebbing of left-wing ideologies, a growing number of serious works are today being devoted to law. Unfortunately, too often these works are content to adopt as their own an attitude that equates the State and law, sometimes they even go further and adorn the latter with all possible virtues, following in this way a see-saw movement that has become customary in the history of thought. It is more judicious, however, to ask oneself under what conditions law satisfies the requirements of justice.

To analyse legitimacy in connection with the dimension of values is to pose the question of the Good in politics and boils down to rehabilitating a normative type of reflection on politics – without, for all that, throwing overboard all the components of positivist analyses. In other words, it is a matter of setting political reflection back on the rails from which political realism, in particular, had driven it: those of responsibility and commitment [*engagement*]. While still being concerned with analysing and comprehending human reality, this approach also aims at fulfilling certain values, including dignity. Without proposing rules of thought and of conduct, one of the ambitions of the present work is, in effect, to show that it is neither possible nor desirable to exclude values, the faculty of judgement, and the question of the Good from political reflection.

In France, the role of formulating analyses that are expressive of value judgements is traditionally entrusted to the intellectuals. The race to strike a pose, as is encouraged by the TV economy, and the highly polemical character of debates over ideas in that country have reinforced this *de facto* situation. Researchers and academics find it all the more difficult to make their voices heard as their very conception of science tends to forbid them from taking a position. In such a context, the present work is animated by the concern to defend and to advance the idea that science is not indifferent to the world in which it evolves and that it attempts to contribute towards the betterment of that world. If we are to believe Marcel Mauss,[1] in science one cannot proceed too slowly, and in matters of practice one cannot wait; it is therefore by advancing at an average speed, which is imposed by taking these two dimensions into account,

---

[1] Marcel Mauss, *Œuvres*, 3 vols. (Paris: Minuit, 1981), vol. III, *Cohésion sociale et divisions de la sociologie*, pp. 579–80.

that political reflection will best be able to confront the truth and the world in which the truth unfolds.

To proceed in this way is therefore to take a detour in order to tackle those questions whose burning character is underscored by the course of contemporary political events. This is a detour that may seem quite long for someone who wants to have immediate answers. Experience shows, however, that patience and the establishment of some distance most often allows one to elucidate that which would not have been seen, had one cast too close and too hurried a glance.

1   What is political legitimacy?

DEFINITION OF LEGITIMACY: THE RIGHT TO GOVERN

The problem of legitimacy, which is central in politics, is not the exclusive property of any one discipline. Philosophy and political science, law, sociology, and political anthropology have all made of it a privileged object of research. The breadth of the literature on this theme suffices to prove the point. With each discipline representing a specific way of understanding reality, it is not surprising that the various points of view being advanced offer marked differences. And if one compares the works of various authors or schools of thought, one finds, even within a given discipline, some major divergencies. Despite these, there exists a common ground for understanding: the idea of legitimacy concerns first and foremost the right to govern. Legitimacy is the recognition of the right to govern. In this regard, it tries to offer a solution to a fundamental political problem, which consists in justifying simultaneously political power and obedience.[1]

To justify power and obedience simultaneously is the first issue involved in the question of legitimacy. Upon this twofold demonstration depend both the right to govern and what results therefrom, political obligation. But in order for this operation to be successful, it has to fulfil at least three complementary conditions that have to do with the domains of consent, law, and norms, these being in reality indissociable. An examination of these three notions will allow one to see in what way they are constitutive of legitimacy.

Consent and legitimacy: from right to political authority

To define legitimacy as the right to govern assumes that consent plays a major role therein. A study of the public character of right allows one better to comprehend this argument.

---

[1] See Raymond Aron, *Democracy and Totalitarianism: A Theory of Political Systems*, ed. Roy Pierce, trans. Valence Ionescu (Ann Arbor, Mich.: Ann Arbor Paperback, 1990), p. 24.

From a general point of view, right serves to determine what is due to each individual, that is to say, it serves to establish the just portion that is to be attributed to him.[2] What is due to each person is precisely what is called 'his right'. Now, the right of an individual has meaning only in relation to an other. The very idea of right presupposes the existence of a community. In a world in which but a single person lived, right would have no room to exist. Indeed, as both the result of a conflict and its antidote, right is connected, on the one hand, to a state of competition between at least two persons for the possession of a given good and, on the other hand, to the creation of a relationship of coexistence.

From this perspective, the public character of right is clear and manifest. Its object being to coordinate the actions among individuals via laws that delimit what is inalienable and, by way of consequence, what has to be respected, right helps to set into place a network of sociability.[3] Such a network allows exchanges to unfold within a fixed framework and under the form of reciprocity, that is to say, in a tangling together of rights and duties. For, to each right corresponds a duty.

Obviously, this public space cannot operate without individual consent. It is, even, the product of the latter. Consent plays, in effect, a decisive role in the mechanisms of reciprocity. A right whose validity is recognised by no one does not possess, properly speaking, the character of a right. Its nature is to be a valid title of property that one enjoys in full security.[4] It has to be recognised in an incontestable manner. Nonetheless, everything that is granted to some being necessarily abandoned by the rest, the rights of individuals can be established only with the aid of a mutual limitation grounded upon a spirit of compromise and concession.

This is the reason why obligation is the sanction that attests to the effective actuality of rights: the feeling that we have a right *vis-à-vis* an individual signifies that we recognise his right – which presupposes, in turn, that this individual also credits us with having our right.[5] In other words, right is an understanding with the other about what constitutes each one's portion and about what is mutually due. In organising an ongoing relationship among individuals, right creates reciprocal expectations that the consent of each allows to be satisfied.

[2] See Michel Villey, *Philosophie du droit*, 3rd edn, 2 vols. (Paris: Dalloz, 1982), vol. I, *Définitions et fins du droit*, p. 146.

[3] For the public, because social, character of right, see Émile Durkheim's *The Division of Labor in Society*, trans. W. D. Halls (New York: The Free Press, 1984), p. 81.

[4] This is what Montesquieu had in mind when he defined freedom as 'that tranquillity of spirit which comes from the opinion each one has of his own security' (*The Spirit of the Laws*, trans. and ed. Anne M. Cohler, Basia Carolyn Miller, and Harold Samuel Stone (Cambridge University Press, 1989), p. 157).

[5] See John P. Plamenatz, *Consent, Freedom and Political Obligation*, 2nd edn (Oxford University Press, 1968), p. 85.

The importance of consent for right in general proves to be even more marked when it comes to the right to govern. Through the decisions they transmit, political institutions commit the society as a whole. Among these decisions, one can distinguish those that relate to the regulation or coordination of individuals or particular groupings and those that concern collective undertakings or actions that mobilise society in its entirety.[6] In this regard, political institutions settle conflicts that threaten the cohesiveness of the community both on the domestic level and on the foreign one. To enact a law, to render justice, and to conduct war are typically political activities. As guarantors of the public space, political institutions are at once the instrument and the expression of right. It is what offers these institutions a position of command and the monopoly on the constraints to be exercised. It is also what places consent at the centre of the right to govern.

Since political institutions act as guarantors of the public space – that is to say, of the relationships of reciprocity that exist among individuals within a given society – it is logical that the role they play in coordinating and in conducting collective affairs will have the character of law only to the extent that they have the accord of the population. The consent necessary to the routine exercise of right also assures its proper unfolding. That is all the more true as the defence of the interests of the community as a whole helps to ensure that the general conditions for the survival of the group will prevail, if need be, over this or that particular right.

Political institutions radicalise in a systematic way the principle of mutual limitation of individual powers, upon which right is based. Far from imposing only negative obligations[7] – as is for example the case in civil law, where each is to remain in his own sphere and to respect the specific right of the other – political institutions require active participation from the members of the community. This contribution of cooperation prises individuals out of their immediate zone of interest and can go as far as the sacrifice of their lives, especially in time of war.

This possibility of a radical limitation upon individual freedom, which lies at the very heart of political life, engenders a need for consent in order to establish the right to govern. The dynamic of rights and duties presupposes the idea of an agreement about what is being abandoned. The result is that, the greater the obligation, the higher is the level of approval needed to establish a rights-based relationship. In order that

[6] Our remarks are inspired here by those of Jean-William Lapierre on political systems: *L'Analyse des systèmes politiques* (Paris: Presses Universitaires de France, 1973), pp. 34–35.

[7] See the remarks of Émile Durkheim on negative solidarity, in *The Division of Labor in Society*, p. 75.

the faculty of political command might be clothed in legal raiment and
not be an unjust use of force, the degree and the value of consent has
to be proportional to the breadth of the obligation being imposed. The
existence of political right is tied to this equation.[8] Acting in the name
of the group could not be a futile formula for a government based upon
consent.

By setting political commands from the outset within a dimension of
reciprocity, consent plays a key role in legitimacy, defined as the right
to govern. It grounds the feeling of obligation and makes of political life
a search for the rules and procedures through which the members of
a community come to an understanding in order to be obligated. From
this standpoint, and in contrast to political actions based exclusively upon
violence, it justifies, within precise limits, a recourse to constraints. This
justification does not eliminate the tension designated by the term *consent*.
To consent is to accept a situation that includes a measure of renunciation, which is manifested in the duty to obey. It is in this sense that the
rights-based relationship between the governors and the governed can be
perceived in terms of political authority. The question of legitimacy leads
to the problem of authority because the latter is a relation of command–
obedience. What distinguishes the latter from the bond of domination–
submission, which rests solely upon the relation of forces among individuals or groups, lies in the fact that to command and to obey together
imply consent. This, indeed, is what Hannah Arendt suggests when she
speaks of political authority:

Since authority always demands obedience, it is commonly mistaken for some
form of power or violence. Yet authority precludes the use of external means of
coercion; where force is used, authority itself has failed ... If authority is to be defined at all, then, it must be in contradistinction to ... force ... The authoritarian
relation between the one who commands and the one who obeys rests ... on ... the
hierarchy itself, whose rightness and legitimacy both recognise and where both
have their predetermined stable place.[9]

Although the word *authoritarian* is generally taken in a pejorative sense,
as a synonym for arbitrary violence, the notion of political authority is tied
to legitimate power.[10] Because it is willed by those who obey, political

---

[8] Michael Walzer treats various aspects of this problem in his book *Obligations: Essays on
Disobedience, War, and Citizenship*, 4th edn (Cambridge, Mass.: Harvard University Press,
1982). See, in particular, the following statement of his: 'In the context of consent theory,
we do not say that the government is just, therefore the citizens are obligated, but rather
that citizens have committed themselves, therefore the government is just' (p. xii).

[9] Hannah Arendt, *Between Past and Future: Eight Exercises in Political Thought*, 4th rev. edn
(New York: Penguin Books, 1983), pp. 92–93.

[10] See the distinction François Bourricaud makes between good and bad authority, in
Esquisse d'une théorie de l'autorité, 2nd rev. edn (Paris: Plon, 1970), pp. 10–12.

authority is a form of constraint that pertains to legitimacy. And it is this will that gives it its efficacy. Acting on behalf of the community, political authority formulates instructions to which those to whom these instructions are addressed conform. It is the right of decision and of action granted to a certain number of men and women; it is the personalisation of the rules the group agrees to ratify. Individuals adhere to it because they see therein both the spirit of the collectivity and the instrument for its preservation.

Consent intervenes at the foundation of legitimacy because it lies at the base of the relationship that is constitutive of right in general and political right in particular. To the extent that those who govern respect the rights of the members of the community, and discharge their specific duties, individuals consent to renounce some of their capacities for action and turn them over to political institutions. In other words, they recognise in the latter the right to govern. The identification of power with right endures so long as consent exists. If consent be withdrawn, that is the sign of a lack of political legitimacy.

Consent is consequently a necessary condition for the right to govern. Nevertheless, it is not a sufficient condition. Indeed, political legitimacy, which validates the relationship between individuals who command and those who obey, cannot rest solely upon consent as it has just been described. Consent sets in motion a procedure whose implementation presupposes some content to which it is fitting to refer and upon which an agreement must previously have been reached. That is why, while it is essential for there to be consent in order to establish political legitimacy, such an establishment can be brought about only in terms of values, which form the substance of rights and duties. This leads us to broach the second condition for legitimacy.

Norms, or the substance of political legitimacy

Legitimacy requires that one take norms into consideration, if only because one of its conditions is that an understanding has to be reached about what the activity of governing is to be. For, to govern is a *de jure* act only after those who command and those who obey have agreed with one another about those values politics makes it its objective to promote. This is what is shown when one analyses the connection between values and right, when one then analyses the connection that exists between values and the identity of a given society, and finally, when one analyses the relationship between political power and the normative aspect of values.

Values constitute the substance of rights. The prerequisite for the existence of a right is a value. Indeed, given that a value, considered in a general way, states what is preferable,[11] it would be contradictory and even absurd to impose respect for what is not desirable, and therefore to erect it into a right. That would boil down, for example, to granting the right to theft, while recognising at the same time that theft is an act to be condemned.

Certainly, not all values engender rights. In order to acquire the status of a right, these values have to be estimable in absolute terms and thus inalienable.[12] Right is therefore established in relation to what is lived as a good. In relation to the latter, it is a means of making things official as well as a way of protecting and promoting them.

By being constitutive of the substance of rights, values provide a foundation for the meaning of law-based practice. Its threefold role of officialisation, protection, and promotion expresses a hierarchy between that which is preferable and that which is less so. Evidently, law-based activity can be accomplished only upon the condition that values are held in common, that is to say, asserted and recognised by a certain number of persons. This sharing of values allows there to be a compatibility among the actions of individuals, and exchange thereby becomes possible.[13]

It is also to this community of values that their content is tied. Held in common and being substantial, they are at once what permits exchange among persons and what is exchanged. Thus, the value of friendship is at the same time that which places two friends in relation to each other and the good they exchange between themselves.

This compatibility is nevertheless not necessarily an assurance of cooperation among individuals. It is often, in reality, even the cause of conflicts. Thus, competition is synonymous with divergencies in interests that lie upon one and the same scale of values. The search for profit, for example, engenders tensions between the concerned parties because they all see therein a good to be desired.

So, in order that commonly held values might really produce a cooperative relationship and not open the way to a multiplication of conflicts, it is essential that the determination of what is preferable, which right initiates, never make one lose sight of the rule of reciprocity. It is when

---

[11] See Niklas Luhmann, *The Differentiation of Society*, trans. Stephen Holmes and Charles Larmore (New York: Columbia University Press, 1982), p. 97.

[12] Starting from a reflection upon an economic approach to law, Ronald Dworkin mentions this problem in his article 'Is Wealth a Value?', in *A Matter of Principle* (Cambridge, Mass.: Harvard University Press, 1985). See, in particular, p. 264.

[13] See Talcott Parsons, *The Social System*, 1st paperback edn (New York: The Free Press, 1964), p. 52.

that rule serves as a paradigmatic reference that values give rise to obligation and not to opposition, thence constituting a factor of integration and not of disintegration. The preservation of the sociability embodied in the group depends upon it.

For a *de jure* situation to be set in place, it is presupposed that there are some values that make allowance for the existence of the public dimension. But this condition does not imply that the substance of rights and duties would be the same for all societies. The form of the public space varies according to the kind of society and the type of political organisation. Thus, although the question of the sharing of wealth is a preoccupation inherent in all life within a group, there exist various ways of allocating resources. The analysis of the terms of the relationship of reciprocity therefore has to take into consideration the tie that exists between the identity of a society and the values it promotes.

The identity of a group or of a society is what assures it its continuity and its cohesiveness. This identity has a two-sided character. On the one hand, social identity determines the way in which a society stands out from its natural environment. On the other, it establishes the way in which individuals belong to their society and, at the same stroke, sets down the conditions for their possible exclusion.[14]

Identity expresses the values of a given society, and it is from their identity that individuals draw out their own qualities, *qua* members of the community. These qualities are not solely modes of being. They are also manifested via actions that can take on a variety of forms. That is the reason why one can describe the identity of a society as the set of actions individuals attribute to one another within the group, at the different levels of its operation.

Values become institutionalised within what Talcott Parsons calls *action systems*. The individuals or associations that go to make up society act within the framework of these systems.[15] Nevertheless, among these values and these action systems, not all concern the structural organisation of the group. Only a tiny fraction of the culture and of the action system of the overall society is really decisive for its identity.[16] This fraction relates to essential values and basic institutions, which are the object of a consensus that lies beyond discussion and that have a type of validity that is foundational. For this reason, each member of the community, taken individually, will feel any destruction of or violence directed at these core values as a threat to his own identity. It is in connection with these core

---

[14] See Jürgen Habermas, *Zur Rekonstruktion des Historischen Materialismus* (Frankfurt am Main: Suhrkamp, 1976), p. 25.
[15] See Parsons, *The Social System*, p. 36.   [16] Ibid., p. 47.

values that the personality of each person as well as the unity of the group are constituted and that it becomes possible to bring out for examination the different forms of collective identity.[17] At once the origin and the horizon of the life of the collectivity, they serve as fundamental norms.

Generally speaking, norms are, first, interpretive criteria that serve as elements for appraising and evaluating reality and, second, guides for action.[18] In this regard, all values contain a normative dimension. As soon as one of them is assigned to a form of behaviour or to an object, that value becomes, for those who adhere to it, a standard of evaluation in terms of which it is deemed fitting to act. There exists, nevertheless, a hierarchy of values, depending upon the extent to which they commit the overall operation of a society. The most universal values are obviously those that express with greatest force the identity of the group. Operating as fundamental norms, it is from them that – symbolically or practically, directly or indirectly – the other norms holding good within society derive.

Indeed, the relationships of reciprocity that exist among individuals in the various sectors of the community's activity are connected to the principles that give the community its specificity. In order that the preservation of the group's identity might be assured, the values that govern activities in the various sectors of society must not contradict these principles. This requirement helps to explain the impact of political institutions and accounts for both the possibility of the right to govern and political power as normative might.

The political function of coordinating and directing society is legitimate only when it expresses the identity of society. But the legitimacy of power remains indissociable from the spreading [*diffusion*] of group values to the entirety of its action systems. Upon the achievement of this task of diffusion depends the right to govern as well as the status of the normative might of political power. The instructions communicated by the latter obligate individuals only to the extent that these instructions correspond to the identity of the community.

In order to contribute to the officialisation, protection, and promotion of the values that are essential to society – that is to say, to their institutionalisation in their quality as legal norms – the established political power has two types of institutions at its disposal: those that create the laws, for example parliaments or constitutional assemblies, and those that apply and ensure respect for these same laws, such as the courts and the

---

[17] See Émile Durkheim's remarks on common consciousness (*The Division of Labor in Society*, pp. 60–61).

[18] See Joseph Raz, *The Concept of a Legal System: An Introduction to the Theory of Legal System*, 2nd edn (Oxford University Press, 1980), pp. 123–24.

police.[19] It is the homogeneous relationship among social and political norms that brings about a continuity between society's values and its laws.[20] In this way, the laws are not only respected but also willed.

Let us put this idea in other terms: the function of legitimacy is to respond to the need for social integration proper to the identity of a society. One has to show how and why existing or recommended institutions have the capacity to organise political power in such a way that the constitutive values of social identity actually do structure reality. To attain this objective of legitimacy presupposes, obviously, a successful empirical outcome: the concrete reality of life within the community has to correspond, in credible proportions, to the stated founding principles. But this objective does not obtain independent of the justificatory force norms harbor within themselves. With political institutions standing as guarantors against all social disintegration by taking measures that are obligatory in character, the corollary of the exercise of power is the imperative to maintain society in its determinate identity. Here we have a criterion that allows us to appraise the legitimacy of political power.

As we have seen, consent does not suffice to engender the right to govern. Some allowance has to be made for values that fulfil the role of fundamental norms. In establishing the content of rights and duties, such values prompt individuals to action and to mutual understanding on the basis of society's identity. They are therefore a mark of political legitimacy and they allow one to understand the place assigned to law in the foundation of the right to govern.

Legitimacy and conformity to the law

The first feature mentioned by most dictionaries in their definition of legitimacy is the relationship that exists between legitimacy and the law. Legitimacy is presented as 'that which conforms to the law'. Still, one needs to be more specific about this idea of legitimacy's conformity to the law.

According to the information reported by those authors who have studied the origin of the word *legitimacy*, this word did not appear before the Middle Ages.[21] Nonetheless, its appearance was preceded by that of the

---

[19] Joseph Raz, *The Authority of Law: Essays on Law and Morality*, 2nd paperback edn (Oxford University Press, 1986), p. 105.

[20] Ibid., p. 100.

[21] For the history of the term *legitimacy*, the reader may refer in particular to Jose Guilherme Merquior, *Rousseau and Weber: Two Studies in the Theory of Legitimacy* (London: Routledge & Kegan Paul, 1980), pp. 2–3.

term 'legitimate' in classical Latin. The latter word served to designate what is legal – that is to say, what conforms to the law. It was used in areas dealing with legal matters and contained explicit political connotations. Thus, Cicero uses the expressions *legitimum imperium* and *potestas legitima* when he refers to legally established power and magistrates or when he distinguishes the legitimate enemy (*legitimus hostis*) from the thief or pirate because of the treaties signed with the former and because such treaties were valid as legal documents.

The signification of the word *legitimacy*, whose employment is observed for the first time in medieval texts, preserves the idea of conformity to the law. The political character of legitimacy is accentuated by a reflection upon the justification of the delegation of power.[22] Legitimacy is identified with the quality of a title to govern and is presented as a legally validated political activity. In this regard, the sovereign does not found the law but holds his authority on its basis. His designation as the sovereign is therefore subordinate to the law, which defines his powers and determines those conditions within which his will can command obligation.[23] After the decline of the idea of a divine guarantee, the development of modern constitutionalism and the growing rationalisation of law helped to expand the role of positive law and highlight the importance of the criterion of legality in the process of establishing legitimacy.[24] This development occurred to such an extent that legal positivism came to reduce legitimate domination to legal domination. Max Weber's analyses testify to this trend.

The dazzling sociology of law developed in Weber's *Economy and Society*[25] is principally a study of its process of rationalisation from charismatic, revealed, and therefore irrational law up to modern law, rational both in its rules of deduction and in its procedures, which becomes increasingly technical in character.[26] Weber describes this process as an inevitable movement towards formalisation, wherein ethical considerations and references to substantive justice tend more and more to be

---

[22] Ibid., p. 2.

[23] The reader may refer to the article by Jean-Fabien Spitz, 'Qu'est-ce qu'un État constitutionnel? La contribution de la pensée médiévale 1100–1300', *Critique* 488–89 (January–February 1988), 129–31.

[24] See Roberto Mangabeira Unger, *Law in Modern Society: Toward a Criticism of Social Theory* (New York: The Free Press, 1976), pp. 61–62.

[25] Max Weber, *Economy and Society: An Outline of Interpretive Sociology*, ed. Guenther Roth and Claus Wittich, trans. Ephraim Fischoff, Hans Gerth, A. M. Henderson, Ferdinand Kolegar, C. Wright Mills, Talcott Parsons, Max Rheinstein, Guenther Roth, Edward Shils, and Claus Wittich, 2 vols. (Berkeley: University of California Press, 1978).

[26] For a description of the different stages of this process of rationalisation, see ibid., vol. II, p. 882.

eliminated.[27] Rational law is a system within which decisions are made not in terms of concrete situations but by following abstract norms that obtain regularity and predictability. The greater the law's capacity to class the particular case under the general one, the more it constitutes a rational system. From this point of view, it is easy to understand why, according to Weber, Anglo-American law is not as rational as Continental law: its empirical character is the mark of a less elevated level of systematicity and rationality.[28] Rational law, being 'devoid of all sacredness of content',[29] therefore does not rest upon values. To this central feature of the Weberian sociology of law corresponds, at the political level, the thesis that the mere formality of the law of the State constitutes the foundation for legitimacy: 'Today, the most common form of legitimacy is the belief in legality, the compliance with enactments which are *formally* correct and which have been made in the accustomed manner.'[30]

The idea that, in the modern State, decisions made in conformity with a legal procedure suffice to establish political legitimacy, without there being a need to base these decisions on values,[31] is tied, for Weber, to the fate of modern politics. According to him, indeed, the impossibility of surmounting the antinomy between formal rights and substantive rights has entailed the ruination of all metajuristic axioms of right. The transformation of formal natural law into substantive natural law, principally under the influence of socialism, has been accompanied by a historicisation and relativisation of natural law, which has led to its annihilation.

Natural law having lost all credibility in constituting the basis for the legal system, the result has been a certain scepticism as regards the function and the groundedness of values.[32] This has allowed the development of legal positivism, which identifies rationality with legality. To this, according to Weber, is added the fact that, on the one hand, the choice of a system of values cannot be grounded – that choice expresses simply the vital interests of a subject who affirms his will to power – and that, on the other hand, the pretension to universality of different competing systems of values renders them irreconcilable.

Thus, formal legality, conceived as a type of legitimacy, plays in the political field the equivalent of the role attributed to objectivity in the

---

[27] Ibid., p. 657: 'The norms to which substantive rationality accords predominance include ethical imperatives, utilitarian and other expediential rules, and political maxims, all of which diverge from the formalism of the "external characteristics" variety as well as from that which uses logical abstraction. However, the peculiarly professional, legalistic and abstract approach to law in the modern sense of the term is possible only in the measure that the law is formal in character'.

[28] Ibid., p. 890.   [29] Ibid., p. 895.   [30] Ibid., vol. I, p. 37.

[31] Ibid., p. 36: 'It is by no means necessary that all conventionally or legally guaranteed forms of order should claim the authority of ethical norms.'

[32] Ibid., vol. II, pp. 873–74.

domain of the methodology of the social sciences.[33] Given that it is impossible to demonstrate the truth of value-systems and in light of their
mutually conflictual relationships, this is the solution involving the lesser
evil. By implementing a rational-legal form of domination, whose best
adapted mode of organisation is the bureaucracy,[34] it keeps politics from
becoming but a dead-end struggle among antagonistic representations of
the world. Law is no longer the expression of founding principles and of
a normative order. It is an instrument, transformable according to the
needs of the moment, that is used in a formal and autonomous way in
order to find a compromise among opposing interests.[35]

Weber's analyses dealing with legal positivism are indisputably quite
penetrating. His remarks on the increasingly technical character of law
and on the decline of value relations recall to mind the fundamental conditions for the development of societies. They connect up with Durkheim's
analyses concerning the fact that political and economic functions, in
breaking free little by little from the religious one, take on a temporal character that is expressed through a more and more technical and
specialised sort of law-based activity.[36] Nevertheless, if Weber's remarks
refer us back to Durkheim's analyses, we discover that the latter does not
make of specialisation and the increasingly technical character of law an
argument that could be used to diagnose its separation from values. For
Durkheim, law has without a doubt lost in modern societies the sacred
character it previously enjoyed in the primitive world, but it retains an
essential social dimension and remains indissociable from the norms of
the society in which it is practised.[37]

It is not obvious that one can pass from an analysis of the growing
formalisation of law to the idea that political right functions, via a pure
formalism, without any reference to values. What poses a problem for
the role Weber assigns to legal positivism is that belief in legality could
constitute an ultimate standard for political legitimacy. Moreover, although he defends the possibility of a purely formal conception of legality, at times he seems to hesitate.[38] In fact, defending the thesis that
legal domination secures legitimation by its technical means alone boils
down to thinking that the performances of the law render representations

---

[33] On this question, check out the remarks of Wolfgang J. Mommsen, *Max Weber and German Politics 1890–1920*, trans. Michael S. Steinberg, 2nd edn (University of Chicago Press, 1984), pp. 449–50.

[34] See Philippe Raynaud, *Max Weber et les dilemmes de la raison moderne* (Paris: Presses Universitaires de France, 1987), p. 193.

[35] Weber, *Economy and Society*, vol. II, pp. 875, 895.

[36] Durkheim, *The Division of Labor in Society*, pp. 119–20.   [37] Ibid., pp. 70–1.

[38] Weber, *Economy and Society*, vol. II, p. 874: 'While it would hardly seem possible to erad-
icate completely from legal practice all the latent influence of unacknowledged axioms
of natural law . . . '.

of legitimacy superfluous. It is to affirm that the efficacy of the State, observed on the formal level alone, and not efficacy such as it is perceived by those who participate in the life of society, produces legitimacy.[39] Now, the idea that legal procedures might be accepted without there being a need to justify them or to evaluate them is incompatible with the notion of legitimacy.

To elevate the positive-legal order to the status of the ultimate standard for political legitimacy implies a submission to the State that goes completely against the idea of legitimacy. Indeed, if what is legal is legitimate solely owing to the fact of its being legal, the result is a passivity with regard to power that is the opposite of the spirit of legitimacy. First, as Weber himself mentions,[40] 'the distinction between an order derived from a voluntary agreement and one which has been imposed' simply dissolves: there is no longer any room for obligation. Second, by limiting the process of evaluating laws to the examination of their formally correct characteristics, the reduction of legitimacy to legality empties this process of all meaning. It suffices that a law be adopted in conformity with accepted procedure for it to benefit from the label of legitimacy, whatever its content may be. Beyond the question of its success in achieving conformity, there can be no recourse to a judgement that a law is illegitimate or arbitrary.[41]

Under these conditions, the very idea of legitimacy is called into question, since one finds it impossible to account for conflicts between legality and legitimacy, conflicts that nevertheless give the theme of legitimacy its importance and its meaning. If the issue at stake is to gauge the validity of a legal order, that process cannot be carried out solely on the basis of the criterion for legality. Upon the distinction between legitimacy and the law and upon its maintenance depend the evaluation of the validity of the law and the decision whether or not to be obligated – that is to say, the possibility of the right to govern.

That legitimacy is not limited to the law and that legality does not suffice to establish the right to govern is shown also by the fact that the law cannot give rise all alone to a belief in legitimacy. One does not adhere to legality for its own sake. For there to be such adherence, it does not suffice that legality might exist and might produce formally correct statements. In this regard, the example of South America is instructive: in numerous countries on that continent there exists a legal culture that places the accent on the need to encompass all social relationships within a systematic legislative framework. The proliferation of laws, decrees, and

[39] See Habermas, *Zur Rekonstruktion des Historischen Materialismus*, p. 274.
[40] Weber, *Economy and Society*, vol. I, p. 37.
[41] Mommsen, *Max Weber and German Politics*, pp. 450–51.

ordinances, the ambition of which is to cover every aspect of social life,[42] does not imply for all that an adherence to legality. For, legalism remains theoretical – indeed, in most cases it is entirely unreal.[43] One can even advance the idea that the inflation of juridical means is greater where political institutions are not legitimate and do not have the capacity to win respect for the laws.

To put it in other terms, let us say that laying down the law [*dire la loi*] does not necessarily make legality synonymous with legitimacy. Without a doubt, it is of decisive import to follow the procedures that have been granted, but that is not enough. In reality, belief in legality presupposes the legitimacy of the legal order that lays down the law.[44] Procedure can legitimate only in an indirect way, through reference to already recognised instances of authority. By way of consequence, legality, or belief in legality, does not form an independent type of legitimacy,[45] but, rather, an indicator of legitimacy.

In this light, belief in legality necessitates two complementary conditions. In the first place, legal statements have to be in agreement with the constitutive values of the identity of society. These values being at once the sources and the guarantees of right, law can pass for being legitimate only on the condition that it be their emanation. It is therefore when legality expresses the identity of the group that it becomes possible to present legitimacy as conformity to the law. If legal decisions that are constraining, yet that are made independently of any violence or manifest threat, are legitimate, that is because they are considered to be the expression of recognised and accepted norms.

This agreement between legal statements and the constitutive values of society concerns all sectors of the community. It is essential in those areas of activity that have to do with the main aspects of the life of the collectivity, and, therefore, in the political field. In order for a law, which commits the overall organisation of a group, to be legitimate and to benefit from the support of individuals, the institutions that lay down and make the law must establish it in terms of the fundamental values of this group.

In the second place, legal statements have to contribute in a credible way to the achievement of society's values. If that is not the case, it leads

---

[42] See Kenneth L. Karst and Keith S. Rosenn, *Law and Development in Latin America* (Berkeley: University of California Press, 1975), pp. 61–62.
[43] See the article by Glen Dealy, 'Prolegomena on the Spanish Political Tradition', in *Politics and Social Change in Latin America: The Distinct Tradition*, ed. Howard J. Wiarda, 2nd rev. edn (Amherst: University of Massachusetts Press, 1982), p. 165.
[44] Jürgen Habermas, *The Theory of Communicative Action*, trans. Thomas McCarthy, 2 vols. (Boston, Mass.: Beacon Press, 1984), vol. I, *Reason and the Rationalization of Society*, p. 265.
[45] Ibid., p. 267.

ultimately to their rejection, and even to the discrediting of values themselves. When values are not given concrete form, they end up seeming unrealisable.

The fact that belief in legality presupposes the legitimacy of the legal order allows one to place the accent on the idea that the functioning of law depends more on the recognition of the validity of the constraint it imposes than on the formal conditions for its application. To affirm the contrary is to confuse the effect with the cause. This confusion is characteristic of those observers who limit their analyses to stable societies with a high level of institutionalisation.[46] That the application of the law issuing from legitimate political instances of authority does not encounter any major opposition would tend to prove that the applicability and the efficacy of the laws constitute a strictly technical problem, one internal to the formulation of legality.

This thesis is so widespread that it is in this spirit that the jurists of South America (to take up that example once again) drone on about the respective merits of a presidential system versus a parliamentary system as ways of ensuring political stability and democracy. The chronic instability of the political regimes in that region shows, however, that neither of these two forms of government is up to the task of resolving anything more than problems of detail and that it is above all on the legitimacy of the political institutions themselves that the efficacy of one or another form of government depends. In order for the comparison of the respective merits of the parliamentary system and the presidential regime to possess some real usefulness, it would be necessary first to have a consensus about the identity of society and about the need to instaurate political institutions that respect and assure the promotion of democratic values.[47]

It is therefore principally from legitimacy that the law draws its efficacy.[48] Whatever the formal qualities of a constitution might be, the latter is incapable of moulding political reality and of serving as a genuine criterion for political actions so long as the rules and procedures it implements do not correspond to the fundamental interests of the community.[49] The authority of the law – or, if one prefers, its effective operation – rests

[46] On the notion of institutionalisation, the reader may consult the remarks of Samuel P. Huntington in *Political Order in Changing Societies* (New Haven, Conn.: Yale University Press, 1968), p. 12.
[47] See Juan Linz's article on 'Democracia presidencial o parlamentaria. Hay alguna diferencia?', in *Presidencialismo vs. Parlamentarismo: Materiales para el estudio de la Reforma Constitucional* (Buenos Aires: Editorial Universitaria de Buenos Aires, 1988), pp. 42–43.
[48] See Raz, *The Authority of Law*, pp. 28–29.
[49] See Jürgen Habermas, *Legitimation Crisis*, trans. Thomas McCarthy (Boston, Mass.: Beacon Press, 1975), pp. 100–01.

upon the belief that legality is the expression of the values of the society. The law contributes to the 'rule of law', a rights-based State, a *Rechtstaat* [*l'État de droit*], but it cannot, all alone, invent it.

In order for the idea that legitimacy is conformity to the law to be defensible, legality has to correspond to the interests of society. It is upon this condition that conformity to the law is a criterion of legitimacy and gives rise to an adherence or to consent on the part of the members of the community. Just power is indissociable from legitimate law. While the fundamental values of the group and the consent of individuals determine the groundedness of the origin of power, the law, thus understood, establishes the precise conditions for its effective exercise within the framework of a *de jure* relationship. From this point of view, it provides some stability for the asymmetric relationship constituted by the command relations between the governors and the governed.

Distinguishing itself from the kind of power an individual grabs by force, legitimate law delimits in a concrete way rights and duties, sets boundaries that are not to be exceeded, and appears as a rule that stands above both the governors and the governed. It is what allows one to say that it is not he or she who holds power, but the law, that is sovereign. *Lex facit regem*, to use the famous medieval saying.

In conclusion, the law really is a condition for legitimacy. Nonetheless, it shares this status with individual consent and society's fundamental norms. Not being an independent type of legitimacy, it has to be justified. In order for legality to intervene in the legitimation process – that is to say, in order for conformity to the law to be indicative of a *de jure* government – the laws must be in accord with the values in which the governed recognise themselves.

Political legitimacy henceforth appears as recognition of the justice of the values a government puts into effect with the help of laws. Thus, it lies at the base of the right to govern and of the organisation of political activity into a *de jure* system of right. Being the expression of the political good, legitimacy boils down to presenting those political institutions it justifies as the best ones possible, indeed, as necessary.

This first approach to the question of legitimacy nevertheless still leaves certain features in the shadows, starting with the political signification of legitimacy.

POLITICAL SIGNIFICATION OF LEGITIMACY

To analyse what legitimacy signifies politically consists in studying what the conception of a political relationship as a *de jure* relationship implies.

From this perspective, it is appropriate to concentrate on three notions that are presupposed in the idea of legitimacy: political differentiation, political responsibility, and political judgement.

Political differentiation and legitimacy

The mechanism of political legitimacy aims at establishing recognition for the right to govern. It is therefore not a matter of doing away with the existence of power. On the contrary, the division that separates those individuals who command from those who obey is that upon which the logic of legitimacy rests. The signification of the right to govern is connected in the first place with this division.

In order to understand how a theory of legitimacy is based upon the separation of the governors and the governed, one must first distinguish it from those political views that find it impossible to justify the power of the State. One must then underscore the fact that the study of political life in terms of legitimacy is equivalent to an analysis of those conditions the division between the governors and the governed has to fulfil in order to be set within the framework of a *de jure* relationship. Finally, one must mention the phenomenon of representation as the essential aspect of the constitution of legitimacy.

Power is obviously not something specific to political life. It plays a major role in the organisation and operation of most groups and associations, be they of an economic, military, or some other sort of order. Its importance is nevertheless heightened in the political field. On account of their functions of direction and coordination, political institutions exert an influence that guarantees the other forms of power and, by the constraints their prerogatives permit them to impose, constitute a major source for (real or potential) limitations on individual freedom. It is for these reasons that political power can be the object of systematic opposition and be considered as being unjustifiable in principle. The need to work for its disappearance or for its destruction proves to be the logical result of this critical attitude.

In this regard, the positions defended, on the one hand, by anarchism and, on the other, in the writings of Marx and Engels, represent the most severe attacks brought to bear against political power identified with the State. Indeed, although the differences are great between the anarchist and Marxist conceptions of power,[50] what they nevertheless

---

[50] For a glimpse of the differences between Marxism and anarchism on the question of the State, see in particular Leszek Kolakowski, *Main Currents of Marxism: Its Origins, Growth and Dissolution*, trans. P. S. Falla, 1st paperback edn (Oxford University Press, 1981), vol. II, *The Golden Age*, pp. 19–21, 198.

have in common is a tendency to criticise political institutions in such a way as to collapse the terms of discussion. In the first place, both confuse state power in a fundamental way with its contemporary historical realisation, the bourgeois State. In the second place, they collapse the State into political or governmental power. In doing so, they broach political relationships either in terms of the relation of forces or in terms of ideality, and they reject in principle every political form that implements a relationship of command and obedience. This leads them to leave in the shadows the question of right and to fail to treat the problem of legitimacy.

In advocating the disappearance of the State, anarchism eliminates what constitutes the very issue of modern political philosophy, namely, how it is possible to reconcile the exigencies of individual autonomy and freedom with the constraints connected with the operation of political institutions.[51] Anarchism purely and simply gives up on trying to find any area of understanding between the individual and the State. Considering power to be pernicious and thinking that all evil comes from impersonal institutions,[52] it interprets past history as a process within whose framework individuals have constantly been prisoners of the State. The latter, which serves only to defend privileges and social ties based upon constraint,[53] must be destroyed.

From this perspective, political power cannot in any case enjoy a legitimate status. It constitutes only a system of infringement upon the individual rights of the majority, for the benefit of a minority.[54] Since nothing could justify political differentiation, it is a matter of abolishing all organisational structures that go beyond the level of direct democracy and of arriving at a complete decentralisation of public life. For anarchism, it is in leaving human beings free to act according to their inclinations that they will become capable of forming harmonious communities.

The Marxist critique of political differentiation is more nuanced, but it leads in principle to the same rejection of political authority. Indeed, while Marx thought that the reorganisation of society after its break with capitalism does not imply the liquidation of the central administration of resources and production,[55] and while he thus opted for a unitary and not communalistic management of communist society,[56] it remains no

[51] See Robert Nozick, *Anarchy, State and Utopia* (New York: Basic Books, 1974), p. 4.
[52] See Kolakowski, *Main Currents of Marxism*, vol. II, p. 20.   [53] Ibid., p. 198.
[54] See Robert Paul Wolff, *In Defense of Anarchism* (New York: Harper & Row, 1976), pp. 71, 112–13.
[55] Kolakowski, *Main Currents of Marxism*, vol. II, p. 20.
[56] On the tension, within Marx's work, between those texts that may be described as statist and those that are communalist, see Pierre Ansart, *Idéologies, conflits et pouvoir* (Paris: Presses Universitaires de France, 1977), pp. 197–99.

less the case that in his view the State as an instrument of coercion is still a transitory formation. History's finality merges with its destruction.

With the abolition of class struggle, the State is destined to disappear. The overcoming of alienation, which implies a total transformation of human existence via the reconciliation of the individual with himself and with his world, passes by way of the elimination of the division between the public sphere and the private sphere. In destroying the class system and the system of exploitation, communism eliminates the need for political institutions and political authority. It puts an end to the difference between civil society and the State, to the oppressive political relationship between the governors and the governed.

For Marx, in contrast to the liberal views of the advocates of Enlightenment, social harmony is obtained not through legislative reforms designed to attune individual forms of egotism to the collective interest but by destroying those antagonisms that originate in the division of labour. Once these antagonisms have disappeared, voluntary solidarity, and not the legal and constraining regulation of institutions, allows one to assure the harmony of human relationships. The end of social inequalities sounds the death knell of political differentiation.[57] The rigid assignment of social and political roles that was the mark of alienated societies will no longer exist.[58] Individual conflicts lose their *raison d'être*. Each then has a responsibility to deploy his abilities to the greatest extent possible, heading in a direction that is necessarily constructive from the collective point of view.

For anarchism as well as for Marxism, it really is a matter of denouncing the bourgeois State's lack of legitimacy and of contributing towards the instauration of a just society. But their theoretical view is in no way set within a logic of legitimacy, conceived as the justification of political differentiation. In reality, the very word does not enter into their vocabulary. Marx's supporters do not miss a beat in presenting this notion as one belonging to a bourgeois theology that is by and large outdated.[59] In establishing that the State has nothing to do with the general interest and that it is exclusively the product of the economically dominant class, they dismiss the possibility of reflecting upon political right. State power being a tool of oppression, it is of no use to seek to ground it in law. The sole political act that is liberatory consists in replacing the realm

---

[57] See Karl Marx and Frederick Engels, *The German Ideology: Critique of Modern German Philosophy According to its Representatives Feuerbach, B. Bauer and Stirner, and of German Socialism According to its Various Prophets*, in *Collected Works*, 47 vols. (New York: International Publishers, 1975–), vol. V, p. 380.

[58] Ibid., p. 47.

[59] See Henri Lefebvre, *De l'État*, 4 vols. (Paris: Union Générale d'Éditions, 1978), vol. IV, *Les contradictions de l'État moderne. La dialectique et/de l'État*, p. 97.

of necessity with the realm of freedom, that is to say, by passing from a coercive situation to a society without a State. In this logic of all or nothing, there does not exist, properly speaking, a right to govern. Law has no validity; it is only an illusion that masks exploitation. As for the realm of freedom, which comes about with the disappearance of social and political divisions, legitimacy does not constitute one of its stakes.

Nevertheless, the history of communism in the twentieth century has shown that it was more difficult than had originally been foreseen to eliminate political differentiation, and that a theory of emancipation that proposes to destroy the relationship of command and obedience could not succeed, and, by way of consequence, had to take the question of the right to govern into account. Once the end of history was recognised as not being imminent, proponents of Marxism–Leninism who did not abandon Marx's eschatological vision and continued to condemn law as anachronistic and ideological[60] – favouring, instead, a kind of emancipation that would be rid of legal and moral rules[61] – were led to broach both political differentiation and the problem of its legitimacy in contradictory terms. The rulers of the young Soviet Union required ever-increasing doses of the State in order to try to reduce disagreements and to attempt to attain a sort of total social homogeneity. The desire to make the instituting and the instituted coincide absolutely,[62] accompanied by the persistence of the State and even its expansion, took the form of an authoritarian intervention on the part of the established political power in all domains of citizens' lives. This omnipresence was presented not as coercion but as the expression of a society that was without division in actuality and in movement [*en acte et en marche*].[63] That is to say, the process of political differentiation was set within a totalitarian dynamic.[64]

---

[60] In *The German Ideology*, p. 209, Marx and Engels state: 'As far as law is concerned, we with many others have stressed the opposition of communism to law, both political and private, as also in its most general form as the rights of man.'

[61] On this question, see Steven Lukes' remarks in *Marxism and Morality*, 1st paperback edn (Oxford University Press, 1987), p. 57.

[62] Here we are inspired by the analyses of Claude Lefort in 'Outline of the Genesis of Ideology in Modern Societies', in *The Political Forms of Modern Society: Bureaucracy, Democracy, Totalitarianism*, ed. and intro. John B. Thompson (Cambridge, Mass.: MIT Press and Cambridge: Polity Press, 1986), p. 222.

[63] See the remarks of Maurice Merleau-Ponty on the Moscow Show Trials: 'Bourgeois justice adopts the past as its precedent; revolutionary justice adopts the future. It judges in the name of the Truth that the Revolution is about to make true; its proceedings are part of a *praxis* that may well be motivated but transcends any particular motives' (*Humanism and Terror: An Essay on the Communist Problem*, trans. John O'Neil (Boston, Mass.: Beacon Press, 1969), p. 28).

[64] See Marc Richir, 'Révolution et transparence sociale', Introduction to Johann Gottlieb Fichte's *Considérations destinées à rectifier les jugements du public sur la Révolution française* (Paris: Payot, 1974), pp. 13–14.

The analysis of power in terms of legitimacy is therefore to be distinguished from a political conception that knows only the alternative
of force and ideality. In the latter case, the rejection in principle of the
possibility of legitimating the separation between the governors and the
governed entails, in reality, as Marxism–Leninism has shown, at the very
least a paradoxical management of this separation. On the other hand,
when one reflects upon the right to govern, one does not consider power
by definition maleficent, nor, by way of consequence, does one consider
the abolition of political differentiation to be a necessary prerequisite for
a communitarian life grounded upon respect for the rights of individuals.

While the analysis of politics from the standpoint of legitimacy presupposes political differentiation, it nevertheless cannot be reduced to
that. It does not uncritically swallow all forms of power, and it is not fundamentally conservative. On the contrary, starting with the governors–
governed distinction, it examines those elements that can make that
distinction acceptable, and it seeks to know whether political power is
set within a relationship of reciprocity as regards the members of the
community. If that is indeed the case, it goes on to analyse the terms of
this exchange, which amounts to considering the political from the point
of view of right and to questioning itself about the conditions for the
constitution of political right. It then becomes a matter of asking oneself
how a just political relationship is established, that is to say, how political
institutions might express and guarantee the constitutive values of the
identity of society. It is within this perspective of political justice, and even
of justice *tout court*, that consent, norms, and the law have been discussed
in the previous pages. The result may be summed up in the following
proposition: for political differentiation to be legitimate, the governors
have to possess a representative status *vis-à-vis* the community.

The justification of political differentiation is in effect tied to the function of representation. It is only upon this condition that the role of coordinating and directing a society may be considered legitimate and that it
has some chance of enduring.[65] Taken in a general sense,[66] representation adopts the organisational modalities that correspond to the various

---

[65] See Jean-Jacques Rousseau: 'The strongest is never strong enough to be the master
forever unless he transforms his force into right and obedience into duty' (*On the
Social Contract, or Principles of Political Right*, in *The Collected Writings of Rousseau*, ed.
Roger D. Masters and Christopher Kelly, trans. Judith R. Bush, Roger D. Masters,
and Christopher Kelly, 8 vols. (Hanover, N.H. and London: University Press of New
England, 1990–), vol. IV, p. 133).

[66] On the contribution the historical dimension of social and political reality makes to the
diversification of formal truths, see Paul Veyne's *Bread and Circuses: Historical Sociology and Political Pluralism*, trans. Brian Pearce, abridged edn (London: Allen Lane/The
Penguin Press, 1990), pp. 293–94.

existing kinds of political systems and regimes; indeed, within such systems and regimes, these modes of organisation correspond to particular political situations. Representation also rests upon the feeling, shared by the members of the community, that the rulers embody the interests of the group and that, in the main, these interests guide their actions.

Representation therefore does not have to be reduced to the specific form given to it in modern society, and especially in liberal-democratic regimes, where it celebrates the autonomy and the reflective potential of both individuals and society.[67] The error, for example, would be to believe that it necessarily implies a delegation to several persons, or that it is constituted solely by a legislative assembly – whereas it is entirely possible that a single individual, the monarch for example, could represent the group.[68]

Those who govern decide and act in the stead of individuals, in accord with them and for them, in proportions and under forms that vary according to the types of polity and according to the context. Thus, the unequal distribution of power, the mark of political differentiation, finds justification, and the position of dominance, by becoming the repository of the spirit of the community, acquires a *raison d'être*.

Representation expresses the political unity of the group as a whole. It is an existential reality that concerns the overall identity of society. To represent is to make manifest, through the intermediary of an individual or an institution, an existent though diffuse reality. Far from being only a symbol, representation is the concrete figure the group adopts, for lack of being able to manifest itself directly; it is the presence of the entire community qua political unity and political will.

For this reason, it can be stated that a characteristic of representation is its public dimension, which manifests itself through the fact that the members of a group recognise themselves in their rulers. This public dimension may even lead one to think that representation is grounded upon a phenomenon of identification, a notion that refers back, it is true, to a rather varied set of situations.[69] Nevertheless, whatever may be the ambiguities of such an identification, it allows one to understand the process whereby individuals come to consider their governors. If the governors are perceived as representatives of the community, that is because, to the extent that they defend and assure the promotion of the fundamental values of the group, the governed themselves identify with them.

[67] See, for example, Pierre Manent's 'Situation du liberalisme', his préface to *Les Libéraux*, 2 vols. (Paris: Hachette, 1986), vol. I, pp. 15–16.
[68] See Julien Freund, *L'Essence du politique*, 3rd edn (Paris: Sirey, 1978), p. 328.
[69] See Bourricaud, *Esquisse d'une théorie de l'autorité*, p. 161.

The identification of the members of the group with the governors is established on the basis of shared values. With rules playing the role of 'value-vectors',[70] the mechanism of identification renders individuals and the collectivity present to themselves. Although they do not manage the community directly, the governed see in political action a recognition of their individual existence and the sign of the collectivity's reality. The phenomenon of identification, which is found again at the heart of political representation and of its public dimension, contributes, in this way, towards providing a basis for political differentiation.

This process never entirely abolishes the distance separating the institutors from the instituted. As expression of the community as a whole and of its constitutive norms, the political representative is not exclusively a private person. Beyond the specific features that go to characterise him as a particular individual, he is an official personage.[71] As such, in contrast to everyone else who does not have to expose his private life, what is personal to him tends to become public. The sphere of his private existence is reduced to a greater and greater extent as his public life grows ever larger. Thus, when the personal qualities of a ruler are praised or criticised, these qualities are praised or criticised less so in their private capacity than from the perspective of evaluating his abilities to work in the group's favour.

The political representative is a public figure before being a private person. But while the identification process brings him closer to the governed, it does not therefore cancel out the division separating him from them. To various degrees and in varying ways, this statement holds good for hierarchical societies as well as for egalitarian ones.

The public character of the political sphere, which keeps the political at a distance from the world of individuals, contains a complementary feature: power that is exercised for strictly personal ends cannot be legitimate. Indeed, as soon as public office is privatised – that is to say, as soon as it serves exclusively private interests – the right to govern is called into question. Whereas the apparatus surrounding the State is justifiable, to a certain extent, when it manifests the powers and grandeur of a society,[72] and therefore of its members,[73] that is no longer the case when there exists

[70] We are freely inspired here by Henry Rousso's remarks on 'memory vectors' in *The Vichy Syndrome: History and Memory in France Since 1944*, trans. Arthur Goldhammer (Cambridge, Mass.: Harvard University Press, 1991), pp. 219–21.
[71] On the dualism of the body in politics, see in particular the classic study by Ernst Kantorowicz, *The King's Two Bodies: A Study in Medieval Political Theology*, 1st paperback edn (Princeton University Press, 1981).
[72] Clifford Geertz points out that *splendour* is one of the three themes that go to make up the etymology of the word *State*; see his *Negar: The Theater State in Nineteenth-Century Bali* (Princeton University Press, 1980), p. 121.
[73] Ibid., p. 129.

a systematic privatisation of political activity. Once the leaders abandon the principle of reciprocity and become strangers to the people they administrate, the identification no longer operates. Every sign of opulence becomes the mark of excess and corruption. This reversal can ultimately make it impossible to provide a foundation for political obligation. It spells the end of the public dimension and, hence, of the governor in his capacity as a representative. Under these conditions, it is not surprising that, in order to distinguish themselves from a bourgeois power that was deemed to be corrupt, modern revolutionary ideals might have made of asceticism one of the virtues of the political good.[74]

Legitimacy and political responsibility

As we have seen, the legitimate exercise of political power is inconceivable when viewed as something strictly private. In order for the members of the community to perceive the governors' position of command as being justified, that position must partake in some explicit way in a dynamic of the common good. The desire for personal success and the thirst for power offer no legitimacy for the rulers' actions. On the contrary, these rulers have to take the good of the group into consideration. In politics, the ambition of an individual becomes justifiable only when it is presented as serving the entire community; it is only when an ambitious person reveals himself to be a statesman authentically concerned with assuring the group's prosperity that his desire for success takes on a genuinely legitimate political value. In this way, legitimate political activity is inseparable from responsibility. The latter is the manifestation of a power that accepts the constraints imposed by the right to govern.

The first of these constraints relates to the fact that he who governs cannot restrict himself to existing for himself in an egotistical way.[75] Unless it is to relinquish all credibility, the established political power needs to justify itself as acting in the service of the group.[76] Here we have a

---

[74] On this question, see for example the remarks of Benjamin I. Schwartz, 'The Reign of Virtue: Some Broad Perspectives on Leader and Party in the Cultural Revolution', in John Wilson Lewis (ed.), *Party Leadership and Revolutionary Power in China* (Cambridge University Press, 1970), p. 161.

[75] See Paul Veyne, *Le Pain et le Cirque. Sociologie historique d'un pluralisme politique* (Paris: Éditions du Seuil, 1976), p. 662. [Translator/editor: The abridged English-language translation, *Bread and Circuses*, pp. 393–94, does not include the passage referred to here.]

[76] See Alexis de Tocqueville: 'In the feudal era, we looked at the nobility in more or less the same way as we regard the government today; one bore the burdens it imposed in consideration of the guarantees that it offered. The nobles had offensive privileges, they possessed burdensome rights, but they assured public order, dispensed justice, executed the law, came to the help of the weak, and ran public affairs. To the extent that the

general truth that concerns all regimes that wish to establish their own legitimacy. Every political ruler who seeks to prove he possesses the right to govern has to satisfy, to try to satisfy, or to pretend to satisfy the needs of the members of the community. Responsibility is a function of group service, which rests upon the rights of individuals and is expressed by a feeling of duty that is tied to the exercise of a public trust. It is, as a consequence, possible to affirm that political relationships that do not evade the question of legitimacy adopt, in one way or another, the form of a protective State.[77]

This general truth may, quite obviously, admit of many variations. The idea of serving the group and the ways in which such service is fulfilled are not everywhere identical. The extent and the content of political responsibility, which are determined by the historical situation and the relations of forces, vary according to political systems and regimes.[78] Analysing political life in the Roman Empire, Paul Veyne points out that the king, like the pilot of a ship, is in the service of the passengers and that he would pass even more easily for being someone who is in their service had he been elected by them.[79] Let us take another example. In democratic regimes, the tasks that pertain to the responsibility of political institutions differ according to whether one is dealing with the Liberal State or the Welfare State. The quite lively controversies that take place between the partisans of one or the other of these two types of State are well known.[80] But whatever variations the notion of service may undergo, this notion becomes irrepressible as soon as the established political power is situated within the perspective of legitimacy.

For a ruler, political responsibility therefore involves, above all, the recognition of the public dimension of his activity. That is the reason why political sovereignty – that is to say, the set of powers at the disposal of those who govern – is not unlimited. For the ruler, not everything is possible. Preoccupied by his legitimacy, he is expected in the first place

---

nobility ceased to do these things, the weight of its privileges seemed heavier, and finally their very existence seemed incomprehensible' (*The Old Regime and the Revolution*, ed. François Furet and Françoise Mélonio, trans. Alan S. Kahan (University of Chicago Press, 1998), vol. I, p. 117).

[77] See Michael Walzer, *Spheres of Justice: A Defense of Pluralism and Equality* (New York: Basic Books, 1983), p. 68.

[78] Ibid., p. 91.

[79] Paul Veyne, *Le Pain et le cirque*, p. 662. [Translator/editor: Again, the abridged English-language translation, *Bread and Circuses*, pp. 393–94, does not include the passage referred to here.]

[80] See, in particular, Pierre Rosanvallon's book *La Crise de l'État-providence*, 2nd rev. and corr. edn (Paris: Éditions du Seuil, 1984), pp. 63–64, as well as Walzer's analyses of the problem of the social coverage of medical expenses in the United States, in *Spheres of Justice*, pp. 88–89.

to make decisions and to conduct actions that express a will not guided exclusively by his impulses and his interests. Without a doubt, political command has always been more or less discretionary in character, to the extent that the relationship of representation that exists between the governors and the governed is not entirely transparent. This fuzziness is due, in particular, to the fact that politics is played out in real time and that, even in advanced democracies, circumstances sometimes become pressing: one cannot consult everyone about everything.

That does not mean, however, that arbitrariness has a free field of manoeuvre. The decisions and actions of the ruler have to respect the rules of the game and take into account the needs of the community. There is no question of heeding one's own will alone, of ignoring procedures, and of launching programmes that go against the very survival of the group.

In another connection, let us note that the acknowledged tasks of the State constitute the touchstone of political responsibility. A governor's legitimacy is therefore evaluated not only upon the basis of his aptitude at deciding and acting in conformity with a society's current laws and with its fundamental principles but also upon the basis of his capacity to obtain effective results. It does not suffice to conform to the letter of those services the State is supposed to render to the community; they still have to be carried out in a credible manner.

The legitimate enjoyment of political command goes hand in hand with its limitation. The unequal distribution of power is justified only by the accomplishment of duties that are considered to be incumbent upon the government. The way in which political responsibility is assumed gives the rulers the right to govern. Far from being absolute, the kind of political sovereignty that accepts the constraint of responsibility is conditional.

To evoke political responsibility is to think that the governors do indeed have at their disposal powers of constraint *vis-à-vis* the members of the community but also that these powers are the mark of a limited sovereignty. The limits imposed upon the ruler set out the framework for legitimate activity, and respect for these limits constitutes at once the expression of responsibility and the instrument for its realisation. Outside these limits, it is just as much the sense of responsibility as the legitimacy of political action that find themselves called into question.

Since political sovereignty conceived in terms of responsibility is conditional, it is worthwhile for us not to lose sight of the aspect of *sanction* that results therefrom. Indeed, the idea of sanction is indissociable from political power as defined in terms of responsibility. A political command that is set within the perspective of the right to govern differs in this respect from absolute power, for the latter rejects any other law but its own and considers that there is no instance of authority by which it might be judged. For this sort of political command, to agree to serve the community within the framework of determinate rules and principles implies a recognition that it is valid for it to be evaluated and a disposition towards allowing the results of its activity to be attributed to itself.[81] What is understood here by the idea of sanction – namely, the possibility of a ruler being condemned for decisions and actions he has authored that have harmful effects throughout the group – is far from constituting a secondary feature in our conception of responsibility. On the contrary, sanctions play an essential role. Without them, and without the relation of cause to effect between a governor and a situation, the idea of responsibility remains abstract, indeed non-existent. In so far as a detrimental event is not tied to its author who, as such, is sanctioned, one cannot genuinely talk about responsibility. In recognising the fact that an individual answers for his acts and in translating this recognition into penal terms, sanctions constitute not only an indicator of responsibility but also that upon which the existence of responsibility rests. *A contrario*, when the decisions and actions of a ruler cease to be imputed to him, political responsibility itself vanishes.

As opposed to a form of political sovereignty that is based exclusively upon force and whose logic is manifested in a refusal to serve the community and to be considered as capable of being at fault *vis-à-vis* this community, the responsible governor grants the principle of blame. This principle does not contradict the notion of immunity. The latter is, in effect, in no way synonymous with licence or impunity. Immunity is involved as an active part of responsibility. The fact that, under certain circumstances and according to precise conditions, the rulers enjoy a situation of immunity is justified only by their status as representatives of the group's interests. It is solely in relation to the common good that immunity offers a protective role.[82] This relationship must therefore be credible, and the individual benefiting from the guarantees immunity procures must not, through his conduct, violate the spirit and the ends of his society. In the contrary case, this protection is lifted and legal action becomes possible. The sanctions that ensue vary, obviously, according to the character and the gravity of the faults committed but also according to the identity of a society and to the kind of relationships that exist therein. Certainly, the more power is institutionalised in a democratic direction, the more the sanctions themselves and the ways in which these sanctions are applied – that is to say, also the conditions of immunity – are strictly

---

[81] See Bourricaud, *Esquisse d'une théorie de l'autorité*, p. 442.

[82] See, for example, the remarks of Jean Gicquel and André Hauriou about forms of parliamentary immunity, in *Droit constitutionnel et institutions politiques*, 8th edn (Paris: Montcrestien, 1985), pp. 853–56.

defined[83] and tend to be better respected. But, in various forms and to varying degrees, all political regimes seeking to establish their legitimacy are careful to set in place some mechanisms that limit their own might.

The importance of the notions of responsibility and sanction is tied to the effort to preserve the existing social and political organisation. These ideas cannot systematically be ignored without endangering the operation of the entire group. There are two reasons for this.

The first reason concerns the fact that the imperative of social peace leads one to think in terms of responsibility and sanction. Thus, differing, for example, from the psychoanalyst and the sociologist, whose work has often had the effect of showing how different determinations may reduce or eliminate free will and, by way of consequence, responsibility,[84] the jurist is much more reluctant to consider an individual who commits an offence as not being responsible for his act. Save for extreme cases,[85] the jurist cannot simply jettison the notion of responsibility, and it is only in relation to responsibility that he considers any external causes that may have contributed to a person committing an offence – at best, in light of attenuating circumstances and under the same heading as the particular conditions within which the fault was actually committed.[86] That does not mean that he would be deeply conservative or reactionary. His role is to guarantee order and, from this standpoint, he has to assign responsibility and to sanction breaches thereof.

In order to safeguard cooperative relations within society, in order to avoid any uncertainty as to who is the author of an offence and to prevent the absence of sanctions from leading to the dissolution of the notions of fault and responsibility, which would thus be an invitation to further disorders, the jurist has to establish the responsibility of the individual who is judged guilty. And the jurist must punish him accordingly.

The second reason accounting for the features of responsibility and sanction that are crucial to the preservation of the group's organisation is more directly political in character. To the extent that the idea of responsibility, as applied to those who govern, has for its corollary the existence of limits for which political action must make allowance, these limits no

[83] See, in particular, the reflections of Dennis F. Thompson concerning political immunity in a democratic regime, *Political Ethics and Public Office* (Cambridge, Mass.: Harvard University Press, 1987), p. 79.

[84] For a view of responsibility based upon freedom defined as autonomy, the reader may refer to Immanuel Kant's *Critique of Practical Reason*, trans. and intro. Lewis White Beck (London: Collier Macmillan, 1956), p. 104.

[85] See the remarks of Herbert L. A. Hart on offences committed by children and persons impaired by mental illness, in *Punishment and Responsibility: Essays in the Philosophy of Law* (Oxford University Press, 1968), pp. 183–84.

[86] For example, with or without premeditation.

longer have any meaning when their transgression entails no sanctions. And when a situation of immunity provided for by a political regime is transformed into systematic impunity, responsibility is emptied of its content. Sooner or later, it is not only the rulers but also the political institutions as a whole that lose their credibility. In excessively protecting its own rulers, the political regime only ends up making itself fragile.[87]

It is fitting, however, to note that even those governors who do not make force into the sole source of their power are often more reluctant to take their failures upon themselves than they are to claim their successes as their own. In this way, it is probably not an exaggeration to say that many of these people dream of passing themselves off as the exclusive authors of whatever is good while never being held responsible for things that go wrong.

Here, the rulers call upon various procedures designed to distract others from lodging criticisms. They endeavour to preserve their credibility by depicting everything that they do not succeed in resolving as a problem that does not pertain to their responsibility.

Thus, politicians today love to boast that they themselves have generated good economic results, yet they do not hesitate, when the figures look bad, to reject any cause-and-effect relationship between their actions and these negative numbers. Invoking the heavy constraints imposed upon national and international systems – which are of a financial, economic, or some other order – they attempt to show how little influence they have over events.

These diversionary tactics are not unrelated to the most perverse kinds of social mechanisms. This is what persuades us that they have their share of bad faith. Such procedures designed to distract can also include the naming of a scapegoat[88] – for example, immigrants who are accused of being responsible for unemployment – and can sometimes lead to witch hunts and persecution, as is testified to, in particular, by the political use of anti-Semitism.

The ambiguity and the reluctance, evinced by those who govern, *vis-à-vis* responsibility and sanctions, as well as the diversionary tactics to which they have recourse, call forth two sets of remarks. Without overestimating the importance of the decisions and actions of the governors as regards society's orientations and its actual operation, and without failing

[87] See Denis Richet, who speaks of a climate wherein absolutism may seem, in the short run, to be reinforced and even strengthened, but wherein, at an underlying level, things are really being undermined. Richet concludes: 'The more absolutism is reinforced, the further it is weakened' (*La France moderne. L'Esprit des institutions* (Paris: Flammarion, 1973), p. 57).

[88] On the relationship between bad faith and the scapegoat phenomenon, see René Girard, *Le bouc émissaire* (Paris: Librairie Générale de France, 1989), p. 179.

to recognise the weightiness of the constraints they may run up against, we can nevertheless state that there exists an individual, and irreducible, dimension that plays a non-negligible role in the organisation of community life. That a statesman responds for his acts does not require that he be freed of all constraints but rests, rather, simply on the choices he makes among several possibilities within a determinate environment.[89] Thus, when a ruler allows himself to be placed within the perspective of legitimacy, he cannot in principle escape his responsibilities. In seeking not to pay the price imposed by the logic of the right to govern, and in yielding to the temptation to make excuses for himself and to grant himself impunity, he sets himself upon the road to illegitimacy.

This is all the more clear when a governor takes responsibility or shuns it according to the advantages he hopes to draw from one or the other position. For, such behaviour is inconsistent and ultimately irresponsible. A moment arrives when the political cost of his opportunism and demagogy becomes higher than that of accepting responsibility, in success as well as in adversity. Systematic recourse to expedients, the search for immediate benefit, and political scheming endanger society's present as well as its future. After all, such behaviour tends to encourage feelings of disaffection from political institutions on the part of the members of the community.

In this regard, it is clear that the governors' sense of responsibility does not work without a comparable sense on the part of the governed. Legitimacy signifies that rulers and ruled are responsible to each other, before each other.[90] This is true to such an extent that in a society where those who govern indulge in an egotistical and complacent use of power, the responsibility of the individuals who make up the group becomes of essential importance. Such responsibility consists in the evaluation of governmental action and in the defence, within the limits imposed by the identity of society and by its relations of forces, of what they consider to be their rights and their freedom. And from this standpoint, the governed have to assume their duties towards the governors only to the extent that the latter assume theirs.

In carefully watching over the relationship of reciprocity that exists between political institutions and the community, and in avoiding all the while the temptation to attribute to the rulers more power than they have, each one of the governed looks with as much care after his own fate as after that of the other members of society. In the end, he contributes to the preservation of the entire group.[91] The duty of each one of the governed is therefore to remind the governors constantly of their duty.

[89] This is quite obviously not specific to political action and holds for every kind of activity.
[90] See Bourricaud, *Esquisse d'une théorie de l'autorité*, p. 443.
[91] See Walzer, *Obligations*, pp. 22–23.

As we have seen, the unequal distribution of political power can be justified only thanks to the office of service rulers assume in relation to society. This office, whose content is determined by the ends and the rules a community gives to itself, implies that, far from being unconditional, political sovereignty has limits. The rulers do not benefit from any status of impunity. The evaluation of political institutions pertains therefore to the problematic of legitimacy, and it raises the question of political judgement.

Legitimacy and political judgement

The notion of judgement has a bad reputation within the scientific world in general and in the world of the social sciences in particular. But as legitimacy is indissociable from the responsibility of political institutions, this notion is an unavoidable one. It prompts one to examine the process by which one evaluates, in connection with the relationship of reciprocity between the established power and society, the rulers' activities, and then to analyse how this process is inscribed within an enquiry as to the rightful foundation of the relationship between the governors and the governed. Finally, the notion of judgement leads one to underscore the importance the status of individuals takes on within the group.

Political reciprocity is always accompanied by an evaluation of the activity of the rulers. The issue at stake in this evaluation is to gauge the claim to right that political command possesses. The result is a judgement, an essential one, that seals the fate of obligation. If the evaluation is positive, obligation is guaranteed. On the other hand, if it is negative, it is expressed, when the occasion presents itself, via attempts on the part of the members of the group either to supply modifications to the details or to make radical changes in the ways society is coordinated and directed.

The process of evaluation and judgement of governmental action has two components. The first concerns the mechanism of evaluation itself. The second is tied to the status of the individual who makes the evaluation.

To evaluate the role of the rulers from the standpoint of legitimacy is to ask oneself whether that role can be characterised by a *de jure* relationship, and therefore whether it is grounded. The appraisal and judgement of political institutions together constitute an enquiry into the rightful foundation of the relation between the governors and the governed. This enquiry includes three complementary levels.[92]

---

[92] We are inspired here, in part, by Gilles Deleuze's analyses of the notion of *grounding* in *Difference and Repetition* (London: Athlone Press, 1994), pp. 272–74.

The first of these levels involves asking oneself what the essential principles are that serve as founding values and that determine at once the origin and the horizon of signification and validity to which political reality has to conform in order to be legitimate. Indeed, in order to be justified, the organisation of the community as it is put into effect by the political authorities has to be in agreement with the originary principles and partake of and aid in the realisation of the qualities they affirm. This required agreement between founding values and political reality has a certain number of implications – including, in the first place, the fact that the fundamental principles render political representation possible. In playing the role of benchmarks, ones that indicate what the relationship between the governors and the governed has to be in order to be grounded, these principles in effect orient the decisions and the actions the rulers have to take in order to have a representational role.

The result is that the correspondence between values and political reality must not, in order to be the expression of legitimacy, be limited to a mere declaration of intention but must be, rather, a concrete defence and promotion of those values at the level of the organisation of the group. That is all the more the case as the originary values and the prescriptive dimension they express not only are not alien to the reality they legitimate but are, on the contrary, interpreted as the very essence of this reality and as its ideal manifestation, that is to say, that towards which it tends. That is why, for instance, the principles of liberty, equality, and fraternity, which are constitutive of the French political identity, cannot be normative without being, to a certain extent, descriptive. If liberty, equality, and fraternity are values that must be defended and promoted, if they are duties that each person owes to himself and to others and that democratic institutions owe to the governed, that is because they are recognised as rights that, as such, correspond to the 'being' of the French citizen. In short, the originary principles allow a person to form for himself an idea both of what reality is and of what it has to be.

The second level of the mechanism of evaluation consists in the effort to relate political reality to the originary principles and to examine whether, in its multiple manifestations, it can be inscribed and, by way of consequence, comprehended within the categories that serve to define those principles. In other words, it is the search for an analogy or a kinship between political reality and the values that are supposed to regulate that reality. Whereas the first aspect of this evaluation bears on what political institutions are to be and what they are to do, having made allowance for the founding principles, here the attention is concentrated on concrete political reality. What exactly do the rulers do? Up to what point are they achieving the values that constitute the horizon of signification and validity of the society within which they decide and act? This connection is crucial, since it leads to the ultimate level of the process of evaluation, namely judgement.

Indeed, the first two levels of the mechanism of evaluation combine in a third: political judgement. After the affirmation of the need for some conformity between the fundamental principles and the political field, and the comparison of values with concrete reality, which gauges whether political diversity is really integrated into the framework afforded by these values, the act of judging finally becomes possible.

Judgement is the culminating point for this evaluation procedure. It is the faculty whereby one states whether a political situation is legitimate or illegitimate. Establishing distinctions and hierarchies, it takes a stand concerning the degree to which the principles are fulfilled in reality. If there exists a credible analogy between political reality and originary values, there is legitimacy. If that is not the case, a negative judgement is pronounced that the institutions in question are illegitimate. Nonetheless, while we have a satisfactory understanding of the way in which judgement results from the act of relating principles to reality, it is important not to neglect the importance of the status of the individual in this process of evaluation.

In fact, the judgement expressed by the governed concerning the rulers' legitimacy cannot be dissociated from the status they occupy within a given society: it is in gauging the benefits that correspond to their status and in considering the way in which those who govern discharge their responsibility towards them that the members of a group judge the rulers' role. In so far as political institutions carry out their function to the satisfaction of each person or social category, those institutions are regarded favourably. In the opposite case, institutions are criticised and conflicts may arise. If no area of understanding is to be found, blocs of frustration form. The consequences for the stability and the legitimacy of the regime depend upon the breadth of frustration and upon the confrontations that ensue.

Judgement concerning the exercise of political power is therefore the logical translation of one's conception of the power to command in terms of legitimacy. From this perspective, the right to govern is measured by the capacity of statesmen to show that their stature attains the heights of the values that ground their community. The legitimacy of those who govern depends upon their aptitude to assume those responsibilities that are considered to be incumbent upon them.

2   Controversies around political legitimacy

The analysis of political life, when conducted from the standpoint of legitimacy, goes against some theses that are judged to be self-evident. Interpreted as belonging to the very birthright of the social sciences, these theses are not always considered in their full detail and often exist in a diffuse and vulgarised way within political thought. In this regard, the problematic of legitimacy developed in the present work goes against two major tendencies.

The first of these tendencies consists in the affirmation that legitimacy, as previously defined, is extraneous to political reality. The second has to do with methodological disputes resulting from the way in which legitimacy is conceived. These two tendencies are obviously not independent of each other. They overlap on many points.

In any case, the questions they raise are serious enough for it to be necessary to account for them. And above all, in parallel with this need, we have to shed some light on their limitations and their contradictions.

POLITICAL REALITY AND LEGITIMACY

To explicate the conditions of possibility for a legitimate relation between governors and governed is to account for an aspect that, even if it does not characterise political reality in full, occupies therein a position of the first rank. This portion of reality, which is manifested in legitimacy, is contested by certain analyses in which it is stated that the right to govern stands in radical contradiction to how political life actually operates. By presenting the arguments that serve to disqualify legitimacy, and by responding to them, we shall have occasion to explore the debates that arise about right, consent, and morality in politics.

Right and legitimacy

Legitimacy consists in taking seriously both right in general and the right to govern in particular. This problematic is, as a matter of fact, the first thing some analysts reject. In order to illustrate their refusal of legitimacy, it is worthwhile to provide an account of those kinds of analyses that maintain that no relationship exists between right and the search for political justice.

RIGHT IN QUESTION

The thesis stipulating that the relationships between the governors and the governed, when set in a legal framework, are not oriented in terms of the public good and do not contribute thereto in any fundamental way emphasises that the decisions of rulers first make allowance, as much as the context permits it, for their particular interests. According to this criticism, the practice of political relations regulated by law reveals that the ultimate purpose of political activity is not the general good but the interests of those who rule. Political right and public good are at once a pretext used to justify the rulers' dominant position and a constraint in relation to which they have to make the necessary arrangements. But they certainly do not determine the real meaning of their political commitment. So, if those who govern happen to have a leadership or regulatory role to play in service to the community, this occurs only in an incidental way. Under certain circumstances, they have to play the game and act accordingly, either in order to satisfy their desire for power or in order to consolidate the power they already hold.

According to this point of view, then, political right is essentially instrumental, and it is used by those who govern in order to attain corporatist objectives. This thesis concerns political situations in which the legal codification of the relationships between the governors and the governed do not occupy a place of the utmost importance as well as types of regimes wherein a higher level of institutionalisation renders taking the public interest into account more credible.[1] In the latter case, far from softening criticisms, the constitution of a political sphere distinct from society creates quite lively feelings of suspicion with regard to those who are the rulers. The reason for this is that to the rationalisation of this exercise of political power corresponds a process of its autonomisation in relation to the rest of the community.[2] As such, the process is characterised in particular by the formation of a group of political professionals and of a technocratic culture specific to them.[3] These factors are complementary and tend to reduce the control of the governed over those who govern.

---

[1] On the connection between the level of institutionalisation and the ability of a political regime to embody the public good, see Huntington, *Political Order in Changing Societies*, p. 24.

[2] Ibid., p. 20. See also Luhmann, *The Differentiation of Society*, pp. 142–43.

[3] Ibid., pp. 96, 140–41. See also Weber, *Economy and Society*, for example, vol. II, p. 958.

The idea that the establishment of a class of professional politicians serves to divert political activity from the general good, thus contributing to the achievement of corporatist objectives, may first be seen in the following statement: from the moment politics is capable of guaranteeing financial support for an individual, it rapidly becomes a full-time occupation whose ends are limited exclusively to a struggle for power. Careerism and the desire to gain access to a comfortable income that is dependent upon the allocation of political posts hamper one's ambition to work for the interest of the collectivity. They combine to become one's main motivation.[4]

From this point of view, the function of legal rules seems less to determine equitably the relations between governors and governed than to set the framework and the terms of the struggle among the members of the political elite, so that this struggle might unfold with a minimum of interference from society. Rather than contributing to the mediation between rulers and ruled, legal rules are, from this standpoint, perceived as serving those who specialise in political affairs and benefit from them. They thus participate in the development of politics for politicos.

To this first consideration is added a second one, which affirms that the professionalisation of political offices provokes distrust on the part of the governed. Indeed, although the battle to become part of the political class may be ferocious, once one belongs the feeling of belonging gives rise to an *esprit de corps* that necessarily creates a distance between people engaged in politics and members of the community. The feeling of estrangement that results from this and the forms of insolence[5] and self-satisfaction that seem tied to the exercise of a public position of prestige are characteristics of a class of professional politicians. This cannot help but generate criticism on the part of the governed.

The technocratic culture of politicians is said by certain analysts to dissociate political activity from the general interest and to orient it in terms of corporatist concerns in three ways. The first of these has to do with the use of the notion of competence: legal rules and procedures, the forms of behaviour politicians have to adopt in relation to one another, and the technical kinds of knowledge that are connected with the management of different facets of the community are presented as making the task of co-ordinating and directing society increasingly complex. This implies that a statesman is not someone who can be whipped up in an instant. Special qualifications and an appropriate training are indispensable if someone

---

[4] See, in particular, Weber's description of the strategies of political parties, in ibid., pp. 1397–98.
[5] See the remarks of Walzer in *Spheres of Justice*, p. 155.

is successfully to take on a political role. Competence constitutes a mark of status.[6]

The collectivity's managerial professionals point to their competence in order to justify their existence as a group. In doing so, they account for the tendency of their prerogatives to be transformed, within the political decision-making process, into a veritable monopoly on power *vis-à-vis* the governed. This appropriation may appear as all the more unacceptable as the competence the governors claim as their own is far from evident, not to mention the fact that they are reluctant to see it measured. In addition, the legal framework within which competence is achieved does not seem fundamentally suited to resolving the problems faced by society but appears to be designed essentially to ensure the defence of the established order within which political personnel participate and from which they benefit.

When one denounces the rift between governors and governed, one can also look at the way in which the laws delineate the field of legitimate political actions. In fact, regulation by juridical means does not mean in principle that it is possible to speak of a right to govern. By identifying legitimate actions with those that enter within the perimeter of the law, codification serves to reduce the terms of political debate to a set of pre-conceived themes that constitute the framework and points of reference for the activity of certified politicians, or, if one prefers, for the activity of those who, recognising themselves within a given regime, act within the limits of the laws that define that regime.

In encompassing the sum of acceptable political combinations and possibilities, the juridical framework therefore produces a routine political life. Only those problems that are manageable within the legal field are considered. Solutions given to these problems arise via deduction: they derive from established juridical arrangements and explicitly refer back to them. The regulation of the relations between governors and governed is therefore pregnant with a political practice, one which shrugs off all questions that go beyond the imposed legal framework and that cast suspicion upon the right to govern affirmed by the regime already in place.

To confine legitimate politics exclusively within the existing perimeter of law entails a reduction of the activities of responsible officials to a positivist dimension. Such a reduction may be formulated as follows: law, and nothing but the law. It easily allows politicians to settle into conservative attitudes and to adopt a defensive posture as regards the established order,[7] and it gives them a way of discrediting social demands

[6] Ibid., p. 156.
[7] Weber emphasises that legal positivism favours a conservative attitude, in particular because the evaluation of actions proceeds first of all according to criteria that concern conformity to the law and not substantive justice. See *Economy and Society*, vol. II, p. 876.

and political behaviours that do not enter into the domain provided for by the legal field. This method of discrediting can be so far-reaching that such demands and behaviours may be denounced and judged as criminal. Generally speaking, it takes on forms that vary according to the political system and regime, to the means employed by opponents, as well as to the relations of forces existing among the contending parties. In this context, politicians seem to take on a task that consists, above all, in preserving a status quo that is geared towards the particular advantages attached to their position.

Those who denounce law as an instance of authority employed by the political class to benefit their personal interests are ultimately reinforced in their position when it seems that legalistic rigidity is challenged mainly at the instigation of the political class itself and for its sole gain. If the legal regulation of phenomena relating to politics is used only for partisan ends, denunciations thereof lead one to think that changes in the laws are basically just operations involving manipulation.[8]

The polemics that occurred in France a few years ago around reforms in the electoral laws feed this type of criticism. From this point of view, far from corresponding to intangible principles beyond whose province there lies injustice, political right seems to be made up of a set of procedures whose very plasticity is used to serve the objectives of those who govern. In this way, the distinction between legality and illegality is supplanted by the idea that law serves the political elites through an arrangement and management of legalities and illegalities that are established according to circumstances and needs.[9] Like commercial business law, where certain texts set out explicitly the way in which other laws can be evaded, political right is not defined by any kind of principled opposition to what is illegal. It involves, rather, the implementation of techniques that shift the boundaries of legality according to the interests of the political class.

These criticisms are obviously accentuated when it comes to evaluating modern political institutions. There are two reasons for this. The first is tied to the process of rationalisation and autonomisation of political activity, as described above. The second has to do with the achievement of this phenomenon of rationalised autonomy within a democratic environment: given the existence of democratic values and the constraints these values impose upon the rulers, the denunciation of these rulers is all the more severe.

---

[8] See, in particular, the remarks of Roberto Mangabeira Unger in *The Critical Legal Studies Movement* (Cambridge, Mass.: Harvard University Press, 1986), pp. 112–13.

[9] We are inspired here, in part, by the analyses of Michel Foucault in *History of Sexuality*, trans. Robert Hurley, 3 vols. (New York: Vintage, 1990), vol. I, *An Introduction*, p. 89, and in *Discipline and Punish: The Birth of the Prison*, trans. Alan Sheridan (New York: Pantheon Books, 1977), pp. 273–74, as well as by the commentaries of Gilles Deleuze in *Foucault*, trans. Seán Hand (Minneapolis: University of Minnesota Press, 1988), p. 29.

Those who question politicians' capacity to do their work as representatives concentrate their attacks in two directions. First, the attacks are directed against the tendency to monopolise the role of representative, which is a result of professionalisation. This attack tends to disparage the first two principles of the democratic system: the principle of the circular flow of goods and of offices and that of the continuity or mediated transparency between the governors and the governed. Next, the attacks are directed against the powers that result from this monopolistic situation. In this regard, one must note that while Anglo-American political institutions have developed within the framework of a very limited right to intervene within society, the size of statist organisations on the European continent has, by placing the community in a situation of dependency, generated a form of political paternalism that could not help but give rise to radical criticisms.

The thesis according to which the end of political activity is not to state and to apply what is just but is, quite to the contrary, to watch over the interests of the politicians themselves stems from a disenchanted, sceptical, even cynical conception of politics. That conception claims to offer a description of reality as this reality is manifested in professional politicians' struggles for power. Taking cognisance of the fact that politicians divert the end of justice towards their own corporatist preoccupations, those who advance this line of criticism think that the laws are only techniques politicians use for their sole advantage. From this point of view, it is only when constrained and forced to do so, under pressure from the collectivity, that the political class consents to look any further than their own particular interests. Taking the general good into consideration is not, for this class, a natural and primary choice.

Let us put this point in other terms: this thesis, which offers us a description of a crisis of representation, ends up denying the fact that legal regulation constitutes an expression and an instrument of legitimacy. There is but a step from there to the conception of political right in particular and right in general as basically being tools of oppression, and that step is quickly taken. It is precisely from this perspective that the Marxist analysis of rights proceeds.

According to Marx and Engels, every State is the product of a division of society into antagonistic classes and constitutes one means of exploitation. This holds, among other things, for bourgeois political institutions. After having played a revolutionary role, the bourgeoisie ceased *de facto* to be a force for progress. Incapable of mastering the tremendous industrial development it itself had prompted, it gave birth to the bourgeois State, which is nothing but the domination of the possessing class over the proletariat. This is the thesis Marx defends when he criticises those theories that are aimed at legitimating the Liberal State. Taking his stand against the arguments defended in Hegel's *Philosophy of Right*, Marx established that the Liberal State is not rationality in actuality, nor is it even the supreme organ that achieves the general interest beyond the contradictions in the system of needs and that transforms the individual into a citizen.[10] It is but the offspring of the economically hegemonic group, and this group justifies its oppressive position by the authority of the laws and through the use of what is the coercive apparatus properly speaking, namely the army and the police.

It is also from this perspective that Marx examines those doctrines that appeal to natural law and that infer therefrom the foundational contract of a legitimate State. According to him, these systems of thought only express, under the guise of a discourse about a supposedly eternal human nature, the claims of the bourgeoisie, now in full economic expansion. The bourgeoisie struggles to instaurate legal-political institutions that allow production to be organised in a way that is favourable to its initiatives and that assures an ever-greater development.[11]

Law is a repressive code because it is the tool of the bourgeoisie. Compared to the feudal world, the bourgeois State is undoubtedly progressive, but it is still only a beginning.[12] It represents only the formal level of rights, which must now be obtained in reality.[13] It is only with the advent of communism that the achievement of human freedom will genuinely be attained. This ultimate stage of history coincides with the withering away of the State and of law-based relationships. It is therefore necessary to denounce the collusion that exists in principle between rights and exploitation, as well as to give up the very idea of a State ruled by right, a *Rechtstaat* [*l'État de droit*].

It is not the case, however, that the entire Marxist constellation of ideas is limited to this theoretical 'hard line'. Thus, the social democrats passed a much more favourable judgement upon liberal institutions.[14] It nevertheless remains the case that the association of the legal framework with oppression constitutes a thesis that has left a very heavy imprint upon the field today. This thesis, which refuses to take seriously the question of right in politics and limits itself to examining the laws in terms of ideology and legitimation procedures, is very widespread indeed. The

---

[10] See Karl Marx, 'Contribution to the Critique of Hegel's Philosophy of Law', in Karl Marx and Frederick Engels, *Collected Works*, vol. V, pp. 61–62.

[11] See Karl Marx, 'On the Jewish Question', in ibid., vol. III, pp. 161–63.

[12] Marx, 'Contribution to the Critique of Hegel's Philosophy of Law', in ibid., vol. V, p. 66.

[13] Ibid., p. 65.

[14] See Kolakowski's remarks on Eduard Bernstein, in *Main Currents of Marxism*, vol. II, pp. 107–08. The reader may also refer to Adam Przeworski's *Capitalism and Social Democracy*, 3rd edn (Cambridge University Press, 1988), in particular p. 3.

works of Pierre Bourdieu are one of the best illustrations of this thesis. Indeed, while emphasising all along what distinguishes them from a strict Marxist approach, these works take over its basic argument and make it their own.

Thus, as Luc Ferry and Alain Renaut have recalled,[15] Bourdieu's writings point up three areas in which the distance he has taken with regard to a certain form of Marxism is claimed to be undeniable. Taking aim at the Althusserian approach and its ambitious attempt to possess the truth of Marx's writings, Bourdieu, in the name of science, first criticises Marxism conceived of as a philosophy: Althusser's research project becomes, under his pen, a variant of the traditional ambitions of philosophy,[16] which may be characterised by the will to rule over empirical knowledge and over the sciences that produce this knowledge.[17] Althusser's alleged science, it is said, proves to be a quasi-metaphysical form of *a priori* thinking that deduces the event from the essence and the historically given from the theoretical model. Bourdieu thus thinks that the famous Althusserian 'break' gives birth only to a science that is lacking in any actual scientific practice.[18] It begets nothing but a consolidation of philosophy.

Next, Bourdieu reproaches Marx's Structuralist readers for their singular lack of a dialectical sense and for their reduction of historical processes to some mechanical effects of economic structures. From that standpoint, subjective practices are nothing but reflections or emanations, whilst in reality, as Bourdieu explains, there is dialectical interaction between objective structures and historical actions, that is to say, between economic structures and people's practices.[19]

Bourdieu underscores one final point. As opposed to the position defended by a vulgar materialism, there really does exist an autonomy of thought in relation to the class struggle.[20]

This distancing from a Marxism judged too simplistic is carried out within the framework of a generalised materialism that calls upon both Weber and Marx.[21] Bourdieu is seeking, in the end, to set up a refined analysis of the social sphere, one liable to offer an explicit account of its laws while at the same time preserving the notions of individual responsibility and freedom.[22] He describes his own approach as a

[15] Luc Ferry and Alain Renaut, *French Philosophy of the Sixties: An Essay on Antihumanism*, trans. Mary H. S. Cattani (Amherst: University of Massachusetts Press, 1990), pp. 155–64.
[16] Pierre Bourdieu, 'La lecture de Marx, ou quelques remarques critiques à propos de "Quelques critiques à propos de *Lire le Capital*"', *Actes de la Recherche en Sciences Sociales* 5–6 (November 1975), 79.
[17] Ibid.   [18] Ibid.
[19] Pierre Bourdieu, *The Logic of Practice* (Stanford University Press, 1990), p. 41.
[20] See Bourdieu's interview in *Le Nouvel Observateur*, 2 November 1984.
[21] Bourdieu, *The Logic of Practice*, p. 17.
[22] Pierre Bourdieu, *Leçon sur la leçon* (Paris: Minuit, 1982), p. 56.

displacement of one's gaze so as to be able to account for ideologies,[23] no longer doing so merely by designating their functions but also by examining their structure as symbolic systems[24] as well as their objectivation in institutions.[25] This commitment takes nothing away from the fact that Bourdieu retains a very Marxist conception of right and of the law. The methodological displacement he endeavours to effectuate does not in any fundamental way affect the critical judgement he brings to bear upon them both.[26]

It is in this light in particular that one can understand the importance Bourdieu grants to the notion of legitimacy, and especially the use he makes thereof. For Bourdieu, legitimacy is the power to naturalise the social order, that is to say, to endeavour to make that order be thought of as going without saying, it being understood that the values of the bourgeoisie are the pivot and the reference point for that order.[27] That these values serve as criteria is the very expression of exploitation. Alienation is what prevents one, or makes it impossible for one, to be present-to-oneself outside of the principles of the dominant class.

If the notions of right and legitimacy are central to Bourdieu, that is because in his works he is attempting to destroy the bourgeois social order's claim that this order goes without saying. In wanting to denounce the legitimacy claimed by the bourgeoisie, Bourdieu examines how right helps to set in place, via the medium of the *habitus*, a social nature. Indeed, for him the *habitus* is at once the generative principle of objectively classifiable practices and the system of classification (*principium divisionis*) of these practices; and it is in the relationship between these two characteristics of the *habitus* that the social world as represented – what Bourdieu calls 'the space of life-styles' – is constituted.[28]

The analysis of the dominant class's claim to legitimacy being conducted then within the framework of an examination of the transformation of law – as code – into *doxa*, Bourdieu states that legal regulation is, *par excellence*, an instrument of naturalisation. It is capable, in time, of passing from some kind of orthodoxy or from a belief identified as a duty to an opinion characterised by immediate adherence to what is perceived as both natural and normal.[29] This is all the more the case as this mechanism for transforming orthodoxy into *doxa* finally makes possible a modification in the perception of the law itself: the abolition of its constraining aspect implies its reinforcement, the legal code and

---

[23] Pierre Bourdieu, 'La force du droit. Éléments pour une sociologie du champ juridique', *Actes de la Recherche en Sciences Sociales* 64 (September 1986), 3.
[24] Ibid.   [25] Bourdieu, *The Logic of Practice*, p. 133.   [26] Ibid., p. 138.   [27] Ibid.
[28] Pierre Bourdieu, *Distinction: A Social Critique of the Judgement of Taste*, trans. Richard Nice (Cambridge, Mass: Harvard University Press, 1984), p. 170.
[29] Bourdieu, 'La force du droit', 17.

its correctness now not only being accepted despite their rigour but also seemingly necessary. This is law made into legitimacy by the exploited themselves.

Certainly, when compared to Marx's analysis, the approach to law proposed by Bourdieu involves a much more detailed account of the functioning of the legal system qua symbolic field. But it takes on the essential features of Marx's way of tackling the question. That laws would only be one means among others for exercising oppression is what Bourdieu is constantly pointing out, even when he is examining how new demands emanating from society are integrated via law.[30] A smoothed-over expression of force, law has a tremendous efficacy that is inscribed completely within the dimension that is alienation. While it does indeed correspond to a phenomenon of rationalisation,[31] the legal space is not that through which reason and justice emerge within the political sphere: it is the fabric upon which false consciousness comes to be imprinted.

It is pointless, therefore, to look in Bourdieu's work for a connection between law and an authentically justified relationship between governors and governed, that is to say, between the regulation of political phenomena and legitimacy. The latter is only the name given to a desire to found exploitation at the level of the collectivity as a whole.

We see that, when law is judged unable to justify in a genuine way the distribution of power between rulers and ruled, it is the very possibility of studying political life in terms of legitimacy that is being set aside. The right to govern cannot be credible when the legal codification of the relations between governors and governed is thought to serve either the political class or the group that is economically dominant within a society. From this standpoint, there is room only for an analysis of institutions conducted exclusively from the standpoint of ideology, legitimation, bad faith, or force.

TOWARDS A MORE BALANCED UNDERSTANDING
OF RIGHT

Our response to this systematically critical view of right and law will be brief. The reason is simple: To reduce law to one element in the apparatus for the defence of the advantages from which elites draw benefit is to offer a description that accounts for only one aspect of its nature and of its function. Certainly, those whose mission is to serve and to apply the law are often its primary beneficiaries, and they do not hesitate, when it proves useful, to turn it into a made-to-order tool. Likewise, it must be recognised that legal institutions do effectively aid in the preservation of

---

[30] Ibid., 19.   [31] Ibid., 17.

a social and political order. In this regard, they play a repressive role that favours the ruling classes. But it is not plausible to remain only on this negative side of the question. Four arguments militate in favour of a more balanced conception of right.

In the first place, who can believe in the possibility of living within society without a set of rights and duties? Unless one is situated in an ideal universe where a natural understanding would reign among people, or unless one has given up all one's relations with others, the management via legal processes of interactions among agents is required for coexistence to be achievable within one and the same collectivity. In the contrary case, the smallest item of daily exchange would give rise to incessant transactions and dissensions, and nothing would prevent those transactions and dissensions from degenerating into generalised conflict.

In the second place, for the governed, right is a means of protecting themselves against the excesses of power that can tempt the governors when no barriers put a brake upon their appetite for power. In fact, starting from the moment the activity of elites is not defined and delimited by a legal framework that establishes reciprocal forms of behaviour, the exercise of command becomes a unilateral practice before which the average members of the group stand dispossessed. Having at their disposal no force equivalent to that of the governors, the governed no longer have the ability, when they do not have the enjoyment of certain rights recognised, to denounce any arbitrary actions. Although they sometimes seem like very fragile shields indeed, rights that are recognised are nevertheless precious elements, ones to which the ruled do not fail to have recourse.[32] Consequently, it is fitting not to neglect their importance.

Moreover, to identify the world of law [*l'instance juridique*] with these negative characteristics alone is to deprive oneself of a way of analysing change. Indeed, if law is used by the governed to defend their interests, it also allows one to describe and to explain the transformations a community undergoes. Thus, not only is it a recording chamber, a way of making official how a society evolves and of noting, in particular, whatever improvements are made to benefit the individuals who make up the collectivity, but it also has, in relation to these modifications and in conjunction with other factors, an active and positive function to fulfil. That function manifests itself in two ways. Generally speaking, we can say that the denunciation of unjust situations cannot take place unless it is based upon a sense of right, in the name of which is expressed the desire to change and to improve social and political reality. From a more particular point of view, let us state that specific claims are exerted on the

---

[32] See, for example, Harold J. Berman, *Law and Revolution: The Formation of the Western Legal Tradition* (Cambridge, Mass.: Harvard University Press, 1983), pp. 43, 556.

basis of the existing legal legacy with which the members of the group are confronted. On the basis of already recognised rights that have become sedimented, the ruled make use of these rights as a lever, bringing out the fact that they have not been respected or are ill respected, or even that they are greatly inadequate. That is to say, there exists a dynamic movement that accompanies the legal dimension, and within whose framework right calls for more right.

Finally, if, under cover of serving the common interest, law had as its exclusive goal the reproduction of relationships based upon domination, it is unclear how it could be described entirely in pejorative terms. Indeed, the world of law must embody, be it only minimally, what it is reproached for not being. Without that, there would be no room to cast such blame upon it. To deplore the repressive dimension of law is also to posit that it is not only that and that it contains potentially, if not actually, some characteristics worthy of one's respect. This is to say that, while challenging all the time the possibility of law playing any positive role, the view that identifies it with a disguised form of repression is appealing to this very possibility in order to develop its own point of view. Clouded by its effort to lodge a protest, it fails to recognise the conditions upon which this conception rests.

Consent, the political subject, and legitimacy

The second type of argument used to devalue the problematic of legitimacy has to do with the question of consent. Let us now turn to that question.

Legitimacy presupposes the agreement of the governed. The members of a community in which a *de jure* political situation exists have a function that, even if it is not the direct exercise of power, confers upon them the status of actor and of subject. They participate in political activity, offering it a support that has a real influence upon the way things go and is, in part at least, the expression of their will. Now, it turns out that this point of view may give rise to some criticisms.

First, some authors think that the consent of the governed has no effect upon the march of political history. Second, the authenticity of the support consent represents is placed in doubt. To the extent that these criticisms contest the reality of legitimacy, it is imperative, after having presented them, to show their limits.

THE ROLE OF THE CONSENT OF THE GOVERNED

Since legitimacy consists in justifying simultaneously both power and obedience, it is clear that the assent of the governed is essential to the setting up of a *de jure* relation. It no less remains the case that, for certain political analysts, the consent of the ruled and, in complementary fashion, their opposition are not determining factors in political life. According to them, the field of political affairs is subject to mechanisms that exclude the possibility that the attitude of the governed might have an influence. Two approaches fit into this outlook. The first is introduced in terms of a study of political reality from the point of view of sociohistorical structures. Those who adhere to this first approach denounce the idea that events can be explained in terms of whether the members of the group offer or withhold their agreement from the rulers, and they see therein only an argument based upon voluntarist and psychologistic premises. In the second approach, it is thought that the exercise of political power is in the hands of an elite that, whatever the regime may be, imposes its opinions upon the rest of the population.

Historical structures and consent

The structural analysis of history. The structural examination of power relations is developed, for example, in systematic fashion in Theda Skocpol's book on the French, Russian, and Chinese Revolutions.[33] Her objective is to provide an explanation of political change and, more specifically, of revolutionary phenomena. The author proposes four main groupings within which it is possible to place the various theories of revolution. Among these groupings, the one pertaining to Marxism takes precedence. For Marx, revolutions are not isolated episodes of violence. Fruits of the class struggle, they are born of the structural contradictions existing within societies.

To this first group of theories are added three others that have appeared more recently and that issue in the main from the American social sciences. Skocpol first mentions those studies that seek to elucidate revolutionary phenomena on the basis of the personal motivations that drive individuals to engage in political violence. She then evokes those conceptions of revolution that, adopting a systemic approach and placing the accent on the dimension of values and the dimension of consensus, state that revolutions are responses on the part of ideological movements to deep-seated imbalances affecting social systems. She mentions, finally, political conflict theories, which explain collective violence in terms of struggles between governments and various organised groups who are contending for power.

Beyond those features that distinguish them from one another and their greater or lesser merits, Skocpol emphasises that all these conceptions

---

[33] Theda Skocpol, *States and Social Revolutions: A Comparative Analysis of France, Russia, and China*, 14th edn (Cambridge, Mass.: Harvard University Press, 1988).

are open to criticism. Indeed, they share three characteristics that point to their limitations and, ultimately, to their inability to explicate, in a satisfactory manner, the true causes of political upheavals. The first of these common characteristics has to do with the fact that all these analyses focus their investigations too exclusively on the national level of conflicts and of mechanisms of modernisation, doing so without ever relating them systematically to international structures and to changes taking place on a worldwide scale. The second common characteristic takes the form of an analytic identification of the State with society, or of a reduction of political and state actions to representations of socioeconomic forces. But the underlying fault, and consequently the most serious one, is the voluntaristic image these views offer of political transformations. It is, of course, this last characteristic that holds our attention here.

For Skocpol, in effect, all these theories presuppose that the emergence of a deliberate effort to rally a portion of the population – generally, the disadvantaged masses and their leaders – is the necessary condition for a revolutionary upheaval to occur. From this standpoint, psychological factors win out over structural explanations. This holds for the Marxist theory, too, even though in that approach one insists upon the structural origin of political phenomena. Now, it is precisely this idea to which she is opposed.

According to Skocpol, the thesis claiming that revolution is the fruit of individuals' intentions is open to criticism in that it suggests that the social and political order rests upon the idea of a consensus of the majority, namely the dominated classes, whose needs are satisfied. In other words, according to this analysis the sufficient reason for engendering a revolution is the loss of consensual support.

In Skocpol's eyes, such a voluntaristic view constitutes a fundamental failure to recognise the conditions for and historical reality of revolutionary movements. Skocpol therefore champions a way of studying revolutions that, while still retaining the positive aspects of political-conflict theories, is based to a great extent on the structural preoccupations of a Marxism that is now rid of its drift towards individualistic explanations and that refines these preoccupations by taking into account the international environment and a non-mechanistic conception of the relations between the State and the economy. In order to explain political upheavals in particular and history in general, one must adopt an impersonal viewpoint and give up the idea that people are causes of either the one or the other. In short, the attitude of the ruled – their consent or dissent – is not decisive for the operation of the political field. The idea that people are the subjects of reality and that they are the contemporaries of a history that is on the march is an illusion, alien to the real determinations at work.

Defence and advancement of consent vis-à-vis *the structural approach.* Without denying the existence of sociohistorical structures and their role in political life, we may say that these structures do not constitute the sole form of causality that conditions political life in a fundamental way. Nor would that form of causality condemn the governed to be only extras in, nay, the mere playthings of, history. The idea of determination via structural factors, one of the most systematic examples of which may be found in Skocpol's book, rests in effect upon a caricatural interpretation of the thesis affirming that the ruled take an active part in politics.

Skocpol interprets the role played by the ruled in political affairs as if it had been stated that they are the sole decisive causes of whatever occurs. After that, she indicates that an explanation of events in terms of the actions of the ruled does not correspond to reality. But her argument begins to look like begging the question. Wishing to establish at any price the superiority of an analysis that views political relations from the standpoint of sociohistorical structures, Skocpol offers an indefensible version of the idea that the ruled can have an impact upon the course of political affairs. Now, to state that the consent of the governed plays a role does not necessarily mean that one considers such consent to be the sole determining factor. To defend the idea that the act of consenting can carry some weight in political reality is, rather, to take cognisance of the shortcomings of a theory stating that the relations between rulers and ruled are determined on the basis of structural factors and to show that the governed, as well as individuals in general, really do act upon reality in concert with sociohistorical structures.

An explanation of the relationships between rulers and ruled that is based upon structural factors contains four major difficulties that undermine its validity. All of them relate to determinism.

The first major difficulty, which is of a general order, is related to the fact that political life is more complex than the structural approach might suggest. Indeed, the confrontation of the Structuralist model with reality does not lead to the anticipated result: no convincing connection exists between this theory and the actual way in which political reality unfolds. The concrete situations examined go beyond the doctrinal framework associated with sociohistorical structures. Such structures do not fulfil the function being attributed to them, that of being principal cause, unless completed by outside conditions. Thus, while emphasising all along that revolutionary phenomena are to be explained essentially by structural factors, Skocpol has to recognise that their impact varies according to the circumstances. This is precisely what leads her to indicate that her arguments cannot be generalised and that, since they do not allow one to know exactly when and how new revolutions will arrive, nor what form they will take, they do not offer any genuine capacity to make forecasts. That does not prevent her, however, from affirming that the need to take conjunctural factors into consideration in order to bring political relations to light does not impair the validity of studies conducted in structural terms. Here is where there is an opportunity to contest her views.

In fact, when the effectiveness of sociohistorical structures reveals itself to be indissociable from non-structural factors, one cannot maintain that only the former are decisive. While everything is determined, not everything is determinable structurally. It is a matter of admitting that the structural elements do not represent the sole form of causality that gives direction at an underlying level to the relationships between rulers and the ruled. One must avoid the speculative illusion. This illusion, which Skocpol's theory does not escape despite an attempt to make allowances for the diversity and complexity of history, introduces in effect a dualism between the essence and the phenomenon. In doing this, she interprets the way in which one event succeeds another on the basis of a principle that is presented as fundamental, and she thus tends to reduce other explanatory factors to mere consequences or accidental manifestations of this principle.

To grant sociohistorical structures the twin status of key to the future and ultimate authority – that is, of a causal category whose function is to be the prime mover[34] – is to forget that these structures are themselves capable of being elucidated through history.[35] Brought into existence by a network of elements mixed in with non-structural factors that are associated with more permanent characteristics, sociohistorical structures cannot be identified with the least conditioned and most general form of causality.[36] It is therefore perilous to describe in too strict a manner the distinction between the level of sociohistorical structures and that of conjunctural elements. It is particularly pernicious to evoke this division from a realist standpoint, considering structural causes to be properties of things and conjunctural factors to be only accidents whose impact is by definition marginal.[37]

---

[34] For a criticism of the prime mover in history, see, in particular, Raymond Aron, *Introduction to the Philosophy of History: An Essay on the Limits of Historical Objectivity*, trans. George J. Irwin (Boston, Mass.: Beacon Press, 1961), pp. 216–19, and Raymond Boudon, *Theories of Social Change: A Critical Appraisal*, trans. J. C. Whitehouse (Cambridge: Polity, 1986), pp. 124–25.

[35] See Paul Veyne, 'L'histoire conceptualisante', in Jacques Le Goff and Pierre Nora (eds.), *Faire de l'histoire. Nouveaux problèmes* (Paris: Gallimard, 1978), pp. 65–66.

[36] See Raymond Aron's remarks in *Main Currents in Sociological Thought*, trans. Richard Howard and Helen Weaver, new edn (London: Transaction Books, 1998), vol. I, *Montesquieu. Comte. Marx. Tocqueville. Sociologists & the Revolution of 1848*, pp. 208–09. In another context, the reader may refer to Lefort's 'L'idée de "personnalité de base"', in *Les formes de l'histoire: essais d'anthropologie politique* (Paris: Gallimard, 1978), pp. 73–75.

[37] Boudon, *Theories of Social Change*, pp. 218–19.

It is worthwhile, on the other hand, to state that these theoretical constructions constitute a mere schema of hypothetical and formal intelligibility. Furthermore, reality is not limited to this schema. And as far as causality is concerned, the structural dimension does not in principle benefit from any sort of preeminence over conjunctural factors.

These affirmations lead to an examination of the second difficulty involved in structural analysis. It can be stated in the following terms: to maintain that only the influence of sociohistorical structures is decisive and that the consent of the ruled is not crucial is to ignore the fact that the latter's activity unfolds on the basis of a range of possibilities and serves to orient, specifically, the course of political affairs. This error becomes clearly apparent when one breaks away from the structural fetishism that has, in the social sciences, become an important paradigm extending beyond doctrinal boundaries.[38] Indeed, one can sift out two lessons from this idea that it is in concert with other equally important factors that sociohistorical structures determine political relationships.

The first lesson consists in recognising that the ruled have the capacity to choose and, by way of consequence, an aptitude for formulating their consent. Indeed, from the very instant one grants that the way in which the relations between governors and governed unfold is not engendered essentially by a structural mode of causality, the process by which political life is determined ceases to be the expression of an explanatory element whose constraining might wins out over other factors. It becomes synonymous with a much more open-ended kind of mechanism in which each, in his own place, is up to the task of intervening.

In the absence of a primordial cause that would stem from sociohistorical structures and would dictate necessary effects, the plurality of elements that go to make up the political context in which the governed live goes to define a relatively fluid sort of world. The diversity of factors conditioning political relations sets out a field of constraints that is, at the same time, an area of resources for the governed.[39] The way in which political reality is organised being the product of various causes, none of which is by its essence preeminent, the ruled are not oriented in a single direction. Not everything is possible, but several paths can be envisaged. That is what puts the governed in a position to choose and therefore to grant their consent or to withhold it.

Let us put it in other terms: the elements that determine reality – and, in particular, within reality, the identity of the ruled and the way in which they interpret their environment – do not constitute a fundamentally rigid

[38] Ibid., pp. 110–11.
[39] We are inspired here, in part, by the analyses of Anthony Giddens in *The Constitution of Society: Outline of the Theory of Structuration* (Berkeley: University of California Press, 1984), in particular pp. 172–74.

form of causality. These elements engender a shifting and contingent setting [*milieu*] in which possibilities (upon which the governed's faculty to
express choices is grounded) arise; for them, choosing consists, then, in
evaluating these possibilities and in making decisions that help to con-
cretise what previously was but a potentiality. The determining factors
thus open up options, and it reverts to the ruled to pronounce themselves
either favourably or unfavourably upon those options.

This obviously does not rule out the fact that their margin of manoeuvre is sometimes quite limited. The content and the extent of what is
possible being connected with the prevailing circumstances, it happens
that, depending upon the type of society in question, the choices placed
at the disposal of the governed may be limited in the extreme and that
their roles may, practically speaking, be preestablished. But on the other
hand, unless one is to fall in the trap of reification (which leads one to affirm that the way in which the relations between rulers and ruled operate
obeys rules whose stability is similar to the kind presumed to characterise
the laws of nature),[40] it is worth recognising that the governed are not, for
all that, entirely lacking in alternatives.[41] The most closed societies never
have enough mastery over the ruled to guarantee that the latter will behave
exactly as expected. On the other hand, to look at a situation from the
outside and to describe it as offering no choice to those who are directly
confronted with that situation does not necessarily correspond to those
people's own perceptions. The governed exceed the bounds assigned to
them by their environment only in relation to that environment or, to put
it in a more radical way, only by being involved parties in an overall critical
process that brings into question the equilibrium of their community.

In this regard, it is fitting to add that, when the ruled do not think
that the options offered to them are opportunities, the resulting crisis
itself presupposes the ideas of possibility and choice. In other words,
one must have a sense of the possible in order to condemn a political
reality that is judged not to have reserved any place for the possible. In
another connection, let us say that it would be absurd to maintain that the
governed might be able to have any dealings with an indeterminate world
or that such would be the condition for them to exercise their freedom.

The point then is to recognise that the evolution of the relationships between rulers and ruled is not written out in advance [*a priori*].[42] Moreover,
this evolution constitutes, at each stage in its history, a definite framework

---

[40] Ibid., p. 180.
[41] Ibid., p. 181. See also Jon Elster, *Ulysses and the Sirens: Studies in Rationality and Irrationality* (Cambridge University Press, 1979), pp. 113–14.
[42] Giddens, *The Constitution of Society*, p. 84. In a more general perspective, see Roberto
Mangabeira Unger, *Social Theory: Its Situation and its Task. A Critical Introduction to Politics, a Work in Constructive Social Theory* (Cambridge University Press, 1987), pp. 135–37.

that, all the while being limitative, still sketches out some possibilities upon which the governed's act of choosing, and therefore their act of consenting, are grounded.

The second lesson that may be drawn from the idea that political reality is not influenced exclusively by sociohistorical structures may be stated as follows: the decisions of the ruled have an impact that modifies the context from which these decisions issue. Indeed, such an impact comes to be inscribed within the network of forms of causality on the basis of which the choices of the ruled are worked out. Bending this network to variable degrees and in varying directions, the impact of these decisions goes on to influence, in concert with other determinations, future decisions and actions. By affecting the combination of diverse factors that go to make up the political setting, this impact brings in additional elements, and the governed's choices and acts will make allowances for them. Modifying the environment, such an impact also weighs upon the evaluation the governed make of the available options as well as of the objectives they deem desirable and achievable. This is to say that how the decisions and actions of the ruled are put into effect is tied up with a world view that events and the interpretation of these events help, within a given context, to formulate.

Thus, someone who is governed transmits to his peers the idea and the desire to act, but only on the condition that his activity might in their view be significant.[43] Such activity must correspond to an option, that is to say, to a goal that coincides with the values of their milieu and with regard to which the lessons of history leave some hope for a reasonable probability of success. If not, it consoles them in maintaining a wait-and-see attitude.

The richer the range of possibilities that serves as a basis for the deployment of acts on the part of the ruled, and the more likely that range of possibilities is to find some concrete expression, the greater the chances that the concatenation of decisions and actions will entail some thoroughgoing transformations. Thus, the activity of the governed can participate in the introduction of factors that counteract the determination of the social and political order by sociohistorical structures and can even be one of the expressions and one of the causes that account for the passage from traditional societies to a modern mode of organisation.[44]

There is a third difficulty against which the structural approach collides. It consists in a misrecognition or underestimation of the fact that the

<hr>

[43] See Paul Veyne, who broaches this question by mentioning, in particular, the role of leaders, in 'L'histoire conceptualisante', p. 78.
[44] See Émile Durkheim (*The Division of Labor in Society*, for example pp. 291, 326–27), who shows that, following the vanishing of the 'segmental' type and with the individual now less closed in than before, society has a hard time containing divergent tendencies. The reader may also refer to Giddens, *The Constitution of Society*, pp. 200–03.

governed have an existence with a specific density. To this dense form of existence are connected some particular reasons for choosing and acting. This third difficulty also consists in a misrecognition or underestimation of the fact that sociohistorical structures do not operate in politics independently of the decisions and the acts to which this life and these motives give rise.

Within limits that are related to the circumstances, the ruled – and this is true, too, of individuals in general – have lives whose originality manifests itself in three complementary ways. First, the bundle of determinations to which one of the ruled is exposed at the outset and in the course of his existence is never entirely identical to the one with which another ruled individual is confronted, even in the most homogeneous of settings: each has a life to which no one else's is comparable. Second, the governed's very activity helps to accentuate the specificity of their respective existences. In engaging in projects to which they seek to give concrete form, they defend the values and interests to which they are attached, and they construct a life whose distinctive character, beyond the more or less marked similarities one person's life offers in relation to another's, increases with the complexity of the actions being conducted. Choosing and acting on the basis of criteria that express at once what they know and what they do not know about their environment, the ruled have a strategy that aims at establishing as harmonious a relationship as possible with that environment. Born indifferent to the world that surrounds them, they endeavour to find, with the aid of the means the context in which they develop furnishes them, an area of understanding with that world, that is to say, with themselves, as well. The process of adapting to reality is a movement in which one appropriates one's milieu. It is mixed up with the mechanism whereby the personal identity of the governed individual is constituted *in situ*.

Finally, it is fitting to underscore the fact that the ruled are not pushed in a given direction without precise reasons. Although they do not depend absolutely upon the ruled, these reasons cannot be reduced to motives alien to the interests of their daily life and to the way in which they preserve those interests. Contrary to what the structural approach, and especially Marxist theory, tell us, the conception the ruled have of their existence and the attitudes that existence implies, as erroneous and limited as they might appear in relation to an ideal point of view, need not systematically be devalued in the name of that ideal itself, nor should those attitudes by described in principle in terms of *illusion*. It must be granted that the motivations that give sustenance to the decisions and actions of the governed may represent good reasons to choose and to act. In short, one must also credit them with the right to live their own lives.

This specific density of one's existence affects, by near or by far, how the relationships between the governors and the governed do indeed unfold. Quite logically, sociohistorical structures do not operate in politics independently of it. In this regard, one must demonstrate one's sensitivity to the meaning of the fact that structural factors do not benefit from a dynamic of their own [*dynamique autonome*]. This boils down to pointing out that these sociohistorical factors, not being able to proceed without the activity of the ruled, have no influence upon the course of political affairs unless they coincide with what motivates the choices of the governed and the actions that result therefrom.[45] Nevertheless, the fact that sociohistorical structures have need of the ruled in order to be effective obviously does not mean that one would have to reintroduce, after having denounced it, the thesis whereby one identifies the governed as neutral and strictly instrumental accessories of the structural dimension. Still being relatively determined by the environment, and in particular by sociohistorical structures, the life of the ruled is not for all that to be reduced to such structures. There exists a process of mutual conditioning between structural elements and the existence of each person. Indeed, if the existence of the governed is oriented by a context within which its most enduring features play a role, those features are, in turn, made possible in part by the characteristics of the activity of the ruled.[46] From this standpoint, such activity is not in principle conservative, and, in terms of the opportunities that present themselves, it takes part in the overall transformation of political reality. This demonstrates once again that it would be injudicious to grant only a minor place to the consent of society's members.

The fourth and final difficulty with the structural approach has to do with the question of responsibility. Being responsible goes hand in hand with giving consent. Indeed, being accountable for decisions and actions supposes the exercise of a kind of freedom that is a property of consent. On this point, the study of political life from the structural standpoint stumbles over three problems.

In the first place, if one thinks that sociohistorical structures influence political relations in a decisive way, does not that mean that one is just having recourse to a sort of explanation that fails to recognise the object it claims to be elucidating? Whereas the analysis of political life in structural terms tends to minimise, nay, evacuate the notion of individual responsibility, the daily unfolding of the relationships between rulers and ruled never ceases to underscore its role. In various forms and to varying degrees, certainly, it implements the idea that the governed and the

---

[45] Durkheim, 'Division', p. 181.   [46] Ibid., pp. 212–13, 220.

governors answer personally for their choices and their acts. There exists, by way of consequence, an incommensurability [*inadéquation*] between the way political reality is known via sociohistorical structures alone and the way in which this reality is in fact organised.

In the second place, the structural study of political development does not rule out a dangerous, because totalitarian, conception of the notion of responsibility. If sociohistorical structures constitute the sole form of causality for the evolution of societies, one is adopting the perspective of a science that is essentially complete, that hypostatises the heuristic tools used to guide one's research efforts and therefore transforms them into dogmatic affirmations whose pretension is to provide an overall account of the real.[47] The history of the twentieth century has shown how this undertaking can be expressed on the level of reality. When the idea of responsibility is subjected to an evaluation of events carried out in terms of an end of history whose accomplishment is presented as both a good and a necessity, the door is left wide open to massive acts of extortion committed in the name of a finality that is judged to be desirable as well as inevitable, and whose consequences the authors do not have to bear because they identify themselves with that finality.

While not entirely renouncing the principle that the governed are individually responsible, especially in those zones of activity where their faculty and right to choose and to act by themselves is recognised, totalitarian societies may be distinguished by the paucity of autonomous spaces granted to the governed. The tighter and tighter grip of this type of depersonalised responsibility, which is grounded upon a view of the meaning of history, leaves the governed dangerously disarmed in the face of the might of those who govern them.

In the third place, the idea that sociohistorical structures are the sole elements capable of having any genuinely decisive influence over the course of political life risks encouraging a process whereby people abdicate their responsibilities and adopt a fatalistic attitude. The weight of structural forms of causality tends to justify past inaction as well as inaction to come, and the rules of conduct are thereby reduced to a morality of disillusionment and the maintenance of a wait-and-see attitude. This risk of fatalism reveals a reversal of the previous situation: whereas the initial intention of this basically Marxist approach to the political via sociohistorical structures corresponded to the desire to forge a tool that

---

[47] See Luc Ferry and Alain Renaut, *Système et critique. Essais sur la critique de la raison dans la philosophie contemporaine* (Brussels: Éditions Ousia, 1984), pp. 162–63, and Luc Ferry, *Political Philosophy*, trans. Franklin Philip, 3 vols. (University of Chicago Press, 1992), vol. II, *The System of Philosophies of History*, pp. 75–76.

would aid in the emancipation of the governed,[48] it now becomes a factor that reinforces, at its own level, the acceptance of the status quo.[49]

Elite theory and the defence of consent

Parallel with this structural approach to political phenomena, there exists another type of argument, which asserts that the governed do not intervene in the unfolding of political life. This argument has to do with the theory of elites and hooks up with the remarks previously mentioned about the professionalisation of political personnel. In this conception, it is maintained that the ruled take no part in political decisions and actions because the governmental process is reduced to the domination of a minority over the majority. This thesis allows of no ambiguity: a small group holds power, it exercises that power unreservedly, as a fact, and it is impossible to conceive of a social and political structure that would head in another direction. It is within this perspective that Gaetano Mosca, to whom we owe the first theory of elites based upon a sociological approach, considers the persistence of the phenomenon of elites to be a basic datum. The existence of a minority that governs to the detriment of a majority thus passed for being such a universal characteristic that Robert Michels, a few years after Mosca, saw therein an operative institutional rule, describing it as an iron law of oligarchy.[50] Such a conception does not signify, moreover, that society is frozen in an eternal opposition between an elite, triumphant in its immobility, and a mass of people condemned to submission. On the contrary, a constant renewal of the individuals who make up the circle of rulers occurs. That is what Vilfredo Pareto shows. For Pareto, the history of human societies is a graveyard of past aristocracies: by a perpetual movement, one elite succeeds another.[51] In no way, however, does this process change the nature of power: a narrow group governs on an ongoing basis. The ruled merely change masters.

[48] See Unger, *Social Theory*, in particular p. 138.   [49] Ibid., pp. 138–39.
[50] Robert Michels, *Political Parties: A Sociological Study of the Oligarchical Tendencies of Modern Democracy*, trans. Eden and Cedar Paul (London: Collier-Macmillan, and New York: The Free Press, 1966), p. 342.
[51] Vilfredo Pareto, *The Mind and Society*, ed. Arthur Livingston, trans. Andrew Bongiorno and Arthur Livingston, 4 vols. (New York: Harcourt, Brace and Company, 1935), vol. III, *Theory of Derivations*, §2053, and *Manual of Political Economy*, ed. Ann S. Schwier and Alfred N. Page, trans. Ann S. Schwier (New York: Augustus M. Kelley Publishers, 1971), ch. 7, §98, p. 312. [Translator/Editor: Coicaud had cited here as his source the French original of Aron's book, *Les Étapes de la pensée sociologique. Montesquieu, Comte, Marx, Tocqueville, Durkheim, Pareto, Weber* (Paris: Gallimard, 1985), p. 466 (which provided, moreover, an incorrect citation of the *Manual*). The quotation and citation were dropped from *Durkheim, Pareto, Weber*, the English-language translation of the second volume of Aron's *Main Currents in Sociological Thought*, p. 182.]

Far from being limited to types of political organisation that are based explicitly upon the confiscation of the instances of decision and action, the government of all by a few is therefore alleged to belong to the essence of political activity. The only things that vary are the composition of the ruling class and the way in which its members accede to power and exercise it. This variation combines with the modalities proper to different political systems and regimes. It suffices to examine how to each particular situation there corresponds a pattern of government by a few. One would thereby establish the inescapable character of the phenomenon of elites. This theory of political relations applies to democratic regimes as well as to other kinds.

Without ever doubting the fact that the governors can trifle with the consent of the governed, it is nevertheless fitting to underscore that one cannot identify in any absolute way all of political practice with this mode of behaviour. Such an amalgamation does not do justice to the respective roles of rulers and ruled.

To be convinced of this, it suffices to indicate that for elites to ignore the point of view of the members of the group is to opt for a method of governance that proves to be, in the shorter or longer run, rather precarious. Indeed, the governors enjoy a secure and stable situation only when the roots of their power plunge deeply into the society they rule and whose activities they coordinate. While they contribute to the fashioning of the social and political spheres through their choices and their actions, the way in which they are obeyed gives expression to a kind of authority that can be solidly grounded or seriously marred. Now, it is apparent that, in order to enjoy the most favourable conditions for the exercise of power, the rulers have need of the consent of the governed. It is preferable that this consent not be only tacit but correspond to a real sense of approval. This assumes that elites and the political institutions they run answer to the expectations of the governed. If not, a crisis ultimately ensues.

Certainly, the support that is required varies from regime to regime, and the need to include the consent of the ruled is not a very significant constraint in certain social and political types of governance, so great is the might the rulers have at their disposal. It remains no less the case that, in order to assure the duration and the legitimacy of their position at the top of the group, these rulers cannot just do without it. There exists, therefore, a mechanism whereby the governed check up on the governors, and this mechanism confers a considerable role upon the consent of the governed. We shouldn't underestimate the fact that elites most often take the lion's share. But to reduce the political to an activity that by definition serves only their interests is to conduct only a partial survey of this sphere.

THE AUTHENTICITY OF CONSENT

The argument that the consent of the governed does not in reality display the qualities attributed to it is another way of creating doubts as to its capacity to contribute to the constitution of a theory of legitimacy. To challenge the authenticity of the act of consent is therefore to identify it with the support from which a regime benefits, as well as with the stability accompanying it, and to show that these two elements do not, after all, produce a situation of legitimacy. In this line of criticism, one devalues the support the governed provide to the social and political order in which they live. A variety of arguments are advanced towards this end. Among them we find, in the first place, one that employs the notion of consensus.

The authenticity of consent questioned

Consent, consensus, and anomie. Starting from the idea that a community is never totally consensual, the approach used here underscores the fact that the differences in status among individuals generate varying attitudes towards power and that the evaluation of the right to govern depends upon the place each person occupies. From this point of view, if a person is counted among the privileged members of the system, the regime's organisation will have every chance of seeming legitimate to him. In contrast, those left out of society will undoubtedly not think the same.

It is not impossible, moreover, that those who yesterday denounced the illegitimacy of the government might tomorrow become its fervent supporters, if the government changes its policy and responds favourably to their demands. And this may be so, whatever the fate of the rest of the members of the community.

Far from being an impartial sort of judgement, consent involves, according to this argument, only a level of satisfaction of individual needs, needs which vary along with changes in people's personal situations and careers. In reducing consent to an exclusively egotistical conception – that is to say, one that tends towards anomie – this thesis challenges the very possibility of legitimacy. How, indeed, could legitimacy work to form a relationship of overall reciprocity between governors and governed, and among the governed themselves, if the act of consenting, which is one of the conditions for its existence, expresses only the triumph of particular interests that clash with one another?

To this first argument it is fitting to add a whole set of additional criticisms. These criticisms contest the idea that the ruled might be up to the task of deliberating and choosing, in full freedom, between the act of consenting and that of standing in opposition.

Consent, prudence, and cultural alienation. These objections can be placed under two headings, one dealing with submission, the other with cultural alienation.

The first consists in a defence of the idea that the support individuals give to a government pertains simply to an attitude characterised by prudence. From this point of view, the fact that an individual backs the decisions and actions of the rulers by remaining silent or even noisily manifesting his support does not mean that he is truly in favour of them. On the contrary, one can think that he acts so in order to preserve his immediate interests. According to this conception, the power of the State and the fear it arouses in the ruled entails on their part an attitude that has nothing to do with consent as defined in terms of freely given assent. For the governed, conducting oneself in conformity with the law and obeying the orders of the rulers boils down to safeguarding the conditions for their security. Extracted under threat of direct or indirect sanctions, the support the ruled grant to a regime is therefore neither active nor authentic. It is on the order of prudence.[52]

For it to become clear that their backing was only a form of submission, all that is required is the appearance of some favourable occasions. One witnesses such occasions in particular when the pressure exerted upon individuals begins to abate.

It is understood that the more the might of the State comes to envelop the life of a society, the more this line of criticism has a chance of seeing its merits recognised as being well grounded. In this regard, although it is aimed initially at non-democratic political forms, and, in particular, totalitarian regimes, it does not spare democracies. While leaving the ruled with rather large margins of manoeuvre, the democracies do not rule out the possibility of applying procedures that involve the intimidation of its members. Thus, as in more authoritarian types of political systems, respect for the laws can in democracies be prompted not by deep-seated convictions but by a concern to avoid repressive measures. In another connection, it may be pointed out that the weight of the State – that is to say, the compass of its bureaucratic antennae and the number of areas in which they intervene – can produce within democratic regimes individual dependency upon public powers. Such dependency may come to resemble a clientelistic system that succeeds in imposing attitudes of allegiance.

The second category of objections has to do with cultural alienation. Stating that the members of a group are in only limited possession of the faculty of evaluating the world in which they live, this line of argument

[52] See Raz, *The Authority of Law*, p. 30.

articulates two criticisms. One is based on ideology; the other denounces what may be called an autarchic interpretation of reality.

The thesis that places consent under the heading of ideological views of society is one familiar to us. Advocating a Marxist type of analysis, it reduces the act of consenting to an emanation of bourgeois domination and of its political expression: representative democracy. This thesis is composed of two elements. In the first, consent, far from being the expression of free will or of the autonomy of individual persons' wills, is considered indissociable from the state of alienation in which they live. Being only an excrescence of the false consciousness engendered by ideology's labour of generalised stupefaction, it cannot be taken as a reliable political notion.

The Marxists are not, moreover, the only ones to think that the governed do not have much of an idea of what is desirable for the community as a whole. The argument has been used on several occasions, and in quite a variety of forms, in particular by conservatives. Thus, during the nineteenth century the opponents of the process of democratisation defended the idea that the majority of the population, and in the first place the workers, did not have sufficient intellectual and moral capacities to express a valid political opinion.[53] Whether this argument issues from Marxism or conservatism, and despite the fundamental divergences that exist between these two approaches, the result is the same: whether they are in the clutches of some bad instincts or of a world view that is manipulated by the bourgeois class, individuals are alienated. False consciousness prevents them from having a correct appreciation of the situation to which they are supposedly giving their consent.

The second element in this effort to discredit consent in the name of ideology refers to the political practice of representative democracies. It describes the support individuals provide within the context of elections as a routine and formal sort of participation that corresponds solely to the ideology promoted and secured by bourgeois democracies. Under these conditions, the act of consenting has no significance in terms of loyalty. In having recourse to an electoral system, the capitalist State wants individuals to adopt and to follow the political rules that have already been decreed, without asking themselves how well grounded those rules are. The stakes involved in consent being always preestablished by the domination of the possessing class, it is a matter only of obtaining the passive support of the ruled, that is to say, their adherence to the limitations on debate imposed by the regime. Thus, elections serve

---

[53] See, for example, William H. Sewell Jr, *Work and Revolution in France: The Language of Labor from the Old Regime to 1848*, 4th edn (Cambridge University Press, 1985), pp. 226–28.

only to make the governed act as guarantor for the choices that perpetuate their inferior status. In instaurating the abstract law of the majority, the bourgeoisie in no way puts its privileges at stake. The mechanism of elections and the act of consenting are full participants in the modes of legitimation of bourgeois capitalism and in the fabrication of its acceptance.

The other criticism designed to reduce consent to cultural alienation has to do with the autarchic interpretation of political life. It consists in asking oneself what authentic consent might consist in when the support afforded a regime is established on the basis of collective norms that offer no alternative. Close, in a way, to the tendency to identify the act of consenting with ideology – since ideology also has to do with a limited and unilateral evaluation of reality – this objection differs, nevertheless, from the former one. In contrast to the practice of the bourgeois democracies, which authorise a certain amount of pluralism in opinions and forms of behaviour, the purpose of this objection is to describe, in effect, a systematic form of cultural imposition that excludes any divergencies. Such divergencies are necessarily judged to be anomic. In this regard, the autarchic interpretation of group organisation is connected in an essential way with an organicist conception of the collectivity, which is lived as totally closed and which celebrates individuals' belonging to a whole within which differences are not tolerated.

This situation, wherein the laws demand absolute compliance, tends to be characteristic of primitive societies,[54] and even traditional ones. It also concerns – subject, obviously, to certain designated reservations – those regimes that wilfully cut themselves off from other national communities and develop an organicist and dogmatic approach to reality: that is, totalitarian regimes. The question here is how, from this point of view, to consider the support afforded the rulers: is it solely the product of individuals' regimentation and an enslavement of their autonomous consciousness and action?

Consent and democratic government. Continuing along the line of this series of questions, a final criticism of consent arises: in the hypothetical situation where the act of consenting can be considered defensible and can constitute a non-alienated commitment on the part of the ruled, does not an act such as this lie exclusively within the bounds of democratic government – which, in contrast to other political forms, rests explicitly on the choices of individuals and offers them freedom of movement and

[54] See, for example, the comments of Pierre Birnbaum on the works of Pierre Clastres, 'Sur les origines de la domination politique: à propos d'Étienne de La Boétie et de Pierre Clastres', *Revue française de science politique* 27:1 (February 1977), 15–17.

thought?[55] So, if consent is one of the conditions for the theory of legitimacy, does not one have to assert that it is a category that is operative only within the framework of democracy? In that case, is not one ruling out the possibility of studying other political regimes from the standpoint of the right to govern?

Defence of the authenticity of consent
The argument designed to deny the authenticity of consent is just as fragile as the objections dealing with sociohistorical structures and elite theory.

Consent is not in principle anomic. The objection that goes to challenge the authenticity of the consent of the governed under the pretext that such consent is the expression of their egotism gives rise to two sets of reflections. First, it is difficult to imagine that the consent of the ruled could be anything other than a process by which they evaluate the role of elites and of political institutions with regard to the material and symbolic goods these elites and institutions are charged with procuring for the members of the community. To judge the governed's act of consenting as egotistical because it cannot be separated from their will to obtain some gain in exchange for their support is a quite unconvincing point of view. Upon what element, if not this one, might the consent of the ruled be grounded? To consent is to renounce a portion of one's autonomy in order to confer it on those who rule. Such an abandonment has meaning only when it has another side to it that occurs for the benefit of the governed and for which the governors are responsible. It is in terms of the services expected from them, as well as of their capacity to take it upon themselves to render these services, that the governors benefit from the support of the ruled. It is, by way of consequence, normal that the ruled take into account, in the act of consenting, their level of personal satisfaction. The error is to see in each one's calculation of his interest the sign of the doubtful authenticity of his consent, which would thus prevent it from being one of the elements required by the right to govern.

Second, the fact that the consent of the ruled might be indissociable from the evaluation of the goods allotted to them does not signify that this evaluation isolates the governed from one another or that, by definition, this evaluation is performed independently of any consideration of the other's fate. There is no question here of ignoring the tendency of individuals to think that social reality is satisfactory overall when their own

---

[55] Cf. the characteristics of democracy according to Claude Lefort, in 'Human Rights and the Welfare State', *Democracy and Political Theory*, trans. David Macey (Minneapolis: University of Minnesota Press and Cambridge: Polity Press, 1988), p. 39.

conditions of life are favourable. It is a question of recognising that the mechanism for evaluating the effectiveness of the rulers and of political institutions, which gives rise to consent, is not based solely on the analysis of the particular situation of each person who is ruled.

In reality, each person's exercise of the act of consenting rests upon a certain amount of concern for the other members of the group. It offers an indication of the experience of the community, of a relationship of reciprocity, within whose framework the governed agree to concede to the governors the power to act as guarantors for exchanges within the collectivity in terms of rights and duties. This attitude is not one of pure generosity: the preservation of the interests of each requires that the fate of the others not fail to be recognised in any fundamental way. In addition to the fact that taking account of the conditions of the other's life is proportionate to the relations of dependency that bind the ruled together, the enjoyment of goods necessitates, in order for this enjoyment to take place in a tranquil way, that these goods be respected by all. That holds as much for private goods as, in a more obvious way, for public goods. Indeed, the latter exist only in as much as they are shared and shareable among the individuals society brings together. Thus, collective security is not obtained without the security of each individual being suitably guaranteed. The common good is nothing without the well-being of each. In other words, the possibility of people living together passes by way of consent. And the communitarian dimension the latter expresses must never be wholly empty. If that is the case, the sense of belonging to the group dissolves and the very idea of consent loses its meaning.

This is to say that the more consent inclines towards an evaluation conducted in strictly egotistical terms, the more it goes against the organisation of the collectivity and the spirit of understanding from which it issues. In the end, such an inclination contributes to a rending of social and political ties.

In conclusion, it is not necessary for consensus to be general for one to be able to think that the act of consenting is valid, especially since unanimity proves to engage in a dangerous form of utopianism. It suffices that the act of consenting integrates the collective level while not absolutising it.

Individuals have the faculty to deliberate and to consent. Let it suffice to mention here five thoughts on the matter.

First of all, prudence does not discredit consent any more than egotism does. Without denying the existence of political violence, we can say that the obedience of the governed cannot be reduced in principle to mere submission. The prudence displayed by individuals does not have, as its corollary, the idea that their consent results solely from their fear.

Next, let us respond to the argument that the ruled do not interpret the various aspects of political life in a lucid manner because they do not have the requisite intellectual capacities. Today, it is impossible to grant much credit to a thesis that has come to illustrate the worst hours of paternalistic conservatism in its various versions.

In another connection, let us add that, without contesting the share of truth contained in the proposition that the ideological dimension has an influence over one's consent, one must avoid identifying consent systematically with a distorted view of political reality. Indeed, such a comparison amounts to turning a critical approach into a dogmatic judgement grounded upon a radical devaluation of the experiences and beliefs of the governed.[56] This dogmatic judgement is all the more problematic as it is necessarily polemical, given that ideology is always someone else's.[57] Without renouncing the theme that one needs to distance oneself from the world as it is lived, which is included within any ideological analysis, one must be careful not to erect it into a very clearly Manichean sort of schema that reduces the opinions of the ruled to the expression of their alienation. To place oneself exclusively at this standpoint is ultimately to forbid the ruled from having any real life except in terms of ideality. It is probably in order to avoid this difficulty that some authors have wanted to break away from a basically pejorative understanding of the notion of ideology.[58] They thus examine its critical function only as one of the aspects of the overall system of representation that is connected with the objective situations of individuals and groups[59] and that, inscribing people's ways of acting and thinking within a universe of signification, takes on an integrative role.[60]

Furthermore, in criticising the act of consenting by limiting it to an ideological view of how the political world operates, is one not maintaining a thesis that is self-contradictory? For, this thesis assumes that he who states it has granted, at least implicitly, the idea that the sphere of ideology does not encompass everything. He must admit, in particular,

---

[56] See Paul Veyne, *Did the Greeks Believe in Their Myths? An Essay on the Constitutive Imagination* (University of Chicago Press, 1988), p. 88.
[57] See Paul Ricœur, in George H. Taylor (ed.), *Lectures on Ideology and Utopia* (New York: Columbia University Press, 1986), p. 2.
[58] Ibid., pp. 3–5.
[59] George Duby, 'Ideologies in Social History', in Jacques Le Goff and Pierre Nora (eds.), *Constructing the Past: Essays in Historical Methodology* (Cambridge University Press, 1985), pp. 152–56, 165.
[60] Ricœur, *Lectures on Ideology and Utopia*, for example pp. 8, 254–55.

that that sphere is not applicable to his own person, to his speech, and to his behaviour.[61]

Let us make one last statement. The fact that the governed members of a primitive, traditional, or contemporary type of autarchic society do not dispose of the necessary detachment in order to evaluate their environment does not in principle, once again, affect the authenticity of the act of consenting.

In the cases of primitive or traditional collectivities, why think that, making allowance for the few options open to the individuals who make up these societies, the attitude of these individuals is not an authentic example of their providing some backing that can be said to have the status of consent? The scope and the content of choices always being relative to the identity of a given community, how can one, under the pretext that the governed's faculty of judgement echoes the organisational conditions of the group to which they belong, affirm that their opinions are valueless? The act of consenting is one procedure for evaluating reality, and its implementation assumes a homogeneous relationship between this procedure and the field it evaluates. One must indeed grant, in principle, that the closure characteristic of these societies does not rule out the possibility of describing the mechanism of consent that operates therein as a kind of support upon which a *de jure* political relationship can be grounded. To defend the contrary thesis and to compare the constraining might of social norms to a totalitarian form of violence, as Pierre Birnbaum does,[62] is to place oneself in the critics' line of fire. For, beyond the methodological error this thesis commits when it assumes an outside standpoint (of which the members of these primitive or traditional collectivities have, by definition, no knowledge), it forgets that those collectivities furnish spaces for deliberation and discussion.[63]

The question of consent calls forth two remarks as regards contemporary social and political organisations that are constructed in such a way that they are systematically skewed by propaganda while also being isolated from other competing national cultures, and that are built upon a simultaneously organicist and totalitarian view of communitarian experience. It is fitting, on the one hand, not to lose sight of the fact that at their beginning, and even over long periods of time, totalitarian regimes can enjoy real popular support.[64] So, without going so far as to identify the support they possess at certain moments in their existence with

---

[61] See Ricœur's remarks on Mannheim's paradox, ibid., pp. 8–9.

[62] Birnbaum, 'Sur les origines de la domination politique', p. 16.

[63] See, for example, Claude Lévi-Strauss, *Tristes tropiques* (Paris: Union Générale d'Éditions, 1966), p. 277, and Boudon, *Theories of Social Change*, pp. 53–54.

[64] For an illustration of this facet of the question, the reader may refer to, among other texts, Ian Kershaw's *The 'Hitler Myth': Image and Reality in the Third Reich*, 1st paperback edn (Oxford University Press, 1989), pp. 5, 254–56, 258.

an unalienated form of backing, it is difficult to ignore such support in principle. On the other hand, it is not so much the authenticity of consent that is at issue in totalitarian regimes as its very exercise. Indeed, although their leaders attach great importance to the backing they receive from those whom they rule,[65] these regimes are set within a logic that is not that of right. There, the governed are not truly authorised to grant or to withhold their support for political institutions and for the men who are in charge of these institutions. They are forbidden access to this margin of manoeuvre. What, on the contrary, is required of them is a kind of adherence that strongly resembles a mystical union.[66] Those who oppose the rulers are treated as enemies who have to be eliminated. In this regard, indoctrination and repression are the two sides of a warlike dynamic of fusion and terror. That dynamic leaves no room for consent and for the respect of law.

Consent and political regimes. The argument that sees in consent a phenomenon limited to democracy also encounters some objections. It is not because the act of consenting plays a central role, and is institutionalised as such, in a democratic regime that its action would remain strictly confined thereto. Consent is exercised on the basis of the resources placed at the disposal of the ruled in a society. What matters, for its existence and its operation to be made explicit, is that there would be a relationship of reciprocity resting upon a mutual recognition of rights and duties, both on the part of the governors and on the part of the governed. Beyond the different forms the act of consenting takes in relation to the social and political types of organisation in question – that is, also in relation to the various forms of democratic government – consent lies at the base of communities that manifest their collective experience via the exchange of services among individuals. In short, consent is not tied exclusively to democracy. It is achieved within a historical dimension.[67] To be convinced of this is to break away from the uncomprehending concept of the individual that, generally speaking, accompanies the idea that sees consent as a phenomenon limited to democracy. This incomprehension is a consequence, in large part exaggerated, of the distinction worked out by Ferdinand Tönnies between the notions of community and society.[68] It is fitting therefore to point out that, while the degree of interdependence

---

[65] Ibid., p. 257.

[66] See Lefort, 'Permanence of the Theologico-Political?', in *Democracy and Political Theory*, p. 234.

[67] See Carole Pateman, *The Problem of Political Obligation: A Critique of Liberal Theory* (Berkeley: University of California Press, 1985), pp. 98–102.

[68] Ferdinand Tönnies, *Community and Society (Gemeinschaft und Gesellschaft)*, trans. Charles P. Loomis, reprint edn (New Brunswick, N.J.: Transaction Books, 1988); see, in particular pp. 33–35.

among agents and the severity of social and political control changes along with the form of collectivities, this does not imply, as Tönnies suggested, that the individual exists within society and remains absent from the community.[69] Although individual differences might be more marked in the modern world, the members of archaic collectivities are, on their own scale, quite dissimilar, one from another.[70]

Such are the responses that can be given to criticisms designed to challenge the idea that the consent of the ruled might be one of the constitutive elements of the right to govern. And, to the extent that it has been shown that it is not possible to contest altogether the notion of consent, it is ultimately the individual conceived as a political actor that proves irrepressible.

Political and moral legitimacy

The examination of political relations from the standpoint of legitimacy is also criticised from the moral point of view. In this regard, three arguments attempt to discredit the study of behaviours and institutions in terms of the right to govern. This rejection is conducted in the name of realism.

REALISM AGAINST LEGITIMACY

Here, disqualification of the right to govern is based first upon an identification of legitimacy with a moral approach to political affairs, then upon the difficulties that are posed when one tries to determine criteria for evaluation from a moral point of view. Finally, this disqualification is tied in part to the methodological problems raised by legitimacy when the latter is conceived as a moral analysis of the relationships between the governors and the governed.

As was shown in chapter 1, although conformity to the law as laid down in the rulers' decisions and actions constitutes a necessary condition for one to be able to talk about a legitimate situation, such conformity is not sufficient. It is equally of prime importance that the rules codifying the practices of statesmen correspond to the fundamental principles to which the members of society consent or adhere. That is to say, the right to govern is indissociable from a normative dimension: it presupposes that the decision makers take into account the values and the constraints that give to a community its identity and its horizon of signification.

[69] The reader may refer to Boudon's remarks in *Theories of Social Change*, pp. 53–56.
[70] Lévi-Strauss, *Tristes tropiques*, pp. 283–84.

It is precisely this connection between the management of political affairs and fundamental principles that the view championed by realism challenges. From this standpoint, it makes a twofold identification: ignoring the relationship that exists between the normative character of legitimacy and the identity of a society, it interprets the prescriptive aspect of the right to govern as a moralising evaluation of political reality. Moreover, it defends the thesis that there is a radical separation between moral imperatives and the activity of those who govern. Morality being identified with precepts that indicate not what political reality is but what it ought to be, and no continuity being established between the Is and the Ought, it looks like morality teaches us nothing about the concrete ways in which the rulers exercise power. The result of this is that, if legitimacy consists in judging the role of the governors in relation to the governed in terms of morality, and if the latter is wholly unrelated to the political field in its effective reality, the problematic of the right to govern reaches an impasse: considering the rift that exists between legitimacy's discourse about politics and what politics really is, no real possible area of understanding exists between the influence norms exert upon the unfolding of political affairs and the actual practice of the rulers. Politics having its own interests, ones divergent from those of morality, legitimacy, then, is no longer anything but an attempt to impose from the outside guidelines for behaviour that do not conform to the reality of power. The right to govern, being alien to real political life, therefore cannot serve to analyse that life and to comprehend it.

This separation of morality from politics, which echoes the collapse of classical political philosophy, boils down to establishing an ontological division between the activity of the governors and the moral approach. Among the Ancients, and in particular in Aristotle, the city was prior to each individual; and man, being naturally incomplete, realised himself fully only by belonging to the community.[71] The fulfilment of the common good is then the essence and therefore also the end of politics. It designates the type of organisation, internal to the city, that assures a harmonious interdependence between the whole and its parts.[72]

As opposed to that view, the realism of the Moderns affirms that the meaning of politics resides in power games. It therefore manifests itself through the rulers' autonomy in relation to morality. The realist attitude thinks that what gives politics its specificity is not a finalism that would orient the decisions and actions of those who govern in terms of the public good – that is to say, that would aim at the constitution of a

---

[71] Aristotle *Politics* 1.2.1253a20–30.   [72] Ibid. 3.6.1278b20–25.

reciprocity established at the level of the collective structure – but very much instead the fact that it constitutes a framework within which individuals endeavour to win out over other individuals. Politics is less the search for conciliation on a communitarian level than a warlike enterprise that reduces itself to relationships based upon competition. Within the same group – or, on the plane of foreign relations, between States[73] – politics is confrontation.

In this regard, it is clear that legitimacy, when identified with morality, far from fitting into the dynamic of the right to govern and from playing the role of a tool for collective integration, necessarily appears as a piece or part added from the outside. It would be indicative of an idealist conception of how political affairs are conducted. It looks like an attempt to pacify politics, an attempt that does not correspond to the barbarity of reality.

From this point of view, the idea of legitimacy has, at best, nothing to do with the relations between rulers and ruled; and at worst, it is used within a partisan framework as a legitimation strategy for the conquest of power. And this critique of the right to govern, which rests upon the clear-cut distinction between the moral attitude and the activity of those who govern, intersects here with the objections formulated against the legal codification of political relationships.

Furthermore, it is not surprising to see this current of thought jointly attacking right and morality, at least if one grants that these domains are two aspects of one and the same process, which aims at forming a network of rights and duties binding individuals and whose recognition by all constitutes both the tool of a community and its expression. Now, when persons are separated by interests they do not want to reconcile or by ones that are not compatible, there is no place for a compromise that would be implemented via right and morality. The latter two being judged deceptive or illusory, their reality as a way of organising reciprocal exchanges is reduced to nothing. In the absence of communitarian relationships, politics is limited to a merciless struggle. One is therefore being realistic by being cynical, always envisaging the worst in order to avoid it and behaving accordingly towards the other.[74]

---

[73] See, for example, Robert O. Keohane, *After Hegemony: Cooperation and Discord in the World Political Economy* (Princeton University Press, 1984), p. 7. The reader may also consult Friedrich Meinecke, *Machiavellism: The Doctrine of Raison d'État and its Place in Modern History*, trans. Douglas Scott, reprint edn. (New Brunswick, N.J. and London: Transaction Publishers, 1998), in particular p. 15.

[74] In chapter 23 of *The Prince*, ed. and trans. David Wootton (Indianapolis, Ind.: Hackett, 1995), p. 72, Niccolò Machiavelli says, 'For you will find men are always wicked, unless you give them no alternative but to be good.'

Being obliged to presuppose that one cannot trust the individuals with whom one is in competition, one must count on oneself in order to avoid reversals of fortune. Rather than hoping that, through the mere workings of right and morality, those with whom we are in competition will recognise the share that belongs to us, we have to anticipate their predatory actions by developing techniques capable of reducing the uncertainty and insecurity those competitors represent.

In other words, in order not to perish, one must be the first to kill; morality and right do not concern political reality because nothing is ever attained in principle in our relationships with the other. There exists no reciprocity among individuals and, therefore, no claim of legitimate possession in the moral and juridical sense. It is a matter of being the strongest, and that's all. Political relationships, as well as life in general, are made up only of the spoils of war. The result is that an approach to the relations between governors and governed from the point of view of morality and right not only does not coincide with what is real but constitutes, in the end, a weapon of the weak. To appeal to the public good is to admit failure. The logical conclusion of political realism is that the evaluation of the relationships between rulers and ruled in terms of legitimacy is only a last-ditch resort, the political viewpoint of the vanquished.

This first type of argument aims to bring into disrepute the study of political life on the basis of the right to govern by identifying the latter with morality. To it is added a second argument that may be presented as follows: under the hypothesis that one grants the existence of a connection between politics and morality and the possibility of the latter intervening in the way public affairs unfold, the examination of the relations between governors and governed from the standpoint of legitimacy becomes extremely problematic. Indeed, if the right to govern, identified with morality, plays a role in politics, one has to be able to determine the criteria for evaluating rulers' decisions and actions. Now, a difficulty of sizable proportions arises here: in terms of what is the choice of criteria to be performed, and where are these criteria to be found? In this regard, the objections put forth mention two paths, each one of which is as much of an impasse as the other.

Both of these paths proceed from a historicist, and non-teleological, position that is characteristic of the modern world.[75] They therefore have as their backdrop the antinomy between nature and history.

---

[75] See Leo Strauss's remarks in *Natural Right and History* (University of Chicago Press, 1950), pp. 7–8.

Along the first path, one seeks sure evaluative criteria by leaning on universal principles. From this point of view, it is a matter of gauging the rulers' decisions and actions in terms of natural law or, if one prefers, on the basis of an idea of human nature. Presented as the basis for any acceptable politics from the point of view of morality, the criteria that serve as the expression of this natural law allow one to evaluate, to approve or to denounce, the behaviours of those who govern.

This approach is far from unanimously accepted. It is usually contested in the name of history,[76] and the objection is that universal principles contradict the historical dimension of reality. This criticism has two aspects.

The first aspect brings out the fact that, although it is claimed that natural law is accessible to human reason and is recognised by all, history teaches us that there is nothing of the sort. There exists, in reality, a great diversity in conceptions of right and justice. It is therefore not possible to reconcile the universality claimed by the values that represent natural law with the historical character of political life. To put it in other terms: no commensurate relationship exists between these allegedly universal criteria and history. The absence of immutable principles of justice renders the existence of natural law impossible. Such an absence invalidates the attempt to ground the moral evaluation of politics upon timeless values.

The second aspect of this criticism may be deduced directly from the foregoing argument. One can formulate it in the following way: these criteria are all the less reliable as they ultimately appear to be the manifestation of a specific culture that aims at imposing its views upon other societies. An expression of a reductive view of historical and political reality, these criteria limit the process of political interpretation to principles that emanate from a particular period and from particular interests. This is to say that, if one wants to defend the idea of studying politics from the standpoint of legitimacy, with legitimacy understood as moral analysis, it is better to refrain from having recourse to universal criteria: they are but an illusion.

The other path, which seems just as difficult to take as the one involving universal principles, constitutes its exact counterpart. In giving up on absolute elements of evaluation and in deciding to interpret reality only on the basis of historical principles, it is apparent that what one gains on the one side, namely criteria for judgement that are suited to the situation, is lost on the other. In opting for immanent evaluative elements, the individual who uses them is both judge and claimant. It is impossible for him to produce true critical interpretations of other cultures than his own.

[76] Ibid., p. 9.

Moreover, it being understood that evaluating political situations on the basis of history consists in defending a point of view that is subject to revision, it seems difficult to consider as reliable an instrument that depends upon a specific context, one which, as such, may change tomorrow. To seek to evade the problem of the incommensurability between the world and principles that transcend reality by appealing to immanent criteria is therefore to expose a moral approach to politics to the limitations of historical relativism. So, even if one agrees to say that legitimacy involves a moral examination of politics that does not fundamentally contradict its real operation, in one way or another it is not possible to find satisfactory benchmarks.

These objections have been addressed to the attempts to resolve the question of how one can determine criteria that would serve to evaluate political life from the standpoint of the right to govern. They lead us to bring up one final line of criticism.

Confronted with the concern to resolve the difficulties involved in the attempts of the Moderns, who seek reliable criteria for evaluating reality, the social sciences have developed the thesis that one must avoid making value judgements. Because neither features selected from outside history nor those chosen from within it seem to furnish one with incontestable evaluative principles, the idea of detachment characteristic of scientific positivism has appeared to be the only solution. From this point of view, the goal of studying social and political reality is not to evaluate or to judge. It is simply a matter of understanding this reality in an objective way and of establishing, as far as possible, the laws that regulate its operation. This, however, generates a tension, one that seems difficult to resolve, between the agenda of the social sciences and the problematic of legitimacy, as identified with morality. Under the hypothesis that the thematic of the right to govern really involves a moral approach to political life, it boils down to making judgements anyway, that is to say, it ends up examining the degree to which reality is in conformity with some principles. Now, the approach of modern science to social and political phenomena goes against such an evaluative practice, since its claim is to be simply a recording chamber for the way reality operates and it rules out any taking of sides.

LEGITIMACY: FOR A MORAL APPROACH
TO THE POLITICAL

In response to criticisms having to do with the moral dimension of legitimacy, let us first emphasise that to dissociate the domain of morality radically from that of politics, and to deduce therefrom that the thesis of legitimacy is incapable of accounting in a satisfactory way for the specificity of societal phenomena, boils down to mistaking the true nature of those phenomena. The realist approach, which reduces political activity to a struggle for power, fails to recognise an essential element: political activity is not to be defined exclusively in terms of relations of force.[77] One is undeniably revealing one's naivety if one fails to grant that the relations between rulers and ruled, and among the elites themselves, very often have a conflictual dimension to them and that personal ambitions play a role of the first rank. It is equally accurate to state that the varied behaviours of leaders – who, beyond differences in regimes, often complacently and hypocritically wallow in their demagogy and corruption and hold in contempt those whom they administrate – leave one to think that cynicism is the only lucid way of perceiving political life. Nonetheless, to halt at these considerations and to affirm that they suffice to explain how the relationships between the governors and the governed function is seriously to underestimate the role the normative dimension plays in the political field. The moral ideas invoked to evaluate the right to govern are one of the aspects of the very reality of the relations between rulers and ruled. To convince oneself of this, it suffices to show in what way morality is internal to the mechanisms whereby the relationships between governors and governed play themselves out and how it is involved therein. One can shed light on this situation by taking four sets of remarks into consideration.

First, were it true that the normative dimension had no connection with the real unfolding of political relationships, it would not be possible to account for injunctions of the ought-to-be type.[78] In fact, to adopt the idea of a separation between the descriptive level and the prescriptive level would make it impossible to elucidate the status of morality, that is to say, to explicate the provenance, content, and applicability of the maxims and rules that constitute morality. To accredit the point of view that maintains that morality is unrelated to reality in general, and to the actual functioning of political phenomena in particular, is to annihilate any likelihood of comprehending where the values come from that express what ought to be, whether it be on the individual level or on the level of the community. To put it in other terms: if it is impossible to infer the axiological field from what is, morality is reduced to a kind of nomadic discourse. It is unclear how, under those conditions, it could have any concrete and familiar resonance for individuals.

Now, the exigency of ethics – and, in particular, the laws and precepts calling for attitudes of reciprocity within a society – is not in principle alien to these individuals. Although the members of a group might never

---

[77] See Aron, *Democracy and Totalitarianism*, p. 23.
[78] See Unger, *Social Theory*, p. 42.

conform completely to the rules of conduct decreed by the collectivity, and although they might not behave in ways that, even in the most optimistic of hypotheses, entirely reflect these rules, these members are not indifferent to them. Thus, the guilt they may feel when they transgress the norms in force testifies to what attaches them to these norms. To account for the influence values exert upon the relations among individuals when these relations take the form of conviviality and cooperation, and not of merciless struggle, would also be an undertaking with a very improbable chance of success, save for the existence of a connection between political reality and morality.[79] Let us also note that when the maxims that are supposed to regulate the exchanges of rights and duties among individuals are not respected, and when the authors of deviant actions do not experience these actions as instances of misbehaviour, to a certain extent they are not, or are no longer, identifying with the organisation of society those maxims at once represent and defend. Their rejection of the axiological order goes hand in hand with the disgrace that in their view characterises the authorities who are there to guarantee the collective organisation of society.

Second, one can advance the idea that morality is all the less alien to the unfolding of political affairs as it is the manifestation thereof. Far from arising from nowhere, rules of conduct are indissociable from a historical context wherein the economic, social, and cultural aspects – to cite only those ones – combine with power-related phenomena in order to produce a specific type of society. Thus, the great principles that go to make up the criteria for political legitimacy in contemporary France – which, as such, guide the practices of those who govern – are not identical to those of the Ancien Régime. They are inseparable from the state of France today and from the place it occupies. Likewise, the norms that preside over our rulers' undertakings cannot be superimposed upon those that prevail in the United States or, still more obviously, in China. The solidarity between moral injunctions and the identity of the collectivities to which they belong, and which they endeavour to orient in one direction or another, therefore shows that it is impossible to dissociate in any radical way these two levels.

In addition, ethical rules are one of the emanations of the political sphere in that they represent the expression of relationships between individuals that unfold in the form of reciprocity. Indeed, they can be inscribed and can participate in this way within a communitarian dynamic only in conjunction with the role government plays in the coordination of actions among the members of a group and in the organisation of their relationships, viewed from the standpoint of right and duties. From this

[79] Ibid.

perspective, the moral concern to take account of the other coincides with the logic of community experience. At their own level, those who govern, of course, also contribute to this logic.

Third, moral considerations exert an influence upon the operation of political life and upon its history, and these considerations therefore give rise to systems of action. Thus, starting from the moment the rulers no longer count systematically on naked violence to install themselves in positions of command, their governmental programmes have to make some reference to ethics. In this regard, the leaders always say that they want what is good. Even the Machiavellian and instrumental use of one's might proceeds in this way. Beyond the efforts at manipulation in which these appeals to the Good may be enrolled, they are a sign of the force of values in politics. Indeed, if the axiological domain did not have any weight or relevance in the relations between governors and governed, what need would there be to invoke it? In addition, far from being superficial, the influence values exert upon political events can change in a determinate fashion the course of the relationships between rulers and ruled. In this way, during the French Revolution, all moral questions became vital political stakes. These questions dictated their law and their logic to the revolutionary conscience and instigated, in concert with some favourable sociological conditions, certain judgements and practices that were defined in terms of ends.[80]

Fourth, political activity constitutes a domain in which the actions of individuals are not to be reduced to their physical components alone but are indissociable from a demand for signification that brings in the normative level. Indeed, in every human activity the agents need to inscribe their ideas and their behaviours, in general and each *vis-à-vis* the other agents, within a horizon of meaning. That is why social and political relations take place within the framework of a network of significations that, when translated into and set within systems of representation, provide codes by which the members of a group come to understand themselves, give themselves a common identity, or else designate their relationships with institutions. And from this point of view, such relations are not independent of the field of values. There are even grounds to state that they presuppose it. Indeed, the meaning of agents' decisions and acts is determined in terms of what is judged good or bad, desirable or undesirable. It is under this heading that we glimpse the strength of the thesis that politics, as a domain of human reality, takes place within a world of signification that implies the existence of a certain concern for ethics.

For example, in order that an organised society might lastingly maintain itself in existence and ensure a minimum of cohesiveness, individuals

---

[80] See François Furet, *Interpreting the French Revolution*, trans. Elborg Forster (Cambridge University Press, 1981), pp. 25–26, 37.

have to believe in its groundedness and, from this perspective, judge that social commitment is superior to strictly personal strategies. Now, in order that the sense of belonging to a collectivity might have some meaning, its members must still think that their exchanges are regulated in a way that is satisfactory overall and that there exists a balance expressive of and allowing for the dynamic of rights and duties. It is therefore required that the relations among the agents themselves be perceived as relationships of reciprocity in which the moral and political dimension, far from being separate, combine in a relatively harmonious manner.

In politics as well as in the case of social phenomena in general, it is not easy to distinguish absolutely the level of facts from that of morality. We do not have, on the one hand, those features that pertain to the way in which the relations between rulers and ruled unfold and, on the other, completely unrelated to them, ethics. To various degrees and in variable forms, reality combines these two fields. Together, they help to constitute the environment in which agents evolve. Since political activity – and, in particular, the coordination and management of the actions of the members of the community – does not take place without reference to the normative dimension, it is therefore false to state that one could provide an exacting description of it while limiting it basically to a struggle for power.

And even if the way in which the relations between governors and governed unfold does not always attain the heights of those principles that determine the boundaries of what ought to be, it does not follow, for all that, that the domain of values does not comprise one of its components. This is why, after having responded to the theoretical objections that go to challenge the validity of studying the relationships between governors and the governed from the standpoint of legitimacy while attacking right, consent, and the ties between morality and politics, it is now possible to pause for a while and look at some criticisms of a methodological kind so as to show, once again, their limitations and their contradictions.

LEGITIMACY THEORY AND THE SCIENCE OF POLITICS

Methodological objections to studying politics in terms of legitimacy

An opposition exists at the methodological level between the various features that today give to the social sciences, and to political science in particular, their basic characteristics, and the elements contained in the analysis of political relationships in terms of the right to govern. There are three notable points of friction. The first has to do with the determination of the object that is to be explained. The second concerns the separation of facts and values. The third is tied to the problem of the verification and validation of statements produced within the framework of the study of political reality.

THEORY OF LEGITIMACY AND THE POLITICAL OBJECT

The methodological difficulties raised by the problematic of legitimacy are tied to the positivist credo driving the social sciences. This credo, which expresses a desire to account for reality – all of reality and nothing but reality – presupposes an empirical orientation towards scientific endeavours whose aim is to arrive at reliable knowledge of social and political phenomena. The effect of this empirical orientation is to privilege case studies or field studies, that is to say, approaches limited to local objects. This is the first point where it conflicts with the study of the political from the standpoint of legitimacy.

The desire to determine a specific field for analysis is in line with the movement of modern science. Its goal is to satisfy the conditions for establishing true statements about reality. It is contemporaneous with the increasing specialisation of research, whether this specialisation be between the major domains of knowledge or within a given discipline. This process provides access to an ever more refined and complex understanding of phenomena, and to it corresponds a growing professionalisation of scientific labour. One witnesses a rapid growth of different approaches to political life. Each one claims a validity of its own and applies techniques and forms of knowledge sometimes so removed from one another that researchers belonging to distinct branches of a discipline have a hard time finding some points of convergence among their respective preoccupations, points that would still permit them to defend the thesis of the overall unity of the political object.

Faced with this division that is affecting scientific endeavours to an ever greater extent, the analysis of the relations between governors and governed in terms of legitimacy finds itself placed in a precarious position. Indeed, reflection upon the right to govern as it is practised in the present volume takes an overall look at the question. Employing various types of analysis, the problematic of legitimacy goes against the specialisation that is today characteristic of the analysis of politics.

LEGITIMACY, FACTS, AND VALUES

The right to govern maintains a basic relationship with the process of evaluating and judging political reality. To argue about legitimacy is to evaluate rulers' decisions and their actions. Under these conditions, it is clear that the debate over the separation of facts and values is at the centre of the question of the right to govern.

The Ancients' political conception was at once descriptive and pre-scriptive. The distinction between facts and values – that is to say, be-tween description and evaluation – was largely, if not totally, alien to their universe of thought. From this point of view, understanding how individ-uals really are allows one, at the same time, to state what they ought to do. At the heart of this doctrine is to be found a theory of essence, and from this theory the laws governing nature and society follow. Within this tradition, there is little or no place for a separation between rules capable of accounting for the relations between various natural or social phenomena and moral or political laws.

The thesis defended by the Moderns is entirely different. The oppo-sition between facts and values, between science and moral judgement, and, by way of consequence, between the rule in the descriptive sense and the rule in the prescriptive sense constitutes one of the bases for their effort to understand reality. From this distinction, which issues di-rectly from the social sciences' adoption of the natural sciences' model of knowledge,[81] it follows that the notion of value represents a danger to the ideal of explanation. From this perspective, to know is to arrive at facts without worrying about those precepts that values command you to follow.

Better still, let us state it in the following way: to know is to treat values as facts. It happens that the majority of the ambiguities of the most important thinkers in modern social and political theory – such as Montesquieu,[82] Marx,[83] and Durkheim[84] – stem from this: while basing their work all along on a clear-cut separation between facts and values, they do not completely give up on maintaining a tie between the two. They do not distinguish clearly, for example, the movement of history from the political good.[85] It is, however, upon this very opposition that they make the scientific ambitions of their method of analysis rest.

This distinction of facts from values, so weighty with consequences in the logic of the social sciences, lies at the heart of Weber's work. With him, the separation between the Is and the Ought is even asserted in the most clear-cut way possible. Weber assures us that the absolute irreducibility

[81] Strauss, *Natural Right and History*, p. 8.
[82] See Louis Althusser, *Montesquieu, Rousseau, Marx: Politics and History*, trans. Ben Brew-ster, new edn (London: Verso, 1982), pp. 23–24.
[83] See Habermas, *Zur Rekonstruktion des Historischen Materialismus*, pp. 10–11, and Steven Lukes, *Marxism and Morality*, p. 3.
[84] See Aron, *Main Currents in Sociological Thought*, vol. II, p. 102.
[85] See Unger's remarks in *Law in Modern Society*, p. 4.

of facts to values necessarily implies the ethical neutrality of the social sciences. The latter can afford us an answer to factual and causal problems, but they remain incompetent when it comes to the question of values.

Weber sharply insists on the role played by values. He states that the object of the social sciences is determined by a value relation and that, without this relation, there would be no focus of interest, nor any reasonable selection of subject-matter, nor a principle for discriminating between relevant facts and irrelevant ones.[86] Nonetheless, he thinks that there exists a fundamental difference between value relation (*Wertbeziehung*) and the notion of value judgement (*Werturteil*).[87] In stating that some measure may in some way have an influence upon political freedom, for example, the sociologist is not taking a position for or against. He has to content himself with giving an explanation of the objects by connecting them back to their causes. This means that social theory does not resolve the crucial social problems values raise. It is not within its province to criticise value judgements that do not contain an internal contradiction.

The reason why Weber opts for an ethically neutral social science is that, according to him, there exists no authentic knowledge of ends. If such a knowledge were possible, it would suffice for the social sciences to apply themselves to researching the appropriate means to attain those ends. They would thus be brought to pronounce valid value judgements in political matters. But, having taken into consideration the multiplicity of value systems of the same rank whose exigencies engender conflicts that cannot be resolved by human reason, the solution has to be left to the free and not rational decision of the individual.

In the absence of a certain knowledge of good and evil, which would permit one to establish grounded distinctions between clashing points of view, it is not possible to decide between these viewpoints or to prove their truth or their falsity. Faced with such an impasse, neutrality and objectivity are the sole paths that remain open for science to follow.

The credo of the separation of facts and values was accepted as an essential element in the shared legacy of the natural and social sciences. A logical, indeed, even psychological, implication resulted therefrom: the more insecure the social sciences felt with regard to the so-called hard sciences or the greater their sense of inferiority concerning their own scientific capacities, the more they have been tempted to exclude from their labours the notion of value judgement by identifying the latter with a partial and relativistic approach.

[86] See Max Weber, ' "Objectivity" in Social Science and Social Policy', in *The Methodology of the Social Sciences*, trans. Edward A. Shils and Henry A. Finch (New York: The Free Press, 1949), pp. 76, 82.
[87] Ibid., p. 98.

The third point of friction between the problematic of the right to govern developed in the present work and the methodological orientations
presently preponderant in the social and political sciences has to do with
the question of validating the statements produced therein.

In the name of objectivity, a person who studies legitimacy from an
overall perspective is denounced and his right to seek to rehabilitate value
judgements is not recognised. The imperative of objectivity is placed in
the service of the most exacting analysis of reality possible. This goal can
be attained only when the results of the analysis are tested, and therefore after a verification procedure that is connected with the possibility
of falsifying one's statements. That is to say, the first two methodological
objections previously mentioned take effect here in a new critique. In
this new line of criticism, it would be pointed out that the problematic
of legitimacy developed in the present work is not falsifiable. The object
under examination is not local. Not allowing one to apply the type of empirical verification procedures that would be authorised when examining
a narrowly circumscribed sort of phenomenon, that object is deemed not
easily measurable. To this objection it may be added that the truth or
falsity of value judgements are not demonstrable, since one can always
oppose some of them with other ones. The study of politics from the
standpoint of legitimacy not being seen as verifiable, it is therefore not
possible to say that it represents a valid view of the processes having to
do with political life.

The objective of the last section of the present chapter is to demonstrate
that the analysis proposed here, while not agreeing with the characteristic
methodological activities currently enjoying majority support in the social
and political sciences, really is valid.

Defence of the study of legitimacy and positivist aporias

Let us now consider, one after another, the three methodological objections mentioned above.

RELATIVISM AND THE SEPARATION OF FACTS
AND VALUES
The separation between facts and values asserted by the advocates of
positivism offers a twofold disadvantage. It entails a resigned attitude on
the normative plane, and it is not consistent with itself.

To affirm, along with Weber, that it is impossible to demonstrate rationally the superiority of one axiological system over another boils down to
stating that one does not dispose of a valid line of argument that would

explain in what way one situation is preferable to another. The notions of neutrality and objectivity tend to take the form of an indifference as to values. It boils down to admitting that, among these values, everything is as valid as anything else [*tout se vaut*].[88] Thus, researchers who appeal to positivism abstain from making a *de jure* judgement about the motives that serve as supports for the requirements of legitimacy. The study of legitimacy is conceived in such a way that one does not encounter any political organisations genuinely embodying the right to govern but only regimes whose possible legitimacy is only a matter of perception.[89] The consequences of this sort of flattening out of the axiological domain, which is conducted in the name of the imperatives of science, are not too dramatic when they have to do with sets of normative principles among which there exist only a minimum of differences. It is another story entirely when radically opposed conceptions of the world clash with each other. From this point of view, the division of facts from values has a doubly negative effect.

First of all, this neutralist sort of reasoning implies a complete inability to recognise what is good or what is evil. How, then, can one denounce certain political situations on the basis of the truth? To the extent that there is no authentic knowledge of the ought-to-be but exclusively a multiplicity of normative systems of equivalent rank, and to the extent that the choices we make in relation to these systems are not rational, arbitrariness reigns supreme. If one cannot have recourse to a discourse that is capable of explaining, in grounded terms,[90] that certain forms of exercising power offer unacceptable features that it is of the essence to combat, one cannot avail oneself of the right to counter, for example, Fascism and Nazism. So, the absence of an axiological hierarchy, as implied by the scientific ideal of neutrality, expresses, even if does not do so deliberately,[91] the inability to establish a grounded separation between those values that are to be promoted and those ones whose spread must be checked.

To champion a distinction between various normative levels and reality for the sake of being scientific leads to a castration of political thought.[92] It exposes one to the risk of a Munich of the mind.[93] This separation

[88] Strauss, *Natural Right and History*, p. 41.
[89] Habermas, *Zur Rekonstruktion des Historischen Materialismus*, pp. 293–94.
[90] Ibid.
[91] See Raymond Aron's introduction to Max Weber's *Le Savant et le politique* (Paris: Union Générale d'Éditions, 1972), p. 39.
[92] See Lefort, 'The Question of Democracy', in *Democracy and Political Theory*, p. 12.
[93] See Alfred Weber's remarks, as reported by Günther Roth, in the introduction to Marianne Weber, *Max Weber: A Biography*, trans. Harry Zohn (New Brunswick, N.J.: Transaction Books, 1988), p. liii.

is all the more problematic as its adherents often believe, in their heart of hearts, in the superiority of the set of axiological principles whose defence, however, they refuse to take upon themselves.

Such behaviour calls forth two sets of remarks. In the first place, to address the most revolting practices with a relativist mental reservation does not mean that one is not really condemning those practices. In the second place, those who adopt this position most of the time are formally protecting themselves against the accusation of sympathy for the idea of an official morality and of an authoritarian conception of such a morality.[94] But above all, they wish to protect the values to which they adhere from any imputation of an aggressive attitude towards other cultures and thus to encourage respect for different traditions.

As the second negative effect of the separation of facts and values, relativism does not constitute the best means of struggling against cultural imperialism. It can even produce the reverse result. Two arguments may account for this phenomenon.

First, relativising the history of a society by setting it in a more general context and by describing it within the flow of past and present civil-isations helps to create among the members of that society a sense of distance in relation to their own life. That distance can remove them from the strength of the traditions that governed their behaviour before the emphasis was placed on the historicity of the conditions for their existence. In this sense, relativism is synonymous with the creation of a hiatus between the world as it is lived and its study from the standpoint of historical plurality. It serves to suppress practices people do not ques-tion when they are identifying themselves instinctively with the milieu in which they evolve.[95]

Second, in order for the relativist approach to help in a fundamen-tal way to further the recognition and safeguarding of the diversity of cultures, the equivalence of axiological arrangements would have to pos-sess an objective character. To indicate that the choices of other groups are qualitatively equal to one's own ought to signify that objectively they are as good. Now, it is precisely this kind of statement that relativism is forbidden to make, since preferences among normative systems is deemed purely contingent. It is therefore difficult to imagine what is likely to offer some legitimate opposition to the person or persons who, at the whim of their moods or their interests, become bent on destroying a given society.

---

[94] See Jacques Bouveresse, *Rationalité et cynisme*, 2nd edn (Paris: Minuit, 1985), p. 64.

[95] The reader may refer to Jürgen Habermas's remarks in *On the Logic of the Social Sciences*, trans. Shierry Weber Nicholson and Jerry A. Stark (Cambridge, Mass.: MIT Press, 1988), p. 27.

If the values that that society expresses are arbitrary, in the name of what would one protest against its annihilation?[96]

In rejecting an axiological reference defined in terms of objectivity, the relativist finds himself caught in the following trap: in parallel with his concern to consider all options as equivalent, he would like to see morally condemned anyone who fails to respect other choices. But that desire stands in contradiction to the premises of his own discourse. The condemnation of an arbitrary point of view is ultimately just as arbitrary.

Beyond these two negative effects, relativism has to face up to one additional problem. Its inconsistency engenders a phenomenon of self-refutation.

In ruling out axiological objectivity, relativism shuts itself up in a vicious circle that prevents it from remaining consistent with the thesis it is endeavouring to defend. This can be explained in terms of a double aporia that constitutes the two sides of one and the same problem.

On the one hand, to the extent that the subject who states a proposition generally has to at least believe in the validity of what he affirms in order to be credible, a relativistic interpretation of the meaning or the content of the truth (to mention only this example) demands a clearly non-relativistic conception of this notion. The corollary of this clause requiring that one hold to one's own argument has a major disadvantage: to affirm the truth of relativism boils down to one's not being relativistic. Relativism is therefore a prisoner here of a process of self-refutation.

On the other hand, the fragility of relativism is all the greater if the preference for a normative system cannot be grounded and expresses only orientations that are not rational, so that the value of truth itself becomes arbitrary. Raymond Aron underscores this difficulty when, in examining the impasses of Weber's thought, he discovers that an insistence on the contingency of decisions interferes with the idea of scientific statements being universal.[97]

It is not only at the level of the negative effects and of the internal inconsistency of relativism, however, that one can detect aporias. In light of the very practice of the social sciences, the separation between facts and values is also unconvincing.

[96] See Hilary Putnam's comments in *Reason, Truth, and History*, 4th edn (Cambridge University Press, 1984), pp. 161–62.

[97] Aron says: 'If everything that is not a scientific truth is arbitrary, scientific truth itself would be the object of a preference, as little grounded as the opposite preference for myths and vital values' (introduction to Weber's *Le Savant et le politique*, p. 40).

SCIENTIFIC PRACTICE AND THE SEPARATION OF FACTS AND VALUES

Those researchers who adopt a resolutely positivistic and empirical approach may very well cry high and loud that they subscribe to the methodological ideals of objectivity and neutrality and that they can account for phenomena without taking a position.[98] In reality, things proceed in a different way. Although they say that they are eradicating from their studies any value judgements, they do not escape their influence. To pretend that the opposite is the case is to confuse declarations of intent with what really happens and to blind oneself to current practices.

It is appropriate, first of all, to take a stand in opposition to the idea that, in the area of the sciences of society, there is no salvation except beyond the realm of value judgements. Authors would compromise the quality of their work if, at a certain level, they did not include those values in their description and in their explanation of phenomena. Thus, a political scientist who is incapable of indicating what distinguishes a democratic regime from a dictatorial government would inevitably, and rightly so, pass for someone who could not propose a minimally satisfactory understanding of political situations. Or else, when studying the personality and the activities of rulers, he who would rank Winston Churchill and Adolf Hitler, Joseph Stalin and Charles de Gaulle, on the same level or who would see no difference between a politician interested solely in might and a statesman concerned with his country's grandeur would end up confusing everything under the pretext that he did not want to take a position. Certainly, he would not be practising his profession very well, from the scientific point of view. If one grants that these discriminating comparisons are based on value judgements, one has to recognise that the researcher in the social and political sciences cannot eliminate them when they are part of the universe of action and thought upon which he is casting his glance.[99]

Second, when one applies the procedures used to construct the object under analysis, the supposed separation between science, which sets out only the facts, and value judgements is largely illusory. To give only one

---

[98] See, in particular, the remarks of Richard J. Bernstein, *The Restructuring of Social and Political Theory* (Philadelphia: University of Pennsylvania Press, 1978), pp. 44–45.

[99] We are directly inspired here by Aron's introduction to Weber, *Le Savant et le politique*, p. 32. See also his comments concerning the historian of art: 'An art historian who could not distinguish between the paintings of Leonardo da Vinci and those of his imitators would miss the specific meaning of the historical object, that is to say, the quality of the work' (ibid.). The reader may also refer to Strauss's *Natural Right and History*, pp. 50–52.

illustration of this point among others, it is fitting to mention the work of Émile Durkheim, whose academic activity always was inspired by a concern to account for social phenomena as things, to study them from the outside, and to furnish a description of them that was as objective and detached as possible.[100] Parallel with this scientific commitment, concrete questions concerning the society of his time constituted very early on the principal topic of his preoccupations.[101] Indeed, throughout his life he did not deny himself the opportunity to express his opinions on these matters of concern. From this standpoint, it may be tempting to establish a distinction within the overall body of his intellectual output: one may think that there exists a difference in kind between the texts that speak, for example, of happiness and of the conditions for a happy existence – texts that would be connected with a social philosophy – and those that, speaking the language of methodological rules, would belong to the science of societies properly speaking. The first group would be treated as materials pertaining to a sociological history of knowledge. They would be studied with reference to Durkheim's beliefs or else in relation to the historical context. On the other hand, the second group would be taken to be solidly established and still valid in the present as guidelines for ongoing research.

This dichotomy between facts and value judgements does not correspond, however, to Durkheim's actual scientific approach. In his work, the most rigorous methodological rules, and those apparently most independent of the axiological dimension, have meaning only to the extent that they are related to the author's preoccupations with social justice and, more fundamentally, to his anthropology. Although he said he was carefully separating out the theoretical problems from the practical questions,[102] it was not possible for him to achieve an absolute division between the two levels. This situation, which is fostered by his conception of sociology as a useful science[103] and by the ambiguities that result therefrom, is obviously not specific to Émile Durkheim. It affects all analyses of social phenomena that assert such a distinction.[104]

---

[100] Émile Durkheim, *The Rules of Sociological Method*, ed. and intro. Steven Lukes, trans. W. D. Halls (London: Macmillan, 1982), pp. 69–70.

[101] On Durkheim's interest in the issues of his time, see the remarks of Jean-Claude Filloux in his introduction to Émile Durkheim's *La Science sociale et l'action*, 2nd edn (Paris: Presses Universitaires de France, 1987), in particular p. 9.

[102] Durkheim, *The Division of Labor in Society*, p. 33.

[103] Ibid.: 'Although we set out primarily to study reality, it does not follow that we do not wish to improve it; we should judge our researches to have no worth at all if they were to have only a speculative interest.' See also Filloux's introduction to Durkheim's *La Science sociale et l'action*, pp. 6–7.

[104] See Bernstein, *The Restructuring of Social and Political Theory*, pp. 109–10; Charles Taylor's article, 'Neutrality in Political Science', published in his *Philosophy and the Human Sciences*, vol. II of his *Philosophical Papers*, 2 vols. (Cambridge University Press,

LEGITIMACY AND THE VALIDITY OF STATEMENTS

We have seen that the third methodological objection liable to be addressed to the problematic of legitimacy has to do with the imperative to test one's scientific results. The following three arguments can be used in opposition to this objection.

The strictly empirical and positivistic understanding of the relations between governors and governed refuses to make allowance for values. It is therefore condemned to take into consideration only a part of the nature of the field to be explained. This is its first error.

Moreover, just because one recognises the major role the normative dimension plays in politics, that does not prevent one from being able to verify the statements produced about the operation of society. On the contrary, it helps give substance to a credible description of social and political reality. As opposed to studies that are carried out within the confines of the fact/value dichotomy – studies that, in their concern not to take a position, end up shunting aside the deep-seated signification individuals attribute to their ways of thinking and living – the analysis of politics from the standpoint of the problematic of legitimacy, without renouncing the use of the technical methods that are used to verify results, completes them and enlarges them by connecting them up with the dynamic and the real logic of the relationships between rulers and ruled.

Finally, as much from the viewpoint of how to determine the object to be analysed as from that of how to implement some cooperation among several disciplines, this overall approach to political affairs is not an obstacle to the effort to work out satisfactory statements that are capable of verification. Indeed, the choice that consists in explicating the various facets of a temporally and spatially circumscribed situation is not the only path open to the observer. To preach exclusively in favour of empirical studies and to discredit any theoretical perspective that would endeavour to construct a more general conception of political operations is to succumb to the myth of the given and to the illusion that one can gain a privileged access to the heart of the phenomena themselves. In addition, the degree of abstraction with which this more general conception is synonymous does not mean that such a conception is content merely to produce theses that are unverifiable because cut off from reality. Although this overall view does not limit its interest, as field analyses do, to the singularity of reality and to its density, it nevertheless does not have to be identified with a fantasy-filled discourse that has no tie with historical reality.

1985), pp. 89–90, and Alasdair MacIntyre's article, 'Is a Science of Comparative Politics Possible?', in *Against the Self-Images of the Age: Essays on Ideology and Philosophy*, 2nd edn (University of Notre Dame Press, 1984), pp. 275–79.

We have explicated the theoretical and methodological objections that are liable to contest the approach to political legitimacy being formulated here, and we have shown their limits as well as their contradictions. We must now bring out the ways in which these debates and these controversies are set within the history of various societies as well as within the history of the sciences.

3 Modernity, rationality of the social sciences, and legitimacy

The history of modern societies and of the analysis of these societies within the framework of the social sciences has led some people to broach the question of legitimacy in ambiguous terms. It has led them to take away from this question its authentic meaning and to deprive it of the possibility of establishing the conditions for a genuine evaluation of the relationships between governors and governed. This is symptomatic both of the philosophy of the social sciences and of the way modernity has developed and has reflected upon itself historically.

In order to demonstrate this point, it will be necessary first to examine the influence scientism has exerted upon the analysis of social facts. A detour by way of Enlightenment thought will then serve as the occasion for explicating how scientific ideals were reconciled there with values, both in works on history and in the ways people organised themselves and lived in a collectivity. Finally, we shall see that, turning against itself, the project connected with modernity's rationality has contributed to a divorce between the scientific analysis of reality and the normative dimension, a divorce that has mortgaged the future of an approach to legitimacy in terms of the faculty of judgement.

SCIENTISM AND THE ANALYSIS OF SOCIAL AND POLITICAL PHENOMENA

The natural sciences' analysis of reality has profoundly marked the modern study of societies. That analysis has served as a reference point, even a paradigm, for such study. In the wake of the scientific revolution initiated in the seventeenth century, the scientific approach to social facts was going to be built up in very large part by borrowing from the natural sciences their main methodological orientations.

Scientific revolution and physical reality

The advent of the scientific analysis of reality took place within the larger framework of a renunciation of the teleological understanding of nature.

That understanding had determined the conception Antiquity, and in particular Aristotle, had bequeathed to the Middle Ages. With this rejection of an analysis of the real from within – that is to say, on the basis of a principle of development that is internal to beings themselves – the examination of natural phenomena 'as a nexus of relations that could be analysed mathematically' was able to thrive.[1] The changes brought about by the scientific movement of the seventeenth century are symbolised by the destruction of the cosmos and the geometrisation of space. The first aspect of these changes is manifested in the annihilation of the world understood as a finite and well-ordered whole – a world in which the spatial structure embodied a hierarchy of values – and by the substitution, for the latter, of a universe of indefinite proportions. This indefinite universe no longer includes any system of classification that could be established in the name of nature; it is united only by the identity of the laws that regulate its parts. The second aspect marks the replacement of the Aristotelian conception of space by a conception that stems from Euclidian geometry. This replacement leads one to consider the spatial dimension as henceforth structurally 'identical with the real space of the world'.[2]

Once the search for causes pertaining to the essence of things has been abandoned, modern physics is characterised by the will to find laws that explain the movements of a mechanism. Since natural phenomena obey an order demonstrated by the regularity of these laws, the kind of science that is born of this revolution involves a constant pursuit of the mathematisation of nature and a no less systematic bestowal of value upon experience and experimentation.[3] It becomes a matter of bringing to light and of modelling cause-and-effect relations, which are treated as hypothetical in so far as they have not been corroborated by observations.

The goal of scientific analysis is to sort out those necessary relationships that bring out the identity of a succession of events with a series of interdependent episodes that pertain to one and the same logic. Under these conditions, only the process of validation by experience allows one to surmount the difference, assumed by the natural sciences to be absolute, between reality and the subject who examines it. It thus renders possible a reconciliation between these two poles.[4]

---

[1] See Karl-Otto Apel, *Understanding and Explanation: A Transcendental-Pragmatic Perspective*, trans. Georgia Warnke (Cambridge, Mass.: MIT Press, 1984), p. 29.

[2] We are directly inspired here by Alexandre Koyré, whom we quote; see the expanded French version of his Preface to *From the Closed World to the Infinite Universe* (Baltimore, Md.: Johns Hopkins Press, 1968): *Du monde clos à l'univers infini*, reprint edn (Paris: Gallimard, 1990), p. 11.

[3] See Alasdair MacIntyre, *After Virtue: A Study in Moral Theory* (University of Notre Dame, 1984), pp. 80–81.

[4] The reader may refer to Apel, *Understanding and Explanation*, p. 30.

At the early stages of this transformation, laws were invoked as the creation of God, but the new physics unleashed a dynamic that led ineluctably from the notion of a divine architect to that of an idle god (*Dieu fainéant*). It ended with the affirmation that He serves no useful purpose. Testifying to this development are Pierre Simon Laplace's theory of determinism and the anecdote, that, when asked by Napoleon about the role God might play in his system, Laplace is said to have answered that he did not have need of Him.[5]

This upheaval in the order of knowledge – supplanting Aristotle's teleological conception, which closely associates the Is with the Ought – involved a sense of suspicion on the part of scientific thought towards such ideas as value, perfection, harmony, meaning, or end. It ultimately brought with it, as Alexandre Koyré explains, the 'utter devalorization of Being' – the Is – 'the divorce between the world of values and the world of facts'.[6]

From the natural sciences to the social sciences

With the triumph of modern science over the ancient view of the world, the organisation and relations between theoretical forms of knowledge and practical ones were profoundly altered. This new type of explanation of the real was perceived as the best means of understanding phenomena. Also, its employment was not limited to physical reality alone but touched a variety of domains, and observers who made it their goal to analyse people's behaviours took it as their point of reference.[7] The sciences of society reset their analysis of social and political questions on the basis of the scientific study of nature, endeavouring thereby to attain an equivalent rigour.

In the matter of explaining social data, scientism has constituted one of the key elements in the intellectual atmosphere where modern political thought has developed.[8] To mention only two examples where what has been called a moral and political physics has been put into effect,[9] it suffices to cite the cases of Thomas Hobbes and Montesquieu. Each in his own way made it his explicit ambition to break with the classical

---

[5] See Koyré, *From the Closed World to the Infinite Universe*, pp. 273–76. The reader may also consult René Thom's préface to Pierre Simon Laplace, *Essai philosophique sur les probabilités*. Suivi d'extraits de *Mémoires* (Paris: Christian Bourgois, 1986), pp. 26–27.

[6] Koyré, *From the Closed World to the Infinite Universe*, p. 2.

[7] See MacIntyre, *After Virtue*, p. 83.

[8] See Habermas, *On the Logic of the Social Sciences*, p. 1, and 'Knowledge and Human Interests: A General Perspective', the appendix to his *Knowledge and Human Interests*, trans. Jeremy J. Shapiro (Boston, Mass.: Beacon Press, 1971), pp. 302–03.

[9] See Louis Althusser's remarks in *Montesquieu, Rousseau, Marx*, p. 17.

approach to societal problems while relying on recently acquired scientific achievements.

As early as the middle of the seventeenth century, Hobbes constructed a theory that makes the attitudes of individuals the material for a science of man, of society, and of the State. The application of the mathematical method to the political sphere signified in his view the elevation, for the first time, of political knowledge to the status of a branch of rational scientific knowledge. To the extent that a correct understanding of the laws of human nature can exist, it is possible, according to him, to establish definitively the conditions for the organisation of a satisfactory collective life from the point of view of reason.[10]

Hobbes tries to preserve the ancient conception of natural law, which is defined in relation to the end of man, but he dissociates it from the idea of human perfectability. For this conception to have a practical value, he deduces it from the real behaviour of individuals and roots it in the needs of agents. In order to know these needs, one must follow the principles by which one arrives at proofs in the mathematical sciences; these sciences constitute the most rational form of scientific analysis because they are completely cut off from the passions. Indeed, explanations for the true causes of the relationships among individuals are obscured by opinions that originate in the passions.[11] Now, mathematics represents the methodology that allows one to elucidate the most powerful of motives, the one that drives men to act and that sheds light upon that mechanism whose basis is to be found in the fear of death – that is to say, one's desire for self-preservation. While gauging the strength of the bond that still connects Hobbes with the tradition,[12] as well as the limitations and incoherencies present in his use of the modern scientific method,[13] it is therefore important to take cognisance of his effort to make political thought rest upon the advancements of science.

Montesquieu entertains the same design: he builds up a scientific theory of societies while relying upon the scientific revolution that occurred within the study of nature. In order that the relationships between governors and governed and their history might become the object of a science, the explanation of political phenomena has to, in his view, cease to borrow

---

[10] See Thomas Hobbes, *Human Nature, or the Fundamental Elements of Policy* and *De Corpore politico: Or the Elements of Law*, reprint of the 1840 edition (Bristol: Thoemmes Press, 1994), pp. xiii–xiv. The reader may also refer to Leo Strauss's reflections in *The Political Philosophy of Hobbes: Its Basis and its Genesis*, trans. Elsa M. Sinclair, 1st Midway reprint (University of Chicago Press, 1984), pp. 136–38.

[11] Thomas Hobbes, *Leviathan* (Harmondsworth: Penguin, 1987), for example pp. 165–68.

[12] See Strauss, *Natural Right and History*, pp. 166–69.

[13] Strauss, *The Political Philosophy of Hobbes*, in particular pp. 153–54, 166–68.

its logic from a transcendent order. One must rid oneself of any temptation to offer an apologetics, in the style of Pascal, and of the pretensions of a theology and morality whose aspiration is to dictate their laws. It is henceforth a matter of judging from a political point of view, that is to say, in terms of an autonomous domain; the goal of the scientific analysis of this domain is to discover both necessity and rationality while bringing to light its own principles.

In order to carry out this task successfully, Montesquieu renovates the concept of law and distinguishes it from its earlier meaning, that is to say, from the ideas of commandment and end, which pertain to the universe of religion and morality.[14] He sets the concept of law directly in the line of the Newtonian revolution. Defined, in its most generally accepted way, as 'the necessary relations deriving from the nature of things',[15] law is not limited to the physical world alone. Its field of action is extended to encompass 'all beings',[16] and it deals with the topics of politics and history – which assumes that it is possible to draw from human institutions themselves something that would allow one to think their diversity within their unity and their change within a constancy, as happens in the area of nature.[17] In other words, the law does not belong to an ideal order. It maintains an immanent relationship with phenomena. Brought out from the facts through study and comparison, trial and error, law's character is that of a hypothesis at the moment of its discovery. It acquires the status of a principle only once it is verified by the varied and numerous data that have been gathered.[18]

With the exception of direct experimentation, Montesquieu's approach is to adopt an empirical scientific attitude that seeks the rule by which his field of analysis operates. The place he grants to facts, to the collection of as large a number of them as possible, and to their observation so that laws might be extracted therefrom induces one to present him as the genuine founder of modern political science. Indeed, while he shares with Hobbes, and a few others, the project of beginning to reflect upon society in a way that would be in harmony with the new requirements of science, he does not have precisely the same object of analysis. Sworn enemy of the abstractions fostered by his immediate predecessors, Montesquieu reproaches those predecessors for still trying to work out a theory of the essence of societies. For his part, he wishes to construct a science of

---

[14] See Althusser's remarks in *Montesquieu, Rousseau, Marx*, pp. 31–32.

[15] See Montesquieu, *The Spirit of the Laws*, p. 3.

[16] Ibid.: 'All beings have their laws; the divinity has its laws; the material world has its laws; the intelligences superior to man have their laws; the beasts have their laws; man has his laws.'

[17] Ibid., p. 4.   [18] Ibid., p. xliii.

concrete human societies by examining the customs and laws of all the peoples of the world.[19]

Whatever may be the features that contrast one thinker's approach to that of the other, Hobbes and Montesquieu, each in his own way, prefigure and illustrate the impact the natural sciences were going to have on the understanding of human phenomena. The shock wave sent forth went on to accompany the development of the modern way of explaining social and political problems. Even if not everyone rallied immediately to the side of scientism, this approach convincingly became one of modernity's basic components.[20] Little by little, the idea that, in the image of the physical sciences, a valid analysis of people's behaviours must contain an objective external description began to make inroads. In order to implement this mode of analysis, one has to conduct studies that claim to be removed from subjective prejudices and from finalistic considerations. Such analyses consist in bringing disparate information together and in processing that information, in bringing to light the correlations, and in formulating hypotheses, models, and empirically verifiable generalisations. The objective is to discover immanent laws that shed light on the operation of living reality and that offer one an ability to make forecasts.

This obviously does not mean that the influence of scientism has manifested itself in a uniform way or that it unfolds in a homogeneous manner. Between the seventeenth century and today, the approach to social phenomena has changed profoundly. Generating numerous debates, the influence physics has had upon the history of the social sciences has been expressed in a variety of ways, depending upon the discipline in question. This diversity calls forth two sets of remarks.

In the name of a scientism that each day identifies knowledge ever more closely with positive science,[21] the social sciences have, starting especially during the second half of the nineteenth century, progressively been constituted into specialities. Yet, an inequality is apparent in the respective levels of development of these specialities. This is the first point.

---

[19] See Althusser, *Montesquieu, Rousseau, Marx*, pp. 19–20: 'As for theoreticians such as Hobbes, Spinoza, or Grotius, they *propose* the idea of a science of history rather than *working it out*...We might say that their science is as far from Montesquieu's as the speculative physics of a Descartes is from the experimental physics of a Newton. The one directly attains in simple natures or essences the *a priori truth* of all possible physical facts, the other starts from the facts, observing their variations in order to disengage their *laws*.'

[20] See Max Horkheimer's article 'Traditional and Critical Theory', in *Critical Theory: Selected Essays*, trans. Matthew J. O'Connell *et al.* (New York: Continuum, 1986), pp. 188–91.

[21] See Thomas McCarthy, *The Critical Theory of Jürgen Habermas*, 1st paperback edn (Cambridge, Mass.: MIT Press, 1981), p. 41.

Nomological studies forge laws relating to empirical regularities on the basis of tested hypotheses; in this case, certainly, such studies have already gone well beyond the sphere of theoretical descriptions of nature and now reach into the domains of psychology and the economy, sociology and politics. But the concrete results attained in these disciplines remain highly variable. It is in psychology, whether qualified as *social* or not, that the idea of an understanding of human phenomena structurally identical to the physical sciences comes closest to being realised.[22] This idea heads in the same direction – even if still only as a rough sketch – as 'the thesis of unified science'.[23] On the other hand, economic research, when it does not pertain to econometrics, complies with the model of an analytic normative science, which presupposes hypothetical maxims for action.[24] For their part, most sociological works remain within a functionalist framework and propose a theory of action that cannot be reconstructed according to an intentional or motivational model of activities.[25] Finally, in the political field a large proportion of what is produced in the academic world is historical in character and makes no claim to be establishing theses of a general order.

In addition, echoing the problematic results and the doubts inherent in a scientific practice that endeavours to apply the model of nature to an object that is resistant thereto, scientism is far from inspiring a consensus about the goals and the ambitions that are to be attained. Between the various possible directions for work to proceed, scholastic debates within each discipline of the social sciences are as frequent as they are feisty. Thus, some think that the basic objective is to devote one's time to refining one's data-gathering techniques and to confine oneself to making empirical generalisations of limited import. In contrast to this, others affirm that only a very elaborate effort at theorisation will allow one to shed adequate light upon the phenomena. Finally, still others recommend a research path that constitutes a compromise between the above-mentioned two tendencies.[26] Also illustrative of the discussions that accompany scientism's influence upon the study of social facts, various classifications of the competing conceptions of science in the social domain have been proposed. Raymond Boudon is the author of one of these proposals. According to him, there are three conceptions of

---

[22] See, in particular, Serge Moscovici, *Psychologie des minorités actives* (Paris: Presses Universitaires de France, 1982), p. 17.

[23] See Apel, *Understanding and Explanation*, pp. 19–20, as well as the introduction to this book by his translator, Georgia Warnke, pp. vii–ix.

[24] Amartya Sen, *On Ethics and Economics* (Oxford: Basil Blackwell, 1987), pp. 10–15.

[25] Apel, *Understanding and Explanation*, pp. 224–27.

[26] See Bernstein, *The Restructuring of Social and Political Theory*, p. 43.

science: the empiricist, nomological, and formal or hypothetical-deductive programmes.[27]

Despite the divergencies separating these points of view, all agree on an approach to social facts that is set upon fostering a type of explanation whose terms are determined in the main by the analysis of nature.[28] In various forms and according to the different specialities, schools of thought, and extrascientific context within which the examination of the phenomena of life in society is carried out and develops, the mode of understanding that comes from the study of the physical world forcefully sets its mark upon the explanatory categories of the social sciences. This mode of understanding engenders splits that play a part in constituting the principal currents of thought. From this perspective, the degree of development and credibility of the social sciences is to be measured in terms of the methodological choices made when describing natural facts. When, compared to these choices, the social sciences are seen to be lacking in rigour or missing a well-determined object, these failings are presented, in the best of cases, as sins of youth that can be resolved with the onset of a greater maturity and, in the worst of cases, as the sign of their pseudoscientific status.

In adopting the mode of explanation that is capable of accounting for physical phenomena, the social sciences, we see, run the risk of being cast to the periphery of legitimate scientific knowledge. They expose themselves to the risk of seeming like the weak link in the chain of knowledge and of provoking thinly veiled expressions of condescension from the hard sciences.

Although the scientistic approach to human facts is set within an intellectual and historical process that ends up, starting basically in the nineteenth century, posing the question of legitimacy in extremely problematic terms, the 'scientisation of politics'[29] does not initially provide any room for a divorce between scientific rationality and the dimension of values. There exists what could be called a cohabitation between these two levels of study of reality. Indeed, while it is undeniable that the concern with being scientific that was worked out by the sciences of nature imposes upon researchers the idea that it is necessary to examine societal phenomena without taking a position, it no less remains the case that no clear rift between scientific description and the axiological plane was, at this initial stage, established. In a variety of forms and to varying degrees depending upon authors and disciplines, these new fields of reflection could not, at the outset, entirely ignore God and morality. They made

[27] Boudon, *Theories of Social Change*, pp. 223–26.
[28] Bernstein, *The Restructuring of Social and Political Theory*, pp. 42–43, 51.
[29] See McCarthy, *The Critical Theory of Jürgen Habermas*, p. 1.

some allowance for one or the other of these two elements, if not for both of them.

In this regard, although thinkers such as Hobbes and Montesquieu inaugurate this tendency to align the theory of society upon the logic of the sciences of nature, their approach does not avoid a real ambiguity. Even if Hobbes's break with religious thinking is hardly debatable,[30] since he affirms that there is no rational knowledge of natural religion[31] and that positive beliefs concerning the divine have to be judged or criticised in terms of the services they render to the State,[32] his approach to the political is not purely scientific: it remains dependent upon morality. Leo Strauss brings out, moreover, the fact that morality is the source for Hobbes's interest in science.[33]

As for Montesquieu, despite the fact that the majority of his examples head in the direction of eliminating the ambitions theology and morality have to dictate their laws, a basic hesitation still exists in his writings. This hesitation has to do with the disappearance of the scientific law behind the commandment-law.[34] The latter is not only the expression of religious and moral values[35] but also corresponds to a very specific political organisation of the world, that of a shaken world that Montesquieu wishes to set back on its foundations.[36]

In other words, although the first steps in the modern analysis of the life of societies are set within the perspective of the ideal of objectivity, the ties with the prior conception are not entirely severed: the contrast between the descriptive and prescriptive levels is not defined in absolute terms. While participating all along in the process of rationalisation and critical distancing that characterises both the development of the sciences of society and the history of modernity, the beginnings of scientism in the study of social and political phenomena do not produce an irremediable break between scientific rationality and moral judgements.

SCIENCE, REASON, AND POLITICS IN THE PROJECT OF THE ENLIGHTENMENT

The rupture between scientific logic and the possibility of a reasonable, *de jure* foundation of human and political history does not occur within the framework of the Enlightenment. On the contrary, the combat for

---

[30] This, despite his denials of the accusations of atheism launched against him.
[31] See Strauss, *The Political Philosophy of Hobbes*, pp. 76–78.
[32] Ibid., pp. 74–75.
[33] Ibid., pp. 129–30, 169–70, and, by the same author, *Natural Right and History*, p. 179.
[34] See Althusser, *Montesquieu, Rousseau, Marx*, p. 39.
[35] Montesquieu, *The Spirit of the Laws*, pp. 4–5.
[36] Althusser, *Montesquieu, Rousseau, Marx*, pp. 40–42.

science goes hand in hand with the struggle for moral progress and for progress in the life of society. Some of the key components of the thematic of the Enlightenment go to account for a convergence that takes place between the scientific point of view and the viewpoint of practical reason. In this regard, Condorcet's reflections are emblematic.

Science and practical reason in the movement of the Enlightenment

The Enlightenment does not constitute a homogeneous world view. The authors and writings that belong to this moment in thought do not form some kind of monolithic whole lacking all diversity. On the contrary, the Enlightenment spirit does not rule out certain real differences in thinking. Beyond the differences engendered by the disparity in national situations,[37] the thinkers in question do not always agree among themselves.[38] Nuanced and sometimes contradictory positions can even exist side by side within one and the same author's work.

Thus, in opposition to an already well-established tendency within the Enlightenment, Rousseau was not inclined to trust in history and progress. More willing than other Enlightenment thinkers to linger over the vices of civilisation rather than over its benefits, he treats humanity's intellectual and technological ascension as equivalent to the Fall spoken of in Genesis. He reduces this ascension to a process that is literally a movement of dislocation, one in which each leap forward corresponds to an increase in depravity.[39] At the moment in his work when there is a dawning awareness of the importance of the historical dimension and of his own connection with the era history is traversing, he is tempted to seek his salvation, not in and through history but outside it, in a contempt for the constraint it imposes, which is thenceforth nevertheless inevitable. From this standpoint, Rousseau becomes Jean-Jacques, the guide for 'beautiful souls' (Hegel) who find frightening the ways of the world and who pursue happiness with the inward conviction of their solitary innocence.

There nevertheless exists another orientation in his work, complementary to the previous one, that connects Rousseau to the project of the Enlightenment. Indeed, insisting all the while upon the fact that progress has negative consequences, he recognises that the return to the state of

---

[37] See Yvon Belaval, 'Le siècle des Lumières', in Brice Parain (ed.), *Histoire de la philosophie*, 3 vols. (Paris Gallimard, 1973), vol. II, *De la Renaissance à la révolution kantienne*, p. 601.

[38] See the remarks of Jean Deprun, 'Philosophies et problématique des Lumières', in ibid., pp. 673–74.

[39] Jean-Jacques Rousseau, *Discourse On the Sciences and the Arts*, in *The Collected Writings of Rousseau*, vol. II, p. 7–8.

nature is not within the grasp of those societies that have wandered away from it. Although, under the present circumstances, the arts and sciences favour and even accelerate the disintegration of social harmony, no principle says that they cannot be used for better ends. They must simply be placed in the service of virtue.[40]

It is through the perfecting of culture, therefore through a deeper denaturation, that one can rediscover a life lived in accordance with the natural universe. This second nature, the fruit of human talent, is not defined as an instinctive balance but is lit up by rationality and sustained by moral sentiment, something the primitive brute does not know about. Rousseau's historical pessimism is counterbalanced by his anthropological optimism, within whose framework man is naturally good. From this perspective, it is possible, according to him, to educate the individual in order that the individual might acquire enough reason to live in conformity with the exigencies of nature.

Parallel to this elimination of the negative aspects of social and political structures, a chance exists – an infinitesimal one, certainly, and much too random a one for him to invoke some sort of mechanical progress or a kind of grace that would save people – to arrive at a relatively happy life.[41] Even if it is only a possibility, the opposition between the natural and cultural planes may be resolved in a progressive movement.

The example of Jean-Jacques Rousseau illustrates rather well the precautions that are to be taken when one endeavours to interpret the Enlightenment. That having been said, let us now mention the principal elements that can account for a convergence between the scientific point of view and that of practical reason within the problematic of the Enlightenment.

In 1784, Immanuel Kant proposed a definition of the Enlightenment. It is probably one of the most satisfying definitions one might ever encounter:

Enlightenment is man's emergence from his self-imposed immaturity. Immaturity is the inability to use one's understanding without guidance of another. This immaturity is *self-imposed* when its cause lies not in lack of understanding, but in lack of resolve and courage to use it without guidance from another. *Sapere Aude!* 'Have courage to use your own understanding!' – that is the motto of enlightenment.[42]

---

[40] Ibid., pp. 12, 21–22.

[41] See Jean Starobinski, *Jean-Jacques Rousseau: Transparency and Obstruction*, trans. Arthur Goldhammer (University of Chicago Press, 1988), p. 302.

[42] Immanuel Kant, 'An Answer to the Question: What is Enlightenment?' in *Perpetual Peace and Other Essays on Politics, History, and Morals*, trans. and intro. Ted Humphrey (Indianapolis, Ind.: Hackett, 1983), p. 41.

In the wake of Kant, the Enlightenment tried to work towards the emancipation of individuals, put an end to the reign of darkness, and improve the conditions of people's existence. From that perspective, we may say that this renovated form of thinking devoted itself to forging the instruments of its struggle and to translating its ideas into reality. Intellectual positions were transformed into actions, ones that remained subordinate to general principles judged according to theoretical standards. That is to say, there perhaps was never a more complete harmony between ideas and life than during the eighteenth century, and this configuration gives to the culture of the Enlightenment its identity and its force.[43]

It is therefore not surprising to note the essential role assigned to the sciences in the process of the liberation of persons. Making allowance for the fact that their alienation is said to originate in the weight of false knowledge, superstitions, and individuals' opacity to themselves and to what is real, the scientific enterprise takes on a critical role as part of the emancipatory movement. For that movement to become possible, one has to produce and to increase the sum of sure scientific knowledge and to disseminate such knowledge to the greatest number. To put it in other terms: one must gain access to a proper understanding of phenomena.

This project enlivens and guides the logic of the Enlightenment, where the love of knowledge is indissociable from the concrete benefits knowledge brings along with it. The Enlightenment project therefore concerns nature as much as society. Just as the physical sciences contribute to the liberation of individuals from erroneous conceptions about the reality of nature, the scientific analysis of society improves the condition of individuals by providing them with certain statements about the social and political universe.

Nevertheless, the Enlightenment gives primacy to social and political questions. There are several reasons for this priority. First of all, in the eighteenth century, investigations into nature were already sufficiently advanced that one merely had to continue along in the footsteps of Newton and his revolution. Second, a rational approach to social facts had just been born. Moreover, as far as the Enlightenment philosopher was concerned,[44] questions relating to society merited special attention. In borrowing from physics its methods and in applying these methods to the elucidation of social and political phenomena, one was made

---

[43] See Ernst Cassirer, *The Myth of the State* (New Haven, Conn.: Yale University Press, 1946), pp. 177, 179.

[44] During the Enlightenment, as Belaval emphasises in 'Le siècle des Lumières', *Histoire de la philosophie*, vol. II, p. 602, the philosopher became known more and more as an honest, upright man as well as a man of letters.

aware of their full meaning and therefore of the practical dimension they implied.

The Enlightenment's ideas about society call for the denunciation of institutions that act as the objective allies of dogmatism and superstition and that hamper the spread of the spirit of rationality. In this context, the politicisation of scientific activity and the contestation of the traditional organisation of life in society, which had previously remained marginal in the theological controversies raised by the new science of natural facts, began to take on a strategic importance. The fight for knowledge thenceforth went hand in hand with the struggle for a new society, one that would permit an adjustment to scientific ideals and principles.

This is to say that the operation of critical unveiling characteristic of the conception of science defended by the Enlightenment manifests itself in the lack of a clear-cut division between the theoretical and practical levels and rests upon an idea of reason that remains within a system of values. This fundamental factor makes it possible to describe and to explain the convergence that exists, within the thematic of the Enlightenment, between the scientific analysis of social phenomena and morality.

In the framework of the Enlightenment, reason extends its reach to theoretical and practical questions. Stemming from no other authority but its very own, it takes a stand not only on problems that concern pure knowledge but also on those that until then pertained to the domain of faith or strict obedience. Reason is not a tool of study that remains indifferent to values. On the contrary, reason is a way of knowing the real that supposes a commitment in terms of axiological choices. From this point of view, we can say that because science is the expression of reason and its weapon, a connection exists between the scientific approach to social and political phenomena and morality, as well as between the level of understanding social facts and that of practice.

On the one hand, scientific rationality plays a guiding role in theoretical analyses of reality. As the application of a method that endeavours to produce a true scientific knowledge of the world, it rests upon experience, since knowledge of the real also passes by way of the accumulation of facts. Scientific study makes use of reason as a methodological means for formulating valid statements and for gaining access, in this way, to a satisfactory conception of phenomena. But on the other hand, and in a way that is indissociable from this first feature, scientific rationality is not to be reduced to its use in the field of theory. Its area of intervention is vaster than a simple description of the way society operates, one that would be void of all value judgements. Opposing ignorance and dogmatism, Enlightenment rationalism took on a militant tone. Enlightenment thinkers wanted the truths expressed about social and political problems to be translated into reality. The idea of reason their scientific view set forth also proposed to instruct individuals in their actions and in their daily life. Just as it is possible to have a rational knowledge of facts, so there exists a knowledge of values that possesses the properties of science, and it is in its name that the Enlightenment launched its calls for change.

To know the truth is therefore both to know and to want what is good. From this point of view, morality and its progress within history prove to be objects of science, and this is so in two inseparable ways. First, this is because science itself participates in the development of good values. The scientific analysis of the phenomena of society, going further than the mere pleasure of knowledge, helps people to liberate themselves from alienation. In setting itself within a dynamic where the conditions of people's existence may be improved, it helps the spirit of justice, whence it arises, to win out – that is to say, to become institutionalised in a life system.[45] Next, this is also because morality is deduced from the conception of reason that underlies Enlightenment science. It is not a set of subjective maxims. It has a rational foundation: that of science. From this perspective, morality is liable to be achieved gradually and is tied to the fulfilment of reason through scientific labour.

It is while keeping these notions in mind that it is appropriate to offer an interpretation of the Enlightenment idea of progress. According to this idea, there exists a cumulative meaning to the unfolding of history, and that meaning takes the form not of Marxist or Hegelian necessity but of a faith in the future that merges with the rational powers of science. This model for an ascending continuity of history also contains the idea that one must share this desirable development with other nations. The idea of dissemination [*diffusion*] expresses the will to achieve a kind of freedom to which all nations have a right. It is in these terms that the French Revolution, in a near-mystical projection of the event it represents, was to endeavour to export its message beyond its borders while underscoring its universal import.[46]

Based on a unified – that is to say, both theoretical and practical – conception of reason, the scientific method of the Enlightenment did not assert any kind of neutrality in relation to values. On the contrary, to know

[45] See McCarthy, *The Critical Theory of Jürgen Habermas*, pp. 5–6.
[46] See Jean Starobinski, *1789: The Emblems of Reason*, trans. Barbara Bray (Charlottesville: University Press of Virginia, 1982), p. 44: 'The French themselves believed that in overthrowing abuse and privilege, in destroying the great citadel of despotism that had overshadowed Paris, and in coming together in the radiance of universal benevolence, they were bestowing on the world a new sun and source of light. As Tocqueville wrote, "No one doubted that the fate of mankind was involved in what was about to be done". This feeling found echoes abroad: "It seems to me", wrote Fichte in 1793, "that the French Revolution affects the whole human race."'

is to commit oneself, to become engaged, to participate in the process of emancipation. Science and morality join together and cooperate in the notion of reason.

Theoretical and practical knowledge in Condorcet

Condorcet's thought illustrates in an exemplary manner the convergence between the scientific point of view and that of values. His *Sketch for a Historical Picture of the Progress of the Human Mind* testifies to this.[47] Although it was written in 1793, under the pressure of dramatic events and ongoing threats, and completed shortly before his death in March 1794, this work is far from merely occasional.[48] It is the fruit of a slow maturation of the author's ideas on questions he held close to his heart, as is attested to by the powerful burst of inspiration that runs through this text.

In the *Sketch*, the model for rational knowledge is furnished by the mathematical sciences of nature. After having brought out the successive stages of development through which human history has passed since its origins, Condorcet arrives at the examination of the modern period, which concerns, according to his classification, the eighth and especially the ninth stage. He then presents the scientific study of natural phenomena as the paradigm for knowledge in general.[49] Believing that observation, experimentation, and calculation are the three tools that have allowed physics to discover the secrets of nature, he states that science has established, through the systematic use of these tools, a method that has elevated knowledge of reality above the opinionated debates of scholastic philosophy.

Following this description of the revolution that has occurred in the explication of natural phenomena, Condorcet places the accent on the effects this revolution has had on the sciences as a whole. He shows how the employment of the methodological tools of physics has been extended into various other disciplines.[50] After chemistry, botany, and anatomy, the new rules soon began to exert an influence upon the arts as well as upon moral and political studies. Contributing to a dynamic of progress wherein reflections in the abstract can bring about the most concrete achievements and vice versa – and where the various sciences

[47] Condorcet, *Sketch for a Historical Picture of the Progress of the Human Mind*, trans. June Barraclough, reprint edn (Westport, Conn.: Hyperion Press, 1979).
[48] See Alain Pons's introduction to Condorcet's *Esquisse d'un tableau historique des progrès de l'esprit humain. Suivi de Fragment sur l'Atlantide* (Paris: Flammarion, 1988), pp. 21–26.
[49] Condorcet, *Sketch for a Historical Picture of the Progress of the Human Mind*, in particular pp. 148–49.
[50] Ibid., p. 164.

do not cease to teach one another – this movement whereby the method-ological choices of physics are disseminated to other disciplines ends up touching an ever-greater number of individuals. In short, rational knowl-edge enlivens and guides the theoretical sciences as much as the practical ones.

What is striking in this relationship that unites science with the question of values is that Condorcet conceives the development of humankind on the model of modern scientific history and its propagation – that is to say, as a process of rationalisation that allies the characteristics of science, and the benefits science brings, with what is historically desirable. To put it in other terms: the good and its progressive fulfilment can be known scientifically because they are the expression of science, which is itself representative of reason. This process is manifested in four ways.

First, from the scientific point of view Condorcet identifies the idea of perfection with a cumulative dynamic. This movement has a direction that is not teleologically oriented in advance (as had been the case among the Ancients and especially in Aristotle) and that also is not bounded.[51]

Second, speaking of progress as a mechanism that is tied to the faculty of learning, Condorcet affirms that, in the face of ignorance in all its guises, the sciences have an educational function and an educational re-sponsibility; they have a duty to take on the task of public instruction. The sciences have to act in such a way that the principles that serve at once as their basis and as their ideals might be able to become, via train-ing procedures, guides for the maximum number of individuals, so that these individuals might be capable of reaching maturity and attaining autonomy.

Third, Condorcet makes the idea of the Enlightenment into a bridge between the scientific notion of progress and the conviction that the sciences contribute to human beings' moral perfection. In the battle of reason against Authority – which is represented, quite specifically, by the reactionary Church – he expects scientific rationality to be capable of offering satisfactory answers to problems of a normative order. Errors made in relation to values are to be explained by the existence of mis-leading philosophies, which themselves rest upon erroneous conceptions of natural phenomena. In contrast, the production of truth in the do-main of practice flows from physical truths.[52] Condorcet maintains the thesis that the moral sciences can attain a level of exactitude and relia-bility equivalent to that of the sciences of nature. Moreover, by being in contact with them, the ethical feelings and judgements of individuals will find themselves greatly improved.

[51] Ibid., pp. 4–5.   [52] Ibid., p. 163.

Fourth, the development of the scientific spirit, its spread [*diffusion*] from the world of research to the universe of practice, and, finally, the possibility people are offered to define themselves in a rational manner are so many factors that, participating in one and the same movement, ultimately entail an improvement in the forms of collective life. And as it happens, these forms come to institutionalise, in political terms, the advances [*les progrès*] made by individuals.[53]

Because the idea of reason is not divided, because it applies as much to the natural sciences as to human nature – between which, therefore, no fundamental difference exists – it proves to be the case that the facts of chemistry, for example, like those having to do with moral and political questions, are mathematisable. One can attain a rational knowledge of them. Thus, the view of science Condorcet is evoking is not limited to an explication of the role norms play in the socialisation of individuals, to cite just this one case. It also expresses judgements. To produce these true statements in the field of practice is also to verify the conformity of values to reason, to distinguish what is desirable from what is not desirable. In the absence of a separation between the analyses of morality and those of science, it is possible to place scientific progress within the perspective of an overall effort to attain perfection – that is to say, of a sense of history – one that, via a process of rationalisation, constitutes the progressive fulfilment of truth and of the good.

To the extent that the unfolding of historical phenomena reveals a growing understanding and realisation of physical and human natural elements, one must not be surprised to see that Condorcet deems it essential that the universal dimension of this movement can be imparted to all societies. Indeed, it becomes a matter of ridding the surface of the earth of the reign of false consciousness, of working for the triumph of science and justice over ignorance and tyranny. Condorcet goes even further: he specifies that the European model of civilisation defended by Enlightenment thinkers and identified with scientific, moral, and political progress expresses principles to which other nations, without yet knowing it, aspire. It is of great import, therefore, to enlighten them about these principles.

It nevertheless remains the case that, despite this beautifully constructed edifice, the thesis of the unity of reason, of the unity of physical and human reality, began to disintegrate starting in the nineteenth century. It is within the context of an exacerbated form of modernity that the objections formulated against the thematic of legitimacy must henceforth be understood.

---

[53] Ibid., pp. 192–93.

RADICALISM OF MODERNITY, SOCIAL SCIENCES, AND LEGITIMACY

The convergence between scientific analysis and the practical dimension, which is at the centre of the Enlightenment project, began to be denounced in the nineteenth century. This conflict generated an ambiguous conception of legitimacy. In order to explain the process that casts doubt upon the reality of a hierarchy of values and the existence of criteria for judgement that are grounded in reason, it is appropriate to develop the following argument. At the level of the evolution of societies, as well as on the plane of the history of the social sciences that accompanies this evolution, the spread of radicalised, supposedly absolute Enlightenment principles provokes a crisis of confidence. It is then that one witnesses a reversal that affects the founding ideals of modernity.

This mechanism leads to a rejection of the tie between science and the domain of the moral and political good as well as, from a more general point of view, to a disenchanted view of the world. This disenchanted world view manifests itself in three ways that have to do with the phenomena of universalisation, emancipation, and rationalisation. Although these three phenomena are indissociable, here they will be examined separately.

Spread of Enlightenment universalism and conflicts between nations

Our analysis of the relationships between scientific activity and the dimension of values in the project of the Enlightenment has shown that the Enlightenment struggled to set up a model whose validity would be applicable to all nations. The type of individual and collective life the Enlightenment was calling for was supposed to be situated in the higher phase of culture. Its standard of measurement was the degree of perfection human communities had attained.

All peoples aspire to an ideal of truth and freedom. It is therefore up to the most advanced ones among them to see to it that those who are the least advanced evolve in the right direction. The extension of the Enlightenment to different societies is identified with the propagation of something of authentic benefit. Now, this ambition to embody the meaning of the world and to read in the adoption of these principles by all individuals and countries the indubitable sign of progress was going to provoke, as it grew, a reversal of perspective: with the spread of Enlightenment values, the dynamic of universalisation was turned upside down and culminated in the affirmation that there are a diversity of cultures and a plurality of viewpoints. This phenomenon took place via a process that includes two complementary aspects: in parallel with the expansion of the area of enlightened civilisation, which wishes to impose a certain line of conduct in the name of reason, the ideals of the Enlightenment became a weapon that was used, according to a timetable and under forms that vary, to claim the right to singularity and to particularity. Two examples allow us to explicate this mechanism. The first concerns the European model's relations with non-European societies. The second has to do with the German historical school.

The way in which the universalism of the Enlightenment influenced the modern West's relations with non-European societies has engendered a twofold movement. On the one hand, the universalism of the Enlightenment contributed to the development of Europe's feeling of superiority in relation to the rest of the world as well as to the enterprise of colonisation. The notion of progress born of the Enlightenment served, in a more or less hypocritical fashion, to justify campaigns of conquest carried out at the expense of peoples deemed backward. The Westerners' aggressive altruism destroyed these peoples' own organisational structures and re-settled them by force in a way of life about which they had everything to learn in order to survive, after having become strangers to themselves.[54] Moreover, the cumulative view of history defended by the philosophers of the Enlightenment broadly favoured the appearance of various evo-lutionist theories over the course of the nineteenth century.[55] From this perspective, we may note, the most progressive thinkers, those who were anxious to break away from evolutionism, did not quite succeed in escap-ing from it entirely. The case of Marcel Mauss as well as that of Émile Durkheim testify to this. Mauss did not really rise up against colonisa-tion, which had been carried out in the name of progress.[56] Durkheim, one of the severest critics of an evolutionist positivist sociology, did not break completely with its theses.[57]

But on the other hand, in parallel with this feeling of superiority that, transmitted via imperialism and neocolonialism, still today profoundly determines people's minds and practices, the message of the Enlighten-ment also leads to the recognition that cultures distinct from the European model also have a right to existence. From this point of view, the European model is perceived as being one anthropological type among others, under

---

[54] See, in particular, the remarks of Georges Balandier, *Political Anthropology* (New York: Pantheon Books, 1970), pp. 159–64.

[55] See Habermas, *The Theory of Communicative Action*, vol. I, pp. 151–53.

[56] See Marcel Mauss, 'L'ethnographie en France et à l'étranger', in *Œuvres*, vol. III, pp. 432–33.

[57] See Émile Durkheim, 'La science positive de la morale en Allemagne', in *Textes*, 3 vols. (Paris: Minuit, 1975), vol. I, *Éléments d'une théorie sociale*, pp. 336–37. See also S. N. Eisenstadt's comments in *Tradition, Change and Modernity* (New York: John Wiley & Sons, 1973), p. 8.

the same heading as the Chinese, Russian, or Indian civilisations. And it does not benefit from any privileged position that would allow it to impose with complete impunity, under the pretext of embodying the true and the good, its system of values upon the peoples with which it finds itself confronted. Now, if this tendency to take into account different forms of human community results from the Enlightenment phenomenon of universalisation, it is because, wanting to extend the realisation of rationalist principles to various other societies, a moment arrived when the refusal to recognise the specificity of non-Western societies, without ever disappearing completely, began to be accompanied by a reversal of the previous situation. In faithful loyalty to the ideals of the Enlightenment, notably those of freedom and respect for individuals, a feeling developed that one has to make allowance for the singularity of indigenous cultures. This change introduced a readjustment into the European civilisation's relationships with societies that were distinct from it. In this readjustment, the legitimate plurality of types of social organisations was underscored. The question was raised of a hierarchy among the systems of values different cultures represent, and it led some to take a stand against analysing societies upon a scale, at whose summit would be found modern Western society.[58]

This reversal of perspective has partially broken the tie that, in the Enlightenment project, had connected scientific activity with the propagation of a set of moral and political norms. From the absence of a division between theory and practice, one has proceeded to the methodological imperative of neutrality, which is the new credo of science in matters dealing with the study of social phenomena.

A product of the tension that exists between the two paths issuing from the Enlightenment – one not doubting in the superiority of European culture and the other wishing to do justice to the diversity of cultures – this credo endeavours to reconcile the pluralism of civilisations with the concern to attain knowledge. It tries to embody faith in scientific knowledge while at the same time renouncing the moral ambitions through which science had its prolongation into the Enlightenment era. It thus opens the path towards relativism. In order to understand in what way this danger took shape in the methodological reflections of Max Weber, it is important first to analyse how German nationalism is in part a product of the Enlightenment and how the German historical school's setting within Enlightenment universalism leads to the affirmation that there are differing points of view on the world.

---

[58] See, for example, Émile Durkheim, 'Une confrontation entre bergsonisme et sociologisme: le progrès moral et la dynamique sociale', in *Textes*, vol. I, p. 67.

Analysing the context in which German nationalism was born in the early eighteen hundreds, Friedrich Meinecke points out that such nationalism is in the first place the consequence of the deep impression left by Enlightenment principles, of the tremendous renewal of energy these principles brought about, as well as of the wilful refusal to submit to the domination of a foreign power – as it happens, France – which no obstacle seemed capable of stopping.[59] It is incontestable that the development of the German national idea resulted in particular from the ideals of the Enlightenment and from their concrete dissemination within the European politics of the time. These ideals contributed to the crystallisation of national sentiment within the Germanic universe. Thus, the values of freedom and self-determination were, for example, tools that allowed the concept of the nation to be broached in programmatic terms. The French Revolution showed that, whatever the disagreements it might engender, the achievement of these values not only is possible but also gives rise to a vitality and to a fervour monarchical regimes are incapable of arousing. In addition, the expansionist dynamic of revolutionary and Napoleonic France, which presented itself as the holder and the defender of the truth of these principles, gave Germany an enemy. Germany became convinced that it would be able to rid itself of this enemy only by raising itself to its enemy's level of power, through reforms and the adoption of some of the traits of modern politics.[60] In other words, the propagation of Enlightenment ideals helped the Germans to make it their ambition to construct an entity within which the unity of the people and of the State would become real and within which self-affirmation would be expressive of the now sovereign nation.

Nevertheless, some other factors were also at work. For example, the fact that Germany had not become fully conscious of itself within the framework of a preexisting political organisation oriented the process of consolidation of the national idea towards an integral nationalism.[61] The constitution of France's collective identity was basically already established in the nineteenth century on the domestic level,[62] as well as on the foreign one, where its uncontested international recognition did not lead anyone to doubt its right to exist. Things were going to proceed otherwise

---

[59] Friedrich Meinecke, *The Age of German Liberation, 1795–1815*, trans. Peter Paret and Helmut Fischer (Berkeley: University of California Press, 1977), pp. 32–33.

[60] Ibid. The reader may refer in particular to chapter 4, which is devoted to the intellectuals and statesmen who took a stand in favour of the reforms, pp. 44–68.

[61] We borrow this expression from Jürgen Habermas, *The New Conservatism: Cultural Criticism and the Historians' Debate* (Cambridge, Mass.: MIT Press, 1989), p. 255, translation altered.

[62] See Bertrand Badie and Pierre Birnbaum, *Sociology of the State*, trans. Arthur Goldhammer (University of Chicago Press, 1983), pp. 105–13.

in Germany. During this era, the German claim to nationhood was still very fragile. Domestically as well as internationally, it developed without attaining a balance between, on the one hand, the universalist axiological orientations of the *Rechtstaat* [*l'État de droit*] and of democracy and, on the other, those particularisms in terms of which national consciousness was defined. At the same stroke, nationalism in Germany achieved national unity to the detriment of the ideals of freedom – especially to the detriment of those ideals that concern individuals (which the bourgeoisie had erected into rights) – and identified distrust of the foreigner with love of country.

In order to ensure unification in a brief period of time, the Prussian State was seen as the trump card of the German world.[63] It could help Germany overcome the provincialism of its different regions and the hostility of the international environment. To the extent that the liberals were ready to compromise on their demands for democratic reforms,[64] or else did not succeed in imposing them upon Prussia,[65] the construction of a collective consciousness, in merging the idea of nation into the statist myth represented by Prussian authoritarian structures, expressed itself through a willingness to peg civil society upon the interests of the State. This pegging of civil society upon statist interests dooms civil society to oblivion.[66]

Political modernisation was limited to the adoption of bureaucratic rationality, and such rationality was treated as being one with the State.[67] It ruled out an institutionalisation of democratic values, which would have been expressed specifically in the sovereignty of a people comprised of citizens who are by right equal. It led to a situation in which the State was everything and in which any dissensions were lived as conflicts and confrontations without ever being tackled in terms of oppositions that could be resolved via legal mediation. This is how things went, as much on the domestic level – since disagreements with political authorities tended to be perceived as acts of disloyalty and treason[68] – as on the foreign one. Apropos of the latter, attitudes of acrimony, resentment, and aggressiveness (born of people's impression that they were not being understood and recognised abroad) were added on top of the fact that the constitution of a national consciousness thus reduced to the omnipotence of the State implied that the conflictual character of Germany's relations with

---

[63] See Friedrich Meinecke, *Cosmopolitanism and the National State*, trans. Robert B. Kimber (Princeton University Press, 1970), for example pp. 234–35, 250–51.

[64] Meinecke, *The Age of German Liberation, 1795–1815*, pp. 32–33.

[65] Meinecke, *Cosmopolitanism and the National State*, pp. 251, 263, 269–70, 317.

[66] See Ralf Dahrendorf, *Society and Democracy in Germany*, trans. by the author (New York: Norton & Company, 1979), p. 199.

[67] See Badie and Birnbaum, *Sociology of the State*, pp. 116–19.

[68] See, in particular, Dahrendorf, *Society and Democracy in Germany*, pp. 198–99.

the rest of Europe would be underscored. Within this context, the notions of collective identity and individuality, when assimilated into statist institutions, gave way to a new view of history. That view 'conceded to the State the right of inner self-determination, of free movement according to its own law'.[69] In short, this approach to nationhood left the door open to a power politics.

The nineteenth-century German historical school contributed to the development of Enlightenment universalism. It participated in the movement that culminated in the affirmation of different national points of view, in and on the world, this affirmation taking on a distinctive slant in the context of German reality. Indeed, this slant has two sides to it.

On the one hand, the historical school was born in Germany by rejecting in the same gesture the doctrines of natural right (to which Enlightenment thinkers granted great importance) and the upheavals these doctrines brought with them (such as the French Revolution). In conferring a central place upon one's traditions, this school refused to endorse that very fracture in favour of which Enlightenment thinkers were militating. It rejected the break between the present and the past as immediately lived. It wanted individuals and peoples to find their way with the aid of a reflective reappropriation of their roots, knowledge of history serving here as the intermediary. For this school, the point was to inscribe the life of individuals and of societies within the unfolding of a set of traditional principles and practices to which they belong and that belong to them.

But on the other hand, it was apparent that, in proceeding in this way, the German historical school was itself getting involved in the process, initiated by the ideals of the Enlightenment, whereby the German nation constructed its own self-consciousness.[70] Because its view was that people's anchorage in a historically sanctioned community of values allowed them to think and to act in a manner suitable to their time, it contributed to the constitution of national feeling, to individuals' identification with the collectivity. The historical school served to prolong and to radicalise, in the particular context of Germany, the ideas of the Enlightenment, while overturning their universalism. By placing the accent on the fundamentally historical character of different aspects of the lives of individuals and of societies, in this regard it participated in the development of a historicist conception of reality, which took the form of an irrationalist and relativistic approach to phenomena.[71]

Thus, in emphasising the importance of one's rootedness in history, in affirming history's primordial influence upon how the thoughts, choices,

[69] Consult Meinecke, *Machiavellism: The Doctrine of Raison d'État and its Place in Modern History*, pp. 393–94.
[70] See the remarks of Habermas, *The New Conservatism*, pp. 5–6, 254–55.
[71] See Aron, *Introduction to the Philosophy of History*, in particular, pp. 291–92.

and actions of individual and collective identities are determined, the German school defended the following two arguments. First, to the extent that the decisions and actions that are put into effect are implemented in terms of their historical anchorage, it proves from the very start to be the case that these decisions and actions do not rest upon the counsels of reason. Expressing no objective or theoretical certitude, nor relying upon such, the orientations adopted are the product of a specific situation,[72] and they remain bounded by the limits of the historical horizon.

Second, because no viewpoint on the world could be grasped that would not be the manifestation or the effect of a historical structure, the result is that one cannot specify for each and every person how one should behave and what one should want. There exists, on the contrary, a belief in the supreme value of diversity and of the uniqueness of positions. This belief leads one to recognise an equivalence among the plurality of views, whether they emanate from individuals or from groups and whether they concern the societies and civilisations of yesterday or today. The German historical school gave articulation at one and the same time to the weight of the historicity of the human condition and to the relativity of entities no form of rationality can choose between or rank hierarchically.

If Max Weber had been content to perpetuate the universalism of the Enlightenment and the reversal mechanism that its radicalisation engenders, he would probably have made allowance for the variety of cultures and opinions without, for all that, exposing himself to the dangers of relativism. But since he was intervening within the framework of German history at that particular time – namely, in an environment in which political life on the domestic and international levels was more conflictual than conciliatory, and where debates over ideas were largely influenced by the orientations of this historical school – he proceeded differently.

Although Weber formulated original solutions to the problems he endeavoured to think through, the specific cultural universe of Germany, combined with the growing tendency towards positivism, drove him to reject sociological rationalism,[73] that is to say, it led him to refuse to accept any knowledge of reality that would, from the standpoint of reason, take into account what is good and what is evil. From this perspective, we may say that he sets himself off from Durkheim who, as an eminent representative of sociological rationalism, conceives objectivity and neutrality as mere methodological guidelines and who maintains the conviction that there exists a tie between scientific theory and what is preferable in terms of norms. In this way, Durkheim limits the relativity between individual and collective viewpoints to a methodological dimension that does not

---

[72] See Strauss's comments in *Natural Right and History*, pp. 26–27.
[73] See Aron, *Introduction to the Philosophy of History*, in particular p. 296.

open the way to an absolute relativism but allows, instead, for a certain optimism as to the future and as to sociology's role in the construction of that future. As for Weber, he argues in favour of a view of science in which the separation of facts and values, professing to be total, offers no solid rampart against the drift towards inflated relativist claims: since the conflictual relations between axiological systems cannot be resolved via criteria that are expressive of what is just, a recourse to principles that would serve as scientific standards is no longer possible; the diversity of positions and the confrontations to which these positions give rise take the form of a war of the gods wherein no one can decide reasonably between the competing claimants.

Given that the truth of which each avails himself cannot be proved, it is Weber's estimation that a normatively neutral attitude constitutes the solution of the lesser evil. It is the best way of respecting the plurality of viewpoints while at the same time saving scientific knowledge from the excesses associated with the will to win over others on the basis of arbitrary value judgements.[74] In excluding such judgements from its purview, the scientific outlook does not impose itself on anyone, nor is it subject to anyone.

To state that conflicts cannot be eliminated, while wanting at the same time to protect the knowledge science offers, assumes one will make an effort to shelter science from axiological antagonisms by allowing an objective approach to social phenomena.[75] This concern with dissociating scientific activity from claims that cannot be evaluated rationally leads Weber to affirm that there is no room to deduce from the variety of value systems the idea of a hierarchy, in terms of which a choice would be made in agreement with the requirements of justice.

Whatever may be its merits, Weber's approach weakens the status of scientific analysis and exposes it to the serious problems of absolute relativism. Considering that his faith in science is not associated with the conception of a reasonable form of reason[76] – namely, a kind of reason that would not be merely instrumental – scientific truths seem to be as little grounded as assertions that do not pertain to science. The methodological neutrality clause leaves one completely bereft of resources in the face of relativistic nihilism, that is to say, unprepared to counter the argument that one preference is as good or bad as any other. The thesis that decisions are contingent turns scientific activity into a disenchanted kind of recourse, one of very random and problematic usefulness, within a world that is likewise disenchanted. This state of affairs quite obviously

---

[74] Apel, *Understanding and Explanation*, p. 8.   [75] Ibid., pp. 14–15.
[76] See Raymond Aron, *La Philosophie critique de l'histoire. Essai sur une théorie allemande de l'histoire* (Paris: Vrin, 1970), p. 267.

has its repercussions on the notion of political legitimacy. From this perspective, political legitimacy does not seem to be up to the task of embodying norms that can determine the conditions for the exercise of power in conformity with an authentic right to govern. It is reduced to the level of a belief, to the idea that one has some legitimacy according to the context.

As we see, while the tie between the dimension of values and science is characteristic of the project of the Enlightenment, it also sets off a movement whereby the universalism of its principles is radicalised. This movement leads, in turn, to a divorce between the theoretical and practical domains, a split Weber resolutely champions. The consequences of such a mechanism are all the more notable as Weberian reflections upon method still serve today as a paradigm in the field of the social sciences: the great majority of researchers adhere more to Weber's position than to sociological rationalism. It is namely within this logic that the objections – and the weaknesses of these objections – addressed to the thematic of the right to govern are located.

Legitimacy and the paradoxes of the desire for emancipation

The value of individual liberation, which comes quite particularly from the Enlightenment, was popularised by the French Revolution. It constitutes one of the major emblems and wellsprings of democratic politics, starting at the end of the eighteenth century. Taking concrete form in the relations between rulers and ruled, its effect has been to place the theme of legitimacy centre stage – but in a way that ultimately proves, from a certain point of view, to be counterproductive.

When the functioning of political life becomes identified in a fundamental way with the notion of the emancipation of individuals – that is, as soon as the respect for and ever-greater achievement of the rights of individuals comes to play a major role in the establishment of a legitimate relationship between rulers and ruled – the conditions required to satisfy the exigencies of the right to govern become very difficult to attain. A reversal of perspective takes place around the question of legitimacy.

The development of Enlightenment principles having to do with individual liberation sets in motion a mechanism of radicalisation within whose framework these principles not only have a foundational status – they help to determine a just politics – but also have to be followed by tangible effects. This tendency to see the level of values joining up with that of reality, through which individual emancipation is sought, is doomed to failure: it is, in effect, impossible to fulfil the basic norms completely. This state of affairs ends up disqualifying a legal approach to social and political relations. One then sees denounced not only the institutions that try to put the founding principles into practice but also the very idea of right. The legal dimension is discredited when it is identified with a highly criticisable way of regulating relationships among agents because that dimension does not express in deeds the values it is supposed to embody.

In this sense, it is appropriate to interpret, in particular, the rejection of the idea that the legal dimension could work in favour of social and political justice. One witnesses the beginnings of such a rejection in the nineteenth century, under the auspices of Marxism. The Marxist project for individual liberation professes to be systematic. It breaks away, in clear-cut fashion, from the rights-based State [*l'État de droit*] worked out by representative democratic regimes, judging it to be strictly formal in character. Regimes based upon representation are evaluated here in terms of an absolute and on the basis of emancipatory ideals that are the manifestation and the goal of a meaning of history that is to be achieved in full and as quickly as possible. Since reality does not adequately fulfil the goals assigned to it, routine legal action as well as right in general are invalidated. The ambition of liberating individuals, which issues from the Enlightenment and is pushed to its extreme by the Marxist logic, leads to a denigration of the problematic of legitimacy.

The desire to emancipate those who are agents becomes all the more involved in this reversal of situation as the recognition of the rights of individuals and of the need to satisfy these rights within a modern democratic framework takes place in parallel with a movement of liberation from transcendence and tradition. This leads the community of people to become aware of itself through its capacity to act in an autonomous way, and it helps to alter the agents' own feelings of responsibility in relation to their existence and to the environment in which they evolve. One of the consequences of this process is to increase the pressure exerted upon political institutions and to accentuate the problematic character of their legitimacy. Indeed, in this new context individuals have the feeling that they can intervene in the course of events. To have this experience is to discover their responsibility and also the responsibility incumbent upon the rest of the community.

In traditional societies, what the rulers are accountable for is minimised by individuals' own feelings of impotency in the face of the mysteries of nature. This feeling consoles them, sending them towards religion and tradition; and, often combined with a pronounced hierarchy, it suggests to the governed that the governors cannot resolve everything. For this reason, the rulers are not exposed in any systematic way to the reproaches of those whom they rule. By way of contrast, modernity's flaunted mastery over the world and the priority given to the rights of individuals accentuate, in modern democratic regimes, the control over political leaders as well as the responsibility of these leaders. Even if they are not expected to take responsibility for everything that affects the collectivity, and while it is granted that their power to intervene upon events is not infinite, the leaders are sufficiently accountable for their decisions and for their acts that the recognition of their right to govern always remains up in the air.

The responsibility attached to the functioning of modern democratic politics leads to an ever-greater questioning of the legitimacy of institutions since its development has coincided with an increase in the number of tasks assigned to the State. The State has constituted, from this perspective, a target of choice for efforts at contestation. Without neglecting the differences that exist, from country to country, concerning the margins of manoeuvre for acceptable intervention in the State's domain, in modern democracy the impact of the State is such that it yields the following result: the might of political instances of authority and the breadth of their responsibilities also constitute one aspect of their vulnerability. With the increase in missions conferred upon political institutions, the number of criticisms likely to be addressed to these institutions grows as well. The level of politicisation of issues rises in proportion to the ascending curve of services the State is charged with rendering. This phenomenon explains – only partially, it is true[77] – the fact that legitimacy constitutes a less central problem in North America than is the case in Europe. In the United States, where the role of state-run institutions has traditionally been limited, legitimacy does not provoke the kinds of polemics to which it gives rise on the other side of the Atlantic.

Let us conclude this chapter in such a way that we might avail ourselves of an overall view of the history of modern societies and of the social sciences. For, it is within the context of this history that criticisms addressed to the problematic of legitimacy are set. It is therefore appropriate for us to evoke here the theme of rationalisation.

Rationalisation, disenchantment, and legitimacy

Rationalisation is the third element in the movement wherein the ideals of the Enlightenment have developed and become radicalised. Through an ultimate reversal of these ideals, the movement leads to a depreciated [dévalorisée] and ambiguous approach to the question of legitimacy.

---

[77] To this feature would have to be added a reflection upon the modes of social integration and political contestation.

As we have seen, in the project of the Enlightenment the connection between the theoretical and practical dimensions was made in the context of a boundless faith in the power of a unified form of reason. Reason's unification was achieved through a process in which individuals are emancipated from immediate and false forms of knowledge – as represented, in particular, by tradition and religion. From this perspective, the objective was for individuals to acquire a distanced view of themselves, and of the environment in which they live, in order to liberate themselves from prejudices, ones they are affected by more than they master. That does not prevent this mechanism, which is supposed to help bring facts and values together, from producing the opposite result.

Development towards a transparent universe rapidly reaches its limits. The achievements of theoretical, ethical, and political knowledge were supposed to manifest and to celebrate the rational unfolding of reality. Instead, this development culminates in a disenchanted world, one in which the establishment of scientifically grounded norms is impossible. The optimism of Enlightenment thinkers gives way to a study of social phenomena that accounts for these phenomena in terms of rationalisation – cut off, in other words, from the idea of their foundation in reason.

The dynamic of knowledge to which the Enlightenment principles gives rise does not attain the goals it had reckoned on achieving. Far from constituting a rational approach to social problems, the social sciences' development of an analysis of the real breaks with the orientation proposed during the eighteenth century. In the project of the Enlightenment, the logic of research and knowledge was guided by the ideal of rationality. That ideal gave it its full meaning as well as set its boundary lines. Yet the ambition to arrive at an ever more complete and radical elucidation of social phenomena brings with it a situation in which its emancipatory value, being attributed to scientific activity, is turned upside down and leads to a break with the initial objectives. An autonomisation of science occurs in relation to the universe of reason. The problematic of rationalisation replaces the quest for reason.

Although an interest in knowledge is never entirely dissociated from the desire to liberate individuals, the production of knowledge tends to trigger a self-sustaining mechanism and to dissolve the tie that previously bound it to the effort to articulate what ought to be.[78] Attitudes and thoughts, whether they pertain to the individual level or to the collective dimension, are not studied in direct relation to the normative plane. The accent is placed on the construction of convincing descriptive schemata,

[78] See the remarks of Hans Blumenberg, *The Legitimacy of the Modern Age*, trans. Robert M. Wallace (Cambridge, Mass.: MIT Press, 1983), in particular pp. 429–34, and the comments of Jacques Bouveresse, *Rationalité et cynisme*, pp. 172–81.

ones capable of accounting for the ways in which individuals and societies evolve within given cultures and contexts but without evaluating them from the standpoint of reason.

Rather than pronounce judgement upon the values of truth, in terms of which individuals and societies position themselves, it becomes a matter of explaining how these individuals and societies behave. One must therefore reconstitute the series of factors that produce the phenomena to be elucidated, but one must do so without placing oneself on the level of practical investment in these values – which is that of the individual and collective agents caught up in the heat of action – and while refusing to analyse one's object explicitly on the basis of a scale of rational values. This approach thus points us towards a description of social and political reality – within whose framework the agents' own understanding, via an existential adherence to the values of their universe, is spurned in favour of a distanced reconstruction. The point of such a reconstruction is to restitute the logic of events. No genuine evaluation is allowed of the reasons individuals invoke in order to justify their actions.

Offering an account of phenomena consists therefore in their study in terms of a network of dependent elements, with history as the framework. From this point of view, the effort to elucidate phenomena consists in retracing the historical sequence of aspects of people's lives in society and in examining the various spheres within which their practices are inscribed, while taking a special interest in the areas of economics, politics, society, culture, and psychology. This orienting of knowledge in the direction of rationalisation gives rise to an explanatory spiral. This spiral of explanations encourages a mechanism of separation from reason.

The consequent divorce is manifested first of all in the fact that the historical analysis of the real opens up the possibility of multiplying to infinity the causes and the levels of approach. These begin to take up all the researcher's attention. Each factor is liable to be a piece in a puzzle to be put back together. The researcher's main energy is then focussed upon accumulating data, which tends to divert him from the practical meanings of the information he has gathered.

It later proves to be the case that, far from being limited to a few objects, this movement of setting things in historical perspective comes to be applied to all components of the lives of individuals. It soon seizes upon values, which are the source for the Enlightenment dynamic and in whose very name its effort to gain knowledge is justified. By historicising, in particular, the ideas of truth and reason, those very ones Enlightenment humanism uses over and over again, the project of the Enlightenment is itself endangered by this approach. By reducing these ideas to the level of immanence – which is, moreover, the level of ordinary reality – it takes away from them their privileged position, upon which depends their status as a criterion for judgement and as a criterion for setting goals. The phenomenon of emancipation through knowledge is thus transformed into a process wherein to learn is above all to detach oneself both from oneself and from the world, while allowing a question mark to hover over the hope of any reconciliation. The radicalisation of the ideal of knowledge leads all the more clearly to an explication of the real in terms of rationalisation since the historical approach is indissociable from a reduction of the problematic of rationality to the level of instrumentality.

Modern societies, in becoming conscious of their identity, define themselves more and more each day by a relationship of mastery over their environment. Parallel to this movement, one witnesses the spread, in the field of the social sciences, of the thesis that it is inappropriate to examine the values through which phenomena take on meaning by tying them especially, if not exclusively, to normative judgements. It becomes a matter, rather, of analysing them in such a way as to concentrate on the strategies individuals implement. In other words, the objective is less to grasp the domain of people's choices and acts, starting from a policy of actively taking values into account, than it is to explicate the instrumental mechanism in which that domain participates.

Thus, in Weber's work this approach corresponds to a study of behaviours in terms of intentionality. The object of sociology is not to state what is good or evil but to reconstruct the intention that lies at the origin of actions of individuals according to the context in which they evolve. As for Marx, he establishes his theory by explicating the relationships among the members of the collectivity on the basis of class struggle, the instrumental combat among individuals for power, while never clearly admitting that his denunciation of right and of morality rests upon an axiological foundation. In this perspective, the problems of society are judged without that judgement ever being explicitly acknowledged. The analysis offers a description of the logic of human attitudes by foregrounding the process of rationalisation and by not fully acknowledging the centrality of value judgements.

As we see, criticisms directed against the notion of legitimacy are, whatever might be claimed, set within a systematic world view. This systematic conception of the world is connected to the way in which societies and behaviours evolve as well as to their analysis within the framework of modernity.

Let us now push our reflections further. Based upon the elements previously established, it now becomes a matter of demonstrating that, in order to be credible, an explanation of political phenomena in terms of legitimacy has to furnish satisfactory answers to a series of questions.

These questions may be formulated as follows. How is one to respect the plurality of viewpoints, both individual and collective, without giving up on the thematic of the right to govern, understood as the expression of the criteria that allow one to determine what is legitimate or illegitimate? To what extent can one account for conflicts without the recommended choice being considered arbitrary? In what way can one make *de jure* judgements in a changing world, or how can one take the historical dimension of the real into consideration while at the same time setting aside relativism and nihilism? In the following chapters, I hope to demonstrate that there exist some answers to these questions and that upon these answers depend the authentic possibility of legitimacy – in other words, the evaluation of political life from the standpoint of justice.

4   Social sciences, historicity, and truth

The way in which the social sciences interpret the historicity of their object explains in part the ambiguity – indeed, the elimination – at the heart of their explanatory efforts, of their recourse to value judgements that state what is and is not legitimate. In order to extract oneself from this situation, one must break away from a conception of science that inadequately accounts for the historical character of social and political phenomena and has negative consequences concerning the status of truth when it comes to studying the relationships between governors and governed.

In fact, if the social sciences do not integrate the dimension of judgement and of values, this is in particular because their description of the historical aspect of phenomena expresses an unhappy consciousness of the good. The inability of the scientific analysis of society to broach, in coherent terms, the thematic of political ethics and of the right to govern is tied to an inappropriate view of the historicity of social facts. This inability is apparent in three ways.

First, the study of societies strictly takes over as its own the explanatory logic of the sciences of nature. In this case, what it does is to subject social and political problems to an analysis that does not accord with their specificity. Taking this specificity into consideration is, however, one of the conditions for setting in place a study of the relationships between governors and governed that is conducted from the standpoint of legitimacy.

Second, theories that strive to think through the historical characteristics of the unfolding of relationships between rulers and ruled and that endeavour to reconcile these characteristics with the requirements of science – as is the case with Marx, Weber, and those who are inspired by these thinkers – do not succeed any better in respecting the historicity of their object. In particular, by emptying right of its substance, they end up underestimating its role.

Third, the social sciences' inability to provide a satisfactory treatment of the question of the good in politics is indissociable from their understanding of modernity. What is proposed is an interpretation of the reflective process of historicisation in the modern world that combines the scientific description of reality with a nostalgia for the absolute. This leads the social sciences to recognise the centrality of the theme of legitimacy only at the price of renouncing its deep-seated critical signification and import.

THE NOMOLOGICAL TEMPTATION AND IIISTORICAL ASPECTS OF SOCIAL FACTS

To show that the social sciences do not account for the specificity of their domain is to underscore the fact that they set in motion an explanatory mechanism that is incapable of elucidating the axiological dimension implied by the historicity of social phenomena. In order to conduct this argument with success, we will have to construct our reflections around three axes. First, we shall mention the description of social facts; inspired by the natural sciences, such a description, we shall see, is driven by the ambition to establish laws. Next, we shall examine the failure of this research programme, tied as it is to the gap that exists between this type of approach and the historical dimension of social and political facts. Finally, we shall note that it is in this spirit that the concern with practical truth is dismissed, replaced by a decision to pay exclusive attention to methodological preoccupations.

The syndrome of searching for laws in the social sciences

If there is one element that symbolises how widespread are the social sciences' borrowings from the scientific study of the facts of nature, it is the will to find laws that conform with those used to account for natural phenomena. This will would seem to determine the social sciences' own view of themselves, that is to say, their view of what their activity ought to be.[1]

From this perspective, the objective of the social sciences is to formulate laws whose validity is to be tested empirically and to establish statements of general import. This will finds its most fervent defenders among authors who are favourable to the idea of the unity of scientific activity. After August Comte and John Stuart Mill in the nineteenth century,[2] today thinkers who situate themselves in the territory of logical empiricism militate in favour of this thesis.[3] The works on epistemology and

---

[1] See MacIntyre, *After Virtue*, p. 88.
[2] See Apel, *Understanding and Explanation*, p. 34.
[3] See Charles Taylor's article, written in French, 'Les sciences de l'homme', *Critique* 399–400 (August–September 1980), pp. 845–48, and McCarthy, *The Critical Theory of Jürgen Habermas*, pp. 137–38. The reader may also refer to Paul Veyne's *Writing*

scientific methodology of Karl Popper, Carl Hempel, and Ernest Nagel testify, in varying ways, to this approach.

These last three authors think, in effect, that the progress of the social sciences is tied to a recognition and development of the similarities that exist between the social sciences themselves and the scientific analysis of nature. Despite the differences between the concepts and techniques specific to these two types of study of reality,[4] and notwithstanding the restrictions the application of the analysis of natural facts encounters in certain social-scientific disciplines, in particular in history,[5] their methods are said to be similar overall and to belong to the one and the same logic of knowledge.[6] The goal of the scientific analysis of social phenomena is to tackle these phenomena in terms of causality and to subsume them under general laws that are conceived of as a schema for their elucidation. Social-scientific activity therefore takes the form of a deduction of the real on the basis of discovered regularities – that is to say, of an inscription of facts within hypothetical-deductive relations. These relations are then said to display a predictive power that determines a technical or instrumental relationship between theory and practice and allows one to justify the utility, for the collectivity, of the analysis of social phenomena.

The failure of the nomological programme and the historicity of social facts

The nomological ambition contained in the scientific analysis of social facts is nevertheless doomed to failure. The results obtained do not, in effect, allow one to establish regularities that are equivalent to the kind brought out in scientific analyses of natural phenomena.[7] This limitation is inherent in the choice of method, for a gap exists between the desire to work out propositions that are intended to be universal in character and the specificity of their object, rooted as it is in its historicity.

The very configuration of the field of action for analyses of social facts ill lends itself to the formulation of systematic laws. One can see it easily when one casts doubt upon the traditionally established split between the theoretical social sciences and the historical social sciences, to borrow

---

History: Essay on Epistemology (Middletown, Conn.: Wesleyan University Press, 1984), pp. 160–61.

[4] See Karl R. Popper, *The Poverty of Historicism*, 2nd corr. edn (New York: Harper & Row, 1964), for example pp. 141–43.

[5] See Karl R. Popper, *The Open Society and its Enemies*, 5th rev. edn (London: Routledge and Kegan Paul, 1966), vol. II, *The High Tide of Prophecy: Hegel, Marx, and the Aftermath*, pp. 261–65, and *The Poverty of Historicism*, pp. 143–47. The reader may also refer to Jürgen Habermas's comments in *On the Logic of the Social Sciences*, pp. 25–29.

[6] Popper, *The Poverty of Historicism*, pp. 130–36.

[7] See Giddens, *The Constitution of Society*, pp. 344–45, and MacIntyre, *After Virtue*, pp. 88–89.

Popper's terminology.[8] This separation states that the goal of the first group of social sciences is to establish generalisations that are immune to considerations of time and space, whereas the second group examines phenomena situated in a specific context. The distinction has to be toned down. The level of formalisation that marks the activity of the economist, the sociologist, or the political scientist – all of whom are anxious to find rules that are constant – cannot mask the fact that they, too, are confronted with a reality that pertains to history. One must not confuse the directions and the ideals of research with the nature of the facts to be elucidated and conclude that that nature is highly alien to the historical universe.

All of the different ways of analysing social facts are historical. A basic constitutive element of their objects is their dimension of historicity. The distinctions existing between them pertain to the plane of knowledge but do not concern the mode of being. It is therefore necessary to take a stand against the idea of a fundamental split that would separate history from the rest of the social sciences; such a dichotomy invites the social sciences to think of themselves as being further along on the road to being scientific. For, the obstacles encountered by the historian in the fulfilment of this nomological ambition hold equally well for those authors who go off in quest of laws in economics, politics, and sociology. That is to say, the impossibility of producing statements of general import is indissociable from the inability of the nomological project to be in conformity with the historical aspect of social-scientific facts, and quite particularly from its inability to take into account in a satisfactory manner the role of values.

The success of the programme that is aimed at establishing conditional rules with constant validity in the social field presupposes that this orientation would be compatible with its own property of historicity. Now, that is manifestly not the case. The situation of the economist, the sociologist, or the political scientist who wishes to construct laws is very different from that of the scientist moving around in the domain of the natural sciences. Indeed, within the framework of the strict determinism of Newtonian physics or of the relatively open determinism brought to light by recent scientific research,[9] the observer accounts for phenomena through statements that are endowed with an undeniable power of resolution. Thus, although physics today recognises a certain unpredictability in the way phenomena unfold, that does not stop it from showing that there exists

[8] Popper, *The Poverty of Historicism*, p. 143.
[9] See Ilya Prigogine and Isabelle Stengers, *Order Out of Chaos: Man's New Dialogue with Nature* (Boulder, Colo. and London: New Science Library, 1984), p. 306.

a science of random events and that randomness obeys constraints that can be calculated.[10]

Things proceed otherwise in the case of social and political phenomena: the causal relationships brought out there are not expressed in terms of necessary relations. The constitutive elements of historical determinism do not allow one to predict, on the basis of previously stated conditions, what situations will come next. Indeed, the historicity of social facts sets them in a singular configuration that can never be reproduced in identical fashion. The result is that the causal relationships connecting them do not explain each other as do the hierarchised laws of a theory in physics.[11] The phenomena that go to make up the field of social studies form a reality that is too diverse for the process of determining the real, in which they participate, to engender constantly the same consequences and for one to be able to establish general laws. It is therefore preferable to give up on the desire to isolate factors that would have an exclusively decisive role in all cases.[12]

There exists, in the historical universe, no sufficient condition that would authorise one to make permanent and automatic deductions of specific effects. No *a priori* causal connection is to be found there, only conditional relationships that are expressive of a particular situation. Of course, the mind's natural propensity to give itself some points of reference and a willingness to subscribe to bona fide scientific rules encourage one to look for systems with decisive conditions, so that the way in which facts do unfold can be established in advance and with certainty. Nevertheless, it does not follow, from the theoretical and psychological interest in this type of determination, that that interest would be an integral part of the historical dimension of social phenomena. As it turns out, there is no fundamental reason why the empirical level and one's intellectual inclination to rely on constant features should go hand in hand.

Faced with the fluctuating character of human reality, the laws the social sciences endeavour to establish appear fragmentary. Compared to the mere historiographical description of facts, regularities that are of general import seem to open onto a higher knowledge, for the aim of their level abstraction is to embrace broad sets of facts and to ensure an explanatory capacity that is not limited to a determinate spatiotemporal context. Yet the gain is not genuine: their lack of precision and certainty are proportionate to their breadth, and their area of validity is practically always inadequate.[13] In isolating one or several elements and attributing

[10] See René Thom's préface to Laplace, *Essai philosophique sur les probabilités*, pp. 22–23.
[11] See Aron, *Introduction to the Philosophy of History*, p. 205.
[12] See Boudon, *Theories of Social Change*, pp. 65–66.
[13] See Aron, *Introduction to the Philosophy of History*, p. 279.

to those elements the status of a decisive form of causality, rules claiming universality prove unable to account for the complexity of social phenomena. They are in fact abusive generalisations that rely, more than once, on begging the question. Thus, to take an example from the theory of social change, we may note that, while, under certain circumstances, the existence of social classes involves conflicts, that does not mean that every class situation necessarily entails antagonistic relations, as Marxism affirmed.[14]

The study of statistics was able to lead those in the social sciences to think it possible to work out laws of general import. Having properly adopted the goal of maximising use of the incomplete information the researcher has at his disposal, statistics were solicited to plead for the existence of systematic determinations and regularities. Here let us take the example of Durkheim. For him, the stability of suicide rates demonstrated the presence of great collective forces, as real as any physicochemical form of energy; externally impelling individuals to act, such forces were thought powerful enough to give them no alternative but to kill themselves.[15] For his part, Pierre Bourdieu, while warning against a blind submission to statistics and against employing them as a scientific alibi,[16] grants them a preponderant position in the procedures used to validate theoretical hypotheses.[17] He makes use of statistics in order to highlight the importance of a structural form of causality within a network of factors that – even if that structural causality breaks away from, and claims that it is irreducible to, what he calls the direct determinism of linear thinking[18] – is valid as a law.[19] Yet the role attributed to a statistical approach offers decidedly too many drawbacks to convince us of its pretensions to be making law in the social domain.

Without contesting the precious support they provide in the social-scientific domain, it is advisable to grant that statistics do not genuinely contribute to the establishment of laws: indeed, they do not escape the contradiction that exists between the need to isolate constant causes and the historical reality of social and political phenomena. Whereas, in the

[14] See Boudon's remarks in *Theories of Social Change*, pp. 184–85.

[15] Durkheim, *Suicide: A Study in Sociology*, ed. and intro. George Simpson, trans. John A. Spaulding and George Simpson, 1st paperback edn (New York: The Free Press, 1966), pp. 309–10. See also pp. 305–07.

[16] See Pierre Bourdieu, Jean-Claude Chamboredon, and Jean-Claude Passeron, *The Craft of Sociology: Epistemological Preliminaries*, ed. Beate Krais, trans. Richard Nice (Berlin and New York: Walter de Gruyter, 1991), p. 10.

[17] Ibid., pp. 65–66.   [18] Bourdieu, *Distinction*, p. 107.

[19] Ibid., pp. 467–68. One will find some hints about the notion of a structural cause, conceived as a variant of conditional laws, in Boudon, *Theories of Social Change*, pp. 13, 93–94.

study of nature, the uncertainty having to do with the properties of the object under analysis decreases with the observation of greater numbers (at least when the status of the natural sciences is not itself appreciably affected by some characteristics of historicity)[20] and renders recourse to statistics decisive, the use of statistics to work out general rules in the social field stumbles upon two difficulties.

In the first place, statistics fail to recognise the weight of contingency. They underestimate the tangle of determinations of varying origins. Participating on an ongoing basis in the constitutive flux of reality, this tangle of heteroclite determinations precludes one from being able to describe in advance those characteristics that influence the way events will unfold. When the observer formulates the question of how, overall, social phenomena are produced historically and solicits the aid of statistical tools in order to explicate what is not immediately detectable, he is assuming an intrinsic determination these tools would have as their mission to highlight and to express on the macroscopic level. He forgets, or does not want to remember, that social and political facts can result from factors that, while not being alien to the context in which they find a place, have a causality that is fortuitous in character, since they pertain to divergent sequences that, aided by circumstances, influence the course of things in an unforeseen way.

The elements under observation are well determined, but they are not the manifestation of laws. Even while granting, in another connection, that the probative force attributed to large numbers does not rest upon fallacious constructions and generalisations (due to manipulation of the numbers),[21] the determinism in question can in itself be the consequence of the accumulation of data that might have been different. From this point of view, certainly, facts tackled on the macroscopic level are seen to evolve in such a way that their coherency cannot be reduced to mere chance. But that does not eliminate the impact of the fortuitous. Thus, it may happen that historical change is not inscribed within an endogenous sequence of events but results, rather, from an innovation of which no previous record had left any trace or from an exogenous factor that throws off kilter a long-established state of equilibrium.[22] As we see, although the researcher who is concerned with working out laws is automatically preoccupied with mass effects, in the universe of social facts the historicity

[20] See Unger, *Social Theory*, pp. 187–91, and François Jacob, *The Possible and the Actual* (Seattle, and London: University of Washington Press, 1982), pp. 28–29.

[21] See the examples mentioned by David Hackett Fischer in *Historian's Fallacies: Toward a Logic of Historical Thought* (New York: Harper & Row, 1970), pp. 104–24.

[22] Furet, 'Quantitative Methods in History', in Le Goff and Nora (eds.), *Constructing the Past*, p. 15.

of events resists their being represented by simple processes involving statistics. The necessary is not the same as the real, and statistics neglect rather than compensate for contingent causes.

In the second place, the use of statistics offers the major drawback of caricaturing the role of individuals. It is at the level of adding together agents' behaviours that statistics detect their influence and their meaning. The actions of individuals, considered on a case-by-case basis, enter only very fortuitously into the dynamic of causal forms. From this perspective, the intention they give to their acts does not correspond to their truth. The place statistics assigns to agents therefore boils down to stating that they participate in a historical flux that is to be distinguished from their personal investment in the world. However, these individuals do not allow themselves to be shut up within the function to which the statistical approach confines them.

Far from being passive subjects whose actions would attain some meaningful consistency and import only after being added up, individuals themselves orient the course of events. They are a source of contingency. Their behaviours are not mere effects of external and prior causes but are also the fruit of decisions that reveal a non-negligible latitude for deliberation. In becoming real, these decisions introduce new, more or less foreseeable elements not only because it is impossible to anticipate completely their effect but also because it happens that the agents in their strategies might want their objectives to remain opaque to the other's view.[23] Each acts within a personal life-horizon, and it is upon this horizon that the unfolding of the domain of societal activities depends. Individuals' investment in the world is a kind of bestowal in whose absence the operation of the spheres of human action – namely, their continuity and their transformations – would not occur.

The failure to recognise the role of individuals in the historical production of reality, as exemplified by statistics, is a characteristic trait of the will to establish regularities of general import in the historical-social field. In order to bring out the constants, one has to minimise, indeed invalidate, the relevance of singularities that resist the effort of formalisation. It is therefore easy to understand, from this perspective, why one tries to conjure away the extent of each person's intervention upon reality. But that does not stop there being a difference between the desire to work out laws within the universe of human facts and the way in which these facts are configured. And the role individuals play in the dimension of historicity that is constitutive of social and political phenomena creates an obstacle to the establishment of *a priori* rules in the social sciences.

---

[23] See MacIntyre, *After Virtue*, p. 104.

Values in human action and the search for laws

At the origin of agents' acts are found intentions that are not simply the expression of subjective motivations. Certainly, the activity of individuals answers to objectives whose goal is to build an existence in which they might recognise themselves and might give some meaning to their gestures. Nonetheless, this mechanism of intentionality exists only by being set within, and by coming to terms with, the domain of intersubjectivity. The latter, as social matrix, also serves to form the identity of individuals and the relationships they maintain with reality. From this point of view, the perception of the environment in which their projects are embodied makes allowances for those constraints of the collectivity that, in a given context, define which acts are possible. In the various social domains of action, these constraints establish, at least when one is dealing with a relatively stable and homogeneous organisation, the technical boundaries of the collectivity and its cultural limits, as well as the place occupied by each individual.

The collectivity's constraints also determine the field of signification, which is manifested in the way the intra- and extracommunitarian aspects of the world are interpreted and which, via a hierarchy of choices, sets its mark upon the various types of activity. Let us put it in other terms: unfolding within the perspective of life projects to be given concrete form within a collective environment, the power of individuals to act participates in a dynamic that is not independent of the norms currently in force. Agents evolve within a universe where the axiological dimension serves as a reference point and a guidepost for their relations with other beings and with things. It is within this framework that their acts take on meaning and have an impact on events, thus contributing to the history of societies.

Now, the social sciences that opt to seek out laws prove impotent to account both for this structure of actions undertaken by individuals and for what that structure implies. Their objective and the methodological positions accompanying them do not accord with the historicity of social facts, which are to be explained in terms of the activity of individuals and of the role the normative plane plays therein. This deficiency is expressed in two ways.

The first has to do with the mode of causal explanation to which social sciences that are in search of laws have recourse. This mode of causal explanation basically takes an interest in individuals only in an external way. It neglects the level of intentionality, and therefore the field of significations and values that enter into play as individual actions unfold. Broaching agents' behaviours as a succession of events liable to empirical observation, studies of social facts that are in quest of rules with constant validity bolster themselves with a conception of causality that does not take into account the agents' more or less acknowledged intentions and the connections these intentions have with the axiological domain. Such studies analyse actions in simple mechanical terms of cause and effect.[24]

There is nothing surprising, moreover, about this conception of causal elucidation. The dimension of values is, in effect, stubbornly resistant to the type of analysis that is used to account for natural phenomena. In attempting to formalise to the extreme people's lived experience, the ways in which one approaches social facts not only stumble over the question of contingency but also bump up against the following difficulty: on account of their diversity and their changing character, values cannot easily be made into well-defined objects of study. And it is even less easy to demonstrate their truth in a manner equivalent to the way in which natural phenomena are analysed.[25] Rather than face up to and offer a solution for the problem engendered by the specificity of the structure of actions individuals undertake, some researchers are tempted therefore to sidestep the obstacle by developing a kind of causal study that does not take into consideration those characteristics that are proper to individual activity as compared to the ones pertaining to natural phenomena.

This causal interpretation of agents' acts is at once the corollary and the instrument by which one adopts, in the area of questions relating to society, a mode of knowledge that issues from the scientific analysis of nature. This borrowing process cannot but preclude one from authentically taking into account the problematic of values.[26] Here we encounter the second deficiency regarding the role of values in individuals' actions and, by way of consequence, in the production of historical reality. Indeed, it is by identifying one's paradigm of knowledge with the programme of offering a scientific explanation of natural phenomena that one prevents oneself from recognising the specific properties of values as well as the role they play in the historicity of societal phenomena.[27] Instead of abandoning the model to which they adhere for validating their knowledge of

[24] See, for example, Pierre Birnbaum's remarks on behaviourism in Birnbaum and Bertrand Badie, *La Fin du politique*, rev. and expanded edn with an Afterword (Paris: Éditions du Seuil, 1983), pp. 19–20. The reader may also consult Gilles-Gaston Granger, *Essai d'une philosophie du style*, new edn (Paris: Odile Jacob, 1988), p. 119.

[25] See McCarthy, *The Critical Theory of Jürgen Habermas*, pp. 155–57, and Gilles-Gaston Granger, 'Logique et pragmatique de la causalité dans les sciences de l'homme', in Markus Aenishanslin *et al.*, *Systèmes symboliques, sciences et philosophie* (Paris: Éditions du Centre National de la Recherche Scientifique, 1978), pp. 141–42.

[26] See Charles Taylor, 'The Diversity of Goods', in Amartya Sen and Bernard Williams (eds.), *Utilitarianism and Beyond* (Cambridge University Press, 1988), p. 129.

[27] See Charles Taylor, 'Le juste et le bien', trans. P. Constantineau, *Revue de métaphysique et de morale* 1 (January–March 1988), p. 50.

the real, researchers in the social sciences here prefer to think that values do not correspond to the criteria of scientific rationality and that it is therefore not possible to take a position in relation to them. The result is a kind of disengagement – indeed, a veritable axiological dumbness. The place values hold in the unfolding of individual actions and, more sweepingly, in the production of historical facts, is sacrificed on the altar of science.

This disengagement explains how the analyses in question, when they do not completely eliminate every reference to the axiological field, treat the latter in a way that pretends not to decide anything about the values expressed by persons in their activities. Limiting themselves to cataloguing people's beliefs and to trying to shed light on how those beliefs evolve by using schematic interpretations that subsume them, these sorts of analyses refuse, at least theoretically, to pronounce themselves for or against those beliefs. One thereby notices a displacement of the idea of truth: the objective of knowledge is not to articulate the way in which individuals think and act on a scale of values but very much becomes a way of describing how they are situated in the world, without seeking to evaluate their behaviour. This orientation is accompanied by more marked attention being paid to the methodological elements involved. Considerations having to do with the ways in which knowledge is worked out come to occupy a place whose preponderance goes hand in hand with the exclusion of any type of analysis that would include a problematisation of the dimension of values.

Without contesting the need to subscribe to rules of method, it seems to us that the phenomenon of methodological inflation and the form it takes are indissociable here from a refusal to evaluate social facts. Studies that content themselves with offering an account of phenomena without taking any position attribute, furthermore, to the processes of validation a decisive role of quality control in the production of reliable knowledge. Such studies are defending the thesis that the credibility of a proposition depends upon its capacity to satisfy the verification procedures of scientific logic. A true discourse about reality would thus exclude value judgements and be content merely to be a registration of events, where the mission of the methodological mechanisms being employed is to appraise how faithful this value-free registration is to what is real and how much it conforms to the imperatives of being scientific.

Thus does the truth of an analysis of how the political field operates feign indifference to the idea of the good. It is presented as a description that corresponds to scientifically approved methodological conditions and offers a neutral report on the beliefs and actions of individuals. One's notion of what is true is identified with the positive results of validation processes that express and determine what can be known with certainty by following the scientific method. Ratifying the exclusion of practical reason, the interest shown in verification procedures and the place reserved for these procedures in the production of theoretical truth illustrates, and at the same time confirms, the idea that values are irrational.

In doing this, the authors who opt for this conception prevent themselves from examining the relationships between governors and governed by integrating in their studies a reflection upon what is rightly grounded and what is not. The problem of justice in politics and that of the legitimacy of institutions therefore do not really get posed. An authentic understanding of legitimacy via an analysis of the way in which the relations between rulers and ruled are organised – which relies upon an approach that would take seriously the themes of responsibility, distribution of goods, and the criteria for evaluating rights and duties within the framework of a historical community – is abandoned and placed on the blacklist of scientific thought.

These considerations go to show how the nomological ambition – to which, still today, large portions of the sciences of societies succumb – manifests an erroneous interpretation of the historicity of social facts. It implies an inability to treat values and, by way of consequence, the problematic of legitimacy, in a satisfactory manner. But a second type of failure to recognise the historicity of human facts also has the effect of preventing one from posing in suitable fashion the problem of legitimacy.

SCIENCE OF HISTORY, RIGHT, AND LEGITIMACY

Some theories of societies analyse social and political facts while endeavouring to respect the specificity of their historical dimension. But they do so in such a way that, concretely speaking, the reflection upon the notion of the right to govern that they produce betrays the idea that lies at its base. This is the case with the Marxist and Weberian approaches to history – whose character, in this regard, is emblematic and exemplary. Although they analyse the historicity of phenomena with very different working agendas, both try to reconcile their point of view on history with a way of thinking about justice and right. Nevertheless, each in its own way also has a conception of history that prevents it from treating the question of values in a satisfactory manner. They thus run the risk of reducing what is legitimate to what is legal. Now, when one does not keep these two levels at a distance from each other, the possibility of assessing and of judging the groundedness of the right to govern is dissolved.

The question of legitimacy in relation to science and the meaning of history in Marx

The Marxist study of social and political phenomena is more concerned with taking historical facts' own characteristics into account than are purely 'scientistic' approaches. That does not mean that the former approach is to be distinguished absolutely from the latter ones. Certain features testify to the existence of numerous points of contact. The attractive power of the scientific explanation of nature undoubtedly played a role in Marx's abandonment of traditional philosophy's analytical method in favour of empirical analyses. Although his diligent readings in English political economy might have sensitised him to the individualist methodology,[28] and although his vast learning might have kept him from neglecting the fact that the richness of what is real outstripped the doctrinal framework he tried to extract therefrom, he was sufficiently marked by the influence of the natural sciences to think that sociology, in particular, not only could dispense with considerations as to the actors' motivations but did not have to make allowances, either, for individuals and for their subjectivity.

Despite the similarities with the natural sciences, the Marxist concern with finding laws which history obeys, far from ruling out his making a commitment on the level of values, is indissociable from it. Beyond the need to gather technical and concrete data about reality, Marx is guided by an interest in knowledge as emancipation. Knowledge and the achievement of the true and the good have to coincide. However, the way in which Marx conceives the historical universe leads him to fail to recognise the historicity of societal phenomena. The result is that his willingness to take on the axiological dimension and to offer a solution to the question of social and political justice, and, by way of consequence, to the problem of legitimacy, ends in a failure.

To understand this process, it is fitting to point out what Marx intends by a *science of history*. There really does exist in the Marxist approach an effort to establish laws of the same type as those articulated in the scientific study of nature. From this point of view, we may say that the Marxist approach seeks to highlight those factors that are capable of explaining how and why an event arises, and what elements are required for it to happen again. It remains the case that these conditional types of rules are not the only modes to which Marx has recourse for his elucidation of the dynamic of history. In his work, the will to explain the phenomena does not correspond to a programme for attaining knowledge that

[28] See Boudon's remarks, *Theories of Social Change*, pp. 66–67.

would be determined by the criteria of empirical science alone. This programme is set within a larger perspective, one that attempts to articulate
the compartmentalised character of historical regularities in tandem with
laws that embrace history in its generality. It is a matter of conceiving the
history of humanity as a unity.[29]

Thus, there are some passages in the first volume of *Capital*[30] whose
object is to define in rigorous terms some basic concepts of political
economy – such as *commodity, exchange, value, capital, surplus-value, rate
of surplus-value, absolute surplus-value, relative surplus-value,* and *wages.*
In working out these concepts, one is led to make nomological determinations that account for relationships among facts over a given period of
time. This is particularly the case for the three laws that govern the variations in 'the relation between the magnitudes of surplus-value and the
value of labour-power'.[31] But the reader would remain blind to their full
meaning if he did not see that these laws are inseparable from mechanisms
that affect historical development in general (such as the constitution of
the bourgeois and proletarian classes and their conflictual relationships)
and aim at elucidating the birth, life, growth, and death of a system of
social organisation (capitalism, in this case) as well as explaining how that
system is going to be replaced by another one, judged superior (communism, understood as man's end as well as his realisation).

Marx therefore implements a theory of the historicity of events wherein
the truth of empirical regularities is set within a finalistic understanding
of the course phenomena follow. Scientific forecasting is based here in
historical prediction. The goal is to state what the direction and the content of the future will be in its totality. Contrary to an effort to establish
laws within a strictly positivist framework, Marxism, by associating conditional regularities with absolute laws,[32] adopts the perspective of an
overall philosophy of history. It is in this way that Marx adopts as his own
the theme of social and political justice and thinks that he has given a
definitive answer to it. Yet, in defending the idea that there is a general
determinism to history, within which the advent of the good will necessarily manifest itself, Marx offers a dogmatic solution to the problem of truth
in the field of human affairs. The way in which the question of justice
and of the legitimacy of institutions is resolved leads then to an impasse.

[29] See Michel Henry, *Marx: A Philosophy of Human Reality*, trans. Kathleen McLaughlin
(Bloomington: Indiana University Press, 1983), pp. 94–97. [Translator/Editor: The
one-volume English-language translation is an abridgement; the reader will find the
full reference in the original citation Coicaud provided: *Marx* (Paris: Gallimard, 1976),
vol. I, *Une philosophie de la réalité*, pp. 199–203.]

[30] Karl Marx, *Capital*, ed. Frederick Engels, 3 vols. (New York: International Publishers,
1967), vol. I, *A Critical Analysis of Capitalist Production*.

[31] Ibid., p. 526.   [32] See Boudon, *Theories of Social Change*, p. 210.

Indeed, the understanding of historicity worked out by Marx carries within it a rigid form of determination, and the consequences are disastrous. It does not offer a faithful description of the unfolding of events, notably at the level of the reality of the modes of production and of their order of succession,[33] but also concerning the role of contingency and that of individuals. That is the reason why the author of *Capital*, as well as his supporters,[34] have had to falsify certain information in order to try to preserve the credibility of their world view.

Furthermore, Marxist predictions are translated into reality via an authoritarian treatment of the problem of social and political justice. In asserting the existence of an overall historical meaning whose achievement is certain, Marx defends the idea of a reason at work in history. He states that the future has secretly been arranged to deliver the good. According to him, individuals act without knowing the ultimate meaning of the historicity in which they participate. Here there is an identification of fact with value. In taking over as its own the Hegelian schema of historical evolution and in draping that schema with all the prestige of science, Marxism opts for an immanent form of moral rationality. Within this rationality, the idea that the good might be able to be established by means of a discussion among individuals is rejected. It is precisely in this that the major difficulty of Marxism resides as regards the notion of justice in history: it entails an overturning of the will to contribute to the fulfilment of justice.

There is obviously no question, here, of contesting the fact that the concern of the author of *Capital* was to ameliorate people's lot or of doubting the tremendous energy and acute intelligence he mobilised to this effect. It seems manifestly clear that the situations of exclusion systematically suffered by those for whom he was fighting might have led him to want to provide them with scientific guarantees of hope and to think that the modalities of political struggle dictated the demand for a monopoly on the truth and for a monopoly on force. That does not keep it from being the case that, in trying too hard to prove this point, he obtained the opposite result: in turning the statement of what is to be into a necessity, he places individuals in a delicate position where the latitude of awareness and action left to them is quite narrow as well as pregnant with grave dangers. Faced with the certitude of being truly right [*dans le vrai*] and with the feeling that what is true will be fulfilled, no matter what happens, individuals have a choice between the following two options: they can collaborate voluntarily with history, acting submissively, or else try to

---

[33] See Unger's remarks in *Social Theory*, pp. 91–92, 100–01, 111–12, 114.
[34] See Boudon, *Theories of Social Change*, p. 210.

change the course of events before that course reaches its goal, running the risks that such an endeavour implies.

To the extent that the idea of justice stems from a dynamic that is absolutely determined, the realisation of that dynamic does not allow for any form of consent that could be worked out during the course of a genuine debate. On the contrary, the alleged custodians of historical truth maintain a monopolistic logic; not only is real dialogue not to be included among the procedures that are constitutive of what is good but that dialogue itself enters into conflict with those procedures. The assurance that one is in direct communication with the general meaning of history renders useless, of course, any discussion worthy of the name, but it also contains the thesis that disagreement is not grounded in right. It is merely a form of deviance to be corrected; in such a case, one has to be brought back to one's senses [*ramener à la raison*], by force if need be.

Within this universe, how is one to tolerate divergent opinions or the articulation of any doubt? To put it in other terms: By adopting the perspective of a complete and perfected science, the Marxist conception of history discredits the exercise of criticism. The consequences of this position for the field of law do not leave room for any surprises.

Here phenomena are explained in terms of a strict determinism that covers history in its entirety. Such an explanatory schema entails the elimination of right, understood as the working out of the conditions whereby one evaluates, in as independent a way as possible, how the political management of human affairs is to be conducted.

When institutions and those who govern champion such a conception of the world, they cannot be challenged without seeing the historical message they are trying to promulgate also called into question. The corollary of treating truth as something definitive and the movement of historicity as its supposed carrier is the requirement that one obey completely the laws of the State. The State makes itself into the interpreter of these laws, while reassuring people that it is itself, as such, nothing but their instrument and servant. Those who claim to embody the meaning of history refuse to recognise the capacity of individuals to criticise legal statements emanating from revolutionary instances of authority. These instances necessarily being right [*ayant obligatoirement raison*], there is no room to question their legitimacy. Political reality inevitably passes for being the very incarnation of rationality, and the distance between what is legal and what is legitimate disappears in so far as this reality is identified in general with the end of history. Now, as we have seen, preservation of this distance is an essential ingredient in any authentic questioning of the way in which rulers discharge their responsibilities. Without it, individuals are deprived of all recourse *vis-à-vis* the officially established power.

This reduction of the right to govern to the law leaves people all the more at a loss, as it is indissociable from a threefold process:

- First, right and morality are reduced to the ways they operate in bourgeois democracy, whence their condemnation *en bloc*. From this point of view, legal procedures, whose mission is defined as being to watch over the well-being of each in the finitude of his personal existence, are not regarded as a fundamental priority. What matters is to be in step with a history whose aim is to achieve universal happiness and that is indifferent to whatever misfortunes may follow therefrom in the daily life of each individual.[35]
- Second, this leads one to raise the problem of the relationships between ends and means in such a way that the absolute character of the finality of history tends to authorise any method whatsoever, provided that it helps to contribute to the ultimate objective. This orientation took on its full meaning as political regimes claiming to be Marxist were installed in power, starting with the Russian Revolution of October 1917. To win out within a hostile environment, the Communists adopted an uncompromising set of practices set within the logic of the dictatorship of the proletariat. The claim was that this move was justified by the finalistic conception of historicity.
- Third, the fiction that one is fulfilling the good, in whose name the very idea of right is discredited,[36] culminates in the establishment of a schizophrenic, nightmare universe in which general emancipation and the achievement of the end of history exist only in the sick and corrupted imagination of the rulers.

Let us mention, nonetheless, that Marxist theory has no monopoly on the sort of dogmatic delusions wherein legitimacy is strictly equated with legality. There is a danger in identifying the right to govern with legality. It appears as soon as the individuals who are in power adopt an absolutist stance that gives unilateral assurance of knowing what is good and that tries to impose it at any price. This risk concerns all political regimes that avail themselves of left-wing or right-wing ideologies in order to assign themselves an ultimate goal whose superiority requires the systematic

---

[35] See Lukes, *Marxism and Morality*, pp. 61–66.
[36] See, for example, the point of view expressed by the Soviet jurist, E. B. Pasukanis, as summarised by Harold J. Berman in *Justice in the USSR: An Interpretation of Soviet Law*, rev. edn (Cambridge, Mass.: Harvard University Press, 1982), pp. 26–29, and Louis Sala-Molins, *La Loi, de quel droit?* (Paris: Flammarion, 1977), pp. 149–60.

abandonment of the right of individuals to break away from the official line, whether that goal has to do with race, the nation, or the proletarian class.[37]

This effort to dissolve the legal in the political in the name of a general historical necessity obviously strikes only at opponents of the institutions that represent the established power. It does not concern the leaders who hold the reins of command of the State. These leaders are not themselves prisoners of legality: they apply the law, change it, and transgress it, as their moods and the imperatives of the moment suit them. The connection they say they have with the truth allows them, in effect, to justify themselves before the masses. Moreover, it is in this way that it is possible to explain their elevation to the status of charismatic and prophetic figures through a cult of personality. Presented as the voice of history, they supposedly are the manifestation of a will that is not arbitrary because it is not, properly speaking, human.

These leaders, who pass for being both the expression and the guarantor of the laws of history, are therefore able to place themselves above human laws. They state that they are the instrument of a historical plan of which mere mortals are naturally unaware but which they themselves know and are helping to achieve. Of course, the more aberrant their orientations, the louder their appeal to the myth of the infallible boss. As such, this infallible boss constitutes the phantasmatic site of historical meaning that authorises the various ways of managing the problem of legality. That said, when the idolatrous love of the leader collapses and the belief in the existence of a privileged relationship between him and history loses its force, the entire organisation of society breaks down. The course of events brought about by this finalistic view, which until then was applauded or at the very least accepted, suddenly is revealed to be both absurd and unbearable.

The Marxist theory of historicity is driven by the ambition to fulfil historical evolution. Although this way of proceeding also enlivens other approaches, it attains in Marxist thought a rarely equalled power of conviction. Indeed, on the one hand, the thesis of historical necessity is developed in Marx's work within the framework of a rationalist conception, and the scientific effort this conception brings into operation has an intellectual depth that leaves a lasting impression. On the other hand, we must recall that the argument is centred around an emancipatory project. It is based upon considerations that have to do with freedom and with the

---

[37] See Jean-Marc Trigeaud, *Persona ou la justice au double visage* (Genoa: Studio Editoriale di Cultura, 1990), p. 119.

threats to freedom contained in bourgeois right; its penetrating analysis thereof cannot therefore completely be ignored.[38]

It nevertheless remains the case that Marxism does not adequately account for the historicity of human phenomena. The disastrous consequences of this failure can be seen in the relations between legitimacy and law. In dedicating itself to the total disappearance of political, social, and economic differentiation, Marxist theory goes against a history that is always in movement. It leads to a paradoxical situation in which the wished for, but never effectively achieved, dissolution of the distance between the real and the ideal entails the elimination of the possibility of an independent questioning of the rulers' right to govern. This is to say that such an orientation fails to recognise the place of the mechanisms of legality and legitimacy which lie at the heart of the dynamic of history.

It is precisely from these difficulties raised by the dogmatic conception of historicity that Weber desired to escape. Now, it turns out that his science of history poses new problems that also thwart the effort to build up an authentic way of thinking about political justice.

The problem of legitimacy in the Weberian view of history

Weber assigns to history no goals that are explicitly known and necessary. Without repudiating his debt to historical materialism, in particular in its understanding of capitalism, he refuses to think that the way in which events unfold fits into an overall plan.[39] This conviction is manifested in an essential way through his denial of the existence of a universal hierarchy of ends, this being a central aspect of the Weberian corpus.

For Weber, in effect, the course of history does not take the form of a general necessity. Thinking that people are led to choose between incompatible values, he defends the thesis that individuals and cultures are opposed to one another without it being possible to decide in a rational way between different viewpoints or to affirm that the evolution in which they participate follows a preestablished direction. The result is that no one can justify the sacrifice of an individual or a group to the interests of a part or of the whole of the collectivity. The fundamental uncertainty hovering over ends entails that the notion of the common good cannot be determined in any rigorous way. In Weber's view, science is incapable of prescribing the manner in which individuals are to live, of teaching

---

[38] See Lukes, *Marxism and Morality*, p. 149.
[39] See Raynaud, *Max Weber et les dilemmes de la raison moderne*, pp. 52–53.

societies the way in which they are to be organised, of educating humanity as to what its future definitely will be, or of militating for the revolutionary advent of an inevitable future.

This haziness about ultimate goals and values has its obvious translation on the level of scientific practice. The objective is not to maintain or to prove that there exists a necessary meaning of history. The Weberian category of the ideal type is one of the major ways in which his rejection of any overall finality manifests itself. Indeed, the mission Weber assigns to social science is to render intelligible individuals' systems of belief and systems of behaviours as well as to establish the order in which phenomena arise. In order to explain reality in causal terms and to interpret it at the same time in a way that makes understanding possible, he combines history with sociology. According to him, the objective of history is to explicate the role of the various antecedents that lie at the origin of an event and to elucidate individual actions, structures, and forms of existence that have a cultural meaning. Sociology seeks to formulate general classifications within which empirical facts have their place.

Between these two disciplines Weber recognises and works out some connections that hang together and complement one another.[40] It is within this perspective that the notion of ideal type is to be situated.

An ideal type is an intellectual construct that is obtained by 'a one-sided accentuation of one or more points of view' or by linking together a 'great many diffuse, discrete' events given in isolation and variable in number. The observer arranges them to form a homogeneous thought-picture.[41] The ideal type, in its conceptual purity, never exactly corresponds to the real. It is a utopia with regard to which the task of the observer is to determine, in each particular case, how far reality approximates it or diverges therefrom.[42] In this regard, the ideal type presupposes a critique of the speculative illusion that consists in deducing the empirical world from the theory and in setting it within a logic of the end of history. It offers a partial grasp of the real that confers upon the understanding, and upon the causal connection that ideal type is itself working out, their fragmentary and open-ended character. It is presented as a mere heuristic tool to which the diversity and richness of phenomena are not to be reduced.

In another connection, and in a complementary way, the notion of ideal type attests to the fact that Weberian sociology is not opposed to

[40] See Weber, *Economy and Society*, vol. I, pp. 19–20.
[41] See Max Weber, ' "Objectivity" in Social Science and Social Policy', in *The Methodology of the Social Sciences*, p. 90.
[42] Ibid.

Marx's version as a static analysis would be to a dynamic study. Without wishing to prove the historical necessity of certain evolutionary changes – for example, the passage from medieval society to capitalism – Weber is perfectly willing to grant the possibility that one might construct ideal types of development.[43] From this perspective, he proposes to extend our knowledge of societies and of their transformations by comparing the reality of history with the ideal types. Thus, for Weber modern capitalism is not the inevitable product of some historical processes that have been elucidated and carefully delimited. It is the largely contingent consequence of multiple factors.

In short, the ideal type does not refer back to hidden entities, nor is it meant to express the finalised character of history. Thus, what separates the Weberian conception of history from the Marxist approach does not reside so much in the content of the sociological analysis as in the status of the scientific concepts.[44] With the help of the notion of the ideal type, Weber seeks to maintain distance between knowledge and being. He excludes a normative explanation of the empirical world that would allow one to evaluate what is according to what ought to be. To the extent that the question of ends remains open, science is, by its essence, in a state of becoming and could not in any case contribute to closing off the indetermination of reality.[45]

Another expression of this uncertainty as to ultimate goals and values is to be found in the distinction – essential to Weberian scientific practice – between the notion of value judgements and that of value relations. Weber introduces these two notions as a means of saving the validity of science. With their help, he hopes to overcome the difficulty connected with the irrationality of values and not to end in an impasse over what domain they represent.[46]

According to Weber, the value judgement is a vital moral affirmation, a way of taking a position that deeply commits the individual[47] and that does not necessarily obtain the agreement of the other. It expresses what each has the right to recognise as a value, what is fittingly to be safeguarded above all or else to be subordinated or sacrificed to a different point of view. Some particular value judgement may be considered fundamental by one individual and devoid of importance by another. For example, some people maintain that one must not compromise on the

---

[43] Ibid., p. 101.   [44] Ibid., pp. 103–06.
[45] See Aron, *Main Currents in Sociological Thought*, pp. 224–25.
[46] Ibid., pp. 229–30.
[47] See Max Weber, 'Critical Studies in the Logic of the Cultural Sciences', in *The Methodology of the Social Sciences*, p. 150.

idea of human equality, whereas in the estimation of others not only is this idea not basic, but it also reveals itself to be against nature and can even involve negative consequences.

In the Weberian logic, a value judgement is personal and subjective. It is thus never the manifestation of a scientifically demonstrable truth. Science, which has universal validity as its specific aim, is therefore confronted with a problem each time it is led to study objects that include an axiological dimension.

The solution Weber proposes in order to surmount this difficulty is to eliminate value judgements from scientific activity and to defend the thesis that what science examines is a *relation* to values.[48] His methodological set-up involves an objective process of selection and organisation.[49] Thus, according to Weber, the sociologist has to think that the idea of equality, to take up once again this same example, corresponds to an area over which individuals have quarrelled and still oppose one another. He therefore will not take a position in these debates and will be content to report them and to catalogue them, thus making of the idea of equality a tool with whose aid he can order the field of reality that is to be analysed.

What is true for the notion of equality is equally true for freedom or for any other value. Weber intends in this way to avoid becoming engaged in endless discussions, while at the same time not preventing himself from treating questions that cannot be examined except by making some allowance for the axiological level.

As we see, relating to values is a crucial procedure in the interpretive mechanisms of the cultural sciences. The distinction between value judgements and value relations aims at resolving the problem of uncertainty as to ends while preserving at the same time the possibility of conducting scientific activities. However, while the utilisation of the concept of ideal types and the recourse to the idea of value relations allow Weber not to fall into the traps to which the Marxist conception of historical change was exposed, they do not rule out the possibility of the science of history generating difficulties of an equivalent seriousness.

In refusing to identify reality with reason understood as the unveiling of an inevitable meaning, the Weberian approach no doubt escapes the dogmatism of the type of historical interpretation Marx inaugurated. Nevertheless, it falls into the opposite tendency. In the refusal to decide about the good in an authoritative manner is hidden an inability to ensure a satisfactory presentation of axiological viewpoints in the domain of history. In making it his objective to account for human phenomena

[48] Max Weber, 'The Meaning of "Ethical Neutrality" in Sociology and Economics', in ibid., p. 21.
[49] Ibid., p. 22.

without judging them, Weber tackles only in indirect fashion and in an attenuated way the dimension of values these phenomena contain. Beyond the fact that systematic axiological detachment does not correspond to the lived experience of individuals, the irreducible character of such a gap, when taken as a principle, is quite problematic for an author whose claim is to be providing an explanation of reality. Moreover, in making it his ambition to elucidate, without taking a position, the horizon of intentionality and signification within which people think and act, Weber is no longer in a position to oppose the triumph of barbarians.[50] For, the non-recognition of the reality of an axiological hierarchy, which underlies the distance he takes from values, prevents him from coming down in favour of certain ones among them and from defending them in relation to other ones.

In the Weberian set-up, the thesis of value neutrality involves a procedure that, all the while expressing axiological detachment, also claims to be a mechanism for protecting the plurality of viewpoints. It is, moreover, because Weber assigns to scientific activity in particular the task of respecting the diversity of opinions that this notion occupies such a central place therein. Nevertheless, by not placing the emphasis on the value of universal community that the requirement of a neutral scientific description presupposes, he renounces the possibility of allowing the neutrality clause, in relying on the logic of tolerance it contains, to preserve those axiological orientations that favour understanding among individuals and cultures. By not linking this neutrality clause explicitly to the humanist dimension, without which it is nevertheless unthinkable, he condemns it to a sterile formalism devoid of any authentic powers to thwart and counteract the values of violence.

This understanding of the duty of scientific activity to stand back and of the conception of scientific truth accompanying this duty is set within the Weberian view of history. It accords with the place and participatory role he attributes to science in the rationalisation process. Blind to the very values that serve as its basic points of support, this understanding is situated within the perspective of a historical evolution that is analysed by Weber as man's gradual effort to take possession of reality and of its historicity. Such a historical evolution goes hand in hand with a growing distrust *vis-à-vis* axiological data that aspire to achieve a foundational status, and it culminates in what we know as the modern world. In this respect, the Weberian interpretation of neutrality and the disenchantment to which it gives rise echo the diagnosis he offers in the field of law regarding both the progress of legal positivism and the tendency, within the

[50] See Aron, *Main Currents in Sociological Thought*, p. 302.

framework of modernity, to establish the legal order as the standard for legitimacy.

Weber's refusal to reduce concrete history to general scientific laws does not rule out his having an overall view of history. In his own way, his ambition is to think through universal history and, at the same time, to explicate the originality of the rise of the West. Thinking that the development of societies, without being necessary, is not for all that arbitrary, in this perspective he accords the rationalisation process a central function in historical evolution. This process is both what Weber proposes to elucidate and the explanatory schema he uses to interpret the course of events.[51] In order to understand this process, it is fitting to take, as a point of departure, the Weberian classification of the forms of activity.

While never contesting the possibility that this classification might be improved upon or enriched, if only because it corresponds to ideal types that do not exhaust reality,[52] Weber brings out four logically distinct forms of activity:[53]

- goal-related rational action, which aims at being effective and supposes the search for a certain kind of agreement between means and ends;
- value-rational action, which requires, on the contrary, that absolute priority be given to the axiological level – which level, whether it be an expression of the ethical, aesthetic, or religious plane, determines the action, whatever its consequences may be;
- affective behaviour, dictated by the immediate state of consciousness, the subject's mood, or his emotional reaction within given circumstances;
- traditional action, ruled by habits, customs, and beliefs, which consists simply in obeying reflexes rooted in long-standing practice.

When enlarged to include the historical totality of lived experience, these forms of activity bring the observer face to face with various operational systems and systems for representing the world. These systems encompass the broad range of conceptions and arrangements possible in individuals' relationships with reality and with one another.

---

[51] See Habermas, *The Theory of Communicative Action*, vol. I, p. 166.

[52] Weber, *Economy and Society*, vol. I, p. 26.

[53] Ibid., pp. 24–26. [Translator/Editor: In translating back into English these Weberian terms for types of social action, I have tried to reflect the author's French versions of these terms. The first, *Zweckrational*, is usually translated, and is translated in *Economy and Society*, as 'instrumentally rational', which downplays the *purposive* or *goal-oriented* character of this type of social action.]

Having made allowance for the ideal character of this classification, Weber indicates that in reality the situations and societies under study frequently give rise to combinations of these forms of activity. These combinations occur in variable doses – even when one of the forms of activity wins out over the others. Moreover, one of them having primacy does not necessarily rule out the resurgence, in the future, of those that currently remain in the background.

Nevertheless, Weber is also suggesting that the rationalisation of action corresponds to a normal development of the faculty of action.[54] In affirming the universal value of this typology, he not only is thinking of its methodological import but also is defending the thesis that it contains a dynamic aspect. This means that rationalisation is the logical result of social activity: as this activity is implemented, rationalisation increasingly tends to take over.

It is this that Weber wants to underscore when he mentions that, in order for an act to achieve the status of an activity, the agent has to communicate to it a subjective signification. He describes social action as that kind which, according to the meaning aimed at by an individual, relates to 'the behaviour of others and is thereby oriented in its course'.[55]

From this point of view, it is apparent that rational acts determined by a goal as well as those defined by their value fully belong to the Weberian idea of activity, since they are characterised, each in their own way, by deliberation and a conscious intention. On the contrary, on account of their unconscious dimension traditional and affective actions hardly achieve the rank of an activity, properly speaking. They lie 'very close to the borderline' between activity and simple observable regularities.[56] There is therefore no room for surprise when Weber states that the natural development of contacts among individuals, as well as their confrontation with the real, unfailingly encourages the passage from mechanical reaction to reflective and meaningful activity. By placing individuals in a position to take initiatives in relation to the many concrete situations they encounter, this natural development leads them to liberate themselves from the pressure of tradition and the emotions and to think more and more by themselves.

In this respect, the growing prevalence of the rationalisation of social activity tends to merge with an appeal to individual responsibility and autonomy. Elsewhere it is said that, although the compulsion of rationality exists everywhere, only in the West – and especially within the framework of capitalism[57] – is this compulsive rationality pushed to the extreme.

---

[54] Ibid., p. 30.   [55] Ibid., p. 4.   [56] Ibid., p. 25.
[57] See Jürgen Habermas, *Toward a Rational Society: Student Protest, Science, and Politics*, trans. Jeremy J. Shapiro (Boston, Mass.: Beacon Press, 1970), p. 98.

Yet this process does not guarantee a real emancipation of individuals. Indeed, Weber interprets the ideal of an autonomous individual and the contribution rationalisation makes to this individual in a way that detaches them from the rationalist context in which they developed.

In the first place, while recognising all along that the notion of autonomy presupposes that the subject might possess the faculty to determine the ends of his action, Weber affirms that this capacity to decide is not the expression of a will freely submitting itself to universal laws. The choice of a system of values ultimately remains arbitrary and contingent. The autonomy of the individual is therefore independent of any objective or practical reason that would in full justice define the finalities of the individual's activity.

In the second place, the rationalisation process undoubtedly concerns each of the spheres of human experience and each set of values, but it affects first the form of action and the internal coherency of world views.[58] The result is that it is difficult to distinguish this process from the expansion of strictly instrumental rationality, which is defined by the growing role attributed to the relationship between means and ends – wherein the question of values does not enter. This is to say that the process of rationalisation ultimately turns against autonomy and transforms into a fate what originally was a decision.[59]

In tending to separate itself off from a rootedness in and a reflection upon the axiological level that would be assumed fully as one's own, the movement towards rationalisation described by Weber therefore involves a procedure for achieving modernisation that nevertheless does not ensure the liberation of individuals. The elimination of its value foundation and the negative effects that elimination has upon the margin of manoeuvre left to individuals is also expressed in the Weberian sociology of political domination and of law.

The central stake involved in Weber's political thought is the question of legitimate command. Logically, in terms of legitimacy the list of ideal types of authority-based relationships ought to correspond to the general classification of forms of activity. However, as Aron underscores,[60] in this inventory only three pure types of legitimate power are catalogued, whereas there are four forms of activity.

Weber thinks that political legitimacy can take on the following properties.[61] First, it has a *rational* aspect, which rests upon belief in the legality

---

[58] See Habermas's comments in *The Theory of Communicative Action*, vol. I, p. 254.

[59] See Max Weber, *The Protestant Ethic and the Spirit of Capitalism*, trans. Talcott Parsons (New York: Charles Scribner's Sons, 1976), for example p. 181: 'The Puritan wanted to work in a calling; we are forced to do so.'

[60] Aron, *Main Currents in Sociological Thought*, pp. 285–86.

[61] Weber, *Economy and Society*, vol. I, pp. 215–16.

of decreed regulations and of the right of those who govern to issue directives. Next, it has a *traditional* dimension, based upon the sense of sanctity of immemorial traditions and upon the recognition from which individuals in command benefit when they appeal to these traditions. Finally, it has a *charismatic* character, which is based upon people's devotion to the exceptional or exemplary qualities of one person as well as upon 'the normative patterns or orders revealed or ordained' by that person.

In view of this classification, it is easy to notice that the failure of these two typologies to coincide with each other is due to the absence of a power relationship that would be the equivalent of value-rational action. The problem that results therefrom has to do with the very peculiar relationship value-rational action has with domination.[62] It testifies to Weber's scepticism with regard to every effort undertaken to ground politics upon a transcendent standard. He evidently grants that, in determining a level that is absolutely valid as well as superior to the negative aspects of the political field,[63] value-rationality has the possibility of playing a major emancipatory role in history. In indicating that value-rationality is not to be reduced to any given historical period, he is recognising that it underlies, in particular, the sort of political activity that is inspired by universalist systems and that this sort of rationality constitutes, under certain conditions, a principle of substantive, and not simply formal, limitation upon the rulers' powers of action. This is particularly so in the case of natural law,[64] which, he states, is 'the purest type of legitimacy based on value-rationality',[65] and of Christianity when the conception thereof is identified with a strict ethic of conviction.[66] Nevertheless, that does not prevent him from defending the thesis that the claim to universality values make in the domain of life in society is doomed to failure. This is manifested in two ways.

First, as soon as those who take a position in terms of values refuse to arrive at a compromise by tempering their intransigence, and as soon as it becomes their ambition to regulate the political dimension completely by eliminating from this dimension the dilemmas of action and the weight of domination this dimension introduces, they fall in an illusion. The illusion in question rests upon the tendency to make a system of claims into an absolute and neglects the political order's own consistency. Whether they rely, for example, upon the will to ground their way of governing upon an evangelical morality or they aim at achieving a harmonious

---

[62] On this question, we are following the interpretation of Philippe Raynaud, in *Max Weber et les dilemmes de la raison moderne*, pp. 161–63.
[63] See Weber, *Economy and Society*, vol. I, pp. 33, 36.
[64] Ibid., vol. II, p. 867.   [65] Ibid., vol. I, p. 37.
[66] Max Weber, 'The Profession and Vocation of Politics', in *Political Writings*, ed. Peter Lassman and Ronald Speirs (Cambridge University Press, 1994), p. 364.

reconstruction of society from the standpoint of the political rationalism that issues from the Enlightenment,[67] those who take positions in
terms of values are deceiving themselves and abusing others. These positions make them believe, wrongly, that it is possible to do away with the
specific characteristics of political activity, to eliminate political domination, and to achieve total social harmony.[68] Even worse, they represent
a dangerous mystification: far from contributing to the disappearance of
violence, those who take positions in terms of values implement a kind
of absolutism that refuses to acknowledge the existence of different ways
of ordering life and the need to respect these ways by working out a
morality that corresponds to their plurality.[69] This sort of absolutism is
not concerned, therefore, with the consequences that might result from
its application. It is set within a logic where the end justifies the means.
It generates a spiral of violence and exacerbates the recourse to force.

Second, to this situation is added the fact that the claims to universality
of various systems of values create an incompatibility among them and
drives them to oppose one another. This situation gives rise to conflicts
that are all the more insoluble as the deepening of those conflicts instigates
a phenomenon of one-upmanship that serves to discredit all suprapolitical
axioms to which the idealists wish to adapt and subordinate the conduct
of political life. The result is a scepticism towards values that favours an
expansion of pure instrumentality. This expansion sets in motion actions
that are oriented towards achieving objectives that supposedly break away
from value determinations.

Although it may be widespread in history, value-rationality therefore
does not constitute, in Weber's opinion, a legitimate form of domination,
properly speaking. It does not respect the specificity of political action.
It does not avoid the violence it condemns and does not achieve the kind
of universal fulfilment to which it aspires.

It is from this perspective that the Weberian sociology of law – and, in
particular, the place the question of legality in the modern world occupies therein – is to be understood. Legal positivism and the role Weber
attributes to it are not unreminiscent, in the area of law, of the status of
neutrality on the plane of scientific methodology and of the scientific theory of knowledge. Certainly, Weber is seeking to resolve in this way the

---

[67] In *Economy and Society*, vol. I, p. 6, Weber cites human rights as one way of illustrating
the fanaticism involved in an extreme rationalism.
[68] See, for example, what Max Weber says in his letter to Robert Michels of 4 August
1908: 'Any thought ... of removing the rule of men over men through even the most
sophisticated forms of "democracy", is "utopian" ' (cited by Mommsen, *Max Weber and
German Politics 1890–1920*, p. 394).
[69] Weber, 'The Profession and Vocation of Politics', in *Political Writings*, p. 362.

antinomies of political action and to shield people from the violence engendered by the systematic application of value-rationality or of the ethic of conviction. However, the weaknesses of his analysis are equivalent to those detected in his conception of scientific neutrality.

The Weberian sociology of law analyses the phenomenon of the rationalisation of the legal field, from its charismatic aspects – which, as it happens, are 'revealed' and therefore irrational – to the rational characteristics, which are manifested in particular in rigorously deductive rules and in the growing technical complexity of procedure in the modern world. In this regard, the study of the evolution of modern natural law occupies a choice position.

Initially, natural law favoured the emancipation of individuals by reducing their dependence upon those who dominate: it restricted the arbitrariness of judgements and undermined the foundations of established authoritarian powers. On the other hand, by contributing, in tandem with legislative rationalism or even with common law, to the progressive destruction of various forms of particular law, it favoured the development of abstract norms and facilitated the mechanism whereby society itself becomes bureaucratised.

In addition, from the beginning of political modernity democratic and liberal principles have presented an ambiguity that natural law would only aggravate as time went on: whereas the idea of equality before the law requires from administrative authorities a rational and formal objectivity, the disinherited masses did not stop demanding that there be interventions from time to time in order to protect their interests or to bring their material situation into line with that of the well-off classes. To a certain extent, the development of natural law gradually serves to integrate these demands for substantive justice. But, according to Weber, socialism constitutes in this regard a decisive break. In particular, by having property originate in the labour of each person, and not in inheritance, monopoly, or contract, and by proposing an eschatological view, socialism works out a critique of formal law that creates an insuperable rift between the latter and substantive law. The impossibility of surmounting this gap contributes towards the ruination of all metajuristic axioms of natural law and culminates in its self-destruction.

Moreover, belief in the foundational role of values has, according to Weber, been wiped out in modernity. The evolutionist theses of Auguste Comte, historicist theories of organic growth, and realist theories of power and of state interests worked together to discredit them.[70]

---

[70] Weber, *Economy and Society*, vol. II, p. 874.

In any case, it is in this way that the destiny of modern politics is fulfilled. Scepticism towards the values that lie at the source of legal rules evacuates the idea of a natural law that would serve as a protective railing against any overreaching on the part of rulers. One can no longer have recourse to higher values in order to oppose overly expeditious practices. As such, this disintegration of natural law cannot be separated from the enlargement of the field of instrumental rationality and from the accentuation of actual submission to the legal authorities.[71] The latter no longer have to justify themselves by making reference to any supreme principles. It suffices that institutions give their choices and their acts the form of law for these to have the character of law. To put it in other terms: what one is witnessing is an identification of political reason with legality and a reduction of legitimacy to law.

In elucidating in this way the triumph of legal positivism and in adhering to the movement that set the legal order as the ultimate standard for what is legitimate, Weber is nevertheless not thinking of renouncing the imperative of justice. On the contrary; for him, values are irrational and the conflicts that set them in opposition to one another are insoluble and are generative of violence. By way of consequence, the axiological detachment of positive law is a way of preserving some possibility of understanding and cooperation among persons. Thanks to a juridical conception that places legitimacy in the same category as a notion of legality claiming to be distinct from values, one defuses the risks contained in the confrontation between irreconcilable demands.

Let us note in passing that it is hard not to recognise that this orientation is itself expressive of an axiological engagement. To wish to avoid the uncontrolled reign of force is to opt for values that endeavour to limit violence as much as possible. This is, moreover, what is being suggested when Weber evokes the possibility of an authentic statesman: by integrating the ethic of conviction into the ethic of responsibility – which amounts to attributing a higher status to the latter, since the ethic of responsibility worries about the consequences of the actions to which it gives rise[72] – the authentic statesman tries to implement reasonable decisions. Such decisions are not to be reduced to the establishment of the appropriate technical means for obtaining an end without taking the axiological dimension into consideration; they presuppose, on the contrary, that some values are taken into account when engaging in political activity.[73] To put it in other terms: it is to the extent that formal law carries with it a

---

[71] Ibid., p. 875.
[72] Weber, 'The Profession and Vocation of Politics', in *Political Writings*, pp. 359–60.
[73] Ibid., p. 367.

minimum axiological investment that it can oppose the dangers a politics conducted solely in the name of values bears within itself.

However, Weber grants a basic importance to the theses of the irrationality and irreconcilability of axiological systems. The role he assigns to formal law is therefore developed only to a small extent in his writings. It remains too embryonic to constitute a solid alternative to his theses concerning the irrationality and irreconcilability of values. The same thing goes, therefore, for legal positivism as well as for the Weberian interpretation of neutrality, as applied to scientific methodology: his capacity to defend the ideals of tolerance remains, under these conditions, very weak.

It is true that the ethics of the authentic politician require that he be rationally accountable for the ultimate motivations and possible consequences of his acts. This ethic is therefore diametrically opposed to brute force. Likewise, from the Weberian perspective the safeguarding of political freedom and, beyond that, the safeguarding of human dignity really do depend upon the survival of institutions and practices inherited from the modern emancipatory period – for example, the rule of law [*État de droit*], checks upon those who govern, and the open and public nature [*publicité*] of our political existence. It is just as incontestable that the critique of the political rationalism of modernity proposed by Weber is not accompanied by a complete subordination to power politics.[74] This critique is opposed principally to the point of view that makes claims to sanctity in politics – which, according to Weber, is a contradiction in terms.[75] But on the other hand, Weber does not give himself the means to think through those features that render possible his concern for tolerance. His analysis of the aporias of modern politics does not allow him to construct a solid defence of democracy. His inability to put into place a satisfactory reflection upon the founding values of democracy coincides with his refusal to assume, from the standpoint of reason, that political choices are rooted in values.

The axiological position having been, in the main, discredited, positive law is not up to the task of being the expression of a practical truth. Concretely speaking, it has been disarmed in the face of the manipulations of which it can become the plaything in the political arena. By detaching it from the level of values in the hope of avoiding the meanderings of the politics of conviction, Weber is exposing the moderating function he sees at work in legal positivism to the possibility of being betrayed and diverted for the benefit of some unscrupulous set of interests. In relation to these dangers, legal positivism is not in a position to appeal to values

[74] Ibid., pp. 354–55.   [75] Ibid., pp. 365–66.

that would have the status of rational foundations and that would allow it to denounce reprehensible actions.

The monopoly on legitimate violence held by the State is not limited by principles and criteria that can pass for being objective. Right therefore cannot even oppose force with the assurance that it is acting in accordance with the truth. As we see, the recourse the governed have at their disposal is rather feeble. It resides uniquely in the hope of being lucky enough to be ruled by authentic politicians who are respectful of human dignity.

While the Weberian adherence to legal positivism allows one to escape the Marxist danger contained in the identification of legitimate law with revolutionary rationality, it tends to give rise to another defect that is no less serious. In wanting to escape from the impasse of materialism and its terrorist drift, Weber obstinately persists in his refusal to anchor modern positive law in a coherently worked out attempt to take practical reason into account. In doing this, he elaborates a conception of legal positivism that is not up to the task of offering an adequate guarantee for the democratic ideal of tolerance. The laws cannot be respected simply because of the fact that they have been promulgated if they do not correspond to the values in which the members of the community recognise themselves.

In addition, it is a manifest error to advance the idea that in modernity formal law is free of all axiological content. This amounts to taking the effect for the cause. How can one not see that formal law itself has to be integrated into a system of domination, which in turn has to be legitimated as a whole in order for legality to be considered as an indicator of legitimacy?

It finally proves necessary to raise the question of the determination of right by values in order that right might not be reduced to an instrument prone to easy manipulation or violation. It is therefore appropriate to demonstrate in a credible way that right expresses and promotes, in a given environment and at a given time, the principles of truth and justice. Otherwise, it constitutes only a simulacrum of justice.

Let us put it in other terms: when the right to govern is said to stem from a procedure that is independent of the substantive domain and is evaluated in terms of the legal character of the rules that are decreed, the distance between legality and legitimacy tends to dissolve. And the problematic of legitimacy, which affords one a critical look at political reality, tends to disappear. As a matter of fact, legal positivism ends up bringing on what Weber wanted to avoid when he endeavoured to formulate a non-dogmatic analysis of political life: under cover of conformity to legality, there is a risk of the rulers attaining impunity and of the ruled becoming alienated.

In failing to furnish the conditions for a rational judgement, the very concept of right, whether political or not, itself loses meaning. Weber's conception of legal positivism is in perfect agreement with the distinction he proposes to make between the notion of value relations, which are scientifically acceptable, and that of value judgements, which are scientifically unacceptable. It also accords with his general approach to the idea of legitimacy, defined as a mere belief. In the scientific, legal, and political fields, one notices that all attempts to establish the validity of a foundation based in values have been foresworn.

Although Weber's humanism prevents him from giving himself over to an attitude of pure indifference as regards values, his conception of positive law ill protects against the eventuality of an authoritarian use of the law.[76] This is all the more noticeable as the thesis about the need to combine the constitutional parliamentary State with a plebiscitary type of leadership and the thesis that tends to subordinate major democratic principles to the interests of national power are added to his theses about the procedural character of legitimacy and about the irreducible aspect of a certain level of violence in political action.[77] Certainly, one must not underestimate the impact of the intellectual climate in which these arguments were formulated, any more than one should underestimate the impact of the confrontations then taking place in Germany between, on the one hand, the radicalised masses and, on the other hand, the advocates of order.

Nevertheless, these circumstances should not induce one to fail to recognise the gravity of the consequences this Weberian tendency to peg legitimacy on legality is liable to justify. It is to this that the work of Carl Schmitt bears witness. However eclectic the Schmittian theories may have been and whatever may be the differences separating them from Weber's own theses, there is a certain continuity between the two. Schmitt developed a conception of political right that could be said to have been encouraged by the considerations the elder thinker developed about the capacities of the law to work out a formal situation of legitimacy.[78]

Legitimacy and legality: from Max Weber to Carl Schmitt

Certainly, Max Weber fought in favour of the democratic institutions that existed in the Germany of his time.[79] His thinking is not, for all that,

---

[76] See Mommsen's remarks in *Max Weber and German Politics 1890–1920*, pp. 409–10.
[77] Ibid., p. 410.   [78] Ibid., pp. 382–83, note 156, and pp. 404–05.
[79] See Max Weber, 'Parliament and Government in a Reconstructed Germany (A Contribution to the Political Critique of Officialdom and Party Politics)', published in appendix II to vol. II of *Economy and Society*; see, for example pp. 1383–84.

wholly unrelated to that of Carl Schmitt. Without going so far as to affirm that Schmitt is Weber's spiritual offspring, as Julien Freund has done,[80] it must be recognised that he draws radical conclusions from premises already present in the Weberian interpretation of legitimacy. In particular, his reflections are designed to push these premises to their outermost limits. They thus serve to implant a view that establishes the irrationality and contingency of decision-making as the principle for the autonomy of politics. Politics is then considered as the antithesis of the rationalistic management of political life and as the expression of a truth that is but the manifestation of the will of the State.

Schmitt's prolongation of certain aspects of Weber's arguments may first be noticed as regards the idea of legal formalism in democracy and of its legitimating power. In order to understand this prolongation, it is worthwhile recalling that, in deeming the type of democracy that is based on natural law to be unrealisable, Weber deduces from this situation that legitimacy and respect for democratic rules do not rest upon fundamental values whose laws would be at once the signs and the instruments for their propagation. Legitimacy and respect for democratic rules depend, on the contrary, upon their conformity with the statutes of state-based instances of authority and with the procedures of the laws that have been proclaimed.[81] It is, furthermore, because Weber grants so much importance to the formal recognition of political acts that he describes the bureaucracy as the purest mode in which legal mechanisms can operate.

Weber is therefore convinced of the impossibility of basing modern democracy on any kind of rationality that is made up of essential values. From this perspective, the formal legalism of the democratic system rules out any ethical limitation on democratic legitimacy. The idea of an unjust use of the law tends to be disqualified. Indeed, in order for the law to be proclaimed as valid, it does not benefit from a grounding in reason, but it does have to fulfil some procedural requirements. This idea sets us on the path towards a decisionist conception of legitimate political activity. Schmitt takes it upon himself to develop this conception.

The fact that, according to Weber, the legality of democracy does not rely upon an axiological plane that would determine in an imperative way the conditions for its legitimacy easily allows one to go so far as to present the State as an entity that is capable of choosing what is or is not desirable in terms of its interests. It suffices for Schmitt to ignore Weber's arguments in favour of a practical rationality and an authentic politics – see in

---

[80] Julien Freund, préface to Carl Schmitt's *La Notion de politique* suivi de *Théorie du partisan*, trans. Marie-Louise Steinhauser (Paris: Calmann-Lévy, 1972), pp. 15–16, note 2.

[81] See Mommsen's analyses in *Max Weber and German Politics 1890–1920*, pp. 402–03.

particular Weber's criticisms directed against the bureaucratic mentality and bureaucratic attitudes in politics[82] and his proposals concerning liberal and democratic reforms[83] – and to exploit the ambiguities in Weber's reflections in order to give free rein to a way of thinking that places the sovereignty of state institutions above all else.[84]

Thus, in his book on Legality and Legitimacy, written during the spring of 1932, Schmitt attacks the Weberian thesis concerning belief in the legitimacy of formal law. He brings out the fact that this thesis allows room for a value-neutral approach to the Constitution, which does not permit one to mount a solid defence of the Weimar Republic.[85] But at the same time, Schmitt avails himself of this thesis in order to affirm that the moral foundations of the legislative parliamentary regime have lost all legitimating power.[86] Taking this situation into account, one has to, according to Schmitt, recognise the need to revise one's conception of politics as well as political practice in order to contribute, in opposition to liberalism and its failures, towards a regeneration of the might of the State.

Let us put it in other words: whereas Schmitt denounces Weber's adherence to formal legalism, he also leans on this formal legalism in order to go beyond it and to affirm the primacy of the State. From this perspective, he works out a theory that, being deduced directly from a critique of the intellectual bases of parliamentarism and taking as its target the type of political thinking that champions a right that is grounded in reason, maintains the idea that the State is above the laws. In politics, the imperatives of order and stability win out over other considerations.

We see that Schmitt's will, made manifest in Legality and Legitimacy, to preserve the Republic against the threat created by extremist parties (whether they be of Nazi or Communist obedience),[87] originates in his concern to safeguard the State. The anti-parliamentarian and authoritarian signification and import of his undertaking situates him, then,

---

[82] Weber, 'Parliament and Government in a Reconstructed Germany...', in *Economy and Society*, vol. II, especially pp. 1417, 1438.

[83] Ibid., for example, pp. 1403, 1419–20, 1426–27, 1439–40, 1461–62.

[84] See the remarks of Joseph W. Bendersky, *Carl Schmitt: Theorist for the Reich* (Princeton University Press, 1983), pp. 10–11, and those of George Schwab, in his introduction to Carl Schmitt, *Political Theology: Four Chapters on the Concept of Sovereignty*, trans. George Schwab (Cambridge, Mass.: MIT Press, 1985), p. xii.

[85] Carl Schmitt, *Legalität und Legitimität* (Munich and Leipzig: Duncker & Humblot, 1932), p. 14. The reader may also refer to Mommsen's comments in *Max Weber and German Politics 1890–1920*, p. 386.

[86] Carl Schmitt, preface to 2nd edn (1926), 'On the Contradiction between Parliamentarism and Democracy', in *The Crisis of Parliamentary Democracy*, trans. Ellen Kennedy (Cambridge, Mass.: MIT Press, 1985), pp. 8, 20–21, 49–50.

[87] Consult Bendersky, *Carl Schmitt*, p. 149.

within the climate of reaction that served to cast opprobrium upon the ideals of democracy in Germany and helped to make itself democracy's gravedigger.

Schmitt's thinking, we said, prolongs Weber's arguments. This prolongation is also made manifest through the themes of charismatic leadership and the plebiscitary process.

From Weber's point of view, the mode of legitimating domination grounded upon belief in legal formalism is less attractive than the traditional and charismatic types of legitimacy, even if, conceptually speaking, it is equivalent. Indeed, legal legitimacy has an abstract dimension to it that is hardly likely to trigger popular enthusiasm. In addition, it offers relatively limited guarantees for assuring not only the stability of institutions but also their dynamism. Apropos of this, its association with the bureaucratic management of society ill predisposes it to produce rulers of an authentically political stature.

That is why, when the problem of constructing the Weimar regime was posed, Weber did not want legal legitimacy to be its sole foundation.[88] In this spirit, and after the failure of his constitutional project, which was aimed at combining the value-neutral formalism of the parliamentary State with the preservation of the monarchy,[89] he pleaded in favour of a regime that unites formal law, as it is manifested in parliamentary and bureaucratic instances of authority, with a Reich president, who would occupy the place of charismatic leader.[90]

In this cooperation between those two modes of legitimacy, the balance leans perceptibly to the side of the presidential figure. Indeed, the establishment of a plebiscitary mechanism, via the direct election of the president,[91] ends up giving this person more weight than the parliament and the bureaucracy. The Weberian objective was thus to endeavour to ensure that the new republican institutions would run properly. While recognising all along the advantages tied to parliamentary and bureaucratic procedures, for him it became a matter of ensuring that the chief of State, even though responsible before the parliament and the masses, would have sufficient margin of manoeuvre to be neither the toy of the parties nor the plaything of the bureaucracy. With the aid of a Reich president who has a popular mandate, it was Weber's wish to inject some emotion and to generate a sense of calling in the management of the nation's affairs.

Schmitt seizes upon this Weberian provision for a presidential post and develops it to its ultimate conclusions. He eliminates the constitutional

[88] See Mommsen, *Max Weber and German Politics 1890–1920*, pp. 386–87.
[89] Ibid., pp. 291–93.   [90] Ibid., pp. 385–86.   [91] Ibid., pp. 339–41, 345.

guarantees foreseen by Weber in order for the president to be able to assume his role of leader in an environment that includes a parliamentary dimension. And whereas the Weberian approach grounds republican institutions upon the parliament and upon a chief of State elected by universal suffrage, Schmitt ignores the first element and accepts only the second as a form of legitimacy.[92] He uses the chief of State in order to discredit the parliament as well as the parties that comprise it. For him, it is a matter of damming up the action of various pressure groups who attack the unity of the nation and strike a blow against its very political existence. In effect, these pressure groups are but adversaries. They do not confront each other within the framework of a friends/enemies division, which is the essence of politics, since upon it rests, according to Schmitt, the State's capacity to impose its will and its sovereignty in decisive cases.[93] Because he wishes for the Reich president, defined as charismatic leader, to be the motive force behind the task of political integration, Schmitt describes him as an instrument for the protection of the State against egotistical particularisms, that is to say, as a means of defence for the Weimar Constitution, which is identified with the German people as a united totality.

The movement by which Schmitt, starting from the Weberian conception of the president, is led to evoke the figure of the chief of State as representative of the people's political will, in opposition to partisan pluralism, is facilitated by the fact that the Weberian thesis of legal formalism is tied to a formal understanding of democracy. The corollary of this understanding is a functional justification of democracy. It is indeed very much from this perspective that Weber contests the idea that the essential finality of a democratic parliamentary regime would be the achievement of the ideals of modern natural law, which have to do with the substantive demands of individuals and with popular sovereignty.[94] This may be explained as much by his convictions concerning the historical process of rationalisation and the irrationality of values as by his works in political sociology, which convince him of the class character of the principles of liberal democracy.[95] Not only does he think that it is not possible to avoid an elitist management of political life, but it is also his view that liberal democracy in reality restricts participation to political parties.[96] Now, to the extent that, in addition to the task of offering a technical check upon the bureaucracy, liberal democracy assigns to participation the mission

[92] Ibid., p. 386.
[93] Carl Schmitt, *The Concept of the Political*, trans., intro., and notes George Schwab (University of Chicago Press, 1996), p. 45.
[94] See Mommsen's comments in *Max Weber and German Politics 1890–1920*, pp. 393–96.
[95] Ibid., p. 394.   [96] Ibid., p. 398.

of selecting leaders of authentically political stature, it is clear that the parliamentary system's inability to fulfil this task in a satisfactory way tempts an author like Schmitt towards anti-parliamentarianism and reinforces his sense that salvation can come only from a charismatic chief endowed with the maximum amount of power.

In another connection, let us note that Weber does not imagine a plebiscitary presidency as parliament's executive organ. He is thinking, rather, that the president has to guide the will of the parliamentary authorities in order to fulfil his personal interpretation of what is good for the nation. It is on the basis of this capacity to win the support of the parliament and of the population that he is responsible before them.[97] Schmitt was able to exploit this viewpoint in order to work out his theory of the charismatic leader.

Weber did not foresee, nor would he have approved of, Schmitt's totalitarian developments of these Weberian arguments. Such developments led Schmitt to subject right to the imperatives of political struggle – that is to say, it led him to affirm that what is decided sovereignly by the authorities in power is legitimate, having made allowance for the priority given to the preservation and consolidation of the might of the State. This connection between our two authors ought not to lead us to think, however, that they shared a community of minds that was unique to them. Set within a specific historical climate, their reflections were formulated in terms that echo the atmosphere of the moment. The point of view adopted by Schmitt, for whom right is not in itself capable of providing answers to questions concerning the legitimacy of power and of political justice, was bolstered by the crisis into which the Weimar regime was sinking on both the domestic and international levels.[98] It is in this respect that he thinks that the sort of conciliation right is supposed to be working towards achieving has in fact contributed towards the weakening of the State. Such a conciliatory effort takes the form of positive laws lacking any axiological basis, a liberal notion of society, as well as its accompanying defence of individuals and their rights. It also takes the form of the regulation of international life via abstract norms. Schmitt emphasises here that the idea of conciliation motivating right generally conceals particular interests that employ this idea in order to achieve their plans under cover of achieving the good. Efforts at conciliation stumble over the fact that politics is grounded upon a logic of confrontation.[99]

[97] Ibid., p. 397.
[98] See Habermas, *The New Conservatism*, pp. 131–32.
[99] Schmitt, *The Concept of the Political*, pp. 66–68.

Schmitt takes as his examples situations in which there is extreme tension in order to show that, in foreign as well as domestic political relationships, right has no foundational status. Only relations of forces count. He states that the framework for political activity is not a communitarian universe within which relationships based upon consensus and compromise, organised in legal terms, are established. Political activity unfolds within a universe where entities engaged in a struggle for their existence tear each other to pieces.[100] Far from being limited by a normally valid legal order, state sovereignty, an integral part of politics conceived as a merciless confrontation, transcends that order. The rulers' exclusive power of decision is the source for what is politically valid.

Breaking with both rationalism and liberalism, the Schmittian conception culminates in the following assertion: the State, which does not really have to render any account to society, no longer has to fulfil even the formal conditions for legitimation required by Weber. In so far as it claims to be placed in the service of the State, the will of the political rulers is valid unilaterally. Their will is the guarantor of the law and of legitimacy.

The anti-democratic character of Schmitt's theories should not lead one to underestimate the quality of his work. That quality is manifest, notably in Schmitt's competence as an expert in matters of public law as well as in his diagnoses of his era – which, into the thirties, are not lacking in clairvoyance.[101] Although opposed to the political positions he took, respected academics, Schmitt's colleagues prior to 1933, were very particular about recognising that quality,[102] before his support of Hitler's regime led them to condemn irreparably both him and his work. It is true that some of his analyses offer an interest that goes beyond the mere framework of historical investigation. This is particularly true of his reflections upon what the State's attitude ought to be in situations of extreme political crisis.[103] It is indeed difficult to avoid the question of how extensive should be the powers of the State and of what measures the State has the right to put into effect when contested by radical opposition forces.

Schmitt resolves this question by recommending the instauration of a state of exception, which is the mark of a statist form of sovereignty that stands above legal norms.[104] In the specific case of the Weimar regime, he

[100] Ibid., p. 53.
[101] See Habermas, *The New Conservatism*, pp. 132–35.
[102] Ibid., p. 133. See also Bendersky, *Carl Schmitt*, for example pp. 169–70, 190.
[103] Schmitt, *Political Theology*, p. 15.
[104] Ibid., p. 12: 'The existence of the State is the undoubted proof of its superiority over the validity of the legal norm. The decision frees itself from all normative ties and becomes in the true sense absolute. The State suspends the law in the exception on the basis of its right of self-preservation, as one would say.'

wished for the Reich president to be able to attribute to himself the powers he deems it good to have in light of the circumstances.[105] Schmitt also considered it necessary to declare unconstitutional and to outlaw political organisations whose explicit aim is to destroy republican institutions.[106]

The question is a basic one: what are the limits within which a democratic regime can, without seriously jeopardising its credibility and its very existence, permit opinions and acts whose avowed aim is, in case of victory, to destroy that regime? Schmitt's response to this question cannot satisfy us and must be condemned, so much does it prepare the ground for the deadly and damaging spread of the brown plague. Without losing sight, of course, of the slippery slope of political terrorism onto which extreme forms of political prohibition and exclusion runs the risk of descending at each instant, one must nevertheless credit Schmitt with having posed the problem. In addition, his arguments serve as a goad for political thinking.

This qualification, which comes to temper the severity of the judgement brought against Schmitt's works, cannot make one forget that the high quality of his thinking is the flip side of a major defect and that this defect burdens his overall conception of the political. In raising the exceptional situation to the status of a revelatory and foundational element of the essence of the political, Schmitt reduces the latter to what is in fact only one of its components. There is no contesting the fact that the political is quickened by relations of force and violent actions. Yet it cannot be summed up in an uninterrupted series of brutal confrontations. Periods of stability and consensus do exist, and during these periods the legal authorities play a major and crucial role as operatives for justice and as instruments for the allocation of material and symbolic goods.

Moreover, when political conflicts occupy centre stage, legal considerations are not totally emptied of all import. This may be seen in two complementary ways. First, the objective behind conflicts is not necessarily the appropriation of power for its own sake. These conflicts can unfold in the name of demands, the achievement of which is deemed by some both possible and necessary. From this perspective, there exists at the heart of the struggle an appeal to right. Second, and this is the corollary of the preceding point, the fact that activity of a legal character may be tied to relations of forces does not imply that such activity constitutes exclusively a veiled way of exercising violence and oppression. Indeed, relations of forces are indissociable from a dynamic in which

[105] Ibid., pp. 6–7.
[106] For more details about this problem, see Bendersky's comments in *Carl Schmitt*, pp. 129, 148–49, 153.

collective beliefs regarding the organisation of life in society become involved in the triggering, development, and outcome of confrontations. It is therefore not power alone, understood in the physical sense, that decides events.

The way in which adversaries line up against each other, the points of contention that set them at odds [*les différends qui les opposent*], and the results of their conflicts all depend upon values. The capacity of these values to arouse, in connection with the identity of society and its evolution, a sense of devotion or to create, on the contrary, a movement of rejection and refusal contributes in full to how these relations of force will be determined. A political action that aims to have a major impact while not taking into account what the members of a community consider to be right is ultimately doomed to failure, even if that may take some time.

By limiting his conception of the political to the characteristics of crises and to a realist perspective, Schmitt abandons himself to a highly warlike view of politics. Such a view of politics feeds the integrational logic of the totalitarian State[107] – and this is so, even though Schmitt was not fully recognised by the Nazis as being one of their own.[108]

The distance between the law of the State and legitimacy, already eroded in Max Weber's works, finds itself reduced to nothing by the analyses of Carl Schmitt. With Schmitt, so-called legitimate politics consists in the legality of the state authority's power of decision. It boils down to forbidding individuals to oppose the choices and actions of the State and thus erases the very meaning of the idea of legitimacy.

As we see, theories that examine social and political phenomena while trying to think as best as they can their historicity in connection with their practical aspects are still incapable of formulating the theme of the right to govern in satisfactory terms. Their interpretation of the history and historicity of social facts prevents them from having an understanding of political reality that would permit them to explicate the conditions that are to be fulfilled in order for the relationships between rulers and ruled to have an authentically legitimate character. Whereas the approach advocated by Marx sins by its dogmatic reading of history, the work of Weber remains a prisoner of his ideas about the war of the gods and the process of rationalisation. Ultimately adopting the credo of positivism, he opens the way to the dangers with which the Schmittian theory of the political is pregnant.

---

[107] See Jean-Pierre Faye, *Langages totalitaires. Critique de la raison/l'économie narrative* (Paris: Harmann, 1972), pp. 377–91, 630, 700–06.
[108] See Bendersky, *Carl Schmitt*, pp. 219–23, 242.

HISTORICITY OF MODERNITY, NOSTALGIA FOR THE ABSOLUTE, AND LEGITIMACY

The inability of Marxist and Weberian analyses to pose in a satisfactory manner the problem of values and of legitimacy is tied to an interpretation of modernity that remains impregnated with a premodern mentality. Indeed, these analyses do not succeed in ridding themselves of an absolutist definition of the truth, which states that the truth draws its credibility from the fact that it is unique and immediately evident.

To shed light on this phenomenon, it is fitting in the first place to point out that the historicity of modernity resides in a movement of self-reflection and that, within the context of this self-reflective movement, the era thus defined appears as an artifact. It is fitting, in the second place, to emphasise that, although they are one of the manifestations of this state of affairs, Marxist and Weberian analyses remain impotent to survey this state of affairs and to draw therefrom some teachings that would allow a reconciliation of the possibility of a practical truth with the consciousness of the historical character of individual and collective forms of existence.

The world as artifact in the experience of modernity

The experience of modernity is tied to the compelling fact that people feel their lives are involved in a history. Individuals and societies perceive themselves as set not in an intangible world but in a successive sequence of phenomena. This mechanism seems to be indissociable from a conception of time wherein the thematisation of movement refers to a temporal unity, which allows one to determine what separates the past from the present and to establish what has changed in the interim. Nevertheless, the historical identity of modernity, which began to be set in place in the sixteenth century,[109] is not confined to the conviction that reality is today not identical to what it was yesterday, or even to the appropriation of the past *qua* the present's memory of it. These features are completed by the idea that there exists a future that is their prolongation. This future takes the form of a time-to-come [*avenir*], which is generative of changes devolving upon individuals. From this perspective, the stake for these individuals is no more or less than the production of the conditions for their own life.[110]

---

[109] See the remarks of George Huppert, *The Idea of Perfect History: Historical Erudition and Historical Philosophy in Renaissance France* (Urbana: University of Illinois Press, 1970), p. 152.

[110] See Marcel Gauchet, *The Disenchantment of the World: A Political History of Religion*, trans. Oscar Burge (Princeton University Press, 1997), p. 177. [Translator/Editor: The

If that is so, it is undoubtedly because modern experience goes hand in hand with the idea that individuals evolve within a context that is largely in their own charge, because they are in good part responsible for their development and for the directions they take in various fields of activity. This faculty of action, which modern people recognise, concerns their relationships with nature as well as the relations that bind them to other individuals. In relation to nature, they do not perceive themselves as passive objects, subject to forces that go infinitely beyond them and in the face of which they must bow down as before a destiny, or upon which they could not have any effect except though prayer and magical rituals. Not confining themselves to a narration and interpretation of nature's mysteries,[111] they impute to themselves the ability to set their mark upon nature. From a power that was to be treated deferentially, the natural universe becomes a domain to be domesticated, a tool to be employed in the service of human needs – indeed, a potential set of occasions to be seized in order to enjoy at one's leisure the pleasures of a newly discovered form of mastery.

To all this is added the idea that individuals belong to a collective type of organisation and are involved in personal relationships over which they can exert an influence. Objective knowledge of nature and sensitivity to the constructed character of one's existence in society are two aspects of one and the same attitude, which boils down to this: that one inhabits an environment, the artifactual status of which seems to be its basic characteristic. In this case as in the other, modern experience implies that individuals conceive themselves more and more as autonomous subjects.

In order for this new awareness to develop, individuals and societies had to break loose from a certain number of givens. A new conception of reality could not be given systematic form without a collapse of the constitutive elements of the premodern community, elements that determined that community's own identity as well as the identity of its members. The passage from the first of these ages to the next required the deployment of three factors as well as of their overlapping effects.

First of all, this change would not have taken place had there not been a decline of tradition. In order to overcome one's inability even to glimpse an alternative to the established order and in order to break away from commandments validated by the past, one had to break with an adherence

phrase in question, 'les hommes qui produisent leur propre monde dans le temps' (people who produce their own world in time), appears in the French original but drops out in the translation.]

[111] For some thoughts on the general typology of modes of discourse and of the corresponding ways of understanding the world, the reader may refer to Jean-Marc Ferry, *Les Puissances de l'expérience. Essai sur l'identité contemporaine*, 2 vols. (Paris: Cerf, 1991), vol. I, *Le Sujet et le verbe*, for example pp. 142, 150.

to socially prescribed rules of conduct and with a mode of organisation that limited changes to minor variations.

Secondly, this change presumed a modification in people's mode of coexistence. As opposed to a universe in which the identity of individuals was defined first of all by group forms of solidarity (stemming, in particular, from ties of kinship), outside of which it was difficult for them to benefit from any status at all, it was necessary for a strategy of individuation to develop. In underscoring both a distance between individual beings that have been freed from rigid enrolment in collective forms as well as face-to-face relationships among them, this strategy of individuation allowed one to recognise in people's choices and actions principles of differentiation and principles for the production of personal lives.[112]

Thirdly, this change in conception of the world would not have been possible had not a detachment from religious values taken place at the same time. Such a detachment involved the disintegration of the role these values played in the establishment of social cohesion through the way in which they weighed upon the perception of the good. In fact, the break with religion's legitimation of the social and political order brought about an upheaval of tremendous breadth. Even if, to a certain extent, Christianity also contributed to the formulation of a historical view of reality – in particular via the doctrine of salvation[113] and Augustinianism[114] – for centuries the religious powers combated this tendency, in particular by stating that the will of God greatly influenced the course of the world and by defending the idea that the hierarchical relationships existing within the immanent organisation of society were anchored in a way that is sacrosanct. In order that the interpretation and investment of social and political phenomena might be expressed fully in terms of historicity,[115] abandonment of the transcendental hypothesis was therefore required.

When the environment is conceived in terms of a history that is in a state of becoming and appears as the product of the thoughts and the activity of individuals, the experience of that environment renders problematic the status of those values that ground the types of conduct engaged in

---

[112] We are freely borrowing here from Gauchet's *The Disenchantment of the World*, p. 156, and from Lefort's 'Société "sans histoire" et historicité', *Les Formes de l'histoire*, pp. 45, 47.

[113] See John Greville A. Pocock, *The Machiavellian Moment: Florentine Political Thought and the Atlantic Republican Tradition* (Princeton University Press, 1975), for example pp. 6–8, 31.

[114] Ibid., pp. 32–36. See also Gauchet's analyses in *The Disenchantment of the World*, p. 153.

[115] Gauchet, *The Disenchantment of the World*, p. 161.

by individuals and societies. The benefit of axiological certitudes, which premodern structures favoured, disappears along with these certitudes. The modern world bestows a historical condition upon its actors, who find themselves plunged into a context where historicity and plurality rhyme with uncertainty. Henceforth, individuals are faced with a plural reality; and within that reality, it is difficult to find principles for living that may be considered certain. The confrontation of their present modes of existence with those of their own past culture, the diversity of individual paths authorised by the society in which they evolve, indeed even the comparison with the customs of distinct civilisations (knowledge of which is now seen as a possibility) induce the people of modernity not to take their situation as a matter of course. This shattering experience affects the credibility of values regulating the conduct of individuals, and this all the more so as religion, seen as a product of history, is itself treated as a possible cause of alienation.

The idea begins to dawn on people that individuals seek to deceive one another. From this vantage point appears the thesis that religion is not only a product of people's activity – which, as such, could not claim to play the role of suprahistorical foundation and guarantor – but also constitutes an invention that serves the needs of individuals in their struggle for power. It is seen as one ideological tool among the panoply of arms placed at the disposal of the mighty.

It is granted that individuals have the faculty to intervene upon the course of events. This then leads to a reluctance to refer phenomena systematically to a transcendent form of causality. The responsibility of agents extends, in particular, to the negative aspects of life. It then becomes conceivable to problematise, in terms of alienation, the sufferings endured within the framework of one's political existence and to show that religious discourse participates resolutely in man's exploitation by man. It is in this way, incidentally, that one must interpret Machiavelli's analyses of the use of religion for partisan ends.[116] One may also note, more generally, that his realistic approach to political relations is the manifestation of a universe that really does perceive itself as the product of a human history and makes it possible to describe political life as being ruled essentially by individual motivations.[117]

---

[116] Machiavelli, *The Prince*, chapter 18, pp. 53–55. See also Claude Lefort, 'Réflexions sociologiques sur Machiavel et Marx: la politique et le "réel"', *Les Formes de l'histoire*, p. 194: 'And if, after having wandered about in Machiavelli, one hadn't halted at any image of politics, it would be necessary . . . surely to recognise that our reflection begins again with his, so as to ask: Is power committed to ruses and society to lies?'

[117] See Pocock, *The Machiavellian Moment*, for example, pp. 156, 159–67.

The experience of modernity is therefore the process through which individuals acquire the conviction that they do intervene in the way events unfold. This experience merges with the idea that they can conceive of and can produce mechanisms to control their fellow human beings, and it is also illustrated by the political manipulations of which religion is the object. It is therefore not surprising to see the benchmark values of society weaken. It is all the more the case considering that the dynamic of self-reflection, in setting up a movement for knowledge that seeks the emancipation of individuals through a permanent increase in the understanding of their environment, pushes one always to want to advance further in the elucidation of the scope and historical characteristics of reality and ends up undermining the principles in whose name this undertaking is being conducted. In systematically subjecting to historical analysis the fundamental values that guide the judgements and acts of the modern agent, the dynamic of self-reflection being referred to here tends to desacralise those values. It takes the risk of breaking loose from the axiological orientations that ground modernity; and while not discrediting them completely, it at least runs the risk of losing sight of their validity. That is to say, the modern project tends to bring its own values into disrepute and to forget the conditions for its own possibility while engaging in self-reflection. It undermines the ground upon which it is built and brings upon itself a sense of crisis as its destiny.

It is precisely this situation that is echoed in the limitations and ambiguities of the previously considered types of explanation for the historicity of social phenomena. Those who adopt these types of explanation position themselves in relation to the uncertainty of the modern world without genuinely facing up to it. They do not truly seek to resolve the problem of the criteria for the right to govern in a way that would allow one to articulate, in tandem with the idea of the political good, an awareness of the plural and changing historical being of modernity.

Uncertainty of values, theory of truth, and nostalgia for the absolute

This is clear as concerns the nomological study of societal facts: to elucidate phenomena in empirical terms while trying to discern some laws is part of an approach that thinks that the uncertain character of history, as experienced within the framework of the modern world, makes it impossible to take a position about values. Weber's attitude is similar in principle, even though he was opposed to pegging the cultural sciences upon the ideals and practices of the scientific analysis of nature. The neutrality he claims for the social sciences testifies to its inability to envisage a political evaluation grounded in reason and a reflection upon the common good. And while the situation is presented in a slightly different way in Marx, the result is ultimately similar. Certainly, the latter does not opt for a separation between facts and values. But he does not, for all that, properly gauge the opening created by modernity. Through his necessitarian conception of history, Marx reinjects a desire for and horizon of absolute truth into a historicised world whose main characteristic is that it no longer can offer precisely this intellectual and moral comfort.

In other words, these various types of analysis of the historical dimension of societal phenomena are emblematic of the way in which the social sciences still today tackle the problem of values, and therefore that of the right to govern. They do not succeed in thinking that what, on the practical plane, has the status of truth might exist within the uncertainty that is specific to modern identity, and in spite of that uncertainty.

The responses these theories give to the questions posed by the historicity of modernity are still impregnated with what must very well be called a premodern mentality. In proving impotent to think through the possibility of offering an ethical evaluation of politics within an unstable universe made up of a plurality of viewpoints that all lay claim to the truth, these responses continue to function upon a schema of truth that is marked by an archaic mind-set [esprit], and they remain dependent upon a model in which the truth is one, permanent, and ahistorical.

There exists, by way of consequence, a nostalgia for a safe and secure environment, one little subject to revision or contestation in comparison with a modern world whose declared ambition is to break up the vast panorama of inherited self-evident truths, sedimented prejudices, and institutionalised certitudes.[118] This is to say that the way in which the above-mentioned forms of analysis of human reality perceive truth in the historical field is less the product of an understanding of the modern universe, which would resolutely participate in the construction of this universe through a reflection and a line of argumentation devoid of afterthoughts, than an approach that has not broken entirely with a world it is nonetheless helping to bury. The reluctance to give oneself over to history reveals the persistence of a nostalgic desire not to cut oneself off from the absolute character from which the truth tended to benefit in premodern times. Thus formulated, the awareness of modern historicity prevents it from adapting itself to the instability of modernity and from granting that it is possible to establish criteria for making de jure judgements.

This influence of the spirit of premodernity upon the interpretation of the historicity of social and political phenomena finds an echo in scientific

---

[118] Ferry, Les Puissances de l'expérience, vol. I, p. 122.

rationality and in the hegemonic situation that rationality attains in the modern world. Indeed, while disqualifying all along traditional and religious beliefs that were previously held to lie beyond discussion, science endeavours from the beginning to take their place. It tends to become the organising principle for one's knowledge of reality. With means that make allowances for the new context, in whose creation and development it participates, science carries within itself from the very start an idea of the truth that attests to a thirst for certainty.[119]

At the moment when science is inaugurating a dynamic of research wherein the process of revising the results is shown to be a motive force for progress, it does not succeed in breaking entirely free from the spirit of premodernity. The artisans of the classical scientific myth[120] find it difficult to live, other than upon the mode of *lack*, the break they bring about with the intellectual and moral comfort that was afforded by the premodern world. They pay a great deal of attention to the conditions of validity and the procedures of verification for the theses they formulate, as is illustrated in an exemplary way at the dawn of modernity by the constant concern Descartes had shown as regards this topic.[121] They also display a desire to formulate overall laws of nature. But all of these worries and concerns cannot be explained simply by their preoccupation with producing scientifically correct statements. They are also the indication of a split, one that is perceived as a loss.

The trauma that occurred sets its mark upon science.[122] For scientists, it is a matter of restoring, through their discoveries, the unity and harmony between man and reality, a unity and harmony they helped to shatter. This is the reason why the rationality of science has become a privileged domain that can be ignored only with difficulty and why its function on the epistemological plane goes hand in hand with, and finds a prolongation in, the key role it plays as social integrator in modern societies.

On the same register of nostalgia, we can mention the works of those contemporary authors who, considering truth to be the product of a human history and of human interests, attack scientific truth and its privileged position in the modern order of knowledge. Certainly, these authors fit right into the movement of historicisation and critical self-reflection that is characteristic of modernity. They even push that movement to its limit, since they deny the validity of the notion of truth as defined in terms of science. But they, too, are spurred on by a nostalgia for the absolute: to think that the historical dimension of scientific activity, with its train

---

[119] We are inspired here by Blumenberg, *The Legitimacy of the Modern Age*, pp. 65–66.
[120] See Prigogine and Stengers, *Order Out of Chaos*, pp. 44–45, 51.
[121] See Blumenberg's remarks in *The Legitimacy of the Modern Age*, pp. 182–83.
[122] Ibid., for example pp. 194–95.

of ideological and personal positions and power struggles, discredits it completely is to betray the persistence in one's own thought of an attachment to an ahistorical conception of what the truth and its elucidation in the domain of science ought to be.

It obviously is not a matter of contesting the positive aspects of the demystification process such analyses contribute. They do indeed help to knock science off the pedestal upon which it had been placed. But one cannot reduce the scientific enterprise to an irrational activity by invoking the fact that it has a history in which it takes on changing forms and frequently finds itself involved in power games where the truth exists only as an alibi. For, that would entail a failure to admit that the process of scientific research culminates in an acquisition of, and a progress towards, knowledge. It would also assume that scientific truth could be cleared of all interference, which seems a difficult proposition to swallow. To denounce science by identifying it with a system that defrauds the truth is still to use the scientific principle of the truth – for, it is indeed difficult to reproach science for not respecting the project of knowledge it claims to be embodying while also judging it at the same time to be intrinsically illusory and deceitful – while continuing to be haunted by a nostalgia for the absolute. Though unavowed, such nostalgia explains how the imperfect achievement of the programme of truth gives rise to a feeling of disenchantment, the consequence of which is to deny the very notion of the truth as a guide to and ideal for scientific activity.

This nostalgic approach to the truth of science is to be found, in particular, in the works of Paul Feyerabend. Championing what he calls an epistemological anarchism, he proposes to carry out a historical and philosophical reflection upon the logic of scientific research. The goal of his reflection is to show that such research has nothing to do with Truth, Reason, Justice, Honesty, and all the other concepts that claim to have a universal signification and import.[123] He also states that scientific experiments on natural phenomena are in large part irrational because of the methods they apply and because they are set within ideological and political clashes.[124] He maintains that the value of truth as well as the other great principles that accompany it and together go to form the ethic of scientific rationalism have nothing to do with what science really is today. Scientific research is simply the continuation of an ever-more proliferating and divergent production of forms of knowledge; in no way is it motivated by a concern to provide a gradual explanation of what is true.[125]

---

[123] Paul Feyerabend, *Against Method: Outline of an Anarchistic Theory of Knowledge*, 6th edn (London: Verso, 1986), pp. 32–33.
[124] Ibid., pp. 299–302.   [125] Ibid., p. 30.

Such an interpretation of the relation between scientific activity and the question of the truth, whose radicalism is tinged with a nostalgia for the absolute, also affects the writings of Michel Foucault. Foucault attacks the idea of truth defended by the scientific rationalism expounded in the human sciences.[126] He wishes to shed light upon the underlying constitutive rules of discourses on truth by examining the historically variable conditions for their genesis. Foucault contests the credibility of the idea of truth, which the human sciences think they represent and on whose basis they try to impose their scientific status. The Foucauldian method endeavours to show that truth is limited to the history of what individuals have called the truth[127] and of their struggles around it. He implies that, behind these conflicts, there exists no benchmark criterion that would allow one to decide rationally among them.[128]

Now – and this concerns Feyerabend's thinking as well as Foucault's – it is not because science is set within a history in which its canons undergo changes and overlap with power relationships that it could be reduced thereto.[129] Scientific rationalism has long benefited from the key role the theme of invariance has played in the validation of values, as well as from an absence of any suspicion of collusion with non-scientific interests. Undoubtedly, this skewed situation goes to justify the efforts these authors have made to shed light upon the weaknesses of scientific rationalism. But the historical character of truth certainly does not authorise them to conclude that it is but a fiction. To adopt that point of view is to remain prisoner of the idea of eternal truth or to remain chained to the rejection of history, a position they have doggedly criticised. To do so is to abandon oneself again to a nostalgic form of absolutism as regards the notion of truth.

What is more, this attitude – which, despite what distinguishes one from the other,[130] Feyerabend and Foucault both share – raises a twofold problem. In the first place, it is self-destructive to the extent that it oscillates between two equally untenable positions. On the one hand, it stands in contradiction to the thesis it is supposed to be defending, since the

[126] See Michel Foucault, *The Order of Things: An Archaeology of the Human Sciences* (New York: Vintage, 1973), pp. 364–67, and Jürgen Habermas's remarks on Foucault in *Philosophical Discourse of Modernity*, trans. Frederick Lawrence (Cambridge, Mass.: MIT Press, 1987), pp. 263–65.

[127] Michel Foucault, 'Nietzsche, Genealogy, History', in *Language, Counter-Memory, Practice: Selected Essays and Interviews*, ed. and intro. Donald F. Bouchard, trans. Donald F. Bouchard and Sherry Simon (Ithaca: Cornell University Press, 1977), p. 144.

[128] Ibid., p. 163. The reader may also refer to Paul Veyne's comments in 'Foucault révolutionne l'histoire', in *Comment on écrit l'histoire*, pp. 204, 230–31, 234.

[129] See Hilary Putnam, *Philosophical Papers*, 3 vols., 2nd edn (Cambridge University Press, 1986), vol. III, *Realism and Reason*, p. 113.

[130] See in particular Bouveresse, *Rationalité et cynisme*, p. 87.

attacks it formulates are supposed to be grounded upon a rational argument and upon the ambition to be true.[131] On the other hand, it can itself be analysed in its own terms and is therefore not superior to the practices it denounces.[132] In the second place, the critique of scientific rationalism is expressed through a conception of research that tends to lose all social purpose [*finalité sociale*]. Contestation of the use of the idea of truth in the natural or the human sciences is not limited to the theoretical aspect of the statements being made. It is also manifested in attacks against the moral considerations that accompany the concern for truth, as is testified to by the critique offered of the principles of justice, duty, and obligation.[133] The result is that the process of acquiring knowledge is no longer set within an ethic of research, understood as a methodically oriented and disciplined will to know, whose aim is to improve reality.

Under such conditions, it is not surprising to see that the consequence of rejecting the rationality of moral values at the scientific level is to harm the credibility of the function they assume on the social level. The corollary to invalidating the idea of truth is criticism of the ethical elements that accompany the rationalist quest for the truth. These ethical elements stand disqualified. Their role as criteria for determining and evaluating people's behaviours, considered valid at the scientific level as well as on the practical plane, is reduced to nothing.

Systematic satirisation – as exemplified, each in his own way, by Michel Foucault and Paul Feyerabend – therefore culminates in a point of view that combines, on both the scientific and practical levels, two questionable attitudes. First there is a kind of utopianism. The concrete forms in which this utopianism is embodied cannot but seem mysterious and indecipherable to uninitiated individuals. For, this operation, which wipes the axiological slate clean, prevents one from appealing to any foundational values. The second feature of this combination is a nihilism that dares not openly define itself as such.

This unilaterally critical conception of the notion of truth is the culmination of the phenomenon of nostalgia for a world that is fully present to itself. The self-reflective movement of modernity is marked by this

---

[131] On this problem, for Foucault the reader may consult Putnam, *Reason, Truth, and History*, pp. 162–63 and Habermas, *The Philosophical Discourse of Modernity*, pp. 282–86. As for Feyerabend, the reader may refer to Bouveresse, *Rationalité et cynisme*, pp. 76–78, 102–04.

[132] For this question, on Feyerabend see Bouveresse's remarks in *Rationalité et cynisme*, pp. 82–83, 88–89. For Foucault, consult Habermas, *The Philosophical Discourse of Modernity*, pp. 276–82.

[133] Feyerabend, *Against Method: Outline of an Anarchistic Theory of Knowledge*, pp. 32–33, 180, 189; Foucault, 'Nietzsche, Genealogy, History', in *Language, Counter-Memory, Practice*, pp. 151–52.

phenomenon from its very beginning. It is the ultimate figure for a kind of sentimentality that is illustrative of the concern to maintain a strict complementarity [*adéquation*] between truth and absolute certitude.

In the modern universe, the nostalgic attitude corresponds in part to a survival reaction in the face of change. Humanly, it is quite understandable. In general, we may say that intellectual and psychological attachment to the conception of the world into which one is born probably never disappears completely, nor does it lose, immediately or entirely, its structuring power. It retains a conditioning force that continues to act so long as the new image of reality is not strong enough to be assumed resolutely in terms that make it break with the past.

It is not surprising, moreover, that the self-reflective dynamic of modernity, which tends to install individuals in the realm of the provisional and the revisable, might be difficult to accept. Chronic instability and the absence of definitive guarantees do not make for a situation individuals easily adopt as their own. Whence the temptation of a nostalgia for pre-modernity. In comparison with modern culture, which is often propelled into a morbid pursuit in search of its identity, such nostalgia gives the seductive and reassuring impression of coinciding with itself.

From then on, a new problem is raised. How is one to define and to defend the exercise of the faculty of political judgement within a historical universe whose self-reflective dynamic promotes a plurality of benchmark values?

5   Study of politics, relation to history, and *de jure* judgement

The analysis of the historicity of social phenomena and of its implications on the practical level is condemned neither to axiological neutrality nor to a dogmatic or disenchanted conception of history. There exists an alternative to these approaches and to the difficulties these approaches generate.

This alternative constitutes a path for research that allows one to establish limits on what is politically acceptable and what is not, amidst a history inhabited by the recognition that change occurs and that there is a plurality of value systems. It allows one to shield the thematic of legitimacy from the aporias to which it is exposed by a consciousness of modernity that is impotent to offer a solution to the problem of good government, even though it places that problem at the centre of its concerns.

This alternative – which does not rule out preserving some of the previously mentioned methodological characteristics of studies of societal phenomena – must articulate an analysis of politics and of the historical field that develops in two complementary directions. First, the utility of an empirical approach to social facts that is designed to elucidate what is politically just remains indissociable from a rehabilitation of the axiological dimension. Second, the alternative envisaged here presupposes a clarification of the relation the analysis of politics has to forms of social organisation.

EMPIRICAL APPROACH, SCIENCE OF SOCIETIES, AND VALUES

In order to offer to political problems solutions that are in accord with what is required when one thinks about right, it is appropriate to make use of some of the views already studied, while correcting them – that is to say, by setting them within a conception of historical reality and of scientific activity that detaches them from their context, which itself gave rise to aporetic situations. From this perspective, one must first underscore the irreplaceable importance of the empirical approach, both as a factor

181

in knowledge and as a guide for method. Next, it is appropriate to demonstrate that, in order to avoid running into an impasse over the theme of legitimacy or proposing an interpretation thereof that amounts to taking away its meaning and its critical resources, empirical analysis has to be understood and applied no longer by contrasting it with the role values play in social and political reality but by associating it with them. This will lead us to a reinterpretation of the notions of objectivity and neutrality.

Importance of empirical data

There could never be a question of depriving oneself of empirical data in order to construct a coherent formulation of the problematic of the right to govern. Certainly, the inability to take a value-based stand on social facts is tied, in part, to the key place occupied by the quantitative recording of observable information. But it is not necessary, for all that, to eliminate references to empirical data in order to arrive at an adequate treatment of the idea of legitimacy. Such data are, in effect, indispensable and irreplaceable.

Generally speaking, we may say that taking empirical data into account is an obligatory stage for anyone who wishes to explicate the characteristics of reality. Such data have an obvious part to play in working out the content of factual propositions. Moreover, they contribute to the testing of the validity of statements by requiring one to move back and forth between reality and the information these statements contain. From cross-check to cross-check, this process refines further and further our propositions about reality, and it generates improvements in our understanding thereof.

This state of affairs is particularly true for the analysis of politics in terms of legitimacy. The effort to explain specific historical contexts is a natural continuation of a theoretical reflection upon the right to govern. There, it appears essential to take concrete data into consideration. The unfolding of political life as well as of the conflicts of which political life serves as the theatre does not manifest itself *in abstracto* but rather in history. It is in particular through the attention one pays to empirical features that one can chart legitimate and illegitimate situations. By bringing in, for example, information about the way in which a regime is evolving, about the degree and form of individuals' adherence or aversion to the way society is organised and directed, the attention paid to empirical features allows one to draw up a sort of rap sheet. While serving as an indicator for the cooperative and oppositional relations existing within society, this rap sheet offers data of the utmost importance about the question of justice.

Nonetheless, these evaluations established via empirical analysis achieve their full import only when they are carried out in conjunction with a reflection upon the problem of the axiological criteria for right – in other words, only when the question of value judgements is taken into account. While the study of relations between rulers and ruled does not exclude recourse to the empirical study of phenomena, neither is it to be reduced thereto. Such a study must be set within a larger context of thought. Within that context, one would be able to articulate this description of political reality in tandem with an investigation into that upon which the formulation of a faculty of judgement integrating the idea of the just depends.

Meaning of values and specificity of social facts

The role of values must be fully recognised. Such recognition is inseparable from the idea that the individual, as subject or actor of history, plays a part in the production and the evolution of social and political phenomena.

It is in terms of these values that individuals think and act and enter into relationship with one another and with their environment. Evolving within a universe of meaning marked out on the axiological plane, they are confronted with an everyday life and a horizon imbued with values. Someone who wants to elucidate social facts while making allowance for their specificity cannot approach them as one would natural reality. The observer of social and political phenomena has to place himself on their level of subjectivity. He must seek to comprehend the motivations and intentions of individuals in as much as those motivations and intentions are guided by the axiological dimension and in as much as they cathect that dimension. Conceived in these terms – and allowing for differences that exist in time and in space among civilisations as well as for diversity within one and the same culture or one and the same society – social phenomena are set within a logic of the true and false that is distinct from the one that governs in the natural sciences.

In order to provide for an empirical approach to the status and role of values that would not betray the thought protocol used to explicate the conditions for *de jure* judgements, one additional factor has to be taken into account. It is important, when presenting empirical information, not to rule out in principle the rationality of the axiological plane that social phenomena contain. It is important not to rule out the hypothesis that those phenomena implement true values, reasons endowed with a coefficient of truth. From this perspective, it is imperative to break away from the point of view that makes mention of the field of values while systematically limiting it merely to a mere narrative of individuals' beliefs. To propose to chart the values with which individuals and societies identify or the ones they reject while refusing to set them within a hierarchy is to forget the specificity of the events that have to do with life in society. It is ultimately to give up taking a stand on the legitimacy of the ties of command and obedience among individuals.

There is no question of contesting en bloc the usefulness of accumulating empirical data. But the issue here is to establish the possibility of reconciling the gathering of empirical data with the formulation of statements that express *de jure* judgements. And when the empirical interpretation of social facts and of the axiological dimension of these facts is conceived solely in the mode of detached observation, it creates a viewpoint that, in claiming to be lacking in any alternative, eliminates from the domain of reflection any treatment of the problem of legitimacy in the strong sense of this notion. Moreover, such an interpretation offers the defect of proposing that one adopt an untenable orientation for one's work. Indeed, the image of a science that fails to take any axiological position is not corroborated by scientific practice: the split it champions in relation to value judgements is, in the best of hypotheses, only partially fulfilled in reality.

Of course, the version of the world science proposes would not be able to correspond exactly to the views individuals have of their own environment. Nevertheless, the gap between the understanding of social and political phenomena defended by researchers who adhere to the conception of axiological neutrality and the understanding that comes from experience argues in favour of studies that are capable of articulating and harmonising those two levels of intelligibility, science and lived experience, without, for all that, reducing one to the other. It is a matter of analysing social reality without subjecting it to the dictates of a naturalistic knowledge of social phenomena. It is a matter of finding a space for some compatibility between the scientific outlook and life, a compatible space that allows one, in particular, to integrate justice into one's reflections.

THE EXPERIENCE OF JUSTICE, IRREPRESSIBLE ELEMENT
OF SOCIAL FACTS

Each person, in his daily existence, feels that some choices and actions are desirable and that others are to be condemned. However, the writings of the advocates of an empirical analysis of social facts that claims to be axiologically neutral go against this experience. This kind of tension also affects authors whose analysis of social life is radically critical and historicising and who, in particular, systematically deny the notions of truth and right. Nevertheless, they do not escape the influence of these notions. That, for example, it is preferable to respect the other rather than kill him is probably something they do not contest.

The convictions dwelling within individuals thus go against the rejection of a hierarchy of values advocated in the neutralist conception of empirical analysis. This is to say that, rather than relating to the world though scientistic positivism, it is more appropriate to try to bring together thought and life.[1]

Of course, it remains difficult to make a determination as to the concept of justice, in particular because the elements proposed to define it change from era to era and according to the type of society in question, as well as in terms of the place individuals occupy within a community and of the interpretation they make of it. Furthermore, the notion of justice provokes disagreements and conflicts that are not easy to settle. In another connection, we may add that the distrust evinced towards the theme of justice is reinforced by three factors. Sometimes it is felt that the principles that lay a claim to the good are not credible in the role they aspire to play as guideline and criterion because those principles are not adequately fulfilled in reality. There is also the idea that individuals, in general, and statesmen, in particular, have a particular propensity towards being self-centred and minimally concerned with others. Finally, collective movements can sometimes bring out hatred, resentment, and violence – as witness, in an extreme and tragic way, the example of Nazi Germany.

Although these considerations seem to reduce the question of what is just to an illusion, they do not get at its importance. The result should even be to press the observer to be concerned about it. Indeed, that justice does not yield a definitive agreement, that its achievement might be uncertain or else never totally satisfying, that it might somehow be diminished by individuals who have adopted a scornful or brutal position – these are all reasons that make it even more urgent to take justice into consideration.

Justice, assuredly, is not part of some automatic mechanism that would necessarily make social facts and individuals bow to its demands. It is nevertheless one of the central experiences of human life. In their existence, individuals cannot avoid being in contact with other people. They need one another to survive and to grow. From this perspective, we may say that they are led to subscribe to and to participate in relationships involving coexistence and cooperation, which implies a sense of reciprocity and therefore a certain idea of justice.

---

[1] See Raymond Aron, *De la condition historique du sociologue* (Paris: Gallimard, 1983), pp. 52–53.

On account of its being immersed in the social dimension, the question of justice in human life manifests itself as much on the personal level as on the plane of collective relations. From the instant individuals come into the world, their existence is indissociable from a tendency to advance in their being.[2] Not being indifferent to what may happen to them, individuals are moved by a logic of self-affirmation[3] that merges with demands regarding the milieu in which they evolve. These demands require favourable responses in order to assure the dynamic continuity of existence. For example, if parents ignore the needs of their child, such neglect runs the risk of traumatising the child and making him fragile his whole life long. From this point of view, we may say that the preservation and prospering of human existence rests upon the fulfilment of demands that call upon the surrounding environment and, especially, the social world. Such demands are lived in terms of needs that are deemed indispensable for life to unfold in a good way but whose chances of fulfilment require the collaboration of the other. In agreeing to see therein an appeal to his sense of responsibility and in accepting to take this responsibility upon himself, the other recognises that he shares a certain community of destiny with the person who calls upon him. It is in this way that individuals, in various and more or less elaborate ways – for example, according to whether one is an adult or an adolescent – are led to think, in the wake of the welcome their demand receives, that justice has or has not been rendered to them. This obviously assumes that individuals are not confronted with adverse situations that would reduce them to a state involving a loss of sense of self [*un état de quasi-indifférenciation*] – a state wherein they would no longer have the capacity to think that their existence is a cause to be defended.

The central character of justice in human existence is also manifested on the plane of collective relationships. Indeed, for one's existence within society to unfold in a good way, it must be tied to the establishment of limits that assign to the members of the collectivity both duties and rights. These rights and duties are a manifestation of the recognition of, and the concern for, the achievement of their mutual interests, under forms and in terms of contents that evidently depend upon the context. The social dimension of life within a community therefore imposes a need to integrate into its direction and organisation some way of taking account of the demands of the individuals who make up the group. When these individuals have the feeling that exchanges are taking place unilaterally

---

[2] See Jacob, *The Possible and the Actual*, pp. 59–60.
[3] See the reflections of Hans Jonas, *The Imperative of Responsibility: In Search of an Ethics for the Technical Age*, trans. Hans Jonas with David Herr (University of Chicago Press, 1984), pp. 81–83.

and are unfolding basically to their disadvantage, their motivation diminishes and ceases to be effective. On the other hand, it is their weaving together that constitutes the fabric of society and, in the main, ensures its operation.

For example, if laws are perceived to be benefiting only a portion, and always the same portion, of the population – without including, be it only in minimal fashion, the needs of the rest of the community and without assuming a regulatory role in the distribution of goods – these laws lose their credibility. Indeed, in this precise case laws cease to remind people (with the aid of sanctions, if necessary) that life in a collectivity implies not ignoring the other totally. The cooperative goodwill of agents who feel injured then decreases accordingly. Under such conditions, relationships among individuals can no longer be entitled to the confidence the notion of justice inspired when it was grounded upon the exercise of reciprocity and the search for compromise. Mutual interest ceases to enliven everyday life and to guide the future of interactions between individuals. An awareness of the relations of force wins out. Already latent, such relations tend to come to the fore, sometimes even dominating the situation when circumstances allow.

The American philosopher John Rawls has worked out two ideas, that of the original position and that of the veil of ignorance, to establish the conditions for a theory of justice.[4] The place they hold may be interpreted in relation to this question of the tie that unites the themes of justice and reciprocity. Rawls states that the procedure that allows one to explicate what is just has to be distinguished from how justice is inscribed in concrete societies. His intention here is to bring out two particular advantages.

First, Rawls thinks that the fictive situation of the agents' original position – wherein these agents are supposed to be rational and well informed about everything except their personal characteristics in the future (they do not know, for example, whether they will be rich or poor) – confers upon them a status of equality. They are thus not tempted, or even in a position, to adhere to a conception of justice that would be solely to their own benefit and to the systematic detriment of others. Indeed, when individuals are not sure they will be placed among the privileged, they prefer to decide in favour of a way of distributing well-being that takes into consideration the individual interests of all.[5] They are

---

[4] See John Rawls, *A Theory of Justice* (Cambridge, Mass.: Harvard University Press, 1971), pp. 136–40 and elsewhere.

[5] We have a feature here that distinguishes the Rawlsian theory from utilitarianism; for the latter, what matters is the sum total or the average amount of this well-being, however it may be distributed.

therefore led to wish to minimise their maximal loss, or maximise their minimal gain.[6]

Via the fiction of the original position, Rawls also wishes to prevent this exposure of the conditions for conceiving and achieving justice from becoming caught in the spiral of the relations of forces and from being held hostage to political struggles or to the way in which these struggles develop.[7] By anchoring the problematic of what is just outside of and upstream from concrete history and its convulsions, the idea of justice can be kept from serving as an alibi for the kinds of swings that may occur when in the name of justice previously disadvantaged individuals, in coming to hold power, replace the kinds of discriminations of which they had fallen victim with new forms of oppression and impose policies that institutionalise revenge, resentment, and exclusionary practices. They forget then the imperative character of the reciprocity clause and the respect for the interests of each that a well-ordered society requires.

Rawls has recourse to this mechanism of the original position in order to work out his conception of justice. In this way, he does his best to see that deliberation on what is just as well as the achievement of justice will not be influenced or undermined by the proliferation of positions that remain indifferent to the fate of the other.

Neutrality and objectivity revisited

The objective of a reflection upon political legitimacy, whose intention is to rely upon empirical knowledge without limiting itself to a value-neutral form of empiricism, is to overcome the rift that separates the latter from human reality. To do that, one must, on the basis of experience, show that some values based in justice do indeed exist and also explicate the way in which these values can be integrated into the analysis of social facts. This implies that one should come up with an ethic of the social and political sciences that rules out the idea that the notions of objectivity and neutrality are to be understood solely in terms of an axiological disengagement. In order to do this, it is fitting to articulate the notions of objectivity and neutrality in tandem with the ideal of tolerance.

The separation of facts from values is not prior to history and morality. It corresponds to a new world view that was built up during the modern era. This division is the product of a way of conceiving reality that combines the break from premodernity[8] with the difficulty one experiences

---

[6] See the remarks of Philippe Van Parijs, *Qu'est-ce qu'une société juste? Introduction à la pratique de la philosophie politique* (Paris: Éditions du Seuil, 1991), p. 83.

[7] Rawls, *A Theory of Justice*, in particular p. 120.

[8] The reader may refer, for example, to Taylor's 'Le juste et le bien', *Revue de métaphysique et de morale*, pp. 34–35.

in trying to attain and live serenely the ideals that break entails. The resulting mistrust regarding the field of values and regarding the domain of historicity in which it expresses itself is thus part of a process in which the scientific study of nature becomes the guiding model for the elucidation of reality. It is in this way that empirical analysis has come to adhere to the thesis that any attempt to account for societal questions in true terms requires that one purge of any value judgements the description and explanation thereof.

Nonetheless, the identification of social phenomena with 'objects' and the will to remain neutral prove to be the products of a specific historical context. The separation of facts from values thus no longer has to be presented as ontological, inevitable, and unsurpassable. It is, by way of consequence, also possible to detach the notions of neutrality and objectivity from a way of conceiving the world that would in principle forbid proponents of these notions from taking a stand in relation to values. They can be understood within the framework of a study of social phenomena that takes values seriously and, from this perspective, develops a kind of analysis that is concerned with integrating the ethical dimension.

Although neutrality is traditionally understood as the refusal to opt for one party against another, it need not limit itself to that interpretation. Its reduction to a total axiological disengagement cuts off access to the resources it can offer for scientific activity and morality. Here, neutrality must be articulated in tandem with a way of thinking that contests neither the validity nor the integration of values in the study of social and political questions. Thus, when neutrality is not associated with a systematic separation from value judgements, it becomes possible to conceive neutrality as a procedure that expresses, even under a relatively polished form, strong convictions. It would seem, moreover, that neutrality highly militates in favour of certain strong convictions. Those holding such convictions deem it essential to respect the plurality of viewpoints, and it is their judgement that the possibility of fulfilling this programme necessitates adherence to the thesis that a hierarchy of values exists.

The neutral attitude thus understood is a way of committing oneself by taking a stand in favour of the right to the diversity of axiological positions. As such, it advocates tolerance. In this respect, it is in no way a stranger to value judgements. Its concern to foster a coexistence among axiological orientations and among the behaviours accompanying them is itself a position. In the neutral attitude, it is not thought that all points of view adopted by individuals or societies are, in principle, of equal value. The imperative of mutual respect intervenes here in the establishment of a classification of values. Its clause regarding tolerance of differences is valid only in as much as these differences do not implement practices involving encroachments and constraints. The neutral attitude rejects the idea that certain points of view can be forced upon others in the name, for example, of the supposed superiority of those points of view. Indeed, in order for the kind of neutrality of which we are speaking to be credible, it has to be completed or continued along the lines of a more active sort of involvement when the context requires. This more active dimension of involvement entails struggle against those who have taken the side of brutality and intolerance.

In other words, in order for it to function as a process that expresses and promulgates balanced relations and compatibility among various points of view, the neutral attitude must not hesitate to intervene in order to stand in the way of individuals and societies bent on destruction. Distinguishing itself from systematic abstentionism as well as from a wait-and-see outlook, the neutral attitude commits to solidarity and actively defends the coexistence of differing viewpoints. It is directly along the lines of this argument that the notion of objectivity must be reinterpreted.

Objectivity, too, is founded upon a value judgement, and first of all upon the impartiality objectivity champions. The willingness to produce the most faithful image possible of the phenomena under study is in itself the mark of a value judgement and the instrument for its fulfilment. In taking on the task of reconstructing, as best one can, the ways individuals think and behave within the various spheres of their lives as well as the events in which these individuals participate, objectivity subscribes to a specific engagement: by endeavouring to formulate accurate statements about collective reality, it commits to offering a fair view of it.

It is also by endeavouring to articulate social facts in tandem with a classification of values that objectivity once again puts a value judgement into effect. In no way does this effort at articulation imply that one is to evaluate the beliefs and attitudes of individuals on the basis of criteria that are foreign to them. It simply consists in describing the way agents live within their cultural and material universe and in examining whether the collective relationships there correspond to cohesive relations or to conflicts, to cooperative ties or to bonds of repression. It then becomes possible, based on the modalities of these relationships and their degree of success, to draw lessons from them about the experience of what is just and unjust within a specific environment.

To be objective, under these conditions, consists in being attentive to information supplied by the attitudes of precisely situated individuals. It does not consist in treating such attitudes as being, by definition, undecidable. Let us put this in other terms: by integrating the dimension of values into one's concern to be objective, one can develop a conception of what is true that, while all along taking into account empirical data concerning social facts, cannot be reduced to the formal corrective properties of the stated propositions but concerns also the very substance of the facts.

Through this understanding of neutrality and objectivity, which interprets them from the standpoint of a dynamic of commitment, it becomes possible to set the empirical approach to social and political phenomena within a scientific ethic. On the one hand, it is affirmed that the neutral attitude militates in favour of respect for a pluralism of viewpoints, in so far as these viewpoints are tolerant and compatible with the positions championed by others. On the other, it is established that being objective consists in analysing social facts in such a way that one endeavours to provide an impartial explanation of them and to broach, in connection with the world views of individuals, the problem of justice within specific contexts. Together, these two features amount to working out a way of analysing existence in society. Far from building themselves up in opposition to a hierarchy of values, an analysis of this sort relies upon such a hierarchy. Neutrality and objectivity thus defined delineate a morality of method that is an integral part of the search for truth.

Furthermore, this set-up could not be limited solely to the empirical dimension of research. It is appropriate to apply it to the social sciences in general, so as to give to the quest for truth a meaning based upon an ethic of commitment.[9] As it happens, this ethic of commitment takes a stand in favour of the ideals of respect and tolerance towards the other. In addition, this scientific morality is indissociable from an ethic of the scientific life itself. One does not go without the other. The study of social facts, which reconciles neutrality and objectivity with the existence of a classification carried out in terms of values, is unthinkable without some form of scientific activity that would come to echo it. The rejection of nihilism in the analysis of social and political phenomena cannot accommodate an embittered and disillusioned way of conceiving and practising science.

From this perspective, it is clear that scientific activity has to develop within an intersubjective space. There, moved by the will to understand, a spirit and dynamic of cooperation intercede. The relationships among scientists, of course, are never exempt from petty acts or conflict. But the desire to dominate and a compulsive craving to be known do not have to win out over creative fervour, risk taking, patience, or any other factor that contributes to the perfectibility of knowledge.

It is all the more necessary to the social and political sciences that this intersubjective space be of good quality, as it tends to offer a form of moral backing. Indeed, given that it is more difficult to demonstrate in

---

[9] Aron, *De la condition historique du sociologue*, p. 53.

an incontestable way the validity of a statement in the social sciences than in the field of the natural sciences, the probity researchers manifest in their argumentation takes on a new dimension. In an area of study where ideas are rarely offered the comforting support of consensus and where the treatment of current themes often gives rise to sharp debates, the integrity of scientists in their search for the truth is a quality that cannot be ignored. Being aware of this situation constitutes one of the ways in which the social sciences acquire meaning and legitimacy, not only as scientific activity but also as social activity. They do so through the positive influence they can exert upon the life of the city.

EVALUATION OF LEGITIMACY AND CONTEXTUAL ANALYSIS OF SOCIAL PHENOMENA

Reflection upon the right to govern, which is open to making determinations about how social and political reality operates in terms of values, has to pose the question of how the analysis of social facts is set within the ongoing flow of history and to respond to that question in a way that renders the judgement reliable. Let us say it in another way: one must elucidate the conditions under which evaluative criteria may be applied by examining the relations between the analysis of social phenomena and history.

In order to undertake this enterprise, we must now examine three arguments. First, we must recognise as a primary reality the fact that the analysis of social phenomena pertains to a historical context and that this rootedness exerts an influence upon the mechanism for evaluation. That should not lead one, however, to interpret and to evaluate societal facts in such a way as to reduce them systematically to the environment in which they are studied. Indeed, it is essential, when deciding about the legitimacy or illegitimacy of political relationships, to make allowance for the principles and modes of organisation that are constitutive of the identity of the societies under consideration as well as for their members' attitudes of adherence or rejection. Still, the society in which the analysis of social facts is set has itself to be concerned with historical truth.

The influence of the historical context on political analysis

Statements about social phenomena are set within a context of, and remain dependent upon, a history. They are not, indeed, the only ones. That proposition also holds good for the theses worked out while analysing natural reality, and, in a general way, for the whole of human practices.

In order to appear and to develop, every activity presupposes its intricate connection within a network of historical determinations. Its present and future configuration is fashioned with the aid of components that go to form the setting in which that activity evolves – including the fact that this dynamic serves to modify this setting by introducing therein some new factors. In any case, it is obviously not inconsequential that the study of social and political facts cannot be abstracted completely from its environment. The setting has an impact upon the description and explanation of social and political facts. The conceptions of justice of John Rawls and Ronald Dworkin confirm this.

THE THEORIES OF RAWLS AND DWORKIN: TWO EXEMPLARY CASES

Whatever may be the points that set these two authors apart, both share a concern not to limit the formulation of the problematic of what is just to concrete communities' particular distributions of goods. As regards the idea of justice, they wish to formulate statements of the highest possible level of generality.[10] Thus having set their hearts upon elucidating the basic structure of a just society, they defend the idea that the evaluation of justice and of injustice should not depend upon the conventions in force at a given moment. This position opens upon a reflection whose claim is to guarantee its own validity through a maximum amount of detachment from real practices and institutions. Rawls and Dworkin therefore implement conceptions of justice that, far from showing a willingness to accept their reduction to the contextual characteristics conveyed by a particular setting, have an ambition that is universalistic and formalistic. Now, the capacity to abstract from the environment, which this type of orientation champions, is contradicted by the facts as well as by the historical anchorage of this orientation itself. This may be seen in two ways.

First, the very will to construct a theory of justice that breaks away from any rootedness in history is an indicator of a particular kind of historical rootedness. Indeed, to raise to the rank of a primordial factor (as Rawls and Dworkin do) some explicit procedures that thought has to follow in order to define and to achieve justice[11] – that is to say, to affirm that the just life is a type of existence that individuals impose upon themselves and construct in an autonomous manner, while determining, with the aid of clearly and formally established rules and criteria for reasoning and deliberation, what they must be and what they must accomplish in

---

[10] See Rawls, *A Theory of Justice*, for example pp. 5–6, 11, as well as Ronald Dworkin, *Taking Rights Seriously* (Cambridge, Mass.: Harvard University Press, 1978), p. 177, and his article 'What Justice Isn't', in *A Matter of Principle*, pp. 219–20.

[11] See MacIntyre, *After Virtue*, pp. 118–19.

order to subscribe to justice[12] – takes us back to a world view that is characteristic of modern culture and more precisely, within the latter, of the liberal project.

The mistrust the idea of any dependency upon history inspires is one of the outstanding traits of the values that issue from the Enlightenment. The feeling not only that it is possible to, but also that one has to, abstract from the historical environment, that this capacity and this necessity attest to the existence and to the power of human freedom and reason, is part and parcel of the development of an understanding of justice whose aim is to establish a line of conduct that will satisfy the exigencies of impartiality and universality, and that therefore cannot be reduced to any particular historical position.[13]

In addition, the connection that exists between the will to break away from any contextual rootedness, as Rawls and Dworkin express it in their formulations of the problem of justice, and liberalism – an emblem of modernity if ever there was one! – finds in these theorists some eminent representatives. Their approach to justice is situated at the very heart of liberal thought. Liberal thought also manifests the will to shield itself from the impact of concrete history. Its initial tendency is to describe individuals as sovereign agents with no identity or commitment other than those they freely choose through their faculty to construct their lives and to influence reality in general. Next, it is an attempt to ground a social order, one in which individuals concerned with emancipating themselves from forms of alienation handed down by traditions appeal to norms of reflection and action that allegedly stem from a universal rationality and that supposedly are, by way of consequence, independent of historical constraints.[14]

Secondly, the detachment from the historical setting advocated by Rawls and Dworkin introduces an incoherency into the structure of their moral theory: in order to operate, this theory requires a substantive dimension, and that dimension does not fail to take root within a historical environment. The procedural conception of justice would not be capable of sorting out those just principles around which a collective existence would be likely to unfold in an equitable manner, should all conventional and contingent data be excluded. The minimalist virtues in which it clothes itself are insufficient. They cannot, by themselves alone,

---

[12] The reader may refer to Taylor's analyses in 'Le juste et le bien', *Revue de métaphysique et de morale*, pp. 38, 49.

[13] Ibid., pp. 35–36, 44–45. The reader may also consult Alasdair MacIntyre, *Whose Justice? Which Rationality?* (University of Notre Dame Press, 1988), p. 6; Brian Barry, *A Treatise on Social Justice* (Berkeley: University of California Press, 1989), vol. I, *Theories of Justice*, p. 8.

[14] See MacIntyre, *Whose Justice?*, p. 335.

motivate the hierarchy of values this procedural conception defines as good, nor can they explain what obliges one to follow the privileged rules to which it suggests that one conform.

Procedure itself assumes a sense of what is just. That sense precedes and guides the kind of deliberation that procedure itself devises and implements.

Thus, placing oneself at the level of the individual, let us say the following: in order that the individual might know that he must relate to rules and know how he must relate to them, he must already have an idea of what is just, and that idea orients his reflection. As we see, the procedural approach is the expression of the content of justice at the same time that it is in its service. The substance of one's awareness of what is just, along with one's set of appraisals of situations, of the desirable and undesirable options it includes, can be determined only in relation to the context in which that substance is deployed. As it happens in this precise case, that context is the culture of a liberal-democratic society.

To be brief: if the rules participate in the establishment of what is just, that is so in as much as these rules are placed within a setting that allows for the elaboration of principles whose content accords with the implementation of a procedural form of deliberation. The values of justice that procedural deliberations help to sift out are values of justice because they happen already to be present at the outset of the reflection.

Even though Rawls states that his conception of justice derives from a 'thin theory' of the good[15] – that is to say, from a theory that is not the manifestation of a conception of justice existing prior to the choice of benchmark principles through recourse to correct rules of procedure – he is presupposing, in reality, a *thick* view of the good.[16] He is taking a strong position in relation to some values that are perceived as just and fundamental and that are culturally distinctive. The values advocated by liberal democracy play a crucial role in the formation of principles of justice as understood by Rawls.[17] Indeed, the two major principles of justice Rawls explicates[18] are recognised as such to the extent that they

[15] Rawls, *A Theory of Justice*, p. 396.
[16] We borrow this qualifier from Charles Taylor's *Sources of the Self: The Making of the Modern Identity* (Cambridge, Mass.: Harvard University Press, 1989), p. 89.
[17] Ibid., pp. 88–89. The reader may also refer to the reflections of Chaïm Perelman, 'Les conceptions concrète et abstraite de la raison et de la justice. À propos de la théorie de la justice de John Rawls', in Jean Ladrière and Philippe Van Parijs (eds.), *Fondements d'une théorie de la justice. Essais critiques sur la philosophie politique de John Rawls* (Louvain-La-Neuve: Éditions de l'Institut supérieur de philosophie, 1984), pp. 208–11.
[18] The first principle Rawls advances is the following: 'Each person is to have an equal right to the most extensive basic liberty compatible with a similar liberty for others' (*A Theory of Justice*, p. 60). The second is presented in these terms: 'Social and economic

tally with individuals' intuitions about what is just.[19] And the content of these intuitions is indissociable from the values of liberal democracy.

For his part, Dworkin indicates that liberalism can be understood in another way than by defining what human beings should be. Here, he is seeking especially to avoid the possibility of exposing the members of the collectivity to the danger of seeing their life dictated by a particular conception of the good, one with which those who hold power themselves identify.[20] The corollary to this idea is the claim that there is a clearcut distinction between the domain of personal existence – within which Dworkin grants that the notion of the good life can legitimately intervene as regards the preferences and existential choices of each person – and that of the overall political organisation of society from which every injunction espousing a model for living has to disappear.[21] But he does not succeed in doing without a theory of the good and the impact it has upon the operation of the community as a whole. Dworkin adopts a point of view that is far from neutral. His theory, which is significative of liberalism, constitutes one way of taking a stand in favour of principles deemed essential to procedural mechanisms. The participation of these mechanisms in the effort to bring out and promote justice takes place within a normative field delineated by values that are considered to be irrepressible.

Dworkin's liberalism does not succeed in distinguishing itself from the kind of conception that decrees to individuals, at least to some extent, what their lives within the collectivity ought to be. The concern not to be the spokesperson for a specific form of existence is bound, in reality, to boil down to favouring particular principles and a particular type of society. According to Dworkin, each individual has a right to demand equality of respect.[22] Dworkin thinks that, on account of its universal character, respect is not to be reduced to some specific content. Yet,

---

inequalities are to be arranged so that they are both (a) to the greatest benefit of the least advantaged and (b) attached to positions and offices open to all under conditions of fair equality of opportunity' (ibid., p. 83).

[19] Ibid., for example pp. 15, 19–20.

[20] Ronald Dworkin, *Law's Empire* (Cambridge, Mass.: Harvard University Press, 1986), pp. 440–41, note 19. The reader may also consult Taylor, *Sources of the Self*, pp. 531–32, note 60.

[21] Ronald Dworkin, 'Liberalism', in *A Matter of Principle*, for example p. 203: 'I do not suppose that I have made liberalism more attractive by arguing that its constitutive morality is a theory of equality that requires official neutrality amongst theories of what is valuable in life. That argument will provoke a variety of objections. It might be said that liberalism so conceived . . . is self-contradictory because liberalism must itself be a theory of the good . . . Liberalism is not self-contradictory: the liberal conception of equality is a principle of political organisation that is required by justice, not a way of life for individuals, and liberals, as such, are indifferent as to whether people choose to speak out on political matters, or lead eccentric lives, or otherwise to behave as liberals are supposed to prefer.'

[22] See Dworkin, *Taking Rights Seriously*, pp. 227, 272–73, and MacIntyre, *Whose Justice?*, p. 344.

along with freedom, such equality constitutes one of the great founding values of liberalism, since it is from the combination of the two[23] that the rights of individuals (and notably freedom of opinion, freedom of religion, freedom of association, or the right to vote) are derived. Equality partakes therefore of a particular world view, one that is convinced of the validity of its principles. Endeavouring to express them, to defend them, and to promote them in reality, it encourages the development of a specific way of life. In fact, it is not possible to explain and to ground, on the one hand, the knack liberal thought has to formulate criteria for justice and, on the other hand, the actions it in reality deploys in order to assert itself and to persevere, other than by its own assurance that it is better than the theories with which it is in competition or eventual conflict.

Liberalism's tendency to present itself as standing at the origin of an open, fluid world in which everything, or almost everything, is possible stems from this very sentiment it has that it possesses the truth as it is defending the values of universality, tolerance, and pluralism. Now, however prone to universality liberal values supposedly are, and however disinclined those who uphold them might be to interfere in people's existence,[24] these values, like any other world view, serve to shape the various dimensions of society and to organise them in a specific way, doing so in concert with the economic, technological, and other resources that are set within the context in which they develop. It is under their influence and in compatibility with them that, in their private as well as public aspects, individuals' ways of living are sketched out and operate. From this perspective, divergencies are acceptable only in as much as they do not constitute a radical questioning of basic principles and do remain within the limits required for them to be safeguarded.[25]

As open and neutral as it endeavours to be, the liberalism Dworkin defends is never open and neutral enough to do without convictions and principles indicating what each individual's existence is supposed to be. This inability to eliminate totally a strong evaluation[26] testifies to a phenomenon that goes beyond the specific case of liberalism and constitutes one of the characteristic and irrepressible traits of life in general. First of all, it has to be recognised that existence implies values – ones

---

[23] Their combination has not failed to give rise to numerous debates regarding the order of preference, the respective weight, and the interpretation the authors in question give to the values that go to make up this combination, as is illustrated in the polemics between liberals and conservatives within liberalism: see Dworkin's reflections in 'Liberalism', in *A Matter of Principle*, pp. 188–91.

[24] The reader may refer to MacIntyre, *Whose Justice?*, p. 346.

[25] Ibid., pp. 342–45.

[26] We borrow this expression from Taylor, 'Le juste et le bien', *Revue de métaphysique et de morale*, p. 40.

that, giving it meaning and a price, guide it in a direction.[27] Next, it must be granted that it is not possible, short of running a risk of schizophrenia, to be at the same time one thing and its opposite.

Obviously, the fact that the theories of justice proposed by John Rawls and Ronald Dworkin do not succeed in abstracting themselves from their setting in no way cancels out the interest of those theories. The obstacles they endeavour to avoid or to surmount while seeking to break away from an anchorage in history – and in particular from the relativism the tendency to peg the conditions and content of justice upon conventions can favour – represent very real dangers. It no less remains the case that, faced with criticisms against their ambitions to ahistoricity and universality, Rawls and Dworkin have been led to adjust, and even to revise, their positions.

Thus, in order to reduce the tension that exists in his book *A Theory of Justice* between the desire to determine, *sub specie aeternitatis*, what conception of justice is to be preferred to all others[28] and the influence the role historical anchorage plays in his understanding of justice, Rawls has been led, in his later writings, to attune his rhetoric to what constitutes, in *A Theory of Justice*, his practice, but without him then wanting to admit it.[29] His revisions are not lacking in breadth. He gives up on the universal import of his categories of analysis. He recognises that the ends of political philosophy depend upon the society to which this philosophy addresses itself.[30] And he comes to affirm that his objective is to construct a theory of justice that is the most reasonable for us. Fittingly, he acknowledges that his understanding of justice corresponds to the conception of the individual belonging to liberal-democratic culture,[31] and that it concerns that culture alone.[32] Rawls almost goes so far as to set the United States and its basic values as the limit for his reflections.[33] Nonetheless, that does not induce him to appeal to a notion of the good life that would precede and that would encompass the meaning of justice.

---

[27] This in no way means that there is only one type of values that expresses the good or that one cannot change one's point of view.

[28] Rawls, *A Theory of Justice*, p. 587.

[29] See Brian Barry, *A Treatise on Social Justice*, vol. I, p. 282.

[30] John Rawls, 'The Idea of an Overlapping Consensus', *Oxford Journal of Legal Studies* 7:1 (Spring 1987), p. 1.

[31] See Rawls's article 'Kantian Constructivism in Moral Theory', *Journal of Philosophy* 73:9 (September 1980), 554.

[32] Ibid., p. 518: 'An immediate consequence of taking our inquiry as focussed on the apparent conflict between freedom and equality in a democratic society is that we are not trying to find a conception of justice suitable for all societies regardless of their particular social or historical circumstances. We want to settle a fundamental disagreement over the just form of basic institutions within a democratic society under modern conditions.'

[33] Ibid.: 'We look to ourselves and to our future, and reflect upon our disputes since, let's say, the Declaration of Independence.'

In championing political liberalism, Rawls states that he is giving priority to a conception of justice that is distinct from a theory capable of enlightening and guiding individuals in all aspects of their lives. He is adopting this position because those who accept the constraints of democratic institutions and its exigencies of freedom and tolerance are all the less inclined to abandon pluralism in favour of a society unified around a single doctrine claiming to run the entire life of each, considering that the conditions in which democratic regimes originate have shown that there exists no general and exhaustive substantive view capable of offering a satisfactory basis for a political understanding of justice.[34]

For his part, Dworkin, too, after opposing the idea of establishing justice on the basis of a conception of the good life, seems to have appreciably modified his point of view. Far from giving up on proposing a doctrine of what constitutes a good existence, he now seems to opt for a properly liberal conception of the good. He thus is committing himself to a way of living that establishes a coherent relationship between personal ethics and political convictions.[35]

As we see, the rootedness of the study of social phenomena in its historical setting is irrepressible. Nevertheless, just because such a study is indissociable from its historical environment does not mean that the judgements it formulates are to be reduced thereto or that these judgements are unable, from the standpoint of legitimacy, to account satisfactorily for characteristics of social phenomena that take place in different settings.

Implementation of judgement and identity of societies

The issues of the social and political sciences frequently correspond to the preoccupations of the society in which they are located. The observer,

---

[34] Rawls, 'The Idea of an Overlapping Consensus', p. 4: 'The social and historical conditions of modern democratic regimes have their origins in the Wars of Religion following the Reformation and the subsequent development of the principle of toleration, and in the growth of constitutional government and of a large industrial market. These conditions profoundly affect the requirements of a workable conception of justice: among other things, such a conception must allow for a diversity of general and comprehensive doctrines, and for a plurality of conflicting, and indeed incommensurable, conceptions of the meaning, value, and purpose of human life (or what I shall call for short "conceptions of the good") affirmed by the citizens of democratic societies.'

[35] Ronald Dworkin, 'Foundations of Liberal Equity', in Grethe B. Peterson (ed.), *The Tanner Lectures on Human Values* (Salt Lake City: University of Utah Press, 1990), vol. XI, pp. 1–119, and more specifically pp. 3–9. Let us mention the article 'Why Liberals Should Care about Equality', in *A Matter of Principle*, where, for example on pp. 205–06, Dworkin seeks to tone down his attachment to the notion of neutrality he defends in 'Liberalism' (also in *A Matter of Principle*), which presages the possibility of this evolution in his thinking. See also the comments of Philippe Van Parijs, *Qu'est-ce qu'une société juste?*, pp. 246–47.

who examines a situation in which he is not an actor, casts a glance, but that glance does not bring back up the same identical impressions as those of the individuals who are actually living through the situation. This is all the more the case when there is a great cultural divide between the phenomena and the observer. How, under these conditions, is one to proceed so that the prism represented by one's rootedness in an environment might allow a margin of manoeuvre that would permit one not to betray the characteristics of these phenomena and enable one to offer credible evaluations regarding the justice or injustice of the relationships between rulers and ruled?

It is appropriate, first of all, to take different societal types into account. Here, we must endeavour, as far as possible, to know their specific characteristics and to integrate them into the judgements being passed. These specific characteristics do indeed enter into the process by which one determines the configuration under analysis. They mark out those orientations that are said to be just and the ones that are condemned. The responsibilities incumbent upon institutions and statesmen, as well as the corresponding expectations on the part of the population, are tied to the identity of this society. Thus, one cannot, when reflecting upon the right to govern, ignore the fact that a particular society's conception of the world delineates the framework within which its members are led to take positions as to its just or unjust character.

This assumes, therefore, that one has made some allowance for the ways in which the identity of societies has evolved over time. It is clear, for example, that the question of legitimacy is not posed today in France in the same terms as it was a hundred years ago. That would be to adopt an anachronistic point of view, wishing to evaluate the past on the basis of criteria for judgement borrowed entirely from the present. Since the end of the nineteenth century, the resources of French society, like the constraints it faces, have changed, thus bringing about modifications in the relations of forces and in demands that are formulated in terms of right, as well as, by way of consequence, in the very idea of what is politically legitimate.

Yet one must also remain sensitive to the differences that exist between societies within one and the same period.[36] The observer who is responding carefully to the question of the right to govern will not treat societies in the same way, depending upon whether they constitute variants of one

---

[36] On analysing societies and the levels of disparity that can exist among them, the reader may refer, for example, to the methodological remarks Louis Dumont makes in *From Mandeville to Marx: The Genesis and Triumph of Economic Ideology* (University of Chicago Press, 1977), pp. 8–9, 14.

and the same system of values – for example, modern democracy[37] – or follow fundamentally distinct logics, such as the egalitarian ideal of democracy versus an organised social hierarchy in India's caste system.[38]

In parallel with this, we may say that the reliability of judgements having to do with legitimacy depends upon the observer's capacity to base his observations upon the viewpoints of individuals who are directly confronted with a given political situation. By helping to forge the identity of the collectivity as well as the identities of that collectivity's members, the values involved in working out the context are so many tools that allow individuals to judge the quality of the social life that unfolds under the auspices of political institutions and to position themselves in relation to these institutions. This positioning on the part of the protagonists is an indication of utmost importance for the study of legitimacy.

That obviously does not stop one from casting a critical glance at social phenomena. The objective is not to carry out an analysis that would rubber-stamp every established situation to the benefit of the official authorities. It is a matter, rather, of inquiring about the degree of justice in a given government, asking oneself whether that government benefits from the support of individuals or whether it arouses their opposition. Thus, the population's attitudes of satisfaction or discontent, which result from the way in which people and institutions embodying the established political power discharge their responsibilities, furnish the observer with top-quality indications of the coefficient of legitimacy existing in the relationships between rulers and ruled. Behaviours that are indicative of

---

[37] See, in particular, Alexis de Tocqueville, *Democracy in America*, ed. Phillips Bradley, trans. Henry Reeve, revised by Francis Bowen (New York: Vintage, 1990), vol. II, pp. 94–97, 297–99. There he contrasts, in terms of the characteristics of each of them, the English, American, and French democratic regimes, according to the relative place granted in a democracy to its cardinal virtues, freedom and equality. England is a country with freedom but not much equality. America has, to a great extent, inherited freedom and developed equality. France, in the wake of the Revolution that broke with the Ancien Régime, seeks principally the reign of equality.

[38] See Louis Dumont, *Homo Hierarchicus: The Caste System and its Implications*, trans. Mark Sainsbury, Louis Dumont, and Basia Gulati, complete rev. English edn (University of Chicago Press, 1980), pp. 1, 3, 4. Societies that belong to completely distinct civilisations and those that share some overall points of reference while at the same time maintaining some differences among themselves due to national peculiarities, do not cover the entire range of possible forms of social arrangement. There exist other cases. There are, for example, societies whose internal diversity goes so far as to combine – not without engendering serious, and sometimes dramatic, tensions – heterogeneous value systems: witness the countries, notably in Africa and Asia, where colonial administrations and then newly independent States have been added to and have mixed with local and traditional cultures. In this regard, the reader may consult Georges Balandier, *Political Anthropology*, pp. 158–64, 172–84, and Clifford Geertz, *The Interpretations of Cultures: Selected Essays* (New York: Basic Books, 1973), pp. 148–50, 238–49, 255–61, 317–23, among other places.

assent or ones that point towards contestation constitute so many sources of information and lessons about the just or unjust character of political relationships.

On the level of thought as well as on that of actions, positions of adherence or rejection are obviously not always in reality displayed in a clear-cut way, notably on account of the risk one might run in manifesting one's opinion overtly. As a consequence, it is also appropriate, in order to detect the actual points of view of individuals, to be attentive to the quality of their participation in collective life by studying their personal motivations and investments. One must, in particular, bring out the extent to which an attitude that endorses a way of governing corresponds to an authentic commitment or is, on the contrary, but a simulacrum of support that answers to the requirements of prudence.[39]

Certainly, information provided through the behaviours of individuals is not always reliable, as witness the cases where people rally to a recommended policy but their rallying is merely symptomatic of a form of alienation engineered by a cleverly orchestrated propaganda campaign. Moreover, there are some dangers in elevating individuals' attitudes to the rank of a decisive criterion in the determination of what justice is, even when those attitudes are in the main the product of a process of free reflection. Such an approach can favour the development of a subjectivist conception of legitimacy – one incapable, therefore, in the absence of rational criteria, of resolving divergencies of opinion and conflicts of interests. It remains the case, however, that, when implemented with caution, the analysis of individuals' attitudes incontestably contributes to the elucidation of the question of the right to govern.

Ethic of truth and society ruled by right

To account for the diverse points of view that exist in the situations under analysis while explicating, when need be, disagreements and conflicts where what is just becomes an issue assumes that the right to know social phenomena for what they are has not been denied. It is to adopt a position that prevents one from considering these phenomena merely as means to be used at one's convenience. And that is something that does not go without saying in all societies.

---

[39] On this subject, see, for example, the situation of Eastern communist regimes, as presented in particular by Moshe Lewin in *The Gorbachev Phenomenon: A Historical Interpretation* (Berkeley: University of California Press, 1989), pp. 25–27, 110. On this same question, but this time within the context of managing manpower in the modern business enterprise, the reader may refer to the observations of Philippe Delmas, *Le Maître des horloges. Modernité de l'action publique* (Paris: Odile Jacob, 1991), pp. 176–78.

Although the description and evaluation of the relationships between rulers and ruled from the standpoint of legitimacy do not escape the pressure exerted by the context in which they are worked out, those who offer such descriptions and evaluations have a duty to fulfil in relation to the domain under examination: not to subject them to operations involving intellectual distortion. Indeed, it is fitting to establish a line of demarcation between the kind of analysis that seeks and desires right through its quest for the truth and the kind that is opposed thereto. For this orientation to be operational, the analysis of political events from the standpoint of legitimacy has to be set in a society that leaves it a certain margin of manoeuvre. Society has to identify sufficiently with the principles of truth and justice so as to, in a general way, conceive and develop its history without systematically repressing those principles and so as to, more specifically, not do harm to these values within the framework of its reflective activities and efforts.

The damages can be considerable if it is the manipulation of facts that wins out. The impact is disastrous not only on the plane of knowledge but also on the practical level. This is quite particularly the case when the facts analysed deal with a still-fresh reality. When the object under study belongs to a society's near past and when it continues painfully to haunt its present, a failure to make allowance for the clause that specifies that one should not distort events does not mean only that one is undermining knowledge and robbing memory. By throwing a veil over the misdeeds that have been committed, one is ultimately making oneself into their accomplice. This ends up casting doubt upon the willingness of institutions to express and to promote truth and justice, whereas these institutions are supposed to be the guarantors thereof.[40] One then risks seeing mistrust developing to the point of discrediting the ideas of right and justice. When these ideas are flouted in a basic way, the reasons for thinking and behaving in conformity with the requirements of duty and solidarity disappear and are replaced by attitudes that tend to privilege short-term personal interest to the exclusion of all else. The way in which everyday existence and the future of the collectivity unfold then become caught up in a deadly spiral.

---

[40] The reader may refer, for example, to the polemics engendered in Argentina in 1987 when, faced with a partial army uprising, President Alfonsin had to, with the exception of the commanders in chief, grant an amnesty to a large number of military officers who had earlier been judged guilty for human-rights crimes perpetrated during the 1976–82 dictatorship. See also the historians' debate in Germany, as discussed in particular in Habermas's *The New Conservatism*, for example pp. 229–40, which was instigated by authors whose writings try to account for Nazism while seeking to minimise and normalise the crimes it committed.

When analysing legitimacy, it is recommended that one show respect for the way in which social phenomena are configured. Such respect is part of a morality of knowledge, that of critical or engaged neutrality. This morality of knowledge is connected to the ethical dimension in general. It is in relation to this dimension of ethics that those who govern as well as the society they rule do or do not align their conduct. Indeed, the approach advocated in the present work induces one to think the following: to the extent that judgements bearing upon social facts do not lose sight of the horizon of truth, their potential plurality constitutes so many complementary approaches. None of the evaluations proposed claims to have in principle a monopoly upon the truth or to stem from the kind of diversity in which everything is equivalent. It is upon this condition that the differences in appreciation liable to separate them not only remain compatible and enrich the mosaic of ways of knowing about reality but also point towards an understanding of political life in terms of right, thus contributing to the latter's development.

By underscoring the importance of the tie between truth and justice, the morality of knowledge deployed in the study of legitimacy is indissociable from what a society has to subscribe to in order to be in step with the search for what is just. The political instances of authority and those who rule these instances have to promote the best possible knowledge of the facts. The strength of this will is an indication of the degree of justice present in society. Thus, when mechanisms used to conceal or manipulate reality are one of basic characteristics of the activities of those who govern, these mechanisms infringe upon ethical imperatives and fail to take into account those rights and duties whose importance those who govern nevertheless sense strongly enough so that they do not take it upon themselves to violate them openly. In this regard, lying about one's responsibility for actions that are deemed reprehensible is not simply a way of hiding them. It is also, upon occasion, to fail to admit it to oneself. The bad faith of government criminals is rarely burdened with scruples when it comes to preserving their own interests.

The credibility of judgements regarding legitimacy depends therefore upon an acceptance and a clarification of relations between the historical dimension of social and political phenomena and the analysis of these phenomena. It nevertheless remains the case that the considerations brought up in this chapter do not exhaust the subject. There is room to supplement them with a reflection upon the experience of meaning individuals have within their community.

6   Community experience, dynamic of possibilities, and political legitimacy

In order to show that it is possible to reconcile the idea of truth with the plurality of historical reality and therefore to think that the diversity of ways of life and the changes that intervene do not rule out the existence of limits to what is politically acceptable, we must complete the arguments offered up till now with a reflection upon community experience. When individuals are sufficiently integrated into a given community, so that they identify with it and are aware of their rights and duties, they have an experience of the just or unjust character of their situation as well as of the responsibility incumbent upon those who govern.

This reflection will take place in three stages. First, it will be shown that the question of practical truths is tied to the domain of meaning and possibilities, which is deployed within the social field. Next, the theme of the judgement of legitimacy will be broached by examining community experience in relation to the dynamic of possibilities. Starting from the idea that one's feeling of belonging to a collectivity cannot be separated from the way in which individuals perceive their rights and their duties, it will be noted that this situation supposes that political institutions are capable of taking note of eventual changes in possibilities and of their impact as they are realised, when these possibilities are conceived by agents as being essential to their well-being. In the contrary case, there is a risk of a rift forming between the political instances of authority and society. If they are not integrated in some way by the established authorities, changes affecting deliberations on possibilities may lead to conflicts that challenge the community's equilibrium. Finally, it will be argued that the achievement of right and of justice is the product of an ongoing effort at adjustment and is indissociable from the theme of the scope [*l'étendue*] of community.

EXPERIENCE OF MEANING, DELIBERATION ON POSSIBILITIES, AND JUDGEMENTS OF LEGITIMACY

We have already seen that the main defect of certain currents in the social sciences, those that identify with the postulates upon which the

205

scientistic, Marxist, and Weberian approaches rest, is their failure to treat the axiological dimension of social facts in a satisfactory fashion. These currents opt for an orientation that prevents them from tackling legitimacy in terms of an authentic reflection upon right. The investigation into the conditions for the possibility and for the existence of the truth in the domain of social and political facts is not carried to its conclusion. In order to overcome the limitations of their analyses and to be assured that the changing and plural character of values capable of serving as criteria for establishing what is just will not be a definitive obstacle to the pronouncement of reliable judgements about legitimacy, it is of the essence to show that the dimension of meaning is at the centre of human experience and, in particular, of life in society.

In order to contribute to the credibility of the procedure by which one evaluates the right to govern, an analysis of the dimension of meaning has to be conducted from the standpoint of how one deliberates about possibilities. In this regard, one first has to examine how the notions of signification, of the possible, and of practical truth are articulated in people's existence within society. It is then appropriate to point out that the responsibility of rulers and of political institutions is to be measured by the yardstick of the decisions and actions determined by these notions.

The domains of meaning and of the possible and the question of practical truths

Because human reality ill lends itself to mechanisms used to demonstrate the truth and because unanimity and definitive answers are rarely present in the operation of life in society, and especially within modern societies, the idea that the domain of values and the domain of human decisions and actions can be inscribed within the categories of the true and the false is a difficult one to accept. Obviously, this situation does not fail to affect the way in which the social sciences account in general for the problematic of meaning in the unfolding of political relations. The social sciences dissociate the question of meaning from the question of practical truths. Thus, it is on account of the supposed impossibility of explicating rationally grounded choices that a positivist empiricism concentrates its ambition upon offering descriptions and explanations of those factors that are most easily quantifiable. It is for this reason, too, that it forsakes the significations surrounding human action. The key feature of any discourse on the truth consists, then, in asking oneself whether the statements being formulated fit with the accepted validation procedures. Weber, for his part, while granting all along a great importance to meaning and to the processes of intentionality, separates off the beliefs held by individuals from the idea of truth. In his writings, it is the irrationality of values that prevents one from establishing any kind of axiological hierarchy. This alleged irrationality of values ends up disconnecting the signification individuals give to their activity in society from any intrinsic relationship with the values of truth and justice. As for the Marxist conception of meaning in history, it is indissociable from a monolithic view of the truth that does not accord very well with a human reality made up entirely of nuances and diversity.

Now, to carry out a reflection upon possibilities seems to be one way of overcoming the difficulty one experiences in articulating the level of signification in tandem with that of practical truths. Indeed, it allows one to establish a connection between the beliefs of individuals and the mechanisms used to evaluate those beliefs. This reflection rests upon the following thesis: a society is a field of possibilities; it is inseparable from the constitutive elements of the identity of the society in which this field is located. This is to say that the decisions and actions that can be envisaged within that particular society depend both upon the society's state of development in its various spheres of activity – economic, political, social, cultural, and so on – and upon the values that give it a normative structure. To be convinced of this, it suffices to note, for example, that the choices and actions accessible to an individual living in France during the Middle Ages are evidently not those of the French today. Between these two eras, these two societies, the axiological framing of collective existence has changed, and it has changed in parallel with modifications occurring in particular within the domain of knowledge and of the technical means at hand. So, the options available to the individuals in these two cases are very different.

To present society as a field of possibilities is therefore to place the accent on the fact that, within a given context, individuals are faced with a range of orientations that are so many ways of manifesting the fact that they have the capacity to choose and to make and do things.[1] The extent of the possibilities offered to individuals constitutes a set of decisions and actions through which individuals can have an impact not only on the way their own existence unfolds but also on the way collective life functions.

Of course, to affirm that society is a field of possibilities in no way implies that anything and everything is envisageable therein; on the contrary. The field of possibilities that includes the set of resources placed at the disposal of individuals is such only within a definite framework.

---

[1] We are freely inspired here by Aristotle's analyses of deliberation in *Nichomachean Ethics*, 3.5.1112a20–30.

In a general way, we may say that the form and the content of these resources vary according to the society under analysis and to the status each person occupies therein. These possibilities therefore unavoidably encounter limitations, which can be classed into two broad categories. Let us nonetheless specify straight off that in a serious crisis situation, where the members of a collectivity disagree with the overall ways in which society is directed and organised, a movement of contestation opposed to the established rulers and institutions most often combines these two categories.

The first type has to do with what is on the order of the unthinkable. To provide a somewhat caricatured illustration of this type of limitation, let us say that a slave in the Empire of the Pharaohs is not up to making an evaluation of his chances of becoming president of the Republic. That just does not enter into his thought options. The imagination of possibilities and the kind of deliberation that is likely to result therefrom are valid only in terms of what individuals are allowed to conceive and to hope for within a specific society.

The second type of limitation impeding the deployment of possibilities is less strict than the first. It is nevertheless of central importance for the questions being broached in the present volume. This one concerns choices and actions that are theoretically and practically conceivable – they are set within the order of the thinkable – but that, to the extent that they express orientations condemned by society, tend to be seen as risky and therefore appear to be very problematic.

THE SOCIAL DIMENSION, LIMITATION OF POSSIBILITIES,
RIGHTS AND DUTIES

This second type of limitation of the field of possibilities is of a kind with the overall culture of a society. Here, the feature that stands in opposition to the realisation of certain possibilities relates to an incompatibility that is perceived and understood on the basis of the constitutive values of the society's identity.

The range of possible decisions and acts individuals evolving within a given society have at their disposal has two dimensions. First, this range of possible decisions and acts is set within a strategy relating to individual success. In this first dimension, one is guided by the concern to reach an objective that would lead to the acquisition of some gain. Here it is a matter of attaining a good the individual believes he can enjoy in terms of what he thinks pertains to the possible. Yet deliberation in terms of one's personal interests does not take place in a void. It is not a solitary undertaking. For, second, deliberation on what is possible inevitably takes place within a social environment. Indeed, it is in relation to what the society's characteristic traits establish as a horizon of possibility that individuals evaluate their individual path and, by way of consequence, the objectives and gains they are likely to decide to pursue. Now, this social dimension, which cannot be avoided in one's personal reflections, carries a limitation on the possibilities each is offered.

In the context of this social dimension, the basic thing is to be careful that the tension between the interests of individuals and the exigencies of collective existence does not reach such heights that social relations are themselves placed in peril. This tension, which varies with the type of society (it is much more pronounced in modern societies, where the individual asserts himself as an autonomous being, than in traditional communities, where the identity and life plans of individuals remain strongly anchored in networks of collective solidarity) has to be contained within the framework of some sort of cooperation. Relationships of reciprocity must be established and must endure between individuals. The relations among the members of society cannot be a one-way street and benefit just a few people, let alone always the same ones. It is therefore important that relationships be placed under the banner of exchange. Beyond differences in the form and content of mutual recognition, the existence of others has to be integrated in some way into the decisions and behaviours of each. If that is not the case, the survival of the social dimension is itself threatened. In the absence of any mutual interest, the continuation and reaffirmation of relationships based upon understanding becomes meaningless.

When this situation – a simple conflict among particular persons – becomes the norm for collective relations, not only is the future of cooperation at the individual level compromised,[2] but so too is the social dimension in its entirety. Short-term calculations win out over long-term ones, and relationships among individuals do not transcend the limits of the present. Based neither upon trust nor upon an investment in the future, such relationships stand in flagrant contradiction to the production of the social dimension and of a collective future. Those who feel that they have been swindled do not hesitate to act when the occasion presents itself. Their reaction may be conducted discreetly, if they must proceed with prudence, or in broad daylight if the risk of conflict is judged to be minimal or if they benefit from a henceforth favourable relation of forces. In any case, within such a context cooperation has now become nothing more than an empty word.

---

[2] See the reflections of Robert Axelrod, *The Evolution of Cooperation* (New York: Basic Books, 1984), for example pp. 7–10.

Deliberative procedures inevitably unfold within the social dimension. This dimension therefore cannot be ignored by the members of the collectivity – unless, of course, one is willing to run the risk of being banned from society or else wants, when this attitude is shared by a great proportion of the population, to contribute further towards the unravelling, if not bursting, of the social bond.

But even when an individual is pursuing his individual interest, he is strongly advised, if he does not want to have to face attacks possibly challenging his grounds,[3] to remain within the limits set by society. The mechanism of deliberation is social in character – which implies that, at the heart of a reflection upon possibilities, there exist some boundaries that are not to be crossed. One has to take into consideration what, in terms of the values and rules decreed by society, is incumbent upon each person. The rights of the other mark out and indicate the duties that must be assumed.

DELIMITATION OF POSSIBILITIES AND SOCIETY'S ENDS

In order to obtain a relatively exhaustive knowledge of this social dimension, which has an impact upon individuals' faculty of deliberation, one must specify its tie with the overall ends of society. These ends orient the community as a whole. They constitute a highly valuable parameter for the determination of possibilities. The establishment of limits that are not to be exceeded under penalty of sanction or of the breakup of society is performed in coordination with the basic principles of the identity of the society concerned. It is in connection with the values that are constitutive of society's present and future that the delimitation of possibilities takes place. Clearly, a community that, for example, conceives the notion of religious tolerance to be one of its basic principles will be very particular about combating those who work for the triumph of one religion over the other ones. Likewise, a society that makes it its duty to ensure a minimum living standard for all its members cannot deliberately let some of these members die of hunger and continue to claim credibility.

To the extent that the ends that determine the overall identity of the community represent a decisive factor for the establishment of what is possible, the compatibility of these possibilities with the ends in question cannot be simply passive in character. It is important, at least when it is society's will to continue along a dynamically rising trajectory, that

---

[3] See Machiavelli's remarks on the constant vigilance the preservation of goods requires in a universe that is dominated by force, and within which, by way of consequence, it is difficult to exercise a right in order to ensure its defence (*The Prince*, in particular, chapter 24, p. 74). See also Claude Lefort's comments in his *Le Travail de l'œuvre. Machiavel* (Paris: Gallimard, 1972), for example pp. 346–48.

cooperative relationships, in which these possibilities are embodied, be expressive of and serve to promulgate in an active way the founding values of that society.

The more the choices and acts of individuals have to do with those strategic areas that are defined by the overall ends and founding principles of a society, the narrower and the more carefully watched is the margin of manoeuvre within which these individual choices and acts are allowed to develop. The extent of one's possibilities contracts; it becomes highly controlled and is subject to codification. Upstream from the decisions and actions likely to take shape within a society's strategic areas of concern, the navigable path is strictly and severely marked out. Downstream therefrom, when the decisions and actions put into effect exceed the limits of the permissible, the authorities do not fail to make harsh use of the various tools of sanction they have at their disposal. In contrast, the field of possibilities is broader, and more flexible, when one's deliberation upon and realisation of possibilities have to do with relatively peripheral issues.

The impact of society's strategic domains, which its overall ends help to establish, differs according to the type of society in question. Thus, the strategic domain supposes a more marked limitation of possibilities in a traditional community – where the higher level of collective forms of solidarity goes hand in hand with a homogeneity and a rigidity in life plans – than in societies of the liberal type – where the attachment to basic values authorises a diversity in individual forms of behaviour. But it is equally possible to notice this phenomenon in relation to societies that, while all belonging to the same system (the democratic system, for example), present local variations.

From this point of view, the difference in the perception of political representation in the United States and France is characteristic. The question of the private life of political leaders is more pronounced in the United States than in France. This is not due solely to an unhealthy curiosity. It is also because there political representation is not, as is the case in France, backed up by a State that, involving it in a universal and abstract conception of the nation, contributes towards its disembodiment. In France, democratic principles, being part of the historical rise of state power,[4] are mediated and guaranteed by a State that claims to be the expression of the public interest and of a secularised form of Providence. In the United States, on the contrary, society dominates the State. This society is made up of diverse communities. While their integration into the American nation is achieved (to a greater or lesser extent, depending upon the ethnic group) in the name of great universal principles, this integration of communities nevertheless remains driven by a desire to

---

[4] See, in particular, Tocqueville, *The Old Regime and the Revolution*, pp. 135–38.

see state institutions and rulers not only make allowances for the cultural particularisms of each community but also act in accordance with moral values that, for some of them, concern the private life of individuals. These values are perceived as being so fundamental to social life as a whole that the responsible political authorities are themselves required to conform to them. In other words, it is less society that identifies with the State than the State that finds itself pegged upon society.[5] The people's representative is in direct touch with the ethic society privileges in private existence. The contractual values of honesty and faithfulness, whose eminent place the Puritan mentality underscores in men's behaviour towards women,[6] ill accommodates a Don Juan attitude from political figures who aspire to the highest offices.

The more the possibilities at issue have to do with the values that structure society and that determine the other ends organising the less strategic spheres of interest, the more the constraints exerted upon possibilities belong to a level of necessity where the survival of society demands that there be no, or else very little, room for compromise. In calculating what is desirable, one is called upon to come to terms with what passes for being necessary. And what passes for being necessary combines what is unthinkable for the collectivity – namely, the first limitation mentioned above – with those choices that risk courting sanctions if they are implemented. The part of the social dimension that enters into individuals' mechanisms of deliberation thereby sets one on the path that points towards a reconciliation of the level of meaning with the question of practical truth. Under the combined influence of scientism and liberalism, observers have largely ignored this dimension, even if recent scientific works are tending once again to recognise its importance.[7]

THE HORIZON OF SOCIAL SIGNIFICATION AND
PRACTICAL TRUTH

The field of possibilities, which is delimited by society's ends, evolves within the horizon of signification these ends determine. In marking out

---

[5] These comparative remarks are obviously not meant to imply that in France the State is separated from society, or that in the United States society is not to some extent under the thumb of the state authorities. It is simply that, in France, more than in the United States, the institutional arrangements make society highly dependent upon the State. This situation developed historically in France in tandem with the centralised regulatory role that devolved upon the State as regards the operation of society.

[6] See, as an illustration of this point, Patrice Higonnet's *Sister Republics: The Origins of French and American Republicanism* (Cambridge, Mass.: Harvard University Press, 1988), pp. 29–30.

[7] See Albert O. Hirschman, *Essays in Trespassing: Economics to Politics and Beyond*, 2nd edn (Cambridge University Press, 1984), pp. 299–304, and Sen, *On Ethics and Economics*, pp. 15–22.

the boundaries for the field of individual reflection and action, the overall ends of the collectivity in effect help to define what has meaning and what is possible. In expressing the basic values that come to establish society's identity, these ends furnish individuals with a guide for meaning and action. They prompt individuals to orient themselves in one direction rather than in another, on the plane of signification as well as on the practical plane.

The possibilities offered to individuals constitute the set of options liable to enter into calculations about what is feasible and what is desirable. This takes place in terms of the universe of meaning worked out by the values society privileges. Better than that, we can say that the possible takes on full meaning to the extent the possible is made probable by those objectives society extends some hope of attaining with success. There is then a convergence between the meaning individuals place in their choices and in their actions and the reality they can envisage interpreting and constructing. In order to illustrate this point, let us point out that it would be absurd to reproach certain Amerindian peoples for having, through the grid of their myths, interpreted the appearance of the Spanish as a return of the gods: they related to something extraordinary with the tools their conception of the world gave them.[8]

Deliberation therefore pertains to a field of possibilities whose configuration depends upon several levels that intervene in complementary fashion in order to calibrate what individuals can or cannot interpret, decide, and do. Without being subject to an absolutely rigid kind of determination, which would leave people no alternatives, this field of possibilities fixes, within a determinate framework, the available options. Assuming that the equilibrium of society is not going through a deep crisis, these options are compatible with its overall ends. And in the universe of signification furnished by these ends, the available options are thought, willed, and implemented in such a way as to open onto concrete realities.

The horizon of meaning the observer is in a position to bring out in relation to his analysis of the domain of possibilities and of ends need not halt at this aspect alone. It also integrates the dimension of practical truth. Indeed, on account of the social dimension, which serves as their framework, the truth of decisions and actions is not to be reduced to their instrumental efficacy. Or rather, this instrumental efficacy brings a truth into play on the practical or axiological level.

The instrumental efficacy of individuals' choices and acts develops within the universe of significations that is fixed in place by society's ends. And these choices and acts are true or false on the practical level in

---

[8] See Miguel León-Portilla, *Visión de los vencidos: relaciones indígenas de la conquista*, 9th edn (Mexico City: Universidad Nacional Autónoma de México, 1982), pp. 33–38.

so far as they conform or do not conform to them. Depending upon their compatibility with these ends, one type of choice and act will be judged to respect or not to respect the rationality of the collectivity, that is to say, to be reasonable in relation to the rights and duties demanded of each person. This can easily be verified. Thus, when an individual infringes upon the code of good conduct of life in the community, he usually adds to this violation – which constitutes a twisting of practical truth – an effort to hide what he has done, so that he may escape the sanction to which he is thereby exposing himself. His concern is to reshuffle the deck so that this violation of moral objectivity – as represented by a requirement to conform to the rules of reciprocity that have been established in a given setting – will not be discovered. The practical error he has made is followed by attempts at manipulation and concealment on the plane of knowledge.

The more decisions and actions enter into contradiction with the meaning in force within a given society, the more they appear erroneous on the practical level. They are sanctioned as such. If the feeling of error goes well beyond the limits of what is considered reasonable, it no longer will be simply a question of a social mistake. The decisions and actions at stake will look simply absurd. Eventually, they could be perceived as not making sense in the context of the experience of meaning attached to a life in society – an outburst that could be perceived as so excessive that it could also be seen as verging on the aberrant, even the inhuman.

This was the experience numerous inmates in the death camps had to face. The situations in which they were thrust were so unexpected, so unimaginable, that they could not have foreseen what was going to happen to them. Even after 1945, the survivors had a hard time believing that such situations could have been possible.[9] It has been said that, in order to survive, people had to give up a part of their human identity and banish their quality of being-a-man, which their torturers had denied them.[10] They had to forget what being a civilised person meant in order to endure the suffering and horror being inflicted upon them. Self-anaesthetisation, forgetting of oneself, and making oneself forget were the means by which one remained a man.[11]

It therefore cannot be said that it is impossible to separate out the true from the false in the way social facts unfold or in the description that

[9] Hannah Arendt, *The Origins of Totalitarianism*, 6th edn with new prefaces (New York: Harcourt Brace Jovanovich, 1979), pp. 439–41.

[10] See Emmanuel Lévinas, 'The Name of a Dog, or Natural Rights', in *Difficult Freedom: Essays on Judaism*, trans. Seán Hand (Baltimore, Md.: Johns Hopkins University Press, 1990), pp. 151–53.

[11] The reader may consult Jean-Pierre Azéma's 'Les victimes du nazisme', in *L'Allemagne de Hitler 1933–1945*, 2nd edn (Paris: Éditions du Seuil, 1991), pp. 322–23.

is offered of them. The statements formulated about social and political reality do not represent merely interpretations liable to endless discussion without the interlocutors being in a position to establish a distinction between those that satisfy the exigencies of truth and those that do not answer to such requirements. That the idea of what is true might have a history, that this history might show us that it has often been used in order to serve partisans objectives, that its content might have undergone profound changes over the course of centuries, and that, during one and the same era, there might have been different systems of truth and of action claiming to embody it to the exclusion of other ones – none of that need induce us to think that the idea of practical truth is a fiction. There is even some danger in thinking that one must either fall back upon those criteria and procedures for construction of the truth that are implemented in the natural sciences or take what is true to be the object of beliefs that are not rationally grounded.

To refuse to give the notion of truth a place and a role in the practical domain is to renounce taking a stand on what is good or bad, and therefore deciding in terms of right. It is to eliminate the possibility of specifying what is true and false both in articulate discourses about social facts and in actions conducted within human reality.

In this regard, historical nominalism and historicism, which refuse to inquire into the conditions for truth in a changing and plural universe, can be considered the Trojan horse for a conservative or reactionary thinking and politics. It does indeed seem very difficult for the advocates of such an approach to stand up to historical revisionism. In order to denounce revisionism, one must first assume that there exist interpretations of history that are true and other ones that are false, and then one must shed light on the benchmarks that allow one to establish this distinction. If that is not done, the task cannot be accomplished.

It is obviously quite acceptable to affirm the thesis that there exists a plurality of possible interpretations about a given phenomenon and to think that such interpretations are connected to the context in which the observers who express them are evolving. But this thesis should not lead one to think that such a plurality is necessarily accompanied by an inability to offer a hierarchy of viewpoints. It must be repeated that the positions individuals take, whether on the level of choice or of action, are set within a social dimension. In this regard, we may say that they unfold within a horizon of possibilities that, while allowing a margin of manoeuvre and permitting the manifestation of diversity, is also limited by what has meaning and what is valued within a given society. The range of possible decisions and acts is defined in terms of their compatibility with the exigencies of reciprocity among individuals, which the social dimension demands in order to endure. The orientations that are sanctioned because they are judged practically incorrect are the ones that go beyond the domain of what is considered reasonable, as determined by the overall ends of the collectivity. Plurality is therefore not a synonym for an absence of limits. One cannot say everything and do everything without offending a society's truths, without violating what conditions therein relationships based upon reciprocity, exchange, and tolerance.

What pertains to the undecidable and to the endlessly debatable is so only in as much as it does not stand in opposition to the possibility of expressing oneself and of living within a community according to the rules of reciprocity set down there. What goes against these rules and threatens them stumbles upon those boundaries that, within a given context, are deemed inappropriate to transgress so as not to abandon the meaning and values of the collectivity in which individuals recognise themselves. It is this state of things that allows one, in offering some reference points, to evaluate the choices and actions of individuals in terms of practical truth. It is clear that this type of argument assumes the existence of an overall agreement among the members of society about the fields of signification and of the possible, and therefore about what passes for being true or just. In the absence of a balanced situation, the dividing line between the principles about which compromise is not allowed and what is simply acceptable dissolves. A period of crisis then ensues regarding the implementation of right.

This is why it is necessary to articulate one's analysis of the domains of meaning, of the possible, and of practical truth in tandem with a study of community experience itself. Before venturing in this direction, however, it is worthwhile to examine in what way the reflections previously presented about signification, possibilities, and the status of what is true on the practical level offer criteria for evaluating the actions of rulers and political institutions *vis-à-vis* the community.

Requirements of the possible, political responsibility, and evaluation of legitimacy

The domains of meaning and of possibilities, which are defined by the overall ends of society, indicate the orientations that are to be respected in order that relationships based upon reciprocity might exist among individuals. In this respect, they delimit the responsibility of political institutions and leaders. These institutions and leaders have to be careful that the satisfaction of those needs that are lived as possible and desirable, nay even necessary, really constitute the present and future reality of the group in their charge. That is what their responsibility to the governed consists in.

Of course, the task considered incumbent upon institutions and upon the responsible authorities is tied in with the identity of society. Their share of the overall responsibility is therefore variable. It changes from era to era, in different types of societies, and according to the situation. And the expectations of the ruled *vis-à-vis* the choices and acts of the political authorities are modelled upon what is supposed to depend expressly upon these authorities. Nonetheless, when societal issues are perceived to be political stakes, they can – if, in the view of the population, they are not resolved – place the rulers in a difficult position.

The risks incurred by those who govern when they do not satisfactorily assume their obligations regarding the areas over which they have responsibility are proportionate to how strategic those areas of responsibility are considered to be. The broader the scope of political responsibility, the more likely the political authorities are to find themselves showered with criticisms. Their strength therefore tends to become a weakness: omnipresent, they court the danger of having to shoulder all alone the responsibility for the difficulties that may arise. Thus, the considerable role played by the State in Communist countries could not help but render the Communist State fragile when faced with protest movements, once these movements were able to express themselves openly. Soviet institutions found it particularly difficult to shift responsibility onto their predecessors for any errors committed – a stratagem Western politicians know so well how to use.

What the governed expect from political institutions and from the people who head up these institutions is for them not to repress those possibilities that are lived as basic to the fulfilment of their rights. On the contrary, their role is to recognise these rights and to safeguard them. The observer will be able to formulate judgements regarding legitimacy based upon the way in which political institutions carry out the job assigned to them, but also based upon the attitude the ruled have towards the rulers. This observer will thus be in a position to evaluate to what extent the rulers are discharging their duties.

In being articulated in tandem with governmental action, the domain of the possible and of the desirable offers one some indications as to the legitimacy of political relationships. The fact that the activity of the ruling authorities might or might not be giving rise to feelings of attachment on the part of the ruled furnishes the observer with information about individuals' assessment of justice and legitimacy.

The rehabilitation of the notion of practical truth and, by way of consequence, of the notion of *de jure* judgement in political matters, therefore must include a reflection upon how various possibilities are deliberated. However, in order for the connection that exists between the domains of the possible and of meaning to be taken into account in a way that might induce one to respond in satisfactory fashion to the problem of practical truth, it is imperative that an agreement exist among the members of society as to those ends society privileges. It is necessary that individuals come to an understanding about the type of society in which they desire to live and about the reciprocity of the rights and duties in which they recognise themselves. That is to say, we must now complement our analysis of the possible and of meaning with an effort to take community experience into account.

COMMUNITY FEELING, EVOLUTION OF POSSIBILITIES, AND RIGHT TO GOVERN

The field of possibilities is connected with a horizon of signification established by the overall ends structuring the organisation of society. It is by heading in this direction that one can provide an answer to the question of practical truths. Indeed, the limits on what is considered reasonable in a community furnishes the means to make *de jure* judgements about the way in which political institutions discharge their duties in relation to the governed. Nonetheless, these limits as to what is considered reasonable are not absolutely stable. They are liable to be displaced, in particular along with changes in the scope of possibilities. Now, such change exerts an influence upon the conditions for one's existence in society as well as upon the expectations of the governed *vis-à-vis* political institutions. Feelings of belonging to a community and attitudes of loyalty on the part of the ruled towards the rulers therefore depend upon the capacity of the latter to gauge the ways in which society is evolving.

In order to demonstrate this point, it is fitting, first of all, to underscore the fact that the fields of possibilities and of significations are subject to changes and that these changes themselves can have repercussions upon individuals' conceptions of their rights and duties. Let us note, secondly, that, depending on their content and upon the rallyings of support from which they might benefit, changes affecting the domain of possibilities participate in a transformation of the givens of community life and of the political balance that reigns there. In this regard, one must examine the greater or lesser degree of strategic importance of the modifications taking place. That will lead us, in the third place, to evoke the different phases the struggle for legitimacy goes through in connection with the plane of practical truths and with the evolutions that take place on that plane.

Dynamic of possibilities, rights and duties in the community

Thus, the identity of a society, as defined by the domains of the possible and of meaning, is liable to experience transformations as time goes on. Even those communities that could be described as being situated outside history or as rejecting history and the change that accompanies it[12] are the theatre for such modifications.[13] Of course, the rhythm may vary and their own modalities may change, but they cannot entirely avoid such transformations. All forms of social organisation experience changes. Such changes are the product of a plurality of causes that generate society's historical identity. This identity expresses itself in relation to itself through its conception of its own temporality, from the memory of its past to the view of its present and its future, through its relationships with other communities, and through its ways of relating to the surrounding natural universe.

These changes are synonymous with a modification in the field of possibilities. In a world that evolves at a relatively slow pace, as is the case with traditional collectivities, the modification of possibilities, when it does not occur in the wake of brutal and radical upheavals of a more or less external sort, does not transform in any fundamental way the existing social balance. And these societies' mastery over their natural environments is not sufficiently strong for the modifications in the field of possibilities to allow the existing social organisation to be grasped as the simple product of the activity of individuals, separately from the order of nature and that of transcendence. It is within the space of social signification, defined in relation to these two orders, that the evolution of possibilities is generally interpreted.

On the other hand, in modernity – which is characterised by a multiplication of possibilities – the fundamental values of the collectivity no longer tend to be perceived solely as an extrahuman sort of constraint to which one must bow down. These values appear instead as the resultant of agents' decisions and acts. Thus, when religion constitutes one of the basic elements of a community, as is the case in traditional societies, the religious attitude of individuals seems to be the mark of their social integration. By way of opposition, we note that in modern societies, where religion is no longer socially so structuring, the faith of an individual tends to pertain to his responsibility alone.

This situation holds for the other major areas of activity, and particularly for that which pertains to the political. What in the premodern world

[12] For a presentation of the different versions of this thesis, see Georges Balandier, *Anthropologiques*, rev. and expanded edn (Paris: Le livre de poche, 1985), pp. 204–15.
[13] Ibid., pp. 238–48.

passes as something given and something over which people have little grasp resides, in the universe of modernity, in the hands of individuals. When social structures are thought of as being produced by people, what previously lay outside the field of action of individuals now constitutes the very matter of what is humanly at stake.

A quick comparison between the theory of deliberation formulated by Aristotle and the contemporary notion of deliberation allows one to shed light on the radical and exemplary dimension this latter notion contains. In the Aristotelian analysis, possibilities are what it is in the power of individuals to do. These possibilities are what pertain to their responsibility. Nevertheless, the scope of possibilities the individual is recognised as having, as the expression and the terrain of their capacity to choose and to act in reality, does not bear upon those values that go to determine what a good society is. Such values are not truly questioned. In Aristotle, the ends corresponding to the good are inscribed within the very essence of nature. The range of possibilities and the human deliberation to which it gives rise are not conceived as meaningful sources for structuring a collectivity based upon justice.[14]

The situation is very different in the modern world. The scope of possibilities is ever enlarging. Such a situation could develop only in the wake of mutual influences between what had meaning in an evolving society and the adjustments that are required with progress in knowledge about the natural and human universe.[15] This ever-enlarging set of possibilities also affects the domain of ends and, by way of consequence, that of meaning.[16] Individuals are led to think that ends and meaning do not constitute a given before which they must simply bow down. They tend to consider both of these as being set within the field of possibilities that are open to them. This is to say that the responsibility of individuals encompasses the ends of the community. Such responsibility drives them to inquire about the type of collectivity in which they wish to live and about the fundamental values they desire to privilege.

Generally speaking, we may say that, far from playing a minimal role in the unfolding of the relationships members of a group maintain with one another, with the political institutions governing them, and, eventually, with the natural environment, transformations in the domain of possibilities play a considerable role therein. Indeed, the existence and the satisfactory operation of relations among individuals in terms of rights

---

[14] On this question, see the comments of Pierre Aubenque, *La Prudence chez Aristote*, 3rd rev. edn (Paris: Presses Universitaires de France, 1986), p. 116. The reader may also refer to the analyses of François Ewald, *L'État providence* (Paris: Grasset, 1986), pp. 555–64.

[15] See, for example, the remarks of Norbert Elias in *What is Sociology?*, trans. Stephen Mennell and Grace Morrissey (New York: Columbia University Press, 1978), p. 63.

[16] The reader may consult Ewald, *L'État providence*, pp. 564–70.

and duties are tied to a world of possibilities that has to be compatible with the identity of the community. Now, when the scope of possibilities is altered, when the agents have the sense that they are benefiting from prospects they did not previously enjoy, the way relationships based upon exchange are organised also tends to undergo a transformation. When a situation that did not previously enter into the domains where individuals can deliberate and act becomes subject to reflection and debate, the new expansion of one's sphere of intervention calls for a redefinition of rights and duties – assuming that one wants the interactions involved in these new possibilities to give rise to relationships based upon cooperation and a sense of justice. Let us put it in other terms: changes affecting possibilities generate an awareness of rights and duties that were not until now perceived as such. They contribute towards a modification in the configuration of right.

Thus, when, in a society, the social, economic, and political hierarchies and partitions that were lived as the way things were – if not a natural state, at least one impossible to change – find themselves denounced as resulting from mechanisms of concealment and indoctrination, disadvantaged individuals no longer tend to accept their condition as fated. With the appearance of new possibilities, these people begin to feel that their rights are being flouted and that their duty to be loyal no longer fits the situation, or that it requires an adjustment.

This extension of one's imagination of possibilities and its impact on right within a collectivity evidently has been an inspiration for an emancipatory conception of the modern social sciences.[17] Indeed, these sciences seek to favour the advent of social relationships judged to be more in conformity with justice, as is testified to by Karl Marx's utopianism,[18] or by Pierre Bourdieu's critical sociology of symbolic violence.[19] Nevertheless,

---

[17] See the reflections of Robert A. Nisbet, *The Sociological Tradition* (New York: Basic Books, 1966), pp. 21–44.

[18] See Jon Elster, *Political Psychology* (Cambridge University Press, 1993), p. 191: 'When reading Marx, one has the impression that his mind is guided by two premises: whatever is desirable is possible, and whatever is desirable and possible will inevitably come to pass. The consequence is a permanent tendency towards utopianism.' [Translator/Editor: The final phrase is my own translation of a sentence in Elster's original French text, *Psychologie politique* (Paris: Éditions de Minuit, 1990), p. 186, which did not appear in the 1993 English-language edition but was quoted by Coicaud from the French original.]

[19] See Bourdieu, *Leçon sur la leçon*, pp. 20–21, or *Distinction*, pp. 380–81. Bourdieu may be reproached for not going beyond the level of critique. Once the liberatory moment of opening up the mind has passed, one must offer some prospects for hope. In wanting too hard to prove that alienation is the basis for the major institutions that ensure social integration and in not asking how things might head in another direction, the sociology of symbolic violence, far from stimulating or motivating individuals to overcome their alienation, runs the risk of leading them to forget their noble ambitions and their enthusiasm, to be haunted by a spirit of resentment – that is to say, to be driven by a hatred of

this coming to awareness can arrive only after the situation has evolved far enough in the direction of new possibilities and towards the readjustment of the rights and duties, which these new possibilities summon forth, that it might become thinkable to put the order of things back into question.

In short, the awareness of new possibilities, their explicit apprehension as issues, and the requirement of new rights and duties all assume that a road has already been travelled towards their recognition. A renewal of possibilities as well as of debates about rights and duties generally occurs in the field of reflection and of social practice only if that renewal has been prepared by changes on the material level (an evolution in economic, technological, and other such conditions) as well as on the non-material one, with convergent effects.

The new possibilities offered to individuals therefore call for a redefinition of rights and duties. From this point of view, the evolution in the conception individuals have of their rights and duties furnishes the observer with information about the conditions required for the implementation of judgements having to do with justice. But in order to pass a judgement of reliable value, one must also pay close attention to the way in which this evolution is effectively expressed in the existence of the collectivity. One has to analyse the degree to which this evolution has been integrated into the community's organisation – which assumes, in particular, that one is taking into consideration the type of society in question and the way in which the ruling instances of authority react to the demands of the governed.

Dynamic of possibilities, rights and duties, integration into community experience, and political responsibility

To the extent that political institutions and political leaders recognise that it is their responsibility to make some allowance for the movements of society, they have to be attentive to changes within the field of possibilities. For them, it is a matter of taking the new situation into account and of integrating the requirements the population formulates about what to it seems possible, desirable, and necessary for its rights to be respected. In resolving to watch over the renovation of the social dimension, they must proceed to make adjustments.

The effort to take into account and to integrate new possibilities, rights, and duties should not take place only at the legislative level. Although this stage may be decisive, it is not sufficient and it has to be followed by effects in the area of practice. The rulers must not be content just to register the

self and of others – and to become cynics, making use of a critical knowledge of society that places that knowledge solely in the service of their career interests, while invoking from time to time a humanism and ethics that are but a facade.

change officially. Not going beyond that point would end up discrediting both legislative procedure and the governing instance of authority. The addition of unenforced laws to other laws is just counterproductive and is liable to lead the members of the group to think that legality is removed from reality and that the legal realm is not assuming its role as mediator or defender of the values to which these members are attached. Legal texts have to be the expression of changes with which individuals identify and have to be translated in a concrete way. If that does not happen, legitimacy cannot hope to benefit in any way from the blessings of legality,[20] and the consent of individuals risks being as fictive as the reality of the laws being issued from the authorities in power.

Of course, the way in which this process of integrating changes is trans-lated into facts and the breadth of the transformations it introduces into collective life remain subject to variations. Social transformations depend in particular upon the strategic dimension found in the new demands. There are some changes that entail only minimal readjustments in rights and duties. Others, by way of contrast, are likely to give rise to thor-oughgoing transformations, to the point where they upset the identity of society.

The strategic character of the new demands is tied as much to the content of the change as to the type of regime in which the change occurs. Thus, it is clear that the reorganisation of rights and duties that results from changes in possibilities will be reduced if these possibilities, far from affecting the basic principles, concern only peripheral aspects of the way in which the collectivity is organised. But in another connection we may observe that, when a regime seeks to impose a systematic form of control, every change in possibilities endangers the overall architecture of society. In a society where a monolithic and alternativeless version of what is possible and permissible exists, contestation is not local and apolitical. Very quickly, challenges call back into question the direction and general organisation of society, since the official authorities pride themselves upon their having assumed responsibility for and achieved mastery over all past, present, and future aspects of their society. A necessitarian and closed view of history – the idea that social reality cannot and should not differ from the image proffered in the official version – makes it difficult to integrate contingency. Such a view confers an inevitably revolutionary role upon contingency and upon the very dynamic of becoming.

The social repercussions and modifications that result from changes in possibilities therefore vary in breadth, depending upon whether or not these possibilities can be integrated. From this perspective, the decision

---

[20] See Silvana Castignone, 'Legittimà, legalità e mutamento sociale', in Antonio Tarantino (ed.), *Legittimà, legalità e mutamento costituzionale* (Milan: Dott. A. Giuffrè, 1980), pp. 53–55.

of the ruling authorities to integrate the renewal of possibilities by proceeding to a rearrangement of rights and duties – that is to say, by incor-
porating them into the legislative field and by watching over how they are
applied in the concrete operation of those domains of society for which
they have responsibility – entails two complementary conditions. First of
all, this assumes a context that favours these new possibilities, one that
induces the established power to take them into account. This favourable
context can result either from the minimal character of the changes the
demand carries within itself or from its irrepressible nature, which forces
the authorities to take it into consideration in order to avoid a conflict or
even breakdowns that could lead to social paralysis. Secondly, the integration of new possibilities assumes that these possibilities do not completely
contradict the social context into which they are seeking admittance. Indeed, those who govern are rarely disposed to accept transformations that
contradict the values they were defending up to that point.

The procedure for integration, when it does take effect, obviously does
not develop all at once, nor does it occur without bumps and jolts. And
that is the case even when the relations of forces are distributed within
the community in such a way that they encourage the opposing parties
to seek compromise.

A demand connected with what is newly possible first tends to be the
object of a debate that goes beyond the initial circle of the actors within
which the demand arose. It then becomes a more general issue that takes
on a political aspect, particularly if the agents agree that it pertains to the
responsibility of institutions. Finally, when the change is accepted, the
demand is integrated into the body of the law, put into application, and
defended in concrete reality. Of course, this entire mechanism takes time,
sometimes even a lot of time. The period required for a change to reach
fruition is not proportionate to the breadth of the transformation involved.
A demand that is not strategic in character can, for this very reason, be
neglected by the governing authorities and be held in abeyance, even
when it is not grounds for any serious dissensions. Conversely, a demand
that is liable to have profound repercussions on the social dimension
can induce the government to make legislation without waiting too long
for the demand to gain favour and to endeavour to make it part of the
landscape.

Here, we are led into the heart of the struggles that unfold around
legitimacy. Indeed, changes affecting the field of possibilities and the way
rights and duties are organised do not always end up being integrated.
Often, the opposing parties do not arrive at a compromise. New demands
that are not integrated can then provoke a breakup of the community.

Identity of the collectivity, struggle of individuals for recognition, and conflicts around political legitimacy

The dynamic of possibilities frequently develops within the framework of relations of forces that do not succeed in surmounting the dimension of conflict. Values that political institutions are responsible for applying are some of the stakes involved in struggles where different parties do not succeed in finding a common area of understanding on what is just and unjust.

Thus, when the breadth of the ensuing conflicts rules out an amicable agreement, the observer is generally confronted with the following situation: a significant proportion of the individuals in question no longer recognise themselves in the way social relationships are organised or in their institutions. Their estimation is that their image of themselves and of what they require is not being translated into concrete reality. They see in the governors' refusal to integrate their demands an attack upon their rights, their personality, and their identity.

The tension aroused by this desire for recognition inevitably becomes conflictual. Not being recognised by the established political institutions, the governed do not recognise themselves in such institutions or in the areas that pertain to the authority of these institutions. The reciprocity clause no longer comes into play. Feeling that their rights are not being respected, individuals no longer are motivated to assume their duties. The interest and the meaning they found in cooperating with others no longer exist. A deterioration of the social climate within the collectivity comes to echo the absence of social morality evinced by the official authorities when they do not respect those values with which agents identify.

This deterioration in the fulfilment of one's duties is manifested by an unwillingness on the part of individuals to respond to the directives of the ruling authorities. But it is also expressed at the level of relationships among individuals: when the deterioration of the social climate has become so profound that it pervades all spheres of society, the ties of solidarity among people tend to come undone. There is then a great danger that things will culminate in a war of all against all. This situation, in which people struggle for justice and for the right to govern, unfolds on several levels.

The tensions are manifested first on the level of speech. The discourse of the official authorities about the way in which society is to be directed and organised becomes the object of criticism. Perceived as a narrative of legitimation, and not of legitimacy, the justification it labours to put into force is denounced as serving partisan interests and not the common good. An analysis of the official discourse in terms of ideology and propaganda then prevails over an attitude that, even if not completely lacking all distance with regard to the ruling institutions, previously lent them support. The criteria of judgement that had yesterday allowed one to evaluate what was acceptable or unacceptable are today denounced as a kind of manipulation, concerned above all with serving specific interests. The structuring discourse had marked out the boundaries of existing possibilities; that discourse is now talked about as being a way of closing off possibilities, whose aim is to perpetuate a certain social and political order. Individuals who think that they have been swindled liken the values used to make classifications and judgements in the collectivity to a power strategy conducted by those who rule.

The struggle for the appropriation of the definition of justice and of right also is expressed on the level of people's practices. In particular, the limits assigned to criminal behaviour begin to deteriorate. In a society that benefits from some social equilibrium, struggles are reabsorbed into compromises that allow cooperation to continue within the collectivity and that contribute towards the determination of what is or is not criminal. By way of contrast, when confrontations find no successful outcome, the borderlines of what constitutes criminal behaviour start to become fuzzy. Sanctions against unlawful actions no longer receive the population's recognition and assent – which are nevertheless required for illegal forms of conduct to be experienced as really illegitimate. The credibility of those institutions that are entitled to say what is good and evil collapses. The judgements they pronounce about criminal behaviour are soon analysed as acts of war and corruption. The individual who transgresses the laws then no longer tends to be judged by public opinion as a criminal but rather as a resistant. It is the political authorities themselves that tend to pass for being the real criminals.

Quite obviously, in order for such a reversal of tendencies to take place, the relations of forces have to play out in favour of the opposition. The opposition must not be reduced to an isolated minority or be cut off from the rest of the community. In order for judgements about criminal behaviour to be turned upside down, what matters is that the criticisms formulated against the government be shared, actively or in an implicit way, by a goodly portion of the group's members. In order for contestation of the official authorities' right to govern to have some impact, such contestation has to have some bearing on areas of strategic interest, in particular on social problems to which the population is broadly exposed. Even if at the outset the criticisms are lodged by a minority, other members of the group can identify with this minority, and these other members will, if the opportunity arises, pass from maintaining a wait-and-see attitude to adopting a more active form of support for the minority's positions.

In order that other members of the group might rally to the minority's positions, the acting minority has to make a correct evaluation of the social relevance of the questions upon which its action bears. It is upon this condition that the minority will, one day or another, be able to gain some backing among the population.

Conflict takes on a violent form when individuals no longer have anything to lose and when the margin of manoeuvre left to them is too negligible for them to be happy with it, or when resentment and hatred have reached a point of no return. Cost-benefit analysis then obeys a logic that no longer has to do with that of routine rationality. For individuals, it becomes a matter of expressing the violence they bear within themselves and of putting an end to their frustration and to the real or psychological death those who hold power are making them endure. Those who have recourse to physical clashes evaluate their chances of coming out the winners of a brutal confrontation with the rulers in terms of the mutually opposing forces. The probabilities of winning out are measured in terms of the capacity of the protesters and of their demands to get the population moving – that is to say, to bring things from a state of discontent, expressed horizontally, to a vertical type of contestation and engagement[21] directed against the governing authorities. But their likelihood of success is also evaluated in terms of the government's attitude, of its determination as well as of its hesitations. When it goes beyond a mere skirmish, a violent clash testifies to how much community life has decomposed.

Violence is not, however, the only way to struggle for legitimacy. Such a struggle may take circuitous forms that, without becoming brutal in character, are indicative of a deep-seated crisis. When these circuitous forms of struggle start to become systematic, they can become as effectively undermining as actual violence can be. Indeed, when individuals evolve within a political order whose legitimacy they deny and when they are not allowed, in particular for reasons of prudence, to express their discontent by speaking out,[22] they can always desert or drop out as a sign of protest. Such desertion can take at least two forms, both of which boil down to a refusal to cooperate with a political regime and a kind of social organisation with which the protesters do not identify. Their objective is then to participate therein to the least extent possible so as not

---

[21] See the remarks of Albert Hirschman, *Vers une économie politique élargie*, trans. from the American (Paris: Minuit, 1986), pp. 63–64. [Translator/Editor: I have not been able to find the English-language original of this book.]

[22] See Albert Hirschman, *Exit, Voice and Loyalty: Responses to Decline in Firms, Organisations, and States* (Cambridge, Mass.: Harvard University Press, 1970), for example pp. 3–5, and his recent restatements of these issues in *Vers une économie politique élargie*.

to betray their own idea of themselves, of their rights, and of what their relationships with the other members of the collectivity should be.

In reality, both these forms of dropping out are variations on one and the same theme. They correspond to the attempts made by individuals to escape the self-exile imposed upon them by the oppressive and alienating situation with which they are confronted.

The first of these boils down to creating the fiction of still being present and involved in those areas of activity where individuals experience alienation. They have recourse to an attitude of passive resistance. This phenomenon is particularly widespread in totalitarian societies. The monopoly on force, the prohibition on expressing opinions that are contrary to the official propaganda, and statist institutions' control over the great majority of activities all serve to bolster individuals in this attitude. When this passive resistance becomes systematic, the social dimension is emptied of its substance and becomes like an empty shell. Everything seems to function according to governmental directives. But this is only an appearance. Individuals invest themselves only minimally in the position that has been assigned to them. Ultimately, the fictive character of this kind of normality appears in broad daylight. The social scene tends to be reduced to one gigantic lie and the wheels of the entire society become locked in place. A schizophrenic system is established wherein reality no longer has anything to do with the description that is given of it. The governed's feigned adherence comes to echo the wooden language of the official spokespersons. In the end, the collective organisation risks falling down like a house of cards.

Emigration is another way of deserting. Indeed, when active contestation is not an option, emigration – assuming that there is some attractive country that will welcome those eager to emigrate – can be one way of registering one's disapproval of the government in place. Leaving the community is a manner of protesting. When this phenomenon is transformed into a mass movement, as in East Germany at the end of the nineteen-eighties, it can imperil the very survival of the country. It nevertheless happens that the governors themselves sometimes may encourage such defections via emigration. They can thus decide to expatriate those troublemakers who in their estimation cannot be coaxed while at the same time closing down the borders for the rest of the population.[23] One thereby closes off access to possibilities that would constitute alternatives to oppression. From this point of view, the complement to the prohibition of freedom of thought is the prohibition of freedom of circulation.

---

[23] In this regard, see the case of Solzhenitsyn and the comments of Serge Moscovici, 'La dissidence d'un seul', appendix to *Psychologie des minorités actives*, pp. 253–54, 259–60.

In as much as an individual fights to improve the living conditions within his community, he has at least not lost all hope. To fight, to contest, to work for a more or less radical change is still to believe in the possibility of building an acceptable political community. By way of contrast, emigration, as discussed here, is nothing less than an abandonment of the belief that a satisfying existence is still possible within the community these individuals are deserting. Those who thus leave the social scene have the feeling that there no longer is a place for them and that in the end they cannot be integrated into relationships based upon reciprocity that take their rights and their duties into account. They do not necessarily relinquish an attachment, tinged with nostalgia, for their native land. But in wishing to break away to the maximum extent from the alienation their homeland heaps upon its inhabitants, they may even be driven to repudiate it. When their native land does not allow them any self-fulfilment, it is their nationality of origin that they are tempted to give up.

RIGHT, JUSTICE, AND THE EXTENT OF THE HUMAN COMMUNITY

As we have seen, in order to explore in a satisfactory way the question of legitimacy one is obliged to find a middle ground between a way of thinking about social reality that remains prisoner of positivism and a dogmatic view of history. To be sure, practical truths do not allow for the ease of proof afforded by empirically verifiable scientific statements. And the values liable to guide the decisions and actions of rulers are not immune to discussions, revisions, and imperfections. But, far from reacting negatively to the difficulty raised by the place and role of the axiological dimension in the social field, political analysis has to endeavour to formulate a way of thinking about justice that integrates the uncertainty surrounding the values of modernity. It has to accept the idea that diversity, change, and imperfections do not eliminate the existence of limits and of a hierarchy of values.

The historical character of the criteria for right and justice, and the experience of community

Progressive theorists who have attacked the notions of right and of justice the most violently have built up their criticisms in part around the disappointment generated by the gap that exists between the exigencies conveyed by these notions and concrete social reality. Since the values of right and justice may not be translated into deeds by the institutions that are supposed to act as the servants of such values, these theorists have a tendency to discredit them, saying that they exist only to benefit power games and relations of forces.[24]

One can interpret the political realism of Machiavelli from this perspective. The place Machiavelli grants to relations of forces is probably connected in part with the new political stakes then appearing, namely with the emergence of the sense of individual rights. While not yet being major enough to give rise to explicit demands on the part of individuals, these stakes, this emerging sense of rights, were nonetheless real enough for Machiavelli to take them into account. He was aware that politics does not respect individual rights (whose advent these stakes were nevertheless heralding) and therefore conceptualised politics as reduced to relations of forces.

More recently, Bourdieu's reflections offer a more clear-cut example of the paradoxical effects of this mechanism of disappointment. In his works, Bourdieu systematically reduces right to symbolic violence. That is because he pays almost exclusive attention to the gap that exists between the contribution right is supposed to make to justice and what is the case on the level of concrete facts. From the existence of this gap Bourdieu concludes that right is nothing but a disguised form of oppression. Now, what one should be asking, rather, is under what conditions, within a given context, right can be right and, therefore, under what conditions it satisfies the exigencies of justice.

Rather than disqualify, in one way or another, an approach to politics in terms of right and justice, research needs to inventory the principles and norms that serve, within a specific context, as criteria for practical truths; and it also needs to examine which factors are liable or not liable to establish their credibility. The values that serve as benchmarks are, we have seen, those ones that ensure social reciprocity. They vary, quite evidently, according to time and place, and their concrete realisation is always tainted with a certain imperfection. But in so far as individuals recognise themselves in them and in so far as these values also seem to these individuals to ensure the proper functioning of reciprocity, they must be taken seriously.

To the extent that certain values allow cooperative ties to be built up among individuals – to the extent, too, that they constitute a horizon of collective definition with which agents identify – they are valid.

---

[24] This mechanism does not operate only in the domain of right. It obeys the following general principle: the more a person is attached to an ideal and is expecting a great deal from it, and the more reality does not correspond to his expectations, the more that person is tempted to deny the value of this ideal as well as the institutions that are supposed to be serving it.

The most strategic ones are those upon which the activity of government bears to the highest degree, for it is in terms of the capacity of governmental activity to express them, to defend them, and to promote them in the community as a whole that its legitimacy will be evaluated. That these values change is not in itself a problem in so far as individuals, in accompanying the movement of history, desire such changes and recognise themselves therein – in so far, that is, as they feel that they are faithful to themselves, to others, and to the environment, and therefore feel that they are continuing a dialogue with their history.[25] By way of contrast, a shortage of legitimacy exists when the values implemented in the decisions and actions of the rulers do not receive the assent of the group's members. Such a shortage exists when these decisions and actions make people strangers to themselves, to others, and, ultimately, to their history in general.

It remains the case that the values that ensure reciprocity do not always guarantee that a society will be heading in the direction of tolerance or in that of the most equitable and integrative distribution of goods. Today more than ever, the values that define what is good and evil depend in large part upon individuals' faculty to want and to will justice. In this domain, there exists no absolute assurance that right and justice will be deployed in a good direction. Thus does it happen that, however small the spread of a spirit of vindictiveness within society, legal procedures sometimes may be used to foster hatred and exclusion. This brings us to tackle a two-sided question. The first side concerns what share of responsibility individuals have in the evolution of the identity of their community, and the second concerns the extent of the community within which relations based upon reciprocity apply.

From the responsibility of people to the extent of the human community

The greater the power of individuals over their environment, the heavier is their responsibility for the way events unfold. That holds for the ruled as well as for the rulers. This phenomenon manifests itself quite especially in modern societies. In order to gauge its breadth, it is fitting for us to analyse its consequences in relation to the functioning of the collectivity and to the values the collectivity privileges, when this phenomenon appears in conjunction with the egalitarian idea.

---

[25] See Ferry, *Les Puissances de l'expérience*, vol. I, pp. 151–52.

EGALITARIAN IDEOLOGY AND REACTIONARY THOUGHT

In a group where differences in status are rooted in a hierarchical conception accepted by all or by almost everyone, individuals do not feel frustrated by the disparities that exist between them. By way of contrast, within a democratic universe, where the principle of equality is sufficiently rooted in mores, this principle can, in combination with the idea that agents share partial responsibility for their failures and successes, lead to thoroughgoing changes in society. It can, for example, give rise to forms of behaviour based upon resentment, which are likely to orient democratic society in directions that go against its basic principles.

In particular, the disadvantaged individual can either accept the privileged status of the other by viewing it as being the result of merit or interpret it as the effect of relations of forces that go beyond him, or he may view his disadvantaged situation as a sign of his failure, without admitting it to himself explicitly and judge that his social environment is responsible for it. In this last case, the individual is likely to give himself over to self-hatred, which will not take long before it turns into a hatred of the other. That is why the logic of resentment can favour the deployment of a reactionary way of thinking, thus poisoning the community as a whole.

The designation of a scapegoat – a mechanism to which every society is always ready to have recourse when confronted with difficulties it does not have the strength or the health to confront by admitting its own errors – is one of the most visible manifestations of the reactionary mind-set. It is not the only one. Be that as it may, here behaviours are adopted that sacrifice social reciprocity to the benefit of policies based upon exclusion. For the individual caught in the grip of this mind-set, it becomes a matter of affirming oneself while denying, to the person with whom one is in competition and who tends to outclass him, the right to exist. Social 'specularity' – the image of oneself that the success or even just the living presence of the other reflects – makes him want to make this other person disappear, for the other's existence is a constant reminder to him of his own failure. Contesting the other's right to live and to be what he is becomes the ultimate proof that allows one to reassure oneself of one's own existence.

Far from seeking to encourage the development of living values, the reactionary individual seeks to accept and justify his situation by bringing the world around him into line with his own situation. As self-hatred includes death instincts, he who undergoes this hatred of self also desires the death of others. It being understandable that it is more pleasant for an individual who hates himself not to die alone and unaccompanied, the person with a reactionary mind-set wishes to see the entirety of the social dimension identify with his malady. The social dimension must come to resemble him to the greatest extent possible, so that exclusion therefrom strikes quite particularly at those who are in the best position to become the object of his resentment. These people can, moreover, be privileged individuals as well as individuals more socially disadvantaged than himself, into whose ranks he sees himself being relegated. Racism finds here one of its conspicuous wellsprings. Ultimately, the social dimension – the dynamic of reciprocity and integration that is deployed broadly when the social body is stretched towards life and progress – is reduced to morbidly compulsive attitudes, collective rituals whose sole aim is to reassure individuals faced with a multiplicity of alien worlds that, they fear, will sweep them away.

In the face of such a situation, each person's responsibility is of the essence. Today the rootedness of transcendent values has to a large extent disappeared. The limits that can be assigned to good and evil can no longer truly claim any kind of transcendency connected with some traditional social structure. As a result, it is principally upon the shoulders of individuals that the faculty of judging what is or is not acceptable, what is or is not reasonable, rests. That is why this faculty of deliberating about and deciding between good and evil should not be perverted or guided by the mind-set of hatred and resentment.

To the extent that individuals are responsible for the establishment of a moral objectivity, privileging good over evil and making life a value that is good in itself depend upon the capacity of these individuals to will the good and to make it happen. In order that resentment and the values of death might not win out over the search for the greatest possible reciprocity and integration, it is of the essence to limit frustrations as much as possible. Life cannot be recognised as a value that is good in itself if the frustrations being endured constitute the unsurpassable horizon of individuals' existences. This is to say that those who govern should not forget the imperatives of justice. Justice is all the more decisive today, and all the more difficult to satisfy, as the modern democratic ideology has made individuals sensitive to their rights. The more their rights are flouted, the greater is their frustration, and the higher is the risk that they will react to their sense of moral and material insecurity by falling back upon themselves. Such attitudes, where people withdraw into themselves, are accompanied by an attack on and exclusion of everything that threatens their fragile individual and social identity.

The problem of political legitimacy fosters the need for a body, individual or collective, to generate positive forms of energy. It is only when animated by a relative serenity that individuals will be willing and able to raise to the rank of objectively moral values principles favouring a common life that is as tolerant as possible and is set upon achieving ideals involving social integration. Harmony among individuals rests upon a harmony with oneself, and that is possible only if each person feels that he and his rights are being respected. Values of moral objectivity determined in this way are liable to change as history evolves. But they will continue to represent a moral objectivity oriented towards reciprocity and integration. Terror can be avoided only if individuals are not themselves terrorised.

SOCIAL INTEGRATION AND THE EXTENT OF COMMUNITY

The resentment individuals may feel when their rights are not being respected presupposes their prior integration into a community. Indeed, one must be an involved party in a collectivity in order to think that one has some rights therein and to regret when these rights are not respected. Quite obviously, when some individuals are not sufficiently integrated into a society to be able to make themselves heard, those who are must give proof of a great moral healthiness in order to speak in their name and really make those individuals' exclusion into an issue without indulging in paternalism. Thus is posed the problem of the extent of the human community.

A government's legitimacy is measured by its power to express, defend, and promulgate the values with which individuals identify within a given collectivity. These values have to be translated into a concrete way of distributing material and symbolic goods that is deemed just. But what is the extent of the community to which these principles apply? It therefore becomes a matter of knowing the borders that delimit the terrain upon which one evaluates justice and, by way of consequence, the duties of governmental action *vis-à-vis* the populace. Knowing the boundaries of the community underlies the following two questions: Who has a right to have rights? Who is sufficiently integrated into the community to think that not only his fate but also that of the others is or is not in conformity with justice? The responses given to these questions represent some of the basic issues at stake.

The history of societies – their evolution and the revolutions through which they pass – is, in effect, made up in large part of struggles that unfold around the question of how the disadvantaged are to be integrated. The issues of justice and of the right to govern are nothing other than debates the disadvantaged succeed in imposing upon the community. Obviously, it is much easier for individuals to obtain recognition and to achieve integration on the level of right when their social utility becomes of itself indispensable. In order not to take the risk of having to make do without their services, the collectivity is led to listen to them. Even at the price of bitter conflicts, the collectivity most often ends up accepting their demands. The objective of the government is to assure itself of their loyalty in order to preserve the proper functioning of the group.

By way of contrast, integration – the recognition of rights and their translation into concrete reality – is more difficult to obtain when the social utility of an individual is not blatantly obvious. The individual is then not up to the task of exerting pressure.

Agents have at their disposal the possibility of being a voice. By virtue of the means their social utility confers upon them to exert pressure, agents can be a voice. This possibility is therefore a first criterion for determining the extent of community and the repercussions the latter can have on the debates around justice. But it is not the sole criterion. Added to it, in effect, is the idea individuals have of themselves, as well as the manner in which this idea is related to their ways of recognising the existence of the other.

To experience the community is to recognise the other as another self. Better than that, let us say that the other is constitutive of each person's identity. But the whole problem is to know in what other one recognises oneself, to know which other – his social and economic status, his race, etc. – is another self and therefore constitutive as such of the identity of each. The answer to this question is decisive. The content given to justice depends upon it.

Indeed, identifying with the other, recognising him as belonging to the same world as one's own, is to act in such a way that his dignity might become in some fashion our dignity, and his indignity our indignity. The admirable or reprehensible acts he commits define us and also engage our responsibility. If that is so, one cannot but experience as an injustice the kinds of behaviour inflicted upon him that one would not put up with for oneself. The injustice imposed on him is also imposed on us. Doing nothing for someone in whom one recognises oneself, and who is suffering, makes the indignity twice as bad. It is to betray him and therefore to betray oneself. That explains in particular the difficulty France still has today in recognising the collaborationist and anti-Semitic behaviour of the Vichy regime and of a number of Frenchmen of that era. To acknowledge these acts is to recognise that France betrayed a certain idea of itself. Such recognition is certainly difficult, since it is, to be sure, rather easier to talk complacently about the France of the Resistance than to acknowledge the existence of a contemptible France that gave in.

The problem of the justice and the duties of the ruling instances of authority in relation to a given population is therefore indissociable from the theme of the extent of the community. It is tied to the manner in which individuals recognise themselves in the other and to the way in which they feel harmed and concerned by the evil the other endures. That is true within the community on the domestic level but also on the international level. In fact, international law has in large part developed in parallel with the recognition of other cultures as a feature of the human community, thus sending back to us our own image and identity. This phenomenon of recognition and identification has to overcome greater or lesser difficulties, depending upon cultural similarities or differences. As it is put into place and as it evolves, it still remains subject to the power relations that exist among competing societies.[26] But that does not change the fact that it is through this phenomenon of identification-recognition that the international community and international law are created.[27] It allows one to extend ever further the experience of community and the implementation of the imperative of solidarity.

[26] See Stanley Hoffmann, *Janus and Minerva: Essays in the Theory and Practice of International Politics* (Boulder, Colo.: Westview Press, 1987), pp. 171–74.

[27] See Friedrich V. Kratochwil, *Rules, Norms, and Decisions: On the Conditions of Practical and Legal Reasoning in International Relations and Domestic Affairs* (Cambridge University Press, 1989), for example pp. 250–56.

Conclusion

Whoever thinks that political analysis has to involve specialised studies will perhaps have been surprised in reading the present work. But as it has seemed to us, it is in adopting a relatively global approach, putting things in historical perspective and taking the operation of society into account, that it was possible to tackle legitimacy without remaining a prisoner of the limitations imposed by prior reflections upon this question.

The social sciences, and in particular political science, have supplanted philosophy in the study of politics. This process is connected to the specialised way in which social and political phenomena have been analysed and to the abandonment of the goal of taking a position on explicitly assumed values. Rather than one asking oneself under what conditions it is possible to preserve the possibility of doing a study of human reality that integrates the level of the Ought without for all that exhibiting dogmatic tendencies, it has generally been preferred to adopt a fragmented approach whose wish is to remain principally descriptive.

The problem of justice, however, and therefore that of political justice, does not cease to be posed to individuals. It is one of the essential issues of life in society. The proof is that those observers who adopt as their own the separation of facts from values soon contradict this idea of separation. In reality, they very quickly break away from the thesis to which they are supposedly adhering – without, unfortunately, ever adapting the theory to their practice.

In order to subscribe to what thinking about legitimacy requires, it is neither necessary nor even advisable to give up on the elements featured in the empirical and positivist points of view. One should still have recourse to these viewpoints while making sure that this is not done to the detriment of the axiological dimension. In order that a science of actions and practical truths might be possible in a changing and plural world, one must look into what modifications should be made to the conventional way of analysing social and political phenomena. It is this spirit that has guided the present work.

Of course, one can see some risks in the decision to tackle legitimacy while taking the dimension of values seriously. Thus, it is more prudent, from the institutional standpoint, to offer the kind of results that are all the more likely to receive approval since they do not go against received ideas. The danger of being sanctioned for errors committed is similarly lessened by such a prudent approach. In another connection, we may state that, allowing for the complexity of the theme of the right to govern, the solutions proposed here constitute only rough sketches. It remains the case that to formulate hypotheses, pose questions whose solutions are not obvious, and try to advance despite the surrounding uncertainty are the necessary steps for progress in knowledge. Imperfect results do not just indicate that reflection is alive and in movement. Such imperfections are also in their own right a full and complete contribution to the collective labour of understanding the world and oneself.

Moreover, the risk and uncertainty the present proposed approach to legitimacy agrees to take on reminds us insistently of the situation individuals find themselves in today in their lives within society. By way of consequence, to take this situation in hand and to take it for an irrepressible element of one's reflection not only entails a refusal to flee one's responsibilities but also is in tune with the object that is to be thought. Indeed, what value can science have when science is not up to the level of its object, when it prefers to keep the old-fashioned conception it has of itself rather than reform itself?

That the problem of justice might today be even more difficult to treat than in previous times need not induce us to sidestep this problem. On the contrary, one should not run away precisely from that which is to be understood.

One must endeavour to rehabilitate the role values play in the unfolding of social relationships. It is on this condition that a problematisation of the idea of legitimacy will allow genuine reflection upon an evaluation of power in terms of right. If the axiological dimension is not taken into consideration, if cooperation among people as it is directed and organised by the political instances of authority is not examined in light of the values with which the individual identifies – and that define his rights and his duties within the collectivity – the very possibility of thinking political responsibility is emptied of its meaning.

Bibliography

Althusser, Louis. *Montesquieu, Rousseau, Marx: Politics and History*. Trans. Ben Brewster. New edn. London: Verso, 1982.

Ansart, Pierre. *Idéologies, conflits et pouvoir*. Paris: Presses Universitaires de France, 1977.

Apel, Karl-Otto. *Understanding and Explanation: A Transcendental-Pragmatic Perspective*. Trans. Georgia Warnke. Cambridge, Mass.: MIT Press, 1984.

Arendt, Hannah. *Between Past and Future: Eight Exercises in Political Thought*. 4th rev. edn. New York: Penguin, 1983.

The Origins of Totalitarianism. 6th edn with new prefaces. New York: Harcourt Brace Jovanovich, 1979.

Hannah Arendt Papers (1949–75). Library of Congress: Courses, New School for Social Research, Morality Lectures, 'Some Questions of Moral Philosophy', p. 024651.

Aristotle. *Politics*.

Nichomachean Ethics.

Aron, Raymond. *De la condition historique du sociologue*. Paris: Gallimard, 1983.

Democracy and Totalitarianism: A Theory of Political Systems. Ed. Roy Pierce. Trans. Valence Ionescu. Ann Arbor, Mich.: Ann Arbor Paperback, 1990.

Introduction. Max Weber. *Le Savant et le politique*. Paris: Union Générale d'Éditions, 1972.

Introduction to the Philosophy of History: An Essay on the Limits of Historical Objectivity. Trans. George J. Irwin. Boston, Mass.: Beacon Press, 1961.

Main Currents in Sociological Thought. Trans. Richard Howard and Helen Weaver. New edn. London: Transaction Books, 1998–99. Vol. I. *Montesquieu. Comte. Marx. Tocqueville. Sociologists & the Revolution of 1848*. Vol. II. *Durkheim, Pareto, Weber*.

La Philosophie critique de l'histoire. Essai sur une théorie allemande de l'histoire. Paris: Vrin, 1970.

Aubenque, Pierre. *La Prudence chez Aristote*. 3rd rev. edn. Paris: Presses Universitaires de France, 1986.

Axelrod, Robert. *The Evolution of Cooperation*. New York: Basic Books, 1984.

Azéma, Jean-Pierre. 'Les victimes du nazisme'. In *L'Allemagne de Hitler 1933–1945*. 2nd edn. Paris: Éditions du Seuil, 1991.

Badie, Bertrand, with Pierre Birnbaum. *La Fin du politique*. Rev. and expanded edn with an Afterword. Paris: Éditions du Seuil, 1983.

Sociology of the State. Trans. Arthur Goldhammer. University of Chicago Press, 1983.

Balandier, Georges. *Political Anthropology*. New York: Pantheon Books, 1970. *Anthropologiques*. Rev. and expanded edn. Paris: Le livre de poche, 1985.

Barry, Brian. *A Treatise on Social Justice*. Berkeley: University of California Press, 1989. Vol. I. *Theories of Justice*.

Belaval, Yvon. 'Le siècle des Lumières'. In Brice Parain (ed.), *Histoire de la philosophie*. 3 vols. Paris: Gallimard, 1973. Vol. II. *De la Renaissance à la révolution kantienne*.

Bellah, Robert N., Richard Madsen, William M. Sullivan, Ann Swindler, and Steven M. Tipton. *Habits of the Heart: Individualism and Commitment in American Life*. Berkeley: University of California Press, 1985.

Bendersky, Joseph W. *Carl Schmitt: Theorist for the Reich*. Princeton University Press, 1983.

Berman, Harold J. *Justice in the USSR: An Interpretation of Soviet Law*. Rev. edn. Cambridge, Mass.: Harvard University Press, 1982.
Law and Revolution: The Formation of the Western Legal Tradition. Cambridge, Mass.: Harvard University Press, 1983.

Bernstein, Richard J. *The Restructuring of Social and Political Theory*. Philadelphia: University of Pennsylvania Press, 1978.

Birnbaum, Pierre. 'Sur les origines de la domination politique: à propos d'Étienne de La Boétie et de Pierre Clastres'. *Revue française de science politique* 27:1 (February 1977).

Blumenberg, Hans. *The Legitimacy of the Modern Age*. Trans. Robert M. Wallace. Cambridge, Mass.: MIT Press, 1983.

Boltanski, Luc, with Laurent Thévenot. *Les Économies de la grandeur*. Paris: Presses Universitaires de France/Cahiers du centre d'études de l'emploi, 1987.

Boudon, Raymond. *Theories of Social Change: A Critical Appraisal*. Trans. J. C. Whitehouse. Cambridge: Polity, 1986.

Bourdieu, Pierre, with Jean-Claude Chamboredon and Jean-Claude Passeron. *The Craft of Sociology: Epistemological Preliminaries*. Ed. Beate Krais. Trans. Richard Nice. Berlin and New York: Walter de Gruyter, 1991.
Distinction: A Social Critique of the Judgement of Taste. Trans. Richard Nice. Cambridge, Mass.: Harvard University Press, 1984.
'La force du droit. Éléments pour une sociologie du champ juridique'. *Actes de la Recherche en Sciences Sociales* 64 (September 1986).
Interview. *Le Nouvel Observateur*, 2 November 1984.
Leçon sur la leçon. Paris: Minuit, 1982.
'La lecture de Marx, ou quelques remarques critiques à propos de "Quelques critiques à propos de *Lire le Capital*"'. *Actes de la Recherche en Sciences Sociales* 5–6 (November 1975).
The Logic of Practice. Stanford University Press, 1990.

Bourricaud, François. *Esquisse d'une théorie de l'autorité*. 2nd rev. edn. Paris: Plon, 1970.

Bouveresse, Jacques. *Rationalité et cynisme*. 2nd edn. Paris: Minuit, 1985.

Cassirer, Ernst. *The Myth of the State*. New Haven, Conn.: Yale University Press, 1946.

Castignone, Silvana. 'Legittimità, legalità e mutamento sociale'. In Antonio Tarantino (ed.), *Legittimità, legalità e mutamento costituzionale*. Milan: Dott. A. Giuffrè, 1980.

Castoriadis, Cornelius. *The Imaginary Institution of Society*. Trans. Kathleen Blamey. Cambridge: Polity Press, 1987.

Condorcet. *Sketch for a Historical Picture of the Progress of the Human Mind*. Trans. June Barraclough. Reprint edn. Westport, Conn.: Hyperion Press, 1979.

Dahrendorf, Ralf. *Society and Democracy in Germany*. Trans. by the author. New York: Norton & Company, 1979.

Dealy, Glen. 'Prolegomena on the Spanish Political Tradition'. In *Politics and Social Change in Latin America: The Distinct Tradition*. Ed. Howard J. Wiarda. 2nd rev. edn. Amherst: University of Massachusetts Press, 1982.

Deleuze, Gilles. *Difference and Repetition*. London: Athlone Press, 1994.

Foucault. Trans. Seán Hand. Minneapolis: University of Minnesota Press, 1988.

Delmas, Philippe. *Le Maître des horloges. Modernité de l'action publique*. Paris: Odile Jacob, 1991.

Deprun, Jean. 'Philosophies et problématique des Lumières'. In Brice Parain (ed.), *Histoire de la philosophie*. 3 vols. Paris: Gallimard, 1973. Vol. II. *De la Renaissance à la révolution kantienne*.

Duby, George. 'Ideologies in Social History'. In Jacques Le Goff and Pierre Nora (eds.), *Constructing the Past: Essays in Historical Methodology*. Cambridge University Press, 1985.

Dumont, Louis. *From Mandeville to Marx: The Genesis and Triumph of Economic Ideology*. University of Chicago Press, 1977.

Homo Hierarchicus: The Caste System and its Implications. Trans. Mark Sainsbury, Louis Dumont, and Basia Gulati. Complete rev. English edn. University of Chicago Press, 1980.

Durkheim, Émile. *The Division of Labor in Society*. Trans. W. D. Halls. New York: The Free Press, 1984.

The Rules of Sociological Method. Ed. and intro. Steven Lukes. Trans. W. D. Halls. London: Macmillan, 1982.

Suicide: A Study in Sociology. Ed. and intro. George Simpson. Trans. John A. Spaulding and George Simpson. 1st paperback edn. New York: The Free Press, 1966.

Textes. 3 vols. Paris: Minuit, 1975. Vol. I. *Éléments d'une théorie sociale*.

Dworkin, Ronald. *A Matter of Principle*. Cambridge, Mass.: Harvard University Press, 1985.

'Foundations of Liberal Equity'. In Grethe B. Peterson (ed.), *The Tanner Lectures on Human Values*. Salt Lake City: University of Utah Press, 1990. Vol. XI.

Law's Empire. Cambridge, Mass.: Harvard University Press, 1986.

Taking Rights Seriously. Cambridge, Mass.: Harvard University Press, 1978.

Eisenstadt, S. N. *Tradition, Change and Modernity*. New York: John Wiley & Sons, 1973.

Elias, Norbert. *What is Sociology?* Trans. Stephen Mennell and Grace Morrissey. New York: Columbia University Press, 1978.

Elster, Jon. *Political Psychology.* Cambridge University Press, 1993.

Ulysses and the Sirens: Studies in Rationality and Irrationality. Cambridge University Press, 1979.

Ewald, François. *L'État providence.* Paris: Grasset, 1986.

Faye, Jean-Pierre. *Langages totalitaires. Critique de la raison/l'économie narrative.* Paris: Harmann, 1972.

Ferry, Jean-Marc. *Les Puissances de l'expérience. Essai sur l'identité contemporaine.* 2 vols. Paris: Cerf, 1991. Vol. I. *Le sujet et le verbe.*

Ferry, Luc. With Alain Renaut. *French Philosophy of the Sixties: An Essay on Anti-humanism.* Trans. Mary H. S. Cattani. Amherst: University of Massachusetts Press, 1990.

Political Philosophy. Trans. Franklin Philip. 3 vols. University of Chicago Press, 1992. Vol. II. *The System of Philosophies of History.*

With Alain Renaut. *Système et critique. Essais sur la critique de la raison dans la philosophie contemporaine.* Brussels: Éditions Ousia, 1984.

Feyerabend, Paul. *Against Method: Outline of an Anarchistic Theory of Knowledge.* 6th edn. London: Verso, 1986.

Filloux, Jean-Claude. Introduction. Émile Durkheim. *La Science sociale et l'action.* 2nd edn. Paris: Presses Universitaires de France, 1987.

Fischer, David Hackett. *Historian's Fallacies: Toward a Logic of Historical Thought.* New York: Harper & Row, 1970.

Foucault, Michel. *Discipline and Punish: The Birth of the Prison.* Trans. Alan Sheridan. New York: Pantheon Books, 1977.

History of Sexuality. Trans. Robert Hurley. 3 vols. New York: Vintage, 1990. Vol. I. *An Introduction.*

'Nietzsche, Genealogy, History'. In *Language, Counter-Memory, Practice: Selected Essays and Interviews.* Ed. and intro. Donald F. Bouchard. Trans. Donald F. Bouchard and Sherry Simon. Ithaca: Cornell University Press, 1977.

The Order of Things: An Archaeology of the Human Sciences. New York: Vintage, 1973.

Fournier, Jacques. With Nicole Questiaux. *Le Pouvoir du social.* Paris: Presses Universitaires de France, 1979.

Freund, Julien. *L'Essence du politique.* 3rd edn. Paris: Sirey, 1978.

Préface to Carl Schmitt. *La Notion de politique suivi de Théorie du partisan.* Trans. Marie-Louise Steinhauser. Paris: Calmann-Lévy, 1972.

Furet, François. *Interpreting the French Revolution.* Trans. Elborg Forster. Cambridge University Press, 1981.

'Quantitative Methods in History'. In Jacques Le Goff and Pierre Nora (eds.), *Constructing the Past: Essays in Historical Methodology.* Cambridge University Press, 1985.

Gauchet, Marcel. *The Disenchantment of the World: A Political History of Religion.* Trans. Oscar Burge. Princeton University Press, 1997.

Geertz, Clifford. *The Interpretation of Cultures: Selected Essays.* New York: Basic Books, 1973.

Negar: The Theater State in Nineteenth-Century Bali. Princeton University Press, 1980.

Gicquel, Jean. With André Hauriou. *Droit constitutionnel et institutions politiques*. 8th edn. Paris: Montcrestien, 1985.

Giddens, Anthony. *The Constitution of Society: Outline of the Theory of Structuration*. Berkeley: University of California Press, 1984.

Girard, René. *Le Bouc émissaire*. Paris: Librairie Générale de France, 1989.

Granger, Gilles-Gaston. *Essai d'une philosophie du style*. New edn. Paris: Odile Jacob, 1988.

'Logique et pragmatique de la causalité dans les sciences de l'homme'. In Markus Aenishanslin *et al. Systèmes symboliques, sciences et philosophie*. Paris: Éditions du Centre National de la Recherche Scientifique, 1978.

Habermas, Jürgen. *Knowledge and Human Interests*. Trans. Jeremy J. Shapiro. Boston, Mass.: Beacon Press, 1971.

Legitimation Crisis. Trans. Thomas McCarthy. Boston, Mass.: Beacon Press, 1975.

The New Conservatism: Cultural Criticism and the Historians' Debate. Cambridge, Mass.: MIT Press, 1989.

On the Logic of the Social Sciences. Trans. Shierry Weber Nicholson and Jerry A. Stark. Cambridge, Mass.: MIT Press, 1988.

The Philosophical Discourse of Modernity. Trans. Frederick Lawrence. Cambridge, Mass.: MIT Press, 1987.

The Theory of Communicative Action. Trans. Thomas McCarthy. 2 vols. Boston, Mass.: Beacon Press, 1984. Vol. I. *Reason and the Rationalization of Society*.

Toward a Rational Society: Student Protest, Science, and Politics. Trans. Jeremy J. Shapiro. Boston, Mass.: Beacon Press, 1970.

Zur Rekonstruktion des Historischen Materialismus. Frankfurt am Main: Suhrkamp, 1976.

Hart, Herbert L. A. *Punishment and Responsibility: Essays in the Philosophy of Law*. Oxford University Press, 1968.

Hegel, G. W. F. *Philosophy of Right*.

Henry, Michel. *Marx*. 2 vols. Paris: Gallimard, 1976. Vol. I. *Une philosophie de la réalité*.

Marx: A Philosophy of Human Reality. Trans. Kathleen McLaughlin. Bloomington: Indiana University Press, 1983.

Higonnet, Patrice. *Sister Republics: The Origins of French and American Republicanism*. Cambridge, Mass.: Harvard University Press, 1988.

Hirschman, Albert O. *Essays in Trespassing: Economics to Politics and Beyond*. 2nd edn. Cambridge University Press, 1984.

Exit, Voice and Loyalty: Responses to Decline in Firms, Organizations, and States. Cambridge, Mass.: Harvard University Press, 1970.

Vers une économie politique élargie. Trans. from the American. Paris: Minuit, 1986.

Hobbes, Thomas. *Human Nature, or the Fundamental Elements of Policy* and *De Corpore politico: Or the Elements of Law*. Reprint of the 1840 edn. Bristol: Hoemmes Press, 1994.

Leviathan. Harmondsworth: Penguin, 1987.

Hoffmann, Stanley. *Janus and Minerva: Essays in the Theory and Practice of International Politics*. Boulder, Colo.: Westview Press, 1987.

Horkheimer, Max. 'Traditional and Critical Theory'. In *Critical Theory: Selected Essays*. Trans. Matthew J. O'Connell *et al*. New York: Continuum, 1986.

Huntington, Samuel P. *Political Order in Changing Societies*. New Haven, Conn.: Yale University Press, 1968.

Huppert, George. *The Idea of Perfect History: Historical Erudition and Historical Philosophy in Renaissance France*. Urbana: University of Illinois Press, 1970.

Jacob, François. *The Possible and the Actual*. Seattle and London: University of Washington Press, 1982.

Jonas, Hans. *The Imperative of Responsibility: In Search of an Ethics for the Technical Age*. Trans. Hans Jonas with David Herr. University of Chicago Press, 1984.

Kant, Immanuel. 'An Answer to the Question: What is Enlightenment?' In *Perpetual Peace and Other Essays on Politics, History, and Morals*. Trans. and intro. Ted Humphrey. Indianapolis, Ind.: Hackett, 1983.

Critique of Practical Reason. Trans. and intro. Lewis White Beck. London: Collier Macmillan, 1956.

Kantorowicz, Ernst. *The King's Two Bodies: A Study in Medieval Political Theology*. 1st paperback edn. Princeton University Press, 1981.

Karst, Kenneth L. and Keith S. Rosenn. *Law and Development in Latin America*. Berkeley: University of California Press, 1975.

Kennedy, Ellen. 'Carl Schmitt's Parlamentarismus in its Historical Context'. Introduction to *The Crisis of Parliamentary Democracy*. Trans. Ellen Kennedy. Cambridge, Mass.: MIT Press, 1985.

Keohane, Robert O. *After Hegemony: Cooperation and Discord in the World Political Economy*. Princeton University Press, 1984.

Kershaw, Ian. *The 'Hitler Myth': Image and Reality in the Third Reich*. 1st paperback edn. Oxford University Press, 1989.

Kolakowski, Leszek. *Main Currents of Marxism: Its Origins, Growth and Dissolution*. Trans. P. S. Falla. 1st paperback edn. Oxford University Press, 1981. Vol. II. *The Golden Age*.

Koyré, Alexandre. *From the Closed World to the Infinite Universe*. Baltimore, Md.: Johns Hopkins Press, 1968.

Kratochwil, Friedrich V. *Rules, Norms, and Decisions: On the Conditions of Practical and Legal Reasoning in International Relations and Domestic Affairs*. Cambridge University Press, 1989.

Kuhn, Thomas S. *The Copernican Revolution: Planetary Astronomy in the Development of Western Thought*. Cambridge, Mass.: Harvard University Press, 1979.

The Structure of Scientific Revolutions. 3rd edn. University of Chicago Press, 1996.

Lapierre, Jean-William. *L'Analyse des systèmes politiques*. Paris: Presses Universitaires de France, 1973.

Lefebvre, Henri. *De l'État*. 4 vols. Paris: Union Générale d'Éditions, 1978. Vol. IV. *Les Contradictions de l'État moderne. La dialectique et/de l'État*.

Lefort, Claude. *Democracy and Political Theory*. Trans. David Macey. Minneapolis: University of Minnesota Press and Cambridge: Polity Press, 1988.

Les Formes de l'histoire. Essais d'anthropologie politique. Paris: Gallimard, 1978.
The Political Forms of Modern Society: Bureaucracy, Democracy, Totalitarianism.
Ed. and intro. John B. Thompson. Cambridge, Mass.: MIT Press and
Cambridge: Polity Press, 1986.
Le Travail de l'oeuvre. Machiavel. Paris: Gallimard, 1972.
León-Portilla, Miguel. *Visión de los vencidos: Relaciones indígenas de la conquista.*
9th edn. Mexico City: Universidad Nacional Autónoma de México, 1982.
Lévinas, Emmanuel. *Difficult Freedom: Essays on Judaism.* Trans. Seán Hand.
Baltimore, Md.: Johns Hopkins University Press, 1990.
Lévi-Strauss, Claude. *Tristes tropiques.* Paris: Union Générale d'Éditions, 1966.
Lewin, Moshe. *The Gorbachev Phenomenon: A Historical Interpretation.* Berkeley:
University of California Press, 1989.
Linz, Juan. 'Democracia presidencial o parlamentaria. Hay alguna diferencia?' In
*Presidencialismo vs. Parlamentarismo: Materiales para el estudio de la Reforma
Constitucional.* Buenos Aires: Editorial Universitaria de Buenos Aires, 1988.
Luhmann, Niklas. *The Differentiation of Society.* Trans. Stephen Holmes and
Charles Larmore. New York: Columbia University Press, 1982.
Lukes, Steven. *Marxism and Morality.* 1st paperback edn. Oxford University
Press, 1987.
Machiavelli, Niccolo. *The Prince.* Ed. and trans. David Wootton. Indianapolis,
Ind.: Hackett, 1995.
MacIntyre, Alasdair. *After Virtue: A Study in Moral Theory.* University of Notre
Dame Press, 1984.
'Is a Science of Comparative Politics Possible?' In *Against the Self-Images of the
Age: Essays on Ideology and Philosophy.* 2nd edn. University of Notre Dame
Press, 1984.
Whose Justice? Which Rationality? University of Notre Dame Press, 1988.
Manent, Pierre. 'Situation du liberalisme'. Préface. *Les Libéraux.* 2 vols. Paris:
Hachette, 1986.
Marx, Karl. *Capital.* Ed. Frederick Engels. 3 vols. New York: International
Publishers, 1967.
'Contribution to the Critique of Hegel's Philosophy of Law'. In Karl Marx
and Frederick Engels. *Collected Works.* 47 vols. New York: International
Publishers, 1975– . Vol. V.
Marx, Karl. With Frederick Engels. *The German Ideology: Critique of Modern
German Philosophy According to its Representatives Feuerbach, B. Bauer and
Stirner, and of German Socialism According to its Various Prophets.* In Karl Marx
and Frederick Engels, *Collected Works.* 47 vols. New York: International
Publishers, 1975– . Vol. V.
'On the Jewish Question'. In Karl Marx and Frederick Engels, *Collected Works.*
47 vols. New York: International Publishers, 1975– . Vol. III.
Mauss, Marcel. *Œuvres.* 3 vols. Paris: Minuit, 1981. Vol. III. *Cohésion sociale et
divisions de la sociologie.*
McCarthy, Thomas. *The Critical Theory of Jürgen Habermas.* 1st paperback edn.
Cambridge, Mass.: MIT Press, 1981.
Meinecke, Friedrich. *The Age of German Liberation, 1795–1815.* Trans. Peter Paret
and Helmut Fischer. Berkeley: University of California Press, 1977.

Cosmopolitanism and the National State. Trans. Robert B. Kimber. Princeton University Press, 1970.

Machiavellism: The Doctrine of Raison d'État and its Place in Modern History. Trans. Douglas Scott. Reprint edn. New Brunswick, N.J. and London: Transaction Publishers, 1998.

Merleau-Ponty, Maurice. *Humanism and Terror: An Essay on the Communist Problem*. Trans. John O'Neil. Boston, Mass.: Beacon Press, 1969.

Merquior, Jose Guilherme. *Rousseau and Weber: Two Studies in the Theory of Legitimacy*. London, England: Routledge & Kegan Paul, 1980.

Michels, Robert. *Political Parties: A Sociological Study of the Oligarchical Tendencies of Modern Democracy*. Trans. Eden and Cedar Paul. London: Collier-Macmillan and New York: The Free Press, 1966.

Mommsen, Wolfgang J. *Max Weber and German Politics 1890–1920*. Trans. Michael S. Steinberg. 2nd edn. University of Chicago Press, 1984.

Montesquieu. *The Spirit of the Laws*. Trans. and ed. Anne M. Cohler, Basia Carolyn Milller, and Harold Samuel Stone. Cambridge University Press, 1989.

Moscovici, Serge. *Psychologie des minorités actives*. Paris: Presses Universitaires de France, 1982.

Nisbet, Robert A. *The Sociological Tradition*. New York: Basic Books, 1966.

Nozick, Robert. *Anarchy, State and Utopia*. New York: Basic Books, 1974.

Pareto, Vilfredo. *Manual of Political Economy*. Ed. Ann S. Schwier and Alfred N. Page. Trans. Ann S. Schwier. New York: Augustus M. Kelley Publishers, 1971.

The Mind and Society. Ed. Arthur Livingston. Trans. Andrew Bongiorno and Arthur Livingston. 4 vols. New York: Harcourt, Brace and Company, 1935. Vol. III. *Theory of Derivations*.

Parsons, Talcott. *The Social System*. 1st paperback edn. New York: The Free Press, 1964.

Pateman, Carole. *The Problem of Political Obligation: A Critique of Liberal Theory*. Berkeley: University of California Press, 1985.

Perelman, Chaïm. 'Les conceptions concrète et abstraite de la raison et de la justice. À propos de la théorie de la justice de john Rawls'. In Jean Ladrière and Philippe Van Parijs (eds.), *Fondements d'une théorie de la justice. Essais critiques sur la philosophie politique de John Rawls*. Louvain-La-Neuve: Éditions de l'Institut supérieur de philosophie, 1984.

Plamenatz, John P. *Consent, Freedom and Political Obligation*. 2nd edn. Oxford University Press, 1968.

Pocock, John Greville A. *The Machiavellian Moment: Florentine Political Thought and the Atlantic Republican Tradition*. Princeton University Press, 1975.

Pons, Alain. Introduction. Condorcet, *Esquisse d'un tableau historique des progrès de l'esprit humain*. Suivi de *Fragment sur l'Atlantide*. Paris: Flammarion, 1988.

Popper, Karl R. *The Open Society and its Enemies*. 5th rev. edn. London: Routledge and Kegan Paul, 1966. Vol. II. *The High Tide of Prophecy: Hegel, Marx, and the Aftermath*.

The Poverty of Historicism. 2nd corr. edn. New York: Harper & Row, 1964.

Prigogine, Ilya and Isabelle Stengers. *Order out of Chaos: Man's New Dialogue with Nature*. Boulder, Colo. and London: New Science Library, 1984.

Przeworski, Adam. *Capitalism and Social Democracy*. 3rd edn. Cambridge University Press, 1988.

Putnam, Hilary. *Philosophical Papers*. 3 vols. 2nd edn. Cambridge University Press, 1986. Vol. III. *Realism and Reason*.

Reason, Truth, and History. 4th edn. Cambridge University Press, 1984.

Rawls, John. *A Theory of Justice*. Cambridge, Mass.: Harvard University Press, 1971.

'The Idea of an Overlapping Consensus'. *Oxford Journal of Legal Studies* 7:1 (Spring 1987).

'Kantian Constructivism in Moral Theory'. *Journal of Philosophy* 73:9 (September 1980).

'The Priority of Right and Ideas of the Good'. *Philosophy and Public Affairs* 17:4 (Autumn 1988).

Raynaud, Philippe. *Max Weber et les dilemmes de la raison moderne*. Paris: Presses Universitaires de France, 1987.

Raz, Joseph. *The Authority of Law: Essays on Law and Morality*. 2nd paperback edn. Oxford University Press, 1986.

The Concept of a Legal System: An Introduction to the Theory of Legal System. 2nd edn. Oxford University Press, 1980.

Richet, Denis. *La France moderne. L'Esprit des institutions*. Paris: Flammarion, 1973.

Richir, Marc. 'Révolution et transparence sociale'. Introduction. Johann Gottlieb Fichte. *Considérations destinées à rectifier les jugements du public sur la Révolution française*. Paris: Payot, 1974.

Riceur, Paul. In George H. Taylor (ed.), *Lectures on Ideology and Utopia*. New York: Columbia University Press, 1986.

Rosanvallon, Pierre. *La Crise de l'État-providence*. 2nd rev. and corr. edn. Paris: Éditions du Seuil, 1984.

Roth, Günther. Introduction. Marianne Weber. *Max Weber: A Biography*. Trans. Harry Zohn. New Brunswick, N.J.: Transaction Books, 1988.

Rousseau, Jean-Jacques. *Discourse On the Sciences and the Arts*. In *The Collected Writings of Rousseau*. 8 vols. Ed. Roger D. Masters and Christopher Kelly. Trans. Judith R. Bush, Roger D. Masters, and Christopher Kelly. Hanover, N.H. and London: University Press of New England, 1990– .

On the Social Contract, or Principles of Political Right, Vol. IV. In *The Collected Writings of Rousseau*. 8 vols. Ed. Roger D. Masters and Christopher Kelly. Trans. Judith R. Bush, Roger D. Masters, and Christopher Kelly. Hanover, N.H. and London: University Press of New England, 1990– .

Rousso, Henry. *The Vichy Syndrome: History and Memory in France Since 1944*. Trans. Arthur Goldhammer. Cambridge, Mass.: Harvard University Press, 1991.

Sala-Molins, Louis. *La Loi, de quel droit?* Paris: Flammarion, 1977.

Schmitt, Carl. Preface to the 2nd edn (1926), 'On the Contradiction Between Parliamentarism and Democracy'. In *The Crisis of Parliamentary Democracy*. Trans. Ellen Kennedy. Cambridge, Mass.: MIT Press, 1985.

Legalität und Legitimität. Munich and Leipzig: Duncker & Humblot, 1932.

The Concept of the Political. Trans., intro., and notes George Schwab. University of Chicago Press, 1996.

Political Theology: Four Chapters on the Concept of Sovereignty. Trans. George Schwab. Cambridge, Mass.: MIT Press, 1985.

Schwartz, Benjamin I. 'The Reign of Virtue: Some Broad Perspectives on Leader and Party in the Cultural Revolution'. In John Wilson Lewis (ed.), *Party Leadership and Revolutionary Power in China*. Cambridge University Press, 1970.

Sen, Amartya. *On Ethics and Economics*. Oxford: Basil Blackwell, 1987.

Sewell, William H., Jr. *Work and Revolution in France: The Language of Labor from the Old Regime to 1848*. 4th edn. Cambridge University Press, 1985.

Skocpol, Theda. *States and Social Revolutions: A Comparative Analysis of France, Russia, and China*. 14th edn. Cambridge, Mass.: Harvard University Press, 1988.

Spitz, Jean-Fabien. 'Qu'est-ce qu'un État constitutionnel? La contribution de la pensée médiévale 1100–1300'. *Critique* 488–89 (January–February 1988).

Starobinski, Jean. *1789: The Emblems of Reason*. Trans. Barbara Bray. Charlottesville: University Press of Virginia, 1982.

Jean-Jacques Rousseau: Transparency and Obstruction. Trans. Arthur Goldhammer. University of Chicago Press, 1988.

Strauss, Leo. *Natural Right and History*. University of Chicago Press, 1950.

The Political Philosophy of Hobbes: Its Basis and its Genesis. Trans. Elsa M. Sinclair. 1st Midway reprint edn. University of Chicago Press, 1984.

Sullivan, William M. *Reconstructing Public Philosophy*. Berkeley: University of California Press, 1986.

Taylor, Charles. 'The Diversity of Goods'. In Amartya Sen and Bernard Williams (eds.), *Utilitarianism and Beyond*. Cambridge University Press, 1988.

'Le juste et le bien'. Trans. P. Constantineau. *Revue de métaphysique et de morale* 1 (January–March 1988).

Philosophical Papers. 2 vols. Cambridge University Press, 1985. Vol. II. *Philosophy and the Human Sciences*.

'Les sciences de l'homme'. *Critique* 399–400 (August–September 1980).

Sources of the Self: The Making of the Modern Identity. Cambridge, Mass.: Harvard University Press, 1989.

Thom, René. Préface. Pierre Simon Laplace. *Essai philosophique sur les probabilités*. Suivi d'extraits de *Mémoires*. Paris: Christian Bourgois, 1986.

Thompson, Dennis F. *Political Ethics and Public Office*. Cambridge, Mass.: Harvard University Press, 1987.

Tocqueville, Alexis de. *Democracy in America*. Ed. Phillips Bradley. Trans. Henry Reeve. Revised by Francis Bowen. New York: Vintage, 1990.

The Old Regime and the Revolution. 2 vols. Ed. François Furet and Françoise Mélonio. Trans. Alan S. Kahan. University of Chicago Press, 1998.

Tönnies, Ferdinand. *Community and Society (Gemeinschaft und Gesellschaft)*. Trans. Charles P. Loomis. Reprint edn. New Brunswick, N.J.: Transaction Books, 1988.

Trigeaud, Jean-Marc. *Persona ou la justice au double visage*. Genoa: Studio Editoriale di Cultura, 1990.

Unger, Roberto Mangabeira. *The Critical Legal Studies Movement*. Cambridge, Mass.: Harvard University Press, 1986.

Law in Modern Society: Toward a Criticism of Social Theory. New York: The Free Press, 1976.

Social Theory: Its Situation and its Task. A Critical Introduction to Politics, a Work in Constructive Social Theory. Cambridge University Press, 1987.

Van Parijs, Philippe. *Qu'est-ce qu'une société juste? Introduction à la pratique de la philosophie politique*. Paris: Éditions du Seuil, 1991.

Veyne, Paul. *Bread and Circuses: Historical Sociology and Political Pluralism*. Trans. Brian Pearce. Abridged edn. London: Allen Lane/The Penguin Press, 1990.

Did the Greeks Believe in Their Myths? An Essay on the Constitutive Imagination. University of Chicago Press, 1988.

'Foucault révolutionne l'histoire'. In *Comment on écrit l'histoire*. Paris: Éditions du Seuil, 1979.

'L'histoire conceptualisante'. In Jacques Le Goff and Pierre Nora (eds.). *Faire de l'histoire. Nouveaux problèmes*. Paris: Gallimard, 1978.

Le Pain et le cirque. Sociologie historique d'un pluralisme politique. Paris: Éditions du Seuil, 1976.

Writing History: Essay on Epistemology. Middletown, Conn.: Wesleyan University Press, 1984.

Villey, Michel. *Philosophie du droit*. 3rd edn. 2 vols. Paris: Dalloz, 1982. Vol. I. *Définitions et fins du droit*.

Walzer, Michael. *Obligations: Essays on Disobedience, War, and Citizenship*. 4th edn. Cambridge, Mass.: Harvard University Press, 1982.

Spheres of Justice: A Defense of Pluralism and Equality. New York: Basic Books, 1983.

Weber, Max. *Economy and Society: An Outline of Interpretive Sociology*. Ed. Guenther Roth and Claus Wittich. Trans. Ephraim Fischoff, Hans Gerth, A. M. Henderson, Ferdinand Kolegar, C. Wright Mills, Talcott Parsons, Max Rheinstein, Guenther Roth, Edward Shils, and Claus Wittich. 2 vols. Berkeley: University of California Press, 1978.

The Methodology of the Social Sciences. Trans. Edward A. Shils and Henry A. Finch. New York: The Free Press, 1949.

Political Writings. Ed. Peter Lassman and Ronald Speirs. Cambridge University Press, 1994.

The Protestant Ethic and the Spirit of Capitalism. Trans. Talcott Parsons. New York: Charles Scribner's Sons, 1976.

Wolff, Robert Paul. *In Defense of Anarchism*. New York: Harper & Row, 1976.

Index

250